Classroom Management in Context:
Orchestrating Positive Learning Environments

CONTENT DIAGRAM

PART 1:
Understanding
Classrooms

1. You and Your Classroom
2. Communications in the
   Classroom Ecosystem

Classrooms
Are Ecosystems

PART 4:
Building Support
Systems

9. Partnerships with
   Colleagues, Parents,
   and Others
10. Taking Care of Yourself

Good Classroom
Management Is
Good Teaching

PART 2:
Orchestrating
Successful Classrooms

3. Diversity in American
   Schools
4. Effective Instructional
   Approaches
5. Preventing Behavioral
   Problems

Teachers Are
Problem-Solvers

PART 3:
Managing Group and
Individual Behavior

6. Dealing with Problem
   Behavior
7. Intervening with
   Individuals
8. Intervening with Groups

Dear Readers—

As you very likely know better than anyone else, classroom management is the number one concern of most people who are studying to become teachers and who have just begun their professional careers as teachers. There are many reasons for this concern. Some have to do with memories that all of us have of a classmate who acted out and disrupted a class. Others have to do with stories in the media. But more important than focusing on why teachers worry about classroom management issues is focusing on ways to prevent these problems. As you read and think about this book's content and complete some of the activities at the end of each chapter, you'll find many strategies, instructional approaches, and foundations for understanding your students. These will help you prevent management problems.

The two key themes in this book are that (1) teachers are problem solvers and (2) good teaching is good management. You will see these themes woven throughout the book. Through its unique ecosystems approach, you will develop an understanding of classrooms as truly dynamic places with all kinds of interactions among the students, teachers, and settings. You are an essential part of that dynamic.

Consider this book as a resource. It is full of strategies and practical approaches you can use from the first day of your teaching career until the last. Enter a dialog with this book. Imagine you are talking with its authors as you read. Question, debate, and interact. Discuss its ideas and your own with your classmates. Mark strategies for classroom management so you can find them easily when you need them in the years to come. As you do these things, you will begin your journey to being an excellent teacher who seamlessly integrates management observations and approaches in classrooms.

Classroom Management in Context

Classroom Management in Context

Orchestrating Positive Learning Environments

Robert H. Zabel
Kansas State University

Mary Kay Zabel
Kansas State University

HOUGHTON MIFFLIN COMPANY   **Boston**   **Toronto**

Geneva, Illinois   Palo Alto   Princeton, New Jersey

Senior sponsoring editor: Loretta Wolozin
Senior associate editor: Janet Edmonds
Senior project editor: Rosemary Winfield
Production/design coordinator: Jennifer Waddell
Senior manufacturing coordinator: Priscilla Bailey

Cover design: Darci Mehall, Aureo Design.

Cover Image: Cover monotype "See, See Them," Copyright © 1993 by Fae Kontje.

Cover Art by: Fae Kontje
represented by: the N.W. Barrett Gallery of Portsmouth, N.H.

Part opener photos: Part 1, Michael Newman/Photo Edit; Part 2, Elizabeth Crews/The Image Works; Part 3, Spencer Grant/Photo Researchers; Part 4, Caroline Ryan Morgan.

Pages 24, 86: From *Savage Inequalities* by Jonathan Kozol. Copyright © 1991 by Jonathan Kozol. Reprinted by permission of Crown Publishers, Inc.

Page 146: From "The Case for Interaction Skills Training in the Context of Tutoring as a Preventative Mental Health Intervention in Schools" by Joseph M. Strayhorn, Jr., Philip S. Strain, and Hill M. Walker, *Behavioral Disorders,* November 1993 (vol. 19, no. 1). Reprinted by permission.

Pages 202–203, 329, 359: Excerpts from *Among Schoolchildren* by Tracy Kidder. Copyright © 1989 by John Tracy Kidder. Reprinted by permission of Houghton Mifflin Company and Georges Borchardt, Inc. for the author. All rights reserved.

Page 205: From Polly Nichols, "The Curriculum of Control: Twelve Reasons for It, Some Arguments Against It," *Beyond Behavior,* 3, 1992. Reprinted by permission.

Printed in the U.S.A.

Library of Congress Catalog Card Number 95-76997

ISBN 0-395-75091-1

3456789-DC-05 04 03 02

*To Frank H. Wood, for his gifts
to teachers, to students, and to us*

BRIEF CONTENTS

CONTENTS

8   Intervening with Groups   265

PREFACE

Your ability to manage your classroom is critical to your success as a teacher. In fact, the management and instructional functions of classroom teachers cannot be separated: *effective teaching includes effective management.* We believe classroom management is more than discipline, and that management cannot be prescribed: to make appropriate management decisions, you must consider the unique mix of students, teachers, settings, and activities within the classroom ecosystem.

For you to manage your classroom effectively, you need to be aware of the ecological nature of classrooms, have many kinds of management skills, and know when and where to use them. As we consider creative approaches to classroom management in this text, we will emphasize two major themes: (1) the classroom is an ecosystem, and (2) teachers are problem solvers.

Our view of classroom management is broad: teachers deal with individual and group behavior continually—often preventing problems. Classroom management is not simply about the narrow domain of student discipline or put another way, coping with behavior problems *after* they occur. As you become increasingly aware of classroom context, you will learn how your classroom works and how it can work. To do so, you will need to think about and understand multiple factors, including your students and the influences on their behavior in your classroom. You must also be able to effectively communicate with students, to use effective instructional approaches, and establish classroom conditions that minimize behavior problems. You must also be able to intervene with students before any problem behavior escalates and spreads to other students. Finally, you should know how to find support from others and how to meet your own professional and personal needs.

OVERVIEW OF THE BOOK

We have organized the book by looking at the whole classroom context, emphasizing its ecological nature and student diversity. Then we consider the role of classroom communication, effective instruction, and preventive planning in minimizing behavior problems. After that we move on to techniques you can use to interfere with problem behavior and interventions for changing the behavior of individuals and groups. Finally, we take a look at ways for you to get support beyond the classroom and to take care of yourself.

To follow this sequence, we have divided this book into four major parts:

1. Understanding Classrooms

2. Orchestrating Successful Classrooms

3. Managing Group and Individual Behavior

4. Building Support Systems

In Part 1, *Understanding Classrooms,* we have included three chapters that should help you develop expectations and attitudes that are both realistic and optimistic about your role as teacher. The first chapter, *You and Your Classroom,* is intended to help you examine your knowledge and beliefs about classrooms, including concerns beginning teachers have about classroom management. We will look at traditional classroom structures and explore the limits of teacher control in such structures. We then propose an ecological perspective on classroom management that places you, the teacher, in the central orchestrating role.

In Chapter 2, *Communication in the Classroom,* we focus on your role as facilitator of student learning and behavior by examining the types of communication, both verbal and nonverbal, that occur in classrooms. We discuss how communication affects student learning and behavior and suggest approaches to help you develop effective classroom communication.

Your understanding of the nature and causes of appropriate and inappropriate student behavior will direct your approaches to classroom management. In Chapter 3, *Diversity in American Schools,* we provide an overview of several perspectives (including biophysical, learning, psychosocial, sociocultural, and ecological) that should help you understand individual and group differences among your students.

In Part 2, *Orchestrating Successful Classrooms,* we describe your role as classroom orchestrater. Much like a symphony orchestra, your classroom will consist of players with differing abilities, skills, and experiences who play different instruments, different music, different parts, sometimes together, sometimes alone, and often with individual variations. Like a conductor, you will direct large, diverse groups of students. Sometimes you will lead the entire group in unison, sometimes you will encourage performances by soloists, and sometimes you will coordinate smaller ensembles.

Earlier we stated our belief that good teaching is good classroom management. One is not really possible without the other. In Chapter 4, *Effective Instructional Approaches,* we describe characteristics of effective schools and teachers' effective instruction and share factors that are relevant to classroom management.

In Chapter 5, *Preventing Behavior Problems,* our focus is on ways you can prevent—or at least minimize—many classroom behavior problems. We stress ways you can prepare and organize the physical environment of your classroom, communicate expectations for student behavior, and become a *withit* teacher who is aware of student behavior and communicates that awareness to your students.

It has been our experience that despite careful planning and preparation, teachers are not able to prevent all classroom behavior problems. In Part 3, *Managing Group and Individual Behavior,* we discuss specific strategies you can use to manage individuals and groups of students. In order to help students learn to control their own behavior, our suggestions are directed toward encouraging and teaching student *self*-management. Where such internally generated approaches are insufficient, however, we also will describe methods that rely more on external control of student behavior.

Chapter 6, *Dealing with Problem Behavior,* focuses on ways you can minimize the growth and contagion of behavior problems within your classroom. We discuss methods you can use to interfere with relatively common but mild forms of disturbing and distracting behavior, that can escalate and spread to other students if they are not attended to.

In Chapters 7 and 8, we describe interventions to change more persistent and pronounced problem behavior. In Chapter 7, *Intervening with Individuals,* we describe strategies for dealing with persistent problem behavior of individual students. We highlight individual contingency management, contracting, time out, mediation essays, methods for teaching self-management, and individual counseling strategies. We will also suggest ways to successfully handle crisis situations like fights or arguments. In Chapter 8, *Intervening with Groups,* we focus on interventions that will help you improve the functioning of your entire class or subgroups within it. Some of the approaches we included here are class meetings, teaching students to understand and appreciate their own and others' feelings and behavior, group contingency management, token economies, and social skills training.

The final part of this book, *Building Support Systems,* extends beyond your immediate classroom environment to explore ways you can find assistance and support for your classroom management efforts. To be an effective classroom manager you will sometimes need to work with others within your school, as well as with students' families, service providers, and available experts within the community. We have found that teachers need to be sensitive to their own needs as well.

Chapter 9, *Partnerships with Colleagues, Parents, and Others,* describes the roles and responsibilities of your professional colleagues in your school and district as well as potential service providers and resources outside of schools, including your students' families. We suggest ways to build partnerships with others within and outside of schools to obtain support, services, and resources that are helpful to your students and yourself.

Finally, in Chapter 10, *Taking Care of Yourself,* we examine factors that can contribute to teacher stress and burnout. We look at ways for you to cope with the challenges of teaching and managing a classroom, to minimize the defeating effects of stress, and to prevent professional burnout.

As authors of this book, we drew on a variety of resources. They included our own experiences as regular classroom and special education teachers of students with learning and behavioral problems, our own and others' research on classroom management issues, and the expertise of other practicing teachers. We have each been involved in education for twenty-five years, working with students from infancy through graduate school. We have both worked as regular classroom teachers (second, third, and sixth grades), special education teachers (emotional and behavioral disorders, learning disabilities, early childhood special education, birth through high school, self-contained, resource, and consulting), and teacher educators (emotional and behavioral disorders, early childhood special education, regular elementary and secondary education). In addition to our professional experiences, we have three children of our own and, in keeping with our ecological philosophy, have learned a lot from our interaction with their teachers in our roles as parents, parent volunteers, and general supporters and observers of the educational process. Foremost in our minds has been the importance of sharing understandings and approaches that will help you establish positive learning environments for all your students and for yourself.

Will we provide *all* the answers to your classroom management questions in this book? Not likely. But we hope we will address many of your questions about classroom management and raise some you perhaps have not yet asked. We hope that you will acquire insights, information, and practical strategies that will make you a more confident, optimistic, and effective teacher. Although we offer no magic wands or even secret formulas, we hope that you come away from this book with the tools to solve classroom management issues. We hope you will gain an understanding of the classroom as a complex ecosystem; recognize the role of communication; appreciate the causes and consequences of student behavior; acquire essential skills in prevention, interference, and intervention with problem behavior; and learn how to use available support systems and to take care of yourself.

SPECIAL LEARNING FEATURES OF THE TEXT

Annie's Journal

At the beginning of each chapter, you will find a new teacher's journal entry. We call her Annie, and her experiences are drawn from incidents in our own professional lives as well as those of friends and colleagues. We present these entries in *Annie's Journal* because they help focus not only on key issues and concerns of new teachers but also on the issues we discuss in the chapter that follows. After each journal entry, you will find a list of questions to help you start thinking about the chapter and how it applies to real classrooms. We encourage you to keep those questions in mind as you read and return to them after you finish the chapter to see how your understanding of classroom management challenges has deepened.

Close-ups

You'll find *Close-ups* in each chapter. They are written "snap-shots" of real teachers and real students in real classrooms, and we hope they will help you see how classrooms are ecosystems and how teachers are problem solvers.

Authors' Dialogues

Another feature we have included are dialogues, *As We See It: The Authors Talk* in each chapter. These are conversations we had that did not seem to fit the format of a text but were about issues we felt were important to discuss. Perhaps they will provide some insight into the collaborative process.

Other Features

At the end of each chapter you will find several additional features to help you reflect on important ideas.

- The *Summary and Review* highlights important ideas in the chapter.
- *Reflecting on Chapter X* suggests activities to stimulate your continued understanding, exploration, and discussion of key issues and questions raised in *Annie's Journal.*
- *Key Terms* and the page numbers they occur on are listed for your easy reference and review.
- *Building Your Knowledge Base: Suggested Readings* lists and briefly describes several books that we hope will be interesting to you and provide opportunities for you to pursue additional information and ideas on your own.

ACKNOWLEDGMENTS

A number of persons have played significant roles in the conceptualization, editing, and production of this book. Many talented people at Houghton Mifflin have shared their expertise and insights, but a few deserve special mention. Loretta Wolozin, senior sponsoring editor, encouraged us to embark on this project and guided its development from an idea to finished product. Throughout the process, she helped us make important decisions about content, organization, and voice, always keeping the audience of readers in mind. Janet Edmonds, associate editor, oversaw technical editing of the manuscript, kept us "on task," and always had kind words about our efforts. Senior project editor, Rosemary Winfield, coordinated the many details of getting the manuscript into print.

Several field reviewers with expertise in classroom management offered suggestions about our prospectus and first draft. We have incorporated many of their ideas. The reviewers were

* Sally Bing, University of Maryland, Eastern Shore
* Robert A. Gable, Old Dominion University
* Kathryn Liptak, University of Kentucky
* Charles Long, Salisbury State University
* Nancy Lourie, San Jose State University
* Donald K. Maas, California Polytechnic University
* Douglas Macisaac, University of Northern Colorado
* Judith A. Ponticell, Texas Tech University
* Donald M. Uhlenberg, University of North Dakota
* Joseph H. Wehby, Vanderbilt University

The book is about context, and we would be remiss if we did not acknowledge the many people who make up the context of our lives. Our parents, friends, colleagues, teachers, and students have contributed to our personal and professional lives in ways too numerous to mention. But it is our children, Laura, Matthew, and Claire, who provide the constant focus and continuing reinforcement that make the context of our lives meaningful and rich. Thanks, guys, for understanding our work, supporting our projects, and putting up with our stress.

We truly hope the information we have provided in this book will assist you on your journey to becoming an outstanding teacher, and we wish you success along the way.

Classroom Management in Context

Understanding Classrooms

Part One, Understanding Classrooms, *includes three chapters to help you develop realistic and optimistic expectations about your role as a teacher and your ability to manage your classroom. The part introduces the two themes that are central throughout this book: the classroom as an ecosystem and the teacher as a problem solver.*

Chapter 1, **You and Your Classroom,** *will help you examine your knowledge and beliefs about classrooms, including concerns about classroom management. Chapter 1 also proposes an ecological perspective on classroom management with the teacher in the central role.*

Chapter 2, **Communication in the Classroom Ecosystem,** *examines the many patterns of verbal and nonverbal communication in classrooms and suggests approaches you can use to promote effective classroom communication.*

Chapter 3, **Diversity in American Schools,** *offers several ways to view individual and group differences in learning and behavior among your students. These biophysical, learning, psychosocial, sociocultural, and ecological perspectives will help you understand variability in student learning and behavior.*

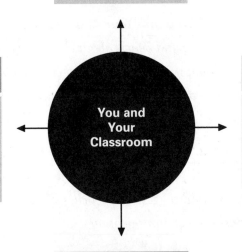

Concerns of Beginning Teachers

- Classroom discipline
- Motivating students
- Individual differences
- Assessing work
- Relationships with parents
- Organizing class work
- Inadequate teaching supplies
- Individual students' problems
- Heavy teaching load and little preparation time
- Relationships with colleagues

The Ecology of Classrooms

Interactive, dynamic environments with four clusters of variables:
- Student characteristics
- Teacher characteristics
- Setting characteristics
- Activities

You and Your Classroom

Traditional Classroom Structures

- Grade and age-level grouping
- Curriculum
- Assumptions of homogeneity
- Implicit curriculum

A New Paradigm for Education

- Outcomes based education
- Active learning
- Inclusion

Chapter 1

You and Your Classroom

Annie's Journal

AUGUST: All right. Here goes. I actually have a job!—a *teaching* job! All the courses, all the papers, projects, exams, lectures, discussions, anxieties—then all the interviews, telephone calls, resumes, smiling faces (particularly mine), more anxieties, waiting, considering alternate careers, waiting, telling people I'm still waiting, and finally . . . *The Job Offer*. I still can't really believe it—I mean, I've signed a contract and everything, but I can't really say I'm convinced that now I'm going to be a teacher . . . fourth grade, Madison Elementary School . . . my own bulletin boards, faculty parking sticker, playground duty, bus duty, reading, math, science, social studies, language arts, drama activities, art projects, school programs, faculty meetings, school board members, *parents*, snow days, flu season, chicken pox (haven't they had that by fourth grade?), special needs students, ADHD, outcomes-based learning, curriculum-based assessment, Arrrrgh! Maybe I should have been a business major—I could be the assistant manager at a quaint pizza restaurant. . . . No. I'm a teacher. I *want* to be a teacher. I've prepared to be a teacher and I'll be a good teacher. Hmm. I sound a bit like "the little engine that could"—or like Stuart Smalley—I'll have to work on that.

I've decided to keep a journal during this first year, so I guess I'd better start thinking professionally about my job and my plans. OK. What do I need to consider first? I mean, besides those things I already wrote down. There's just so much to think about! I don't know what to worry about first—I mean, high on my list is whether the kids will like me or not. Is that professional? Maybe I'm just supposed to worry about whether I'll be a good teacher and be able to motivate them and teach them and understand them and nurture them and help them and guide them and—there I go again. One thing at a time, girl. Then there are the other teachers. . . . What if they think I don't know anything? What if they're right? What if no one else uses whole language? What if they give me all the really difficult kids (that happens to first-year teachers, doesn't it)? I've heard that advice about not smiling until Christmas—should I do that? What if all the kids get up and leave the room on the first day and I don't know how to get them back? What if I say "Good Morning!" and no one answers me? What if *none* of them speaks English? What if they're all really gifted and they know a lot more about science than I do? What if I can't find the school?

I've got to stop this. After all, this is what I prepared for, planned for, and dreamed about. Like they say in *Into the Woods,* be careful what you wish for, it might come true. STOP. This IS what I want . . . I know that. . . . I have two weeks before school starts and I need to decide what to do first. Lists—that's a good idea. OK. First, the kids. I have a list of all their names. Just think, in only two weeks I'll have faces to go with these 27 names. . . . I'll know what Felicia looks like, what Ron usually wears, what Samantha likes to do during recess, whether Lee is a boy or a girl, what Keisha's favorite subject is. . . . That's the exciting part of all this—knowing we'll be a part of each other's lives for the next nine months and maybe beyond. I remember some of my teachers really well. In fact, I've been thinking about them a lot lately, both the good and the bad ones. Great. Four years of college and I'm thinking about MY fourth-grade teacher and how she did it.

Back to the kids. I wonder if I should look at their folders before I meet them. I remember talking about that in a class once. . . . Is it better to form your own opinions about kids and then look at the records, or should I read the files first so I know what to expect? . . . I'll have to think about that. I wonder what I did with that really excellent classroom management text I had at school. I need to get into my classroom and think about room arrangement. I know environment is really important, and I want it to be welcoming and exciting. Posters maybe? I should put up some stuff to get them excited about what we're going to be doing. What *are* we going to be doing? That's up to me now, isn't it? Perhaps if I don't sleep, eat, talk to anyone, or leave the classroom before August 29 (*The First Day*), I can read all the textbooks and know what I'm doing. Not practical. OK. I go to the school, I see the room, I pick up copies of all the books, I get organized—wait! What about the inservice days? What will those be like? Will there be tests? Will we wear name tags? Will I be the only new person? What should I wear? I can't believe this. I am about to embark on my profession, my chosen career of challenging and leading young minds, and I'm concerned about what to wear to the inservice meetings. Get a grip, girl. First impressions are important, though, and I want them to see me as an equal.

OK. Tomorrow I go to *my* school and start to get organized. Why do I feel like a combination of Neil Armstrong stepping out of the space capsule and Scarlett O'Hara at the top of the stairs?

**FOCUS
QUESTIONS**

✳ What do you think Annie is most worried about?

✳ What should Annie do when she gets to her classroom tomorrow?

✳ Do you think teachers should look at students' files before meeting their students?

✳ What sorts of things should a teacher plan for the first day?

✳ What *else* should Annie be worrying about at this point?

✳ Annie has two weeks before school starts. What might be the best way to schedule that time in her school ecosystem?

CONSIDERING YOUR ROLE AS A TEACHER

Do I have the knowledge, skills, personality, and experiences to be an effective teacher? How will my students respond to me? Will they like me and respect me? What kind of school and classroom will I have? How will I work with other teachers, administrators, and parents? Will I be prepared for the demands of the job? Should I have majored in business or gone to law school instead of this?

As you consider your future role as teacher, you may ask yourself questions such as these. You may vacillate between anticipation and apprehension, eager for the opportunity to begin applying your knowledge and skills, but also questioning your preparation and competence. In fact, most of us continue asking ourselves such unanswerable questions throughout our professional lives.

Teachers who feel apprehensive or even ambivalent are not alone.

If you have ambivalent thoughts and feelings about teaching, you are not alone. All teachers, even those who have taught for many years, must balance a basic confidence that we have something to offer with our doubts about how well we can accomplish that task. In his portrait of an experienced fifth-grade teacher Tracy Kidder (1989, p. 5) writes,

> On nights before the school year started, Chris used to have bad dreams that her principal would come to observe her, and her students would choose that moment to climb up on their desks and give her the finger, or they would simply wander out the door. But a child in her classroom would never know that Mrs. Zajac had the slightest doubt that students would obey her.

Today, teachers in American schools face the challenge of operating in complex roles to teach increasingly diverse students. They are also on the front lines of school reform agendas that demand improved academic outcomes *and* more equitable educational opportunities—goals that are not always compatible. Demographic projections for the twenty-first century suggest that the

In the future, teachers will assume more responsibility for accommodating increasingly diverse students.

socioeconomic, cultural, and linguistic diversity of American students will continue to grow. Also, teachers will likely have to assume greater responsibility and a larger role in accommodating diversity and addressing the nation's social and economic challenges. Consider the following:

- The minority population of the United States will be approximately one-third of the total by the year 2000.
- In many schools, including the nation's 25 largest districts, minority students are now in the majority.
- Approximately 2 million school-age children with limited English proficiency live in the U.S.
- The number of students with identified learning and behavioral disabilities has increased dramatically over the past 20 years, and the vast majority of these students are now educated in regular classrooms.
- Increasing numbers of children are considered "at-risk" for school failure as well as for failure within our society in general.
- Nearly one-half of American children are born into single-parent families or will at some time live in a nontraditional family.
- A majority of mothers of elementary school students are now employed outside the home.
- Children constitute a large and growing proportion of America's poor.
- About 500,000 American children live in foster homes.
- Many children are unsupervised by adults for much of their time outside of school.
- For some children, neglect, abuse, violence, drugs, alcohol, and gangs are features of everyday life.

Forces ranging from economic factors to demands for greater accountability are bringing about changes in classrooms.

Economic factors, concerns about educational outcomes, and equity issues are contributing to a variety of changes in "business as usual" in America's schools. Congress, state legislatures, and school boards have become less willing and able to provide additional financial resources and personnel even as educational needs expand. Also, programs that have "pulled out" students from mainstream classrooms to provide specialized services have been criticized for not establishing their efficacy. Policy makers and the public are demanding greater accountability—established outcomes—from educators (Goals 2000: Educate America Act, 1994; National Commission on Excellence in Education, 1983; National Education Goals Panel, 1991). In addition, many parents, educators, and others are concerned that segregating subgroups of the school-age population on the basis of their language, behavioral, and/or learning characteristics only exacerbates those differences and contributes to social stratification.

Inclusion and OBE are two aspects of new classroom environments.

All of these forces are encouraging the full **inclusion** of diverse learners in regular classrooms and **outcomes-based education** (**OBE**) (discussed later in this chapter) for all students. Inclusion involves including all students in regular classrooms. In the near future most individual student needs will be met in mainstream classrooms, and classroom teachers will provide services formerly considered "special," "remedial," or "compensatory." Consequently, schools need teachers who are prepared to work effectively in these new classroom environments. To be an effective teacher, you will need the following kinds of understandings and skills:

- Realistic expectations of classroom life,

- The ability to create and sustain environments conducive to the intellectual, social, and emotional growth of *all* your students,

- The ability to analyze classroom contexts and solve problems related to disruptions of instruction,

- The ability to collaborate with other educators, parents, and service providers, and

- Confidence, enthusiasm, and stamina.

If this sounds like a tall order, it is.

REALITY SHOCK

Experienced teachers will tell you that the shift from being a student to being a teacher can be dramatic—sometimes even traumatic. Researchers who have studied the transition from preservice teacher to first-year teacher have referred to it as "reality shock" to indicate how a person's optimistic notions about teaching are confronted by the sometimes harsh realities of everyday life in classrooms. "In general, this concept is used to indicate the collapse of the missionary ideals formed during teacher training by the harsh and rude reality of everyday classroom life" (Veenman, 1986, p. 143).

Early teaching experiences may differ dramatically from a new teacher's idealistic expectations.

Reality shock involves recognizing and adapting to the complexities of teaching. Your early teaching experiences can create cognitive dissonance—a sense that your previously held expectations about teaching do not correspond with the realities of the job. New teachers deal with cognitive dissonance in a variety of ways. Some come to believe the problems reside in their students or themselves. They adopt control-oriented forms of teaching, become conservative and pessimistic about what they can accomplish, and lose confidence in their teaching abilities.

Of course, not all beginning teachers have a totally bleak experience. Despite reality shock, most new teachers report that they like their jobs and are happy with their career choice. There is no question that teaching is intellectually, emotionally, and physically demanding. Yet, as witnessed by the large

Despite reality shock, teaching is one of the most fulfilling and rewarding professions.

numbers of teachers who make teaching their life's work, it can also be an incredibly satisfying and rewarding profession.

Have you thought about why you want to become a teacher? The reasons people choose to become teachers and remain in the profession have been widely researched (e.g., Darling-Hammond, 1990; Feinman-Nemser & Floden, 1986). In his classic study, *Schoolteacher* (1975), Daniel Lortie identified three potential types of rewards associated with teaching: extrinsic, ancillary, and intrinsic. Extrinsic rewards include material benefits such as salary and benefits and perceived social status. Ancillary rewards include conditions of the workplace and schedule, such as location, travel convenience, job availability, vacation opportunities, and comfort and safety. Extrinsic and ancillary rewards are important to all of us, although anyone hoping to get rich in a high-status, "cushy" job with short working hours is advised to look elsewhere because a teacher's salary and status are modest, job conditions are highly variable, and working hours are typically long.

Intrinsic rewards, however—those positive feelings and thoughts associated with teaching—are far more significant in most of our decisions to become teachers and to remain in the profession. The following are potential intrinsic rewards:

- Enjoyment from working with children and young adults,

- Satisfaction from having a positive influence on student development and achievement,

- Enjoyment of teaching activities and subject matter,

- Stimulation from collegial involvement and support, and

- Satisfaction from providing meaningful service to others.

These, of course, are fairly global potential rewards, and every teacher identifies his or her intrinsic rewards differently. Some teachers, for example, are attracted to working with young children; others prefer teaching adolescents. Some are interested in a particular field of study or activity such as music, literature, art, athletics, mathematics, history, auto mechanics, or theater, and they want to continue studying and sharing their passion for that interest with others. Some teachers find it especially rewarding to work with students at-risk or with disabilities. In our conversations with other teachers, we have found that most teachers believe that they are contributing to the future of their communities, country, and humanity in general by participating in the development of younger generations.

Most teachers believe that they are contributing to the future by helping younger generations.

While there is no way to be fully prepared for the challenges of your first teaching job, there are important attitudes, understandings, and skills that will help prepare you and buffer the inevitable reality shock. Throughout this book we will offer ideas and information that can help you develop realistic expectations and useful skills while retaining your optimism and enthusiasm about teaching.

As We See It: *The Authors Talk*

Bob: It's hard for me to balance the "reality" of teachers' experiences with the ideal—the way it ought to be.

May Kay: You mean the perception that university people don't understand reality—the "ivory tower syndrome"?

Bob: That's part of it. Although most of that difficulty comes from the way that "reality" differs from place to place. You get a whole different set of realities when you look at rural schools in Nebraska, or reservation schools in South Dakota, or midsize suburban schools in Pennsylvania. And what about age level? Is reality the same in elementary, middle, junior high, and high schools? When we talk about "reality shock" in teaching, whose reality are we talking about?

Mary Kay: I guess we have to keep trying to point out the similarities in these various situations, rather than dwell on the differences. All new teachers, for example, share some of the same concerns Annie voiced in her journal. The day before school starts should probably be made a national holiday—National Nerves Day—because teachers, students, and parents are lying awake at night wondering what the next weeks will bring. And that happens no matter where you live or how old you are.

Bob: That's true. I suppose we need to focus on the shared realities, rather than the specific differences—otherwise this book would get awfully long.

CONCERNS OF BEGINNING TEACHERS

Most prospective teachers have many concerns about teaching. If you did not, that itself would be a concern! Teaching is a complex and challenging profession that requires preparation and self-examination. Like many other people who plan to teach, you may wonder about the adequacy of your professional preparation (academic and otherwise) for providing instruction appropriate for your students. You may wonder about the prescribed curriculum and how you will operate within it, infuse it with additional material and activities, make adaptations, and organize and sequence learning. You may wonder about the physical features of your classroom and school, its location, equipment, instructional materials, and supplies, and how they will enhance or constrain your teaching. You may wonder about your relationships with parents and with the other teachers, administrators, and support personnel with whom you will work. You may wonder whether you will have enough energy and how you will motivate your students. But most of all, you may wonder about your students—what they will be like, the quality of your relationships with them, and how you will deal with behavioral and emotional differences and difficulties.

The concerns of many who plan to teach are concerns about classroom management.

Directly or indirectly, these are all concerns about classroom management. It may be reassuring to know that most beginning teachers have similar concerns, and these concerns persist even for experienced (also called "master") teachers. In a review of a large number of studies of the problems experienced by teachers during their first years of teaching (Veenman, 1986), the following were most often identified:

- Classroom discipline,
- Motivating students,
- Dealing with individual differences,
- Assessing students' work,
- Relationships with parents,
- Organizing class work,
- Insufficient or inadequate teaching materials and supplies,
- Dealing with individual students' problems,
- Heavy teaching load resulting in insufficient preparation time, and
- Relationships with colleagues.

Classroom "Discipline"

Beginning teachers often identify classroom discipline as their major concern.

Beginning teachers cite classroom discipline as their primary concern (Veenman, 1986). While we do not know exactly what teachers mean by this term, it seems reasonable to think that classroom discipline reflects their concerns about dealing with perceived student misbehavior. However, Veenman's review reveals little about types of discipline problems, their seriousness, or teacher solutions. Are the perceived discipline problems of beginning teachers due to their own personality and attitude characteristics or the adequacy of their professional preparation? Are they due to school characteristics such as support from administrators, colleagues, and parents, support services, materials and supplies, or features of the physical environment of classrooms and schools?

Some behavior that is identified as "misbehavior" sometimes indicates that students are engaged in learning.

If we assume that discipline problems reflect teachers' concerns about classroom misbehavior, we have to ask, "What exactly is 'misbehavior'?" How would you define misbehavior? Would you begin listing behavior like "talking out," "leaving seat," or "not doing work"? If so, you might soon realize that these behaviors are not necessarily *mis*behavior. For example, in some classrooms, and under certain conditions in *most* classrooms, "talking out" indicates students are engaged in learning as they answer questions, participate in discussions, or help one another.

We believe that emphasizing discipline in classroom management is limiting and misguided for two reasons. First, discipline suggests that problem behavior represents deviance on the part of offending students—that problems are "owned" by students who must conform to established standards of conduct. Second, discipline emphasizes actions teachers take *following* student misbehavior to suppress or modify behavior.

Ecological Factors

Behavior identified as "misbehavior" often reflects ecological factors.

In place of emphasizing discipline, we offer a broader view that emphasizes *ecological factors* and suggests that problem behavior often reflects these relationships between people and their surroundings. Effective classroom management requires that you recognize the ecological nature of behavior and focus on ways you can arrange, structure, and operate the classroom to *promote* functional behavior and to *minimize* misbehavior. We would mislead you, however, if we suggested that you will never encounter disruptive, distractive, or destructive student behavior that needs correction (after all, we did promise a realistic perspective in this book). Consequently, we include approaches you can use to redirect, modify, and—when necessary—suppress misbehavior when it persists. Our main focus is on emphasizing approaches you can use to establish positive learning environments that motivate and involve students, encourage cooperation and caring, *and* minimize and prevent misbehavior.

Effective classroom management involves understanding features of classroom ecosystems.

A first step in classroom management involves understanding the multiple interactive features of classroom ecosystems. An **ecosystem** is an interaction system of organisms with their environments. In this book we use an ecological orientation to understand classroom behavior and management, and we stress that student behavior does not occur in isolation from the classroom ecosystem—and that conditions in your classroom can encourage or discourage misbehavior. You and your students live within several ecosystems, including homes, classrooms, schools, and communities. Our primary focus here will be on the classroom ecosystem, although we continuously acknowledge the influences of these other ecosystems on life in your classroom as well.

Home, community, and school ecosystems influence life in the classroom ecosystem.

"Misbehavior" can be understood only in the context of the classroom structures where it occurs (Doyle, 1986). All behavior occurs in context, and as you will see in the discussion of classroom ecology later in this chapter, the appropriateness or inappropriateness of student behavior depends on how well it fits the expectations of the classroom ecosystem. Before we introduce the ecological analysis, however, we want to look at some features of traditional classroom structures.

TRADITIONAL CLASSROOM STRUCTURES

Most schools are organized around the age and grade level of students.

In some schools, students progress through the curriculum at their individual rates.

In U.S. schools, the most prevalent organizational structure has been the age- and grade-level level groupings of students. Although there are variations among states, school districts, and schools, children typically start school when they are five or six and continue through twelve grade levels. Schools are usually divided into elementary schools (sometimes primary- and intermediate-level schools), junior high or middle schools, and high schools. Grade levels correspond with the chronological age of students, and most students advance one grade per year. Generally, the age range in a classroom is no more than about two years, so that, for example, most first graders are six or seven and most fifth graders are about ten or eleven.

The underlying assumption of this age and grade arrangement is that similar expectations and curriculum are appropriate for students of about the same age and developmental level. A relatively small percentage of American schools are arranged not according to age and grade delineations but are "continuous progress" schools, where students progress through the curriculum at their individual rates, or "open schools," where learning is individualized according to the interests and needs of each student.

What goes on in classrooms is the **curriculum**. *Curriculum* refers to what is taught, as well as to when, how, and to whom it is taught. The academic curriculum consists of content or subject matter, and its organization or sequencing. It differs according to grade level, with higher grades building on what students learn in lower grades. The curriculum is usually divided into distinct subject matter areas: at the elementary level, these areas are usually reading, language arts, mathematics, social studies, and science, as well as physical education, music, and art. At the middle and secondary levels, these academic subjects continue, but typically there are more curricular choices within them and a wider variety of study areas. For example, high schools usually offer courses in foreign languages, forensics, and vocational education (such as auto mechanics, carpentry, office skills, drafting, and home economics). Although there are many variations in the administrative structures of schools at all levels, elementary programs generally have self-contained classrooms, consisting of a group of students assigned to a single teacher for most instruction; secondary programs generally are departmentalized with students moving from teacher to teacher for different subjects throughout the school day.

This is probably not new information, though. It sounds a lot like everyone's school experience and what one would expect to find in any classroom. So what is wrong with this seemingly logical organization of schooling?

ASSUMPTIONS OF HOMOGENEITY

One of the features of the age and grade structure and the uniform curriculum described above is an implicit assumption of homogeneity. We assume that similar expectations and experiences for learning and behavior are appropriate for all children of similar ages. However, this assumption is far from valid for two reasons. First, children do not develop at uniform rates, and second, classrooms are not uniform, homogeneous environments. For example, despite the *apparent* uniformity of curriculum within a grade level, there is no universally accepted academic curriculum. Academic content, learning objectives, activities, and experiences at any given grade level are not uniform within individual schools, let alone across school districts, states, or the country. Even in the same school, one third grade is not identical to another third grade. In one, the teacher may emphasize some areas of the curriculum more than a teacher in another class. Different instructional materials and resources may be available and used differently. In one class, instruction may be primarily didactic, involving the whole class, followed by independent seatwork; in another, a teacher may divide the class into small groups with similar academic skills; in a third, a teacher may use cooperative learning groups of students with different abilities and skills.

Every class is different because of unique characteristics that interact with one another.

Of course, even if there were a national first-grade, sixth-grade, or tenth-grade curriculum with established content, sequence, and instructional procedures, no two first-, sixth-, or tenth-grade classrooms would be exactly alike because every class is a unique mixture of students, teachers, and setting characteristics that interact with and affect one another. Any teacher who has taught a particular grade level for more than one year recognizes that each class is unique. The uniqueness of every class is one of the real challenges and pleasures of teaching.

If you think about your own experiences in elementary and secondary classrooms, you will probably remember students who did not conform to the "ideal" or "typical" expectations for their age and grade levels. Individual students at every grade level vary in their cognitive, physical, social, and emotional development. For instance, approximately 10 percent of all students are formally identified as having educationally significant disabilities and receive special education services for learning and behavior problems. Another 10 to 20 percent (or perhaps more) do not meet eligibility requirements for disabilities but do have learning problems that place them *at-risk* for educational failure (Will, 1986).

An analysis of the educational performance of American students indicates that the top 20 percent have excellent academic credentials by any measure, and the next 40 percent do fairly well and are capable of eventually graduating from college. However, "the lowest 40 percent of students are in very bad educational shape, a situation caused mostly by problems they brought with them to the kindergarten door, particularly poverty, physical and emotional handicaps, lack of health care, difficult family conditions, and violent neighborhoods" (Hodgkinson, 1993, p. 622).

These 30 to 40 percent of students who are not responsive to the usual curriculum and instructional approaches pose a tremendous challenge. As a result of their learning and behavior problems, they are often considered educational failures. Some are retained at grade level, some are consigned to low-achieving "tracks," and some are placed in compensatory, remedial, or special programs outside of regular classrooms. Many eventually drop out of school. Because they have few job-related skills, they are at greater risk of becoming unemployed or underemployed, poor, and dependent on welfare and of encountering other social problems.

To date, schools have neither created nor solved societal problems.

While our schools have not created these societal problems, neither our schools nor our society has successfully addressed them. In many respects, it is the schools, as well as the students, who have failed. It might be said that there is a mismatch between the expectations, curriculum, and organizational structures of schools and the learning and behavioral characteristics of many students.

THE IMPLICIT CURRICULUM

In addition to the apparent academic curriculum, there is an implicit or "hidden" curriculum in traditional classrooms. It is important to recognize that student and teacher behavior is influenced by more than just academic endeavors. In a classroom, much learning involves social behavior and interpersonal relationships.

Crowds, praise, and power are the three common structural features of classroom ecosystems.

Although every classroom is unique, you will also find some common features of classroom ecosystems. Phillip Jackson (1990) identified three structural features of classrooms: *crowds, praise,* and *power.* Jackson says that classrooms are typically *crowded* places where students (and teachers) function in groups. As in any group endeavor, some type of order must be maintained to ensure fairness and safety. Consequently, as teachers, we often serve in the role of "gate keepers" who manage the flow of classroom dialogue and movement, as "supply sergeants" who allocate limited space and material resources, as "judges" who grant privileges and delegate responsibilities, and as "timekeepers" who see that activities begin and end on schedule. One pervasive feature of classrooms is that students spend a lot of time waiting and taking turns. Another is that we expect students to behave as if they were alone—not talking, not looking, not communicating with one another—when, in fact, they are in the midst of a crowd.

Students have traditionally been expected not to communicate with each other even though they are in the middle of a crowd.

Praise—and its counterparts *criticism* and *disapproval*—are also ever-present in classrooms. According to Jackson, student performance (whether academic, personal, or social) is constantly under public scrutiny. Students are evaluated by teachers and other classmates. Their performance is also

The counterparts of praise are criticism and disapproval.

compared to the performance of others. Students are questioned, quizzed, and tested in ways that rarely occur in "real life": when was the last time someone asked you to diagram a sentence with thirty people watching you? In this sense, a student's successes and failures are part of the public record in classrooms. By the same token, teacher successes and failures are apparent to all students in the room.

Although *power* relationships exist in all social systems, Jackson asserts that there are sharp differences in the authority of teachers and students in classrooms. As teachers, we have authority over what students are expected to do and how they should behave. We expect students to be obedient by conforming to our wishes. Teachers exercise their power over students in different ways. Some use their position and status as well as praise and punishment to enforce obedience and conformity. Others use their position to guide students toward self-management of their behavior.

There is a wide range of ways that teachers exercise power over students in their classrooms.

Additional insights into the general features of classroom life that correspond with those described by Jackson and that speak to its ecological complexity have been offered by Walter Doyle (1986), who identified six classroom features: *multidimensionality, simultaneity, immediacy, unpredictability, public climate,* and *history.*

Multidimensionality

Multidimensionality means that many different activities, events, and tasks occur in classrooms. Classrooms are often crowded places with twenty, thirty, or even more individuals with different personalities, abilities, histories, and interests. Teachers must keep records, follow schedules, store and pass out supplies, as well as monitor, compile, and evaluate student work. A variety of subjects and activities occur in a variety of formats. Individuals and groups come and go, and any event can have multiple effects. For example, if you direct one student to pick up some paper next to her desk, you may distract other students from activities in which they are engaged.

Simultaneity

Teachers often need to manage, monitor, and direct many things at the same time.

Many things occur at the same time in classrooms, and teachers must monitor and regulate several activities *simultaneously.* At any given moment, you may be providing individual instruction to a few students doing seatwork (some of whom are paying attention, some of whom are not), while another group is working in a cooperative learning team. Several more students are working at independent learning centers, and others are preparing to leave the room for special services. At the same time, a student injured on the playground is returning from the nurse's office.

Immediacy

Effective teachers often have to make decisions on the spot rather than rely solely on planned events.

Classroom events proceed rapidly, creating an element of *immediacy*. In the example above, for instance, you must try to keep the independent learners at work, keep an eye on the cooperative group, make sure that the students going to special classes are ready to go on time with all their supplies, *and* make sure that the student who was hurt on the playground catches up with the rest of the class without disrupting others. As we know from our own experience as teachers, there is never time in these situations to pause to reflect on how the class is progressing. Teachers have to be able to make decisions on the spot if they are to stay ahead of their students.

Unpredictability

Doyle also notes that classroom events often develop in *unpredictable* ways. Distractions and interruptions frequently occur. You can't always prepare for circumstances such as the playground injury, a thunderstorm, a breakdown of the heating system, a visit from the principal, a spilled jar of paint, or a new student joining your class, let alone control events outside the classroom that affect your program. A single, unanticipated event like the playground injury will influence not only the injured student's behavior and learning but also that of the rest of the class.

Public Climate

Classrooms are also very *public* places. If one of your students is ill, others will be aware of it and affected by it (we all remember the poor soul who threw up on our third-grade teacher). If two students argue and you intervene, everyone else in the classroom is a participant observer and learns something about his or her classmates and about your ability to handle the incident. Furthermore, the arguing students and their responses to your intervention are affected by the presence of an audience. Teachers act in fishbowls (Lortie, 1975) where everyone can see and judge their behavior. In fact, classrooms offer few opportunities for privacy for either teachers or students.

History

History consists of the common experiences, values, expectations, and patterns of behavior that are established as a result of the hours that are spent and events that occur in classrooms. Experiences early in a school year are especially critical in laying a foundation for later events, as behavioral norms and routines become established. Also, the influence of history is not limited to a single year or classroom but extends back to student and teacher experiences in previous years. Students' prior educational experiences influence how they interpret and respond to their current experiences.

As a prospective teacher trying to grasp the complexity of classroom life, you might be overwhelmed by our discussion of the classroom ecosystem. Doyle's description is especially daunting when you have not yet seen your school and classroom, met your students and colleagues, or explored other aspects of your ecosystem. Don't panic. We believe that being aware of these classroom features helps prepare you for that first class.

In addition to understanding common features of classroom life, you should also be aware of some dramatic changes in American education that are fundamentally modifying these traditional conditions. We believe that the changes we have outlined in the following section have important implications for classroom management.

A NEW PARADIGM FOR EDUCATION

*In recent years what has been called a **paradigm shift** has been occurring in education.*

Over the past few years there has been growing attention to what has been called a **paradigm shift** in American education. This means that fundamental changes are occurring in both the conceptualization of education and also its form. Due to increasing awareness that the traditional educational approaches are failing to adequately prepare a significant proportion of students to be effective citizens, a nationwide movement toward **outcomes-based education (OBE)** has emerged. Implicit in "Goals 2000: Educate America Act, 1994" is the identification of *national* standards for student performance across curricular areas to guide state and local OBE plans (National Educational Goals Panel, 1991; Ysseldyke, Thurlow & Shriner, 1992). While there are various models of OBE, or "standards based education," they share several common features: (1) identification of goals or outcomes to be achieved, (2) determination of criteria for meeting the outcomes, and (3) demonstration of mastery.

KEY FEATURES OF OUTCOMES-BASED EDUCATION

In OBE, it is recognized that desired results must drive educational practices.

One key feature of OBE is a recognition that *educational practices must be directed by outcomes,* or desired results. In other words, educators must first determine educational goals—the important understandings and skills students should acquire—and then design instructional approaches to meet them. Important goals must be identified by knowledgable persons, including professional educators, parents, and community members at the district and school level.

In OBE, criteria for meeting established goals are also established.

A second key feature of OBE is determining *criteria for meeting the established goals.* That is, educators need to determine how to assess student accomplishment—how to know that students understand concepts and can perform skills. When you are a teacher, you may use *authentic assessment* instead of standardized tests that compare each student's performance to national norms. Authentic assessment includes evaluating actual student performance, often by using *portfolios,* or collections of student work and accomplishments.

Instruction in OBE occurs until students have mastered skills and concepts.

A third key feature of OBE is its emphasis on *mastery learning.* Students are not simply taught, tested, and graded with some achieving and others not achieving established criteria. Instead, instruction continues, using different approaches, materials, and formats, until students have achieved mastery of the important skills and concepts.

IMPLICATIONS OF OUTCOMES-BASED EDUCATION

Obviously, there are dramatic implications of outcomes-based education for the operation of your classroom. If it is widely implemented, the typical school and classroom of the twenty-first century may look quite different from the traditional approaches we discussed earlier. Although there will be differences in the ways OBE is implemented, the following classroom implications have been identified by Spady (1992) and others (e.g., Champlin, 1991; King & Evans, 1991):

- Educational programs will be less time-bound (e.g., with grade levels and time allocations for curriculum subjects) and more flexible to meet individual learner characteristics.

- Assessment will involve less comparison among students according to national, state, district, and classroom norms and more criterion-based evaluation (authentic assessment) of established outcomes.

- There will be less emphasis on interstudent competition and more on collaborative models of student learning.

- There will be less emphasis on covering traditional curricular content and more on ensuring important learning outcomes.

- There will be less emphasis on academic tracking and special programs for students and more on mastery learning for all students.

- Classrooms will be less isolated, discrete entities consisting of a single teacher and a group of students and more integrated environments involving collaboration among general and special educators as well as student movement among groups.

ACTIVE LEARNING

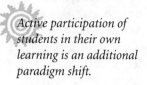

Active participation of students in their own learning is an additional paradigm shift.

An additional paradigm shift that is sometimes associated with OBE is a movement toward more **active learning** by students. *Active learning* refers to the active participation of students in their own learning and includes journal writing, cooperative groups, multimedia presentations (viewed and created), learner-centered curriculum, and critical thinking. Even though active learning and teaching to objectives have been proposed in the past (e.g., Dewey, 1902; Piaget, 1954; Tyler, 1949; Whitehead, 1932), the predominant instructional model in American schools has been "mechanistic" or didactic, with the teacher as dispenser and students as recipients of information, knowledge, and skills. The most prevalent instructional model has been lecture-recitation-drill. Although this approach can effectively transmit certain kinds of information, it is not as effective in helping students understand and apply their knowledge and skills.

A central element in the emerging active learning paradigm is that *real understanding and knowledge result from activities that enable learners to actively participate in the learning process,* not from passive consumption through rote memorization and drill. We are recognizing that demonstration, application, and experimentation through "hands-on" activities are essential to meaningful learning. This active learning has been characterized as "organic" as opposed to "mechanistic" (Salz, 1990). Traditional mechanistic instruction has tended to divide learning into its supposed component parts, which has often resulted in fragmentation of skills. For example, a mechanistic approach to reading could include teaching subskills of reading: phonics, vocabulary, spelling, and grammar. An active learning or organic approach to reading, however, would utilize a "whole language" curriculum, which does not break down reading into subcomponent skills but treats it holistically. Because active learning is important to effective teaching, we have written more about it in later sections of this book, especially in Chapter 4.

CHALLENGES FOR TEACHERS

The shift toward outcomes-based education and active learning, together with the movement toward greater inclusion of students with disabilities, should ultimately benefit both students and teachers. However, communities and schools will differ in their commitment and progress in these areas. OBE, active learning, and inclusion also challenge teachers to adopt new orientations and approaches to instruction and classroom management.

The educational innovations implicit in this paradigm shift will not diminish the importance of classroom management skills. In fact, we think it is likely that these changes will make your job even more complex and demand greater skills. For example, students with learning and behavioral disorders and other

OBE, active learning, and greater inclusion will increase the importance of classroom management skills.

disabilities will usually attend school in regular classrooms rather than in segregated educational programs where specialists work with them. Thus, your classroom will likely include students with more diverse characteristics than in the past. Also, classroom teachers can no longer rely on an established curriculum to direct their instruction. You will need skills in design, delivery, and adaptation of a variety of forms of instruction to help your students achieve established outcomes. Increased individual and small-group instructional formats will require that you use different management skills than whole-class instruction.

In addition, teachers will no longer be able to measure student learning solely on the basis of curriculum material covered, student grades, and standardized test scores. Instead, you will have to develop and collect more direct, authentic evidence of student performance. Teachers will also need to coordinate their activities with other educators as their students move among classrooms and instructors and as they function as members of collaborative teams. All of these changes mean that you will use a variety of creative approaches to classroom management. Understanding the ecological nature of classrooms can be the first step in developing the necessary skills.

A number of creative approaches will help teachers manage their classrooms.

THE ECOLOGY OF CLASSROOMS

Creative classroom management includes concern for the classroom and school ecosytems. It means you must understand, appreciate, and accommodate the differences in personality, ability, and experience of your students and yourself. Creative classroom management also involves understanding how the physical and psychological environment affects your students and you, and how it affects interactions between you and your students. Here are criteria that will help you define any ecological analysis:

- *It focuses on the interactions between persons and their environments.* Individual behavior has a reciprocal relationship with the physical and social environment where it occurs. Individuals both influence and are influenced by their environments.

- *It describes an ecosystem as a whole, rather than isolating a few features.* An ecosystem, such as a classroom, is imbedded in larger school, family, community, and cultural ecosystems; and within a classroom itself, smaller subsystems may exist.

- *It treats attitudes, feelings, and perceptions of individuals within an ecosystem as being as important as their actual behavior* (Hamilton, 1983).

Understanding the classroom as an ecosystem is key to developing management skills.

A classroom ecosystem is an interactive, dynamic environment that we can describe in terms of four clusters of variables: *students, teachers, settings,* and *activities.* We could describe each of these clusters in many ways. An exhaustive listing of all possible characteristics of each of cluster is impossible, but Figure

FIGURE 1.1 How Elements of a Classroom Ecosystem Can Intersect

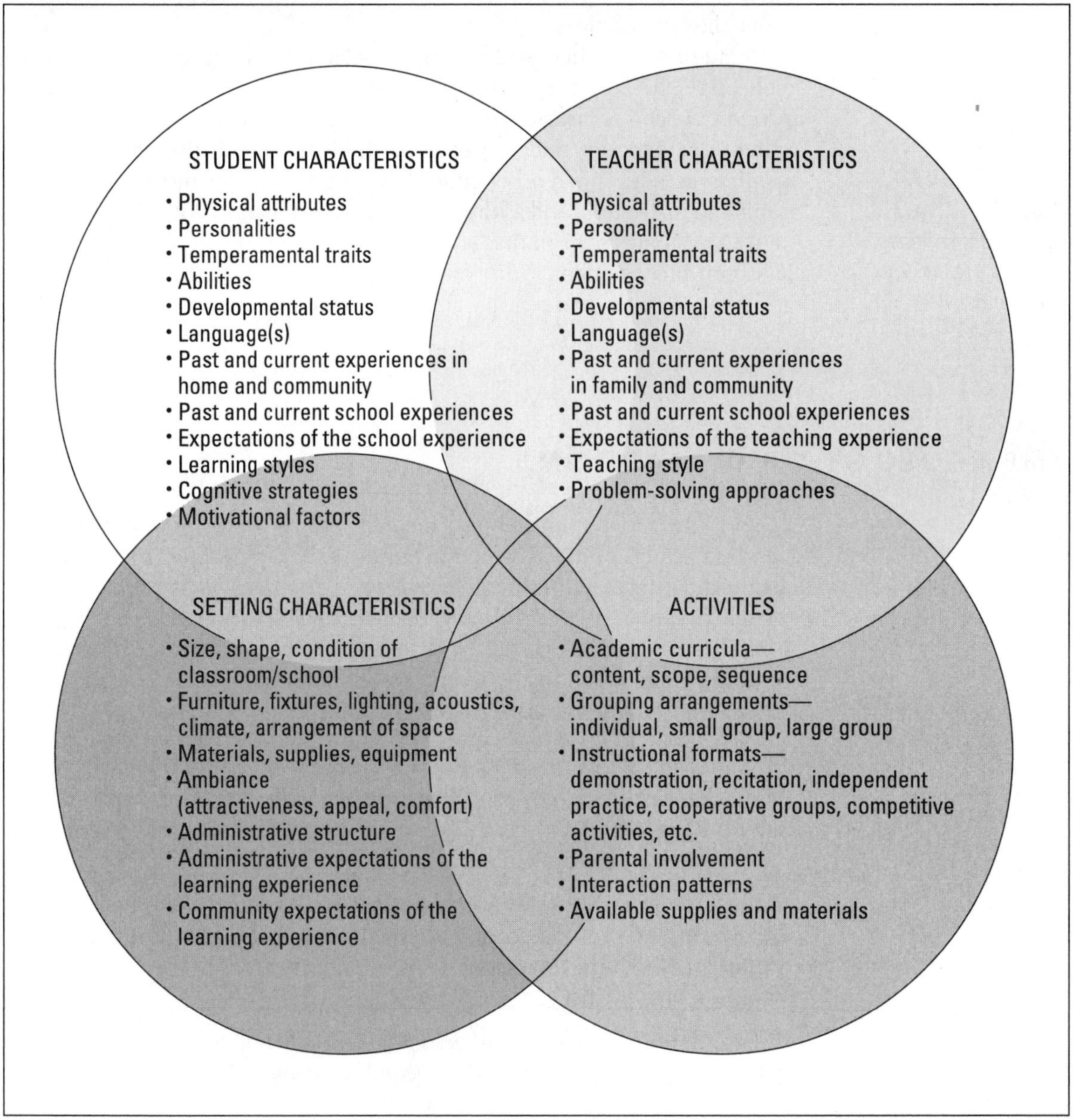

STUDENT CHARACTERISTICS

- Physical attributes
- Personalities
- Temperamental traits
- Abilities
- Developmental status
- Language(s)
- Past and current experiences in home and community
- Past and current school experiences
- Expectations of the school experience
- Learning styles
- Cognitive strategies
- Motivational factors

TEACHER CHARACTERISTICS

- Physical attributes
- Personality
- Temperamental traits
- Abilities
- Developmental status
- Language(s)
- Past and current experiences in family and community
- Past and current school experiences
- Expectations of the teaching experience
- Teaching style
- Problem-solving approaches

SETTING CHARACTERISTICS

- Size, shape, condition of classroom/school
- Furniture, fixtures, lighting, acoustics, climate, arrangement of space
- Materials, supplies, equipment
- Ambiance (attractiveness, appeal, comfort)
- Administrative structure
- Administrative expectations of the learning experience
- Community expectations of the learning experience

ACTIVITIES

- Academic curricula— content, scope, sequence
- Grouping arrangements— individual, small group, large group
- Instructional formats— demonstration, recitation, independent practice, cooperative groups, competitive activities, etc.
- Parental involvement
- Interaction patterns
- Available supplies and materials

1.1 shows you how the elements of a classroom ecosystem could intersect one another.

SIGNIFICANCE OF PHYSICAL SETTING

Every feature of a classroom ecosystem can affect students, teachers, setting, and instruction.

As you can see, it would be an ultimately impossible task to identify all the features of a classroom ecosystem. To describe even the physical characteristics of a classroom, we face the dilemma of how specific we should be. For example, desks or work tables are common features of the physical setting, but not only the number of desks and tables but also their match with student sizes, their comfort, condition, suitability for activities, and arrangement are significant. In other words, every feature of a classroom can affect students, teachers, setting, and instruction.

Consider a student who has a desk that is too small, uncomfortable, falling apart, ill-equipped with space for storage of supplies and assigned activities, and placed at the end of a long row hidden from your view. How might this student's thinking, behavior, and attitude be affected by these setting characteristics? What influences might these "desk conditions" have on *your* interaction with the student? Would this student's behavior be different if he or she sat at a more comfortable desk, in good condition, with adequate storage and surface working area, near you?

Or consider a classroom where there are no individual desks. Instead, students sit or stand at round tables with a group of four other students who are working on cooperative learning tasks. Or a student sits alone working on programmed learning tasks at a computer table. In each of these scenarios, the students' behavior, feelings, and learning (and *your* behavior, feelings, and instruction) are directly affected by the nature of the classroom furniture, its condition, and its arrangement as well as by the multitude of additional characteristics of the setting, other students and teachers, and activities.

The direct result of disparities in educational funding is diminished programs in poor school districts.

In *Savage Inequalities* (1991), Jonathan Kozol shows how disparities in educational funding result in striking inequities in resources, materials, equipment, facilities, and personnel between affluent and poor school districts. The result is that better-funded schools can offer more enriched experiences for their students while poorly funded schools can afford only diminished programs. Even within individual schools, whether relatively well or poorly funded, disparities are often evident in the resources teachers find and the ways they use them. The accompanying Classroom Closeup on "Contrasting Classroom Ecosystems in a Chicago School" contains Kozol's descriptions of two very different classroom ecosystems in the same poorly funded school in the Lawndale area of Chicago.

As a student or teacher, which of these classrooms would *you* prefer? Striking differences between the two classrooms highlight their physical and psychological characteristics. The first classroom, relatively barren and cold,

Classroom Closeup

Contrasting Classroom Ecosystems in a Chicago School

Classroom 1

The room is sparse—a large and clean but rather cheerless space. There are very few of those manipulable objects and bright-colored shelves and boxes that adorn suburban kindergarten classrooms. The only decorations on the walls are posters supplied by companies that market school materials. . . . Nothing the children or teacher made themselves. . . .

In a somewhat mechanical way, the teacher lifts a picture book of Mother Goose and flips the pages as the children sit before her on the rug. . . .

The children recite the verses with her as she turns the pages of the book. She's not very warm or animated as she does it, but the children are obedient and seem to like the fun of showing that they know the words. The book looks worn and old, as if the teacher's used it many, many years, and it shows no sign of adaptation to the race of the black children in the school. (Kozol, 1991, pp. 44–45)

Classroom 2

The classroom is full of lively voices when I enter. The children are at work, surrounded by a clutter of big dictionaries, picture books and gadgets, science games and plants and colorful milk cartons, which the teacher purchased out of her own salary. An oversized Van Gogh collection, open to a print of a sunflower, is balanced on a table-ledge next to a fish tank and a turtle tank. Next to the table is a rocking chair. Handwritten signs are on all sides: "Getting to know you," "Keeping you safe," and, over a wall that holds some artwork by the children, "Mrs. Hawkins's Academy of Fine Arts." Near the windows, the oversized leaves of several wild-looking plants partially cover rows of novels, math books, and a new World Book Encyclopedia. In the opposite corner is a "Science Learning Board" that holds small packets which contain bulb sockets, bulbs and wires, lenses, magnets, balance scales and pliers. In front of the learning board is a microscope. Several rugs are thrown around the floor. . . .

The 30 children in the class are seated in groups of six at five of what she calls "departments." Each department is composed of six desks pushed together to create a table. One of the groups is doing math, another something that they call "math strategy." A third is doing reading. Of the other two groups, one is doing something they describe as "mathematics art"—painting composites of geometric shapes—and the other is studying "careers," which on this morning is a writing exercise about successful business leaders who began their lives in poverty. (Kozol, 1991, pp. 47–48) ✳

communicates distance between teacher and students. In contrast, the second classroom communicates the teacher's warmth and involvement with her students. She has designed a comfortable, engaging environment to facilitate the students' learning. You can imagine how each of these classroom environments would affect the learning and behavior of students. How would they affect the teacher's behavior?

Physical features of a classroom *are* important to student learning and behavior, but they reflect and influence social and emotional features as well. In the contrasting classroom descriptions in the Classroom Closeup box, there are differences in the available equipment, resources, instructional materials, and supplies. However, the two different classroom environments also reflect two teachers' very differing approaches to teaching and learning.

SIGNIFICANCE OF TEACHING STYLE: INVITATIONAL TEACHING

In the first classroom the teacher is just "going through the motions." The classroom arrangement, use of materials, and instructional approaches seem ungrounded in any guiding philosophy or purpose. The teacher of the second class, however, knows what she wants to achieve and has deliberately designed her classroom to meet those goals: "'This is the point of it,' she says. 'I'm teaching them three things. Number one: self-motivation. Number two: self-esteem. Number three: you help your sister and your brother. . . . The most important thing for me is that they teach each other'" (Kozol, 1991, pp. 48–49).

Although she may not express her teaching style using the same terms, this teacher practices **invitational teaching**, which asserts that "the primary goal of teaching is to cordially summon individuals to see themselves as able, valuable, and responsible and to behave accordingly" (Purkey & Stanley, 1991, p. 16). She communicates her philosophy in the ways she has designed the classroom environment and in her choices of instructional content and activities as well as how show talks with students.

Student motivation and achievement can be linked to a teacher's trust, respect, optimism, and intentionality.

Invitational teaching reflects an attitude, or a philosophy, about teaching and teacher-student relationships. It draws from the ideas of Carl Rogers (see *Freedom to Learn*, 1969, and *A Way of Being*, 1980), who urged teachers to intentionally communicate their respect and caring for their students as unique human beings. Invitational teaching also draws upon research that links student motivation and achievement with positive teacher expectations (Brophy, 1987; Good & Brophy, 1991). The cornerstones of invitational teaching are developing *trust, respect, optimism,* and *intentionality.*

Trust is established when you use cooperative, collaborative activities to develop *inter*dependence in your classroom, among students, yourself, and others who may be present. An integral goal of invitational teaching is to trust students to take an active role in their learning—to focus more on what students *can* do than what they cannot. A corollary of trust is communicating mutual *respect,* as "manifested by the teacher's caring and appropriate behavior, as well as by places, policies, programs, and processes created and maintained by teachers" (Purkey & Stanley, 1991, p. 18). You communicate respect by being reliable and trustworthy, by setting reasonable expectations for students, by holding students accountable for their academic and social behavior, and expecting them to be respectful in turn. Invitational teachers are also *optimistic*. You communicate an optimistic belief that your students will learn when "the classroom appearance, the discipline policy, the academic program, the organizational process, and the actions of people" communicate optimism about their ability to succeed (Purkey & Stanley, 1991, pp. 24–25). Finally, invitational teachers demonstrate their *intentionality* by deliberately selecting and using instructional and management approaches that serve their instructional goals. Your consistency and dependability communicate intentionality and purposefulness to your students.

Teachers' beliefs and attitudes generate their instructional and management practices.

If trust, respect, optimism, and intentionality sound more like attitudes and beliefs about students and teaching than specific classroom practices, they are. However, *your beliefs and attitudes generate your instructional and management practices.* We believe that student behavior and academic performance are in large measure a reflection of how students think and feel about themselves, about their teachers, and about their schools. When you trust and respect your students, when you are optimistic about their competence, and when you intentionally design classrooms for them, you are likely to have students who trust and respect you and their classmates, and who achieve and behave in caring, cooperative ways. Speaking of ties between teacher-student relationships and student behavior, Morgansett (1991) comments, "In the classroom students who feel accepted by their teachers are more likely to do what the teacher asks of them (e.g., assignments) and less likely to do things that make teachers' lives difficult (e.g., disrupt)" (p. 261).

THE CLASSROOM AND OTHER ECOSYSTEMS

Although to this point we have been considering classrooms as distinct ecosystems, they actually have indistinct boundaries and overlap with other interaction systems. As we noted earlier, a classroom exists within other ecosystems such as the school and community. Within the school, for example, there can be several distinct ecosystems with different participants, settings, and activity characteristics. Ecosystems within schools include other classrooms, lunchrooms, playgrounds, gyms, school busses, hallways, and administrative offices.

In addition, teachers and students participate in ecosystems outside of school, including homes, neighborhoods, and communities. Figure 1.2 depicts various levels of ecosystems.

Students' experiences in ecosystems outside and inside school affect their behavior in the classroom ecosystem.

It is important to recognize that each of these interaction systems affects and is affected by the others. Your students' experiences in the larger contexts of their school, home, neighborhood, and community influence their thinking, feeling, and behaving in your classroom just as your experiences in the broader ecosystems that you inhabit affect how you think, feel, and behave in school. In the same way your classroom experiences and those of your students affect those broader environments.

FIGURE 1.2 Various Levels of Ecosystems

Classroom

Home

School

Neighborhood

Community

Region

Nation

World

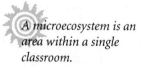

A microecosystem is an area within a single classroom.

While we can identify the larger ecological contexts that encompass classrooms, we might also consider *areas* within a single classroom as *microecosystems*. For example, you may have several groups of four or five students working on cooperative learning activities in separate areas of your classroom for thirty minutes every day. You may have learning centers comprised of participating students, setting characteristics, and activities. In most classrooms these internal ecosystems are fluid and constantly changing rather than static.

Nothing that happens in a classroom occurs in a vacuum. You do not teach under laboratory conditions where you can control all the variables and always predict outcomes. This is why teaching often has been referred to as an art, as opposed to a science. Like all forms of art it requires a blending of technique and creativity. Good teaching combines your personality with your skills as influenced by the students, settings, and activities you encounter.

THE TEACHER'S ROLE AS FACILITATOR

Given the ecological nature of classrooms, we can never fully control all aspects of the classroom environment. As a teacher, you are only one element—albeit a critical one—of a multifaceted, interactive, dynamic system. In addition, you generally have limited influence over your students' lives outside your classroom and no direct influence on their lives before they enter our classrooms. You also have limited influence over the physical setting of a school and classroom and over the resources available.

However, as a classroom teacher *you are the most critical determinant of your classroom environment.* More than any other element, *you* will guide the learning and behavior that occur in your classroom. You will communicate expectations, arrange the physical setting, determine the "psychological" atmosphere, motivate your students to learn and behave, devise and implement instructional and other activities, and set the tone for interactions between your classroom and the larger worlds of the school, community, and society. You will communicate your classroom leadership skills in everything you say and do. As teacher, you are the leader of your classroom.

Teachers have their authority tested every day and must be able to demonstrate that they have the energy and skills deserving of their leadership role (Wood, 1991). In addition, you must recognize and help meet your students' individual and group needs. You must know your students and show that you like them by being fair and objective and not rejecting, isolating, or scapegoating individuals. In addition, to be an effective classroom leader, you must dependably reward desirable group behavior and discourage inappropriate behavior (Wood, 1991).

Given the limitations and opportunities of the classroom teacher, we think it is helpful to view teaching as facilitating the learning and behavior of your students. A facilitator understands the ecological nature of classrooms and seeks to establish a good fit, or balance, among the unique elements of students, teachers, settings, and activities. An effective facilitator is foremost an effective communicator. In the next chapter, we focus on classroom communication or classroom discourse. We will examine the many ways teachers and students communicate in classrooms and study ways you can use communication to manage your classroom.

The teacher is the most important determinant of the classroom environment.

Effective teachers reward desirable group behavior and discourage inappropriate behavior.

SUMMARY AND REVIEW

In this chapter, we have stressed the challenges and opportunities facing classroom teachers and the importance of an ecological perspective of classroom management. We discussed implications of teachers' concerns about "discipline" and student "misbehavior" and suggested more ecological approaches to understanding and dealing with behavior in context.

Despite assumptions of homogeneity in traditional classrooms, today's classrooms are actually complex, dynamic social interaction systems inhabited by diverse individuals and groups, including those that are defined according to racial, ethnic, cultural, social status, gender, and educational (dis)ability characteristics. Classrooms are characterized by both an explicit and hidden curriculum that influences academic instruction and classroom management.

Revolutionary changes—described as a major "paradigm shift"—are occurring that will influence the ways you teach and manage your classroom. Increased inclusion of diverse learners in regular classrooms, outcomes-based education, and active learning are three developments that demand even greater competence in classroom management than were needed in the past.

The goal of the effective teacher is to recognize and appreciate the diversity of classrooms and attempt to facilitate the learning and behavior of all students. In the next chapter, we will examine in more detail a critical feature of classroom management—communication.

REFLECTING ON CHAPTER 1

As Annie worried about her new job and her new class in the journal entry at the beginning of this chapter, she focused on her personal feelings about the first days of school. As you have seen in this chapter, there were a lot of other things she could have worried about! Teaching today is a complex and difficult task, one that incorporates many skills, attitudes, and situations that were not present, or at least not acknowledged, in classrooms a decade or two ago. Talk with your classmates about the changes and differences in your own experience:

- How similar or different are the schools you attended from those in the community where you live now?

- How did your school experience differ from that of your parents?

- What kinds of ethnic, social, or language diversity do you have in your own family? (What languages are spoken, what holidays are celebrated, what traditions do you continue?)

Key Terms

inclusion (p. 8)	outcomes-based education (p. 8)
ecosystem (p. 12)	curriculum (p. 13)
paradigm shift (p. 18)	active learning (p. 20)
invitational teaching (p. 25)	

Building Your Own Knowledge Base: Suggested Readings

Jackson, P. (1990). *Life in Classrooms.* New York: Holt, Rinehart and Winston. Reissued in 1990, this classic 1968 examination of the "hidden curriculum" takes the reader inside classrooms.

Kidder, T. (1989). *Among Schoolchildren.* Boston: Houghton Mifflin. A sensitive, engaging account of the experiences, thoughts, and feelings of an elementary classroom teacher in Holyoke, Massachusetts, over the course of a school year.

Lortie, D. (1975). *Schoolteacher.* Chicago: University of Chicago Press. A sociological analysis of the challenges and rewards of teaching.

Veenman, S. (1986). Perceived problems of beginning teachers. *Review of Educational Research, 54,* 143–178. Reviews and summarizes the results of studies regarding the concerns of new teachers.

References

Brophy, J. (1987). Synthesis of research on strategies for motivating students to learn. *Educational Leadership, 45,* 40–48.

Champlin, J. R. (1991). Taking stock and moving on. *Journal of the National Center for Outcome-Based Education, 1,* 5–8.

Darling-Hammond, L. (1990). Teachers and teaching: Signs of a changing profession. In W. R. Houston (Ed.), *Handbook of research on teacher education* (pp. 267–290). New York: MacMillan.

Dewey, J. (1902). *The child and the curriculum.* Chicago: University of Chicago Press.

Doyle, W. (1986). Classroom organization and management. In W. C. Wittrock (Ed.), *Handbook of research on teaching* (3rd ed.). New York: MacMillan.

Feinman-Nemser, S., & Floden, R. E. (1986). The cultures of teaching. In M. C. Wittrock (Ed.), *Handbook of research on teaching* (3rd ed.). New York: MacMillan.

Good, T., & Brophy, J. (1991). *Looking in classrooms* (5th ed.). New York: Harper & Row.

Hamilton, S. F. (1983). The social side of schooling: Ecological studies of classrooms and schools. *Elementary School Journal, 83,* 313–334.

Hodgkinson, H. (1993). American education: The good, the bad, and the task. *Phi Delta Kappan,* (April), 612–623.

Jackson, P. W. (1990). *Life in classrooms.* New York: Holt, Rinehart and Winston.

Kidder, T. (1989). *Among schoolchildren.* Boston: Houghton Mifflin.

King, J. A., & Evans, K. M. (1991). Can we achieve outcome-based education? *Educational Leadership, 49,* 73–75.

Kozol, J. (1991). *Savage inequalities: Children in America's schools.* New York: Crown.

Lortie, D. (1975). *Schoolteacher.* Chicago: University of Chicago Press.

Morgansett, L. (1991). Good teacher-student relationships: A key element in classroom motivation and management. *Education, 112,* 260–264.

National Commission on Excellence in Education (1983). *A nation at risk: The imperative for educational reform.* Washington, DC: U.S. Government Printing Office.

National Educational Goals Panel. (1991). *The national education goals report: Building a nation of learners.* Washington, DC: U.S. Government Printing Office.

Piaget, J. (1954). *The construction of reality in the child.* New York: Basic Books.

Purkey, W. W., & Stanley, P. H. (1991). *Invitational teaching, learning, and living.* Washington, DC: National Education Association.

Rogers, C. (1969). *Freedom to learn.* Columbus, OH: Merrill.

Rogers, C. (1980). *A way of being.* Boston: Houghton Mifflin.

Salz, A. (1990). The roots of revolution in education. *Educational Forum, 54,* 389–405.

Spady, W. G. (1992). It's time to take a close look at outcome-based education. *Communique, 20,* 16–18.

Tyler, R. W. (1949). *Basic principles of curriculum and instruction: Syllabus for education 360.* Chicago: University of Chicago Press.

Veenman, S. (1986). Perceived problems of beginning teachers. *Review of Educational Research, 54,* 143–178.

Whitehead, A. N. (1932). *The aims of education and other essays.* London: Williams and Norgate.

Will, M. (1986). Education of children with learning problems: A shared responsibility. *Exceptional Children, 52,* 411–415.

Wood, F. H. (1991). Cost/benefit considerations in managing the behavior of students with emotional/behavioral disorders. *Preventing School Failure, 35,* 17–23.

Ysseldyke, J. E., Thurlow, M. L., & Shriner, J. G. (1992). Outcomes are for special educators too. *Teaching Exceptional Children, 25,* 36–50.

Forms of Classroom Communication

- Communication and classroom management
- Verbal communication
- Nonverbal communication
- Paralanguage

Framing

- Power
- Solidarity
- Self-disclosure
- Humor
- Turn-taking
- Dialogue

Communication in the Classroom Ecosystem

Cultural Compatibility in Classroom Communications

- Classroom social organization
- Sociolinguistics
- Cognition
- Motivation

Gender and Classroom Communication

- Gender patterns in teacher-student interactions
- Social learning factors
- The students' beliefs

Chapter **2**

Communication in the Classroom Ecosystem

Annie's Journal

SEPTEMBER: Well, I've survived the first two weeks of school. I can't say they've exactly flown by, but I do feel good about getting this far. Most of the things I worried about didn't happen. I did find the school, no one got up and left the first day refusing to come back, they all speak enough English to communicate with me—although Rafael and Lupe are still working with the ESL teacher three times a week. I don't feel completely comfortable with that situation yet—I need to find the time to talk with Gloria (our ESL teacher) and find out how I should be modifying things in class. Lupe in particular doesn't seem to be following what I'm saying a lot of the time, but I'm afraid if I slow down too much or try to repeat, I'll lose the other kids.

That reminds me of something I noticed the other day. Before I started teaching, I always thought about "my class" as though they were a solid mass or a single organism—kind of like coral. I didn't really think of them as individuals with different moods, needs, personalities, etc. That sounds really stupid when I write it down. I guess what I mean is that I didn't think about how hard it would be to *balance* all those different selves as I tried to go about my business as a teacher. For example, I have kids who like to move along really quickly when we're having a discussion. Asif, for instance, has lived in several different countries and has really neat things to say when we talk about different parts of the world. But some of the other kids, Terrell and Aaron in particular, just look out the window during these discussions and don't seem interested at all. How do I balance those differing needs? Or are they differing styles?

I also worry about this when I ask the class questions. I mean, I remember all the stuff I read about how teachers call on boys more often, and about how wait time is important, but when you have four or five kids waving their arms in the air saying "I know! I know!" it's hard to ignore them and call on someone who doesn't even look interested! In fact, I don't know that I should. I mean, if I call on someone who didn't raise a hand and who doesn't know the answer, then they'll be really embarrassed and that certainly won't encourage future volunteering. . . . And another thing—I try to be positive and reinforcing when I do ask them questions. I don't put anyone down if they don't know or if they get it wrong, but there are still several kids who never volunteer. I think they know the answers, but they just don't raise their hands. . . . How do I get them to *want* to participate?

OK—this is therapeutic—what else am I worried about at this point? Let's see . . . there's Matt who sits at his desk with his arms folded across his chest and seems to be daring me to teach him anything . . . There's Rolandria, who's my shadow. Every time I turn around, there she is—which isn't so terrible, except I want her to get to know some of the *kids* (she's new to the school this year), not just the teacher. . . . There's Nketi (boy, did I worry about pronouncing *his* name before school started!), who has informed me at least six times that he's going to be a doctor, so all he needs to learn is math and science . . . and Carla, who has not stopped talking since the first minute she walked in the room. I worry about some of the students I haven't gotten to know very well yet—like Justin, who is so quiet I could forget he's there. I don't mind the quiet part, but he looks worried all the time—maybe that's just the way he looks. . . . I'm really concerned about Danny and Tremaine, however. They're quite a pair . . . always together, whispering, giggling, starting stuff. If there's a burst of noise, they're at the center of it. There was a fight on the playground yesterday, and guess who were the first spectators? . . . I don't know what to make of them yet, but I'm watching!

I had to drop the idea of not smiling until Christmas—just couldn't pull it off—but I do hear myself raising my voice and saying "No!" and "Quiet down, please!" much more often than I'd like to. I hope that's just first-of-the-year energy and that we'll get past it soon. I want to communicate positive things to the kids, let them know that we're on this adventure together, but I don't really know how to do that yet. I try to use positive language, walk around the room so I'm near the kids, vary my voice—all that stuff—but it's a lot to remember! (Speaking of remembering, yesterday I forgot we were supposed to go to art and the secretary had to ask me over the intercom if we were coming—not *too* embarrassing. The kids loved it.)

FOCUS QUESTIONS

✳ How should teachers deal with the kind of question-asking dilemma Annie has?

✳ How might teachers approach the difference in discussion interest that Annie describes?

✷ What are some communication issues Annie needs to think about?

✷ How might having a diverse group of students influence a teacher's communication strategies?

HOW CLASSROOM MANAGEMENT AND COMMUNICATION FIT TOGETHER

In the last chapter, we discussed the concept of the ecosystem and how it can be applied to classrooms. If we accept that model, then how does a term like *classroom management* fit? If we are conscious of and responsive to all the elements of the classroom ecosystem, aware of how each action affects all the parts of the system, and of how we in turn are affected by those responses, what does that mean for classroom management?

When we consider management in other contexts, it is clear that managers often have tools that we, as teachers, do not. For example, professional sports teams are managed (sort of), but those managers have multi-million dollar contracts at their disposal to modify the behavior of the players. Hotels and stores are managed, but those managers select their employees and can fire anyone who doesn't conform to their expectations. Corporations or even individuals may have money managers or business managers, but they manage resources and somewhat predictable commodities more than they manage people. Teachers, however, are classroom managers with no control over who signs up, no freedom to "fire" those who don't conform, and no reinforcers in the multimillion dollar range to encourage peak performance.

Teachers do not have all the same tools that managers in other contexts have.

So how does management fit the ecological model of classrooms? Very carefully—with sensitive planning, careful implementation, constant evaluation, and ongoing concern for the results and responses generated by the intervention. What are the tools of a classroom manager—a teacher? Clearly not money or power or ability to select those they manage. Instead, teachers' tools for classroom management are found in communication. They include an understanding of the content and process of communication. We are often dismayed by programs or books about classroom management (or more often about discipline) that take a cookbook or instruction manual approach. Effective classroom management is not a matter of looking up the problem and applying the listed solution. It is established in the everyday interactions between teacher and students—the classroom discourse, the body language, the verbal and nonverbal messages about what is appropriate and inappropriate behavior. To borrow a term from those other managers, the bottom line is this: *Effective classroom management is a function of effective classroom communication.*

A teacher's management tools are found in a variety of forms of communication.

A key point to bear in mind is that effective classroom management results from effective classroom communication.

In this chapter, we explore some apparent and not so apparent aspects of classroom communication. We examine forms of classroom communication, features of effective and ineffective communication, and the influence of individual and cultural variations in verbal and nonverbal communication. We also suggest ways you can understand and use communication to facilitate learning and create positive, caring, cooperative environments in your classroom.

FORMS OF CLASSROOM COMMUNICATION

A classroom is a communication system in which there is an interchange of ideas, feelings, and information among students and teachers. When you consider classroom communication, what comes to mind? You might first think of how teachers speak and write as they teach. As a teacher you will instruct, explain, direct, provide feedback, and demonstrate ideas, information, and skills using spoken and written language. Your students will exchange thoughts and information with you and with one another using both spoken and written language. Certainly, these kinds of instruction-relevant communication are critical in classrooms.

A student's success or failure in school often reflects his or her social relationships with teachers.

In addition to instruction, classroom communication determines social relationships. Students and teachers communicate their attitudes, motives, and feelings about learning, about school, and about themselves and others in the ways they interact with one another. A student's success or failure in school is largely a reflection of the social relationships that are developed between the child and his or her teachers (McDermott, 1977). When students are considered problems, that is often evidence of miscommunication or a breakdown of communication.

Verbal (spoken and written) communication is important, but classroom communication takes additional forms that directly and indirectly involve behavior and learning. Furthermore, verbal communication is more than just words. Whether people are writing or speaking, the ways they put words together—their intonation, emphasis, and context—communicate meaning. So classroom communication involves more than spoken and written language; it includes *all* of the verbal and nonverbal interchanges among students, teachers, and anyone else who is in the classroom.

Nonverbal communication can support verbal communication or confuse and contradict it.

Nonverbal communication takes many forms, including how far away people stand from each other, their positions, gestures, facial expressions, eye contact, and other body language. Sometimes your nonverbal behavior supports your verbal communication, as when you smile while saying something positive. Sometimes, however, nonverbal behavior confuses or even contradicts verbal communication, as when you show no expression or frown while saying something positive.

Classroom communication also involves what you do *not* say and do as well as what you *do* say and do. For example, when a student does not answer your questions or follow your instructions, that nonevent might communicate several possibilities: the student does not hear your question, does not understand the question, does not realize the question is directed at him or her, does not know the answer, or does not want to answer the question.

At another level, aspects of the *physical environment* and what we call the *psychological milieu* are forms of classroom communication. The way you arrange classroom furniture communicates attitudes and expectations for student behavior. The physical environment partly determines the kinds of interaction that are likely to occur between you and your students. Consider, for example, how the arrangement of a single element of your classroom, such as the location of your desk, could promote or inhibit communication, instruction, or traffic flow. In Chapters 4 and 5 we will see how your classroom's arrangement and decor communicate attitudes, values, and feelings about yourself, your teaching philosophy, and the activities you expect to occur.

Furniture arrangement and other aspects of the physical environment also communicate attitudes and expectations.

BECOMING AWARE OF VERBAL AND NONVERBAL COMMUNICATION

Communication is a very broad and complex topic, and we will by no means say all there is to say about it in this chapter. Our aim here is to help you become more aware of the role of verbal and nonverbal communication in classroom behavior. We will point out some aspects of classroom communication that appear to be universal, as well as those that reflect sociocultural and individual differences. Understanding as much as possible about communication is an important aspect of being a successful problem-solver in your classroom.

As we mentioned earlier, classroom communication is not a one-way street, with teachers simply transmitting information *to* students. Rather, communication is both *interactive* and *dynamic*. It is interactive in that it requires at least two persons exchanging information. Your instructions, lectures, or demonstrations do not communicate unless your students understand them. Communication involves both expressive language (saying, doing) and receptive language (hearing, seeing, understanding) by both teachers and students. As a teacher, you express thoughts, motives, and feelings to your students, who must be able to understand you. Likewise, your students express their thoughts, motives, and feelings, which you and others must understand.

Classroom communication is *dynamic* in that you and your students continuously adjust and adapt to the changing nature of the communications that occur. Classroom communication is anything but a static or simple

In interactive communication, at least two people are expressing and hearing thoughts, motives, and feelings to each other.

Dynamic communication requires that people adjust to the changing nature of communications.

give-and-take interaction. There are many opportunities for miscommunication, which may be considered behavior problems. For example, when students are uninvolved, distracted, inconsiderate, disruptive, or stubborn, that may indicate that they do not understand what you are trying to communicate or that you do not understand what they are trying to communicate. In more extreme situations, withdrawal, arguments, or fights may result from miscommunications. For example, in your effort to comfort a distraught student, you might approach the student, smile, and place your hand on the student's shoulder—all of which could reinforce your comforting words. However, if the student sees your smile as insincere, your words as abrupt, and your body language as communicating social distance rather than warmth, the student will not experience your behavior as reassuring.

Linguistic and Cultural Differences

Recognizing linguistic and cultural differences in language is important for effective classroom communication.

Teachers must be especially sensitive to linguistic and cultural differences in the ways they and their students display and interpret verbal and nonverbal behavior. Obviously, a student's lack of proficiency in the language of instruction interferes with communication and, in some cases, leads to misconceptions about the student's abilities. Also, a student's family and cultural background can lead to different interpretations of your nonverbal behavior than you intend. One student may experience your smile and pat on the shoulder as your effort to provide reassurance; another student, though, may experience your smile and pat as intrusion into his or her personal space. By the same token, you may find a student's slang, nonstandard dialect, or profanity inappropriate or offensive, but in that student's home, this type of communication may not be inappropriate or offensive.

Because of linguistic and cultural differences, behavior considered inappropriate in school may be fine in the home.

Some students are especially sensitive to how they are treated by authorities (like teachers) and how their peers see them treated. The important reference group for establishing their sense of respect is not so much their teacher as their peers. This phenomenon exists to a degree in all classrooms. In the inner city, the "code of the streets" reflects this demand for respect (Anderson, 1990, 1994). The central feature of this code is a willingness on the part of youth to engage in violence if necessary to gain or retain respect from others. The youths communicate in their facial expressions, gait, and verbal expressions, as well as clothing, jewelry, and grooming that they take care of themselves and will not be intimidated. The purpose is to deter aggression by others (Anderson, 1994).

Clearly, the kinds of behavior Anderson describes are not limited to interactions that occur on the streets. They are also powerful influences on children's behavior in schools and classrooms.

Classroom communication patterns always reflect the larger ecosystems in which students live. Even students who use the same patterns of communi-

Teachers may not always be familiar or comfortable with students' expectations about language but they need to become aware of these expectations.

cation we try to promote in our classrooms bring expectations and meanings about verbal and nonverbal communication that we are sometimes unfamiliar or uncomfortable with. There is no right or wrong type of verbal and nonverbal communication. What is essential is that you be sensitive to the individual and group differences in verbal and nonverbal behavior in your classroom and become more aware of your own behavior. Teachers need to understand teacher and student patterns of communication in their classes and make sure their students understand them as well.

VERBAL COMMUNICATION

Most classroom teaching uses spoken language, but the spoken language of classrooms is very different from conversations outside of school (Cazden, 1986, 1988). For one thing, teachers control talk in most classrooms, both to avoid verbal collisions and to provide instruction.

Spoken language in the classroom is very different from the spoken language outside of school.

Because spoken and written language are involved in most instruction and evaluation of student performance, and are integral to the identities of students and teachers alike, they deserve attention: "All human behavior is culturally based. Ways of talking that seem so natural to one group are experienced as culturally strange to another" (Cazden, 1988, p. 67). Variation in ways of speaking is a fact of life. Students come to school from families, neighborhoods, and ethnic and linguistic backgrounds that influence how they speak and how they understand spoken language. "Differences in how something is said, and even when, can be matters of only temporary adjustment, or they can seriously impair effective teaching and accurate evaluation" (Cazden, 1988, p. 3).

Verbal/Analytic Versus Visual/Holistic Language

Verbal/Analytic language often does not meet the instructional needs of students with language and/or cultural minority backgrounds.

In most traditional classrooms, the curriculum emphasizes **verbal/analytic language** over **visual/holistic language.** In verbal/analytic language, teachers instruct students by using rules, abstractions, and verbal descriptions; they assume that students will understand the concepts by learning the parts. They assume that students learn from verbal instructions, as when a teacher asks them to add numbers with paper and pencil. Visual/holistic, or global instruction, however, starts with the whole concept gradually revealing its parts. Students learn concepts by observing and doing, as when a teacher has students group tangible objects together to see what they add up to. Some students, including those with language disabilities, flounder when confronted with verbal/analytic instruction because they have difficulty processing spoken and written language; students with language or cultural minority backgrounds are often less fluent and comfortable with this instruction.

Classroom communication patterns often fail to match the needs of students from linguistic and cultural minorities (Cummins, 1989; Garcia,

1994; Heath, 1983; Tharp, 1989). This is a significant problem since a sizable proportion of American students represents language or ethnic minorities, and the population is growing: "In less than two decades, one-half of the students in the U.S. schools will be nonwhite and Hispanic—and half of these students will speak a language other than English on their first day of school" (Garcia, 1994, p. 38).

African-American students, in a study of recently desegregated classrooms with white teachers, were reluctant to answer teachers' questions primarily because of a discontinuity between students' home language and school language (Heath, 1983). Teachers who have students who are more comfortable using a nonstandard dialect (e.g., black English vernacular) could begin with content and types of talk that are familiar to the students and gradually introduce new, less familiar kinds of talk (e.g., standard English). In other words, teachers should "contextualize" instruction (Health, 1983), drawing on students' experience, previous knowledge, and schemata (or ways of thinking).

Contexturalized instruction is relevant to students and uses language that they are comfortable with.

Contextualization means making instruction relevant to the lives of students and using communication that is compatible with the patterns students feel comfortable using. In language, as well as in other types of instruction, teachers should attempt to place instruction in a meaningful context, drawing on the personal, everyday experiences of students and stimulating thought and discussion of relevant personal experiences before introducing new material (Tharp, 1989). For example, in social studies, teachers could use actual photographs of the students' community and ask questions about the neighborhoods. Teachers could use peer models in photographs, audiotape "appropriate" classroom discourse, and even discuss with students different ways of asking and answering questions (Health, 1983). These kinds of approaches can help you make instruction more relevant for your students. Contextualization involves using culturally based materials and approaches including visual/holistic processes that can benefit both minority- *and* majority-culture students and can be particularly useful to underachieving students:

> If schools themselves take seriously the task of teaching, then there are universalistic teaching/learning strategies that are desirable for all students at this time in North American history. These features include varied activity settings, language development activities, varied sensory modalities in instruction, responsive instructional conversations, increased cooperative and group activities, and a respectful and accommodating sensitivity to students' knowledge, experience, values, and tastes. (Tharp, 1989, p. 356)

IRE, a form of public evaluation, rately occurs in adult-adult interchanges.

Instruction-Response-Evaluation.   How many times in informal conversation or even in formal conversation do you ask people questions for which you already know the answer? Probably not very often, yet in classrooms this happens all the time. Not only do teachers ask questions when they know the answers, but they also evaluate the answers. This pattern is known as as **IRE:**

teacher Instruction, student Response, teacher Evaluation (Cazden, 1988). Here are two examples of an IRE exchange:

Teacher: John, spell *carrot.* (*Instruction*)
John: *C-a-r-r-o-t* (*Response*)
Teacher: Right. (*Evaluation*)

or

Teacher: What time does the clock say, LaShawna? (*Instruction*)
LaShawna: 10:35. (*Response*)
Teacher: Yes. The time is 10:35. (*Evaluation*)

This known-answer questioning followed by evaluation of the response happens rarely except in adult-child interactions. It is important to realize that the above interchange is not just a simple question but a form of public evaluation. Teachers need to choose their words and responses carefully in these interactions. Consider the side effects when a student often gives answers the teacher judges to be wrong. The logical outcome is for that student to avoid being asked questions, to withdraw, or to create some distraction to sidetrack the questionner. Any of these responses might be seen as forms of classroom misbehavior.

The Teacher-Talk Register.   Teachers have other conventional language usages that comprise what Cazden calls a *teacher-talk register* (Cazden, 1988). Although there are differences in communication styles among teachers, there are also some common characteristics of teacher talk that appear to be part of the teacher role. One prominent feature of the teacher-talk register is teacher dominance over classroom talk. On average, teachers do about two-thirds of all the talking in classrooms, even though there may be twenty or thirty students in the classroom. If it is true that "the person who talks is the person who learns," we must have some pretty intelligent teachers out there! An additional feature of the teacher-talk register is that teachers may interrupt student-talk but may not be interrupted by students. In fact, teachers may reproach students for talking without permission or for interrupting, although teachers themselves may engage in any of these behaviors.

Most teachers dominate classroom talk and may interrupt students.

Suggestions for Use of Spoken Languages

Teachers should be sensitive to how they use spoken language in the classroom.

It is important to be sensitive about the ways you use spoken language in the classroom, since it not only affects your students' understanding of the academic curriculum but communicates social relationships and personal identities. You should use language that your students understand—clear vocabulary, meaningful syntax, and familiar metaphors. You should also try to be aware of how language communicates to your students their roles and personal value in your classroom. To this end, be aware of the following (Cazden, 1988):

- Teachers inevitably constrain their students' freedom and often publicly criticize their behavior and work.
- Teachers often soften those constraints and criticisms by using various politeness strategies.
- The seriousness of any act to student and teacher depends on social distance and relative power.

As We See It: *The Authors Talk*

Mary Kay: Do you suppose our readers are beginning to yearn for those "cookbook" approaches to management that we talked about earlier?

Bob: Probably. We read some where you looked up the problem and were provided with a three-sentence solution—not with the suggestion that you examine not only *what* you say but *how* you say it!

Mary Kay: I really wish that stuff worked: it would make everyone's life easier. But it's clear that this kind of attention to communication in its various forms is becoming critical in every field. Look at the "spin doctors" that are a part of every politician's inner circle; the consultants that train lawyers in verbal and nonverbal strategies and in how to "read" how jurors will vote; and even the emphasis in medicine on an effective "bedside manner." All those forms of communication have been defined as critical to their fields.

Bob: I guess it's no surprise that teachers, whose careers rest on communication, need to spend time thinking about how and what they're doing.

May Kay: True. But I still think it would be nice if those look-it-up cookbooks worked. . . .

Bob: Reality again.

Mary Kay: Back to work.

NONVERBAL COMMUNICATION

Most people are not fully aware of how their nonverbal communication affects others, even though it is extremely important.

Spoken and written language may be the most obvious forms of communication in classrooms, but nonverbal communication is tremendously important and may even constitute the majority of human communication (Birdwhistle, 1970). People are generally less aware of nonverbal than verbal communication. You are probably more aware of what words you use (vocabulary) and how you put them together (syntax) to express yourself than you are about your nonverbal behavior (body posture, eye contact, facial expressions, vocal pitch and volume, pauses, and proximity to others). You also may be less aware of how the nonverbal behavior of students affects *you*. Yet nonverbal behavior constitutes an aspect of language that can communicate as much—and sometimes more—than verbal language.

Metacommunication is how people communicate their words.

Different forms of nonverbal behavior are sometimes called **metacommunication,** which means "communication about what is being communicated" (Bowers & Flinders, 1990). Some broad dimensions of metacommunication are **proxemics, kinesics,** and **paralanguage.** Proxemics is the physical distances and positions between or among persons who are communicating. Kinesics is body language, like facial expressions, gestures, and posture; and paralanguage consists of voice qualities like pitch, volume, and rhythm. Each of these dimensions can add to verbal communication or serve as an independent form of communication. Although we will look separately at these dimensions of nonverbal communication as they relate to the classroom, remember that they often occur simultaneously with verbal communication.

Proxemics

Have you ever felt uncomfortable because someone invaded your personal space while talking with you? As the word indicates, *proxemics* has to do with proximity—the space or distance among the people who are communciating—and how those distances and changes in distances influence communication.

One way to communicate with students is to make decisions about your proximity to them.

Distance.   As a teacher you communicate with your students by modifying your proximity to them, both intentionally and unconsciously. The physical space between you and your students communicates your different roles and status within the classroom social system. For example, to communicate with the class as a whole you may stand at a particular spot such as the chalkboard or lectern, where all students can face you. If you want to communicate with individual students, however, you may approach their desks or have them come closer to you and direct your communication to them individually. Awareness of proxemics can help you solve a number of problems in class such as inattention and distractability.

Although there are individual and cultural variations in use of space, closer proximity generally denotes more intimate communication, and greater distance is more public. These distances are distinct and can be referred to as intimate, personal, social, and public zones (Hall, 1966). (See Figure 2.1.)

Your physical distance from a person you are talking with often expresses the nature of your relationship.

Intimate interactions are those where participants are only six to eighteen inches apart. They are considered intimate because this closeness allows for intense awareness of physical features, most notably facial expressions, and physical touch. Lovers and parents and children express affection for one another within this intimate zone. When others approach us this closely, however, we may perceive them as invading our personal space, or being aggressively "in our face," and we may back away.

FIGURE 2.1   The Four Zones That Signal the Nature of Social Relationships

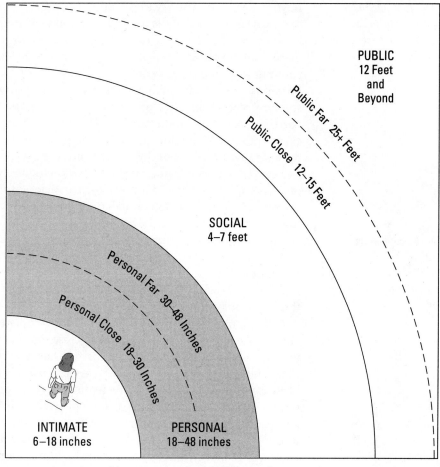

Source: From *The Hidden Dimension* by Edward T. Hall. Copyright 1966, 1982 by Edward T. Hall. Used by permission of Doubleday, a division of Bantam Doubleday Dell Publishing Group, Inc.

The *personal* zone has a close phase, about eighteen to thirty inches apart, and a far phase, about thirty to forty-eight inches apart. The close phase still allows easy physical contact like touching, while the far phase allows personal communication without raising one's voice.

Most impersonal business and casual social interactions occur in the *social* zone, where participants are four to seven feet apart. The *public* zone involves more formal communication and also seems to have a close phase of twelve to twenty-five feet and a far phase beyond twenty-five feet. These distances often entail individual to large-group communication such as lectures or demonstrations.

Where students choose to sit in a classroom reveals information about their preferences and/or cultural variations.

When you are allowed to choose, where do you usually sit in a classroom? In your classes, do you try to sit "up front" near the instructor? Do you prefer seating near the back of the room? Or do you seek some middle ground neither too close nor too far away from the instructor? Do you sit in about the same place in all of your classes, or does your location depend on the class? Students communicate their involvement in a class by the seats they choose. These positions indicate individual preferences or cultural variations. Generally, students who sit in the "front and center" near the teacher are more active participants in the class. Sitting in the back or on the periphery of a classroom can communicate a reluctance to participate. Thus, shy, withdrawn students distance themselves from the teacher and other students to avoid interaction. Academically insecure students may position themselves away from the center of academic activity to hide their inadequacies. Students who are bored or interested in something other than the class activities are also likely to distance themselves from the locus of activity.

Most people have different levels of comfort with distances between themselves and others.

In addition to having individual preferences, people have different levels of comfort near others. Consider, for example, differences in how persons greet one another. In one culture, they may stand several feet away from one another nodding or bowing. In another, they may shake hands, smile, and nod. In a third, they may hug and kiss one another.

For example, among Arabs, Latin Americans, Greeks, and Turks, children are socialized to comfortably engage in close social interaction and to perceive persons who maintain greater personal distance as aloof and unfriendly. In other cultural groups, however, such as the Japanese, closer proximity is more likely experienced as possibly threatening. Even among Europeans and European-Americans, there can be striking differences in proxemics. Greeks, Italians, and French, for example, are generally more comfortable in closer face-to-face interactions accompanied by frequent physical contact like pats and hugs than, say, English or Germans. In an often-cited study of cultural differences in the number of times couples in cafes touched each other, Jourard (1966) found that couples in San Juan, Puerto Rico, touched each other 180 times per hour compared to 110 times per hour for Parisian couples. However, couples in Gainesville, Florida, averaged just two contacts, and English couples never touched.

It is important to be aware and informed about acceptable and unacceptable touching.

Of course, not all touches communicate the same thing. Among American children it is generally more acceptable to touch others on the outside than the inside of the body line (Nowicki & Duke, 1992). Touching on the inside of the body line (inside arms, sides of chest, or inside legs and thighs) is emotion-laden, experienced as a violation of personal space, and taboo. When students violate these touch standards, teachers usually consider their behavior inappropriate and aggressive. Because of its highly emotional overtones, we think teachers should be cautious about touching students. In Chapter 6, we will consider appropriate uses of proximity and touch controls to influence student behavior.

This teacher is using the personal zone while encouraging the student in her multiplication work.
(Elizabeth Crews/ The Image Works)

Communication with students becomes more equal when teachers are close to them physically.

How Proxemics Affects Communication with Students. Teachers need to be aware of how proxemics affects communication with students and can be used to support different kinds of classroom activities. Each zone usually involves alterations in other forms of communication, such as facial expressions, gestures, tempo, volume, tone of voice, and body stance. At greater distance from the teacher, students are more likely to be passive recipients of instruction. Closer proximity between you and your students tends to encourage more equal two-way communication. For example, you might use the intimate zone for consoling a distraught student, while speaking in a hushed, slow manner, squatting next to him or her, and placing your hand on the student's shoulder. You might use the personal zone when instructing or helping individual students, social distance when you are working with a small group, and public distance when you provide an all-class demonstration, lecture, or group recitation.

As you determine the kinds of interaction that are most likely to facilitate communication in your classroom, you will want to consider your students' individual and cultural preferences in personal distance as well as how spacing

*Teachers can use
personal distance
strategically to manage
their classrooms.*

will enhance or interfere with effective communication. You also can use personal distance strategically in classroom management. For example, greater distances between you and some students during a demonstration or presentation may provide a more impersonal tone and seem to allow some students to become distracted and inattentive. To counter this, you can simply move closer to those students, while continuing your discussion or presentation, to inhibit their distracting behavior. This is an example of using proxemics to solve a problem.

You can use intimate or personal zones when you want to have a serious discussion with a student about specific behaviors or incidents, since this close proximity emphasizes the close relationship between the two of you and minimizes the involvement of other students in your discussion. Often you can adjust seating arrangements to allow for proximities that facilitate your communication and instructional goals. It is usually easier for you to move, however, than your students.

In addition to distance, other types of proxemics such as **level** and **precedence** also communicate relative position or status. *Level* refers to the relative height of interacting individuals; *precedence* refers to position in front or back of one another.

Level.   You can also use these kinds of proxemic conditions to promote or impede communication. For example, relative power and status of people are affected by *level.* Consider, for example, a ritualized activity such as religious services, where the worship leaders' status is enhanced because they are stationed at an altar above their congregation. The higher level not only allows greater visibility but also strengthens status differences between the leader and the worshippers.

In classrooms, you use level to promote communication as you address your whole class during group recitation by standing at the chalkboard, overhead projector, or behind a lectern. For other kinds of communication, however, you may want to relax level barriers by "getting down to the kids' level"—sitting next to, leaning over, or squatting by students to encourage more informal communication with individuals or small groups.

*Teachers can use
communication levels to
strengthen instruction
and achieve other
purposes.*

Both unequal and equal levels of teacher-student communication reinforce teacher-student and student-student status relationships in classrooms. Teachers can deliberately use communication levels to promote their instructional goals. Higher levels tend to confer higher status and authority on teachers (or students, for that matter) who "have the floor" and to promote transmission of information and knowledge from higher- to lower-level individuals. Equal levels, on the other hand, indicate more equal status and tend to promote more interaction among participants at the common level. Thus, if your purpose is to convey information efficiently to your entire class, standing in front of them usually works best. On the other hand, if you want to encourage leadership by individual students who are demonstrating something or presenting to the rest of your class, you can have the presenters stand in front of the group while you sit down or move to the side or back of the room. If your purpose is to promote interactive discussion *among* a group of students, you can sit down with them, thereby reducing level distinctions.

Precedence. *Precedence* relationships also influence communication as, for instance, when students line up during transitions or take turns in an activity. For example, a teacher can use place in line as a kind of within-group status by calling on students to line up when they show they are "ready." Teachers also establish their precedence in relationships with students by positioning themselves at the front or rear of lines, or by being outside of a line of students walking down the school hallway. While we may assume that these precedence distinctions are not very important, consider how eagerly some students wave their hands to be called on first or squabble over their place when lining up. For some students, higher precedence seems to confer higher status within a group. As a teacher, you will want to avoid setting up situations where students fight over positions, while sometimes using them to encourage healthy competition. At the same time, you will want to be sensitive to cultural variability. In some cultures, for instance, a traditional form of deference to authority is for children to follow adults or for females to follow males. In other cultures, just the opposite ("ladies first") is considered appropriate.

Students' positions in front or back of one another can be very important to them.

Kinesics

Have you ever been in a situation (perhaps purchasing a used car) where you were trying to judge the other person's honesty and where you understood the person's words but were uncertain how true they were? What kinds of information did you look for to help you ascertain the other person's honesty or sincerity? Did you look for clues in eye contact, facial expressions, and gestures? Have you ever tried to deliberately mislead someone (perhaps setting up a surprise birthday party) by controlling your emotional expressions? If you have either tried to understand another person's expressions and gestures or used them yourself to communicate, you were relying on *kinesics,* or body language.

Students' body language can communicate important information to teachers.

Kinesics offers information about how feelings, intentions, and motives are communicated. Body language can function independently of the verbal language and proxemics we discussed above or together with them. Among the most prominent forms of body language are facial expressions of emotion, eye contact, hand gestures, body movements, posture, and other positionings of the body (see Figure 2.2). These forms of nonverbal behaviors can communicate very specific information. For example, a student may say, "I'm not angry," but the expression on her face, her rigid posture, and her clenched fists may tell a different story. Just as "a picture is worth a thousand words," a person's demeanor can tell you much about how he or she feels and may confirm or call into question what that person says.

FIGURE 2.2   Prominent Forms of Kinesics or Body Language

People use **KINESICS OR BODY LANGUAGE**

Dress and Grooming

Body Movement

Eye Contact

Facial Expressions or Emotion

Facial muscle movements and even micromovements can reveal a person's true feelings.

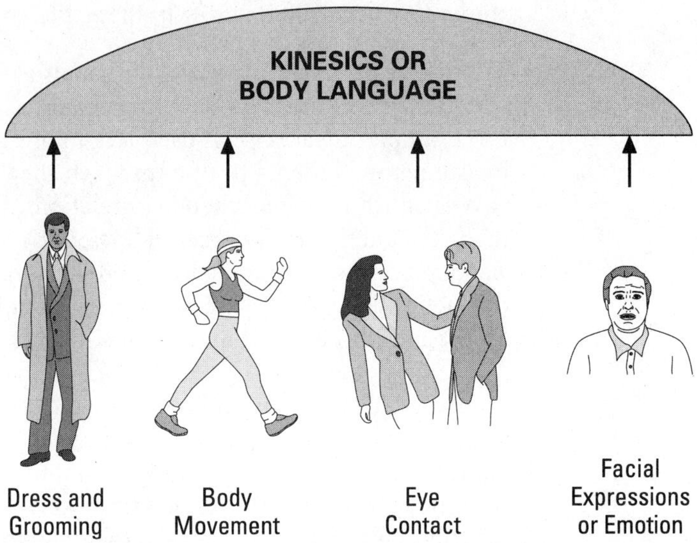

Facial Expressions of Emotion.   Your face is the primary way you communicate affect—the emotions you feel—although other body language (muscle tension and posture, for example) also give information about these emotions. Facial expressions are also our primary source of information about how other people feel. Carrol Izard (1971; 1977) and Paul Ekman and his colleagues (Ekman & Friesen, 1975; Ekman, Friesen & Ellsworth, 1972) have extensively studied human communication of emotions in *facial expressions*. Ekman, for example, has identified basic emotions (happiness, sadness, fear, anger, surprise, and disgust) that are communicated by distinct patterns of facial muscle movements. These facial expressions are both innate and learned forms of communicating emotions. Human beings use both natural and stereotyped facial expressions. Consider, for instance, how children react with happy faces when they see something funny or with a look of disgust when they smell something distasteful. Children also learn to deliberately put on a happy face or an expression of disgust, or fear, or anger, or another emotion when the situation calls for that emotion.

People show their natural or deliberate communication of emotions. As children grow, they learn how to express and understand facial expressions from parents, siblings, friends, and others, as well as the media. Some families are more expressive or more guarded in emotional expression; some cultures encourage or discourage forms of emotional expression. Because these influences vary individually and culturally, there are individual and cultural differences in the expression of emotions.

People also learn to express emotions in stereotyped forms by intentionally showing certain emotions even when their underlying feelings are different. Actors, of course, deliberately imitate emotional expressions to communicate feelings, but all of us, to a certain degree, and with varying success, deliberately engage in emotional expression. We also sometimes try to hide emotions we have learned are inappropriate or unacceptable in particular contexts. However, our true feelings may emerge anyway, even in the tiniest movement of facial muscles (Ekman, 1982).

Although there are similarities in forms of emotional expressions across cultures, all cultures do not encourage these expressions to the same degree.

There appears to be a good deal of similarity in the forms of emotional expressions across cultures, although they may be displayed and interpreted differently. When people in different cultures (some isolated from other cultures) were filmed with a hidden camera, they showed remarkably similar behaviors: "The similarities in expressive movements between cultures lie not only in such basic expressions as smiling, laughing, crying and . . . anger, but in whole syndromes of behaviour" (Eibl-Eibesfeldt, 1972, p. 299). The "eyebrow flash" is a momentary (about one-sixth of a second) emotional expression—a raising of the eyebrows—that communicates a person's readiness for contact with another, as in greeting, approving, seeking confirmation, flirting, thanking, and emphasizing a statement. The eyebrow flash is a kind of yes statement that invites social interaction and often is accompanied by smiling and nodding. In some cultures, like that of Samoa, an eyebrow flash signals approval or agreement. In other cultures, like Japan's, however, people tend to suppress eyebrow flashes because they are considered indecent (Eibl-Eibesfeldt, 1972).

The same form of nonverbal expression can mean different things in different cultures. In many cultures people nod their heads to indicate yes and shake them to indicate no. This pattern is probably inborn, since even infants who are blind and deaf perform them. However, even this kind of inborn pattern can be modified by learning and by cultural influences. For example, Ceylonese express agreement by swaying their heads back and forth, rather than nodding. Greeks indicate yes by nodding, but to indicate no, they jerk their heads back, often closing their eyes and lifting their eyebrows (Eibl-Eibesfeldt, 1972).

There are, of course, individual as well as cultural variations in the ways people understand and use facial expressions. We all know some people whose faces readily and transparently communicate their feelings and others who are less expressive. Facial expressions and other body language are fundamental to our judgment about the appropriateness of another person's behavior. When nonverbal behavior does not match spoken words, we may question a person's honesty. If a person's emotional expression seems inappropriate for a particular situation, he or she may be considered odd or unbalanced.

Identifying emotion in basic facial expressions is difficult for children who have emotional and behavior disorders.

As a group, children who have been identified as having emotional and behavioral disorders appear to have difficulty identifying emotions in basic facial expressions (Zabel, 1978; Walker & Leister, 1994). It is unclear the degree to which learning or constitutional factors, or some combination, account for this deficiency. Many children may be socially rejected by their peers because of problems of nonverbal communication, including their use of facial expressions, gestures and posture, and eye contact (Nowicki & Duke, 1992). These kinds of deficits might even be considered a type of disability: *dyssemia* (*dys* = difficulty; *semia* = using signs) (Nowicki & Duke, 1992). While we are not convinced that nonverbal skill deficits should be considered a disability condition, we agree that nonverbal behavior exerts a tremendous role in communication and social relationships. In some severe emotional/behavioral disorders, such as autism, schizophrenia, and depression, there are pronounced abnormalities in emotional expression that are likely due to biophysical factors. For example, a central feature of autism is language abnormalities involving both verbal and nonverbal forms. Children with autism often are *echolalic,* repeating sounds, words, or phrases often out of context; they often perform *stereotypic behavior,* repeating motor movements that seem to have no function. Children with autism appear to have particular difficulty understanding and expressing emotions.

Eye Contact.   Have you ever felt uncomfortable when someone stared at you, or have you averted your gaze from someone who "caught your eye"? No doubt you have stood in a crowded elevator or bus and felt discomfort from others' staring eyes (as well as from the close physical proximity to strangers). A feature of nonverbal communication that is closely related to facial expressions is *eye contact.* We make eye contact with others during communication to determine how they are understanding and reacting to us and to obtain information about their feelings and motives. During conversations we look into the other person's face about 30 to 60 percent of the time (Nowicki & Duke, 1992).

Eyes have been called "the windows of the soul," and indeed they do tell us a good deal about a person's thoughts and feelings. Looking into another person's eyes is a physiologically arousing activity. The amount and intensity of eye contact partially defines your relationships with others and your judgments about their behavior. In mainstream American culture, prolonged direct eye contact tends to make us feel uncomfortable and causes us to look away (unless, of course, we are in love). Limited eye contact, on the other hand, can communicate disinterest, nervousness, or hostility. A person's degree of eye contact influences our impressions of him or her as friendly, shy, hostile, or indifferent.

Limited eye contact can communicate distance while prolonged contact can communicate familiarity and comfort.

Generally, more prolonged eye contact communicates greater intimacy or familiarity; less contact communicates more social distance. People with autism have great difficulty communicating and establishing social relations, even with close family members. In addition to verbal communication problems, a major contributor to the social incompetence of persons with autism is a pronounced lack of eye contact, sometimes called *gaze aversion*. Even as infants and toddlers, children with autism often avoid looking directly into another's eyes, perhaps because the arousal that accompanies the eye contact makes them intensely uncomfortable. As a result, they seem aloof, distant, and noninvolved.

While an autistic child does not *learn* gaze aversion, some differences in eye contact are likely a result of cultural learning. Among Navajo people, for example, children learn that it is impolite to look directly into another person's eyes and so turn and look down or away when an adult is speaking to them (Tharp, 1989). Anglo teachers who are unfamiliar or uncomfortable with this culturally mediated gaze aversion sometimes interpret it as disrespect, disinterest, or lack of attention.

Body movement is another important way people communicate with each other.

Body Movements. Hand gestures, body movements, posture, and other positionings of the body are additional ways we communicate feelings, intentions, and involvement with others. In your college classes you might consider how effectively and naturally your instructors' movements help communicate what they are saying. Also consider how you and other students nonverbally communicate your involvement and interest to your instructor through your eye contact, nodding, posture, or facial expressions. Sitting on the edge of your chair, looking intently at your instructor, nodding, or responding with facial expressions all tend to communicate understanding and involvement. Closing your notebook, looking at your watch, staring out the window, reacting with blank facial expressions all communicate disinterest or confusion.

A teacher's dress and grooming also communicate information about attitudes and values.

Dress and Grooming. A person's dress and grooming constitute another type of body language. We sometimes have preconceived notions of what is appropriate dress for specific occasions, and when others do not share those notions, or choose not to conform to them, our response can be disapproval. (Parents and their preadolescent and adolescent children often have these sorts of conversations, sometimes with raised voices and accompanying negative body language.)

Schools usually have rules concerning dress, such as no caps or colors that might have gang significance, shirts with certain slogans or labels, or other forms of *communicative dress*. Teachers must be aware of school rules and the reasons for them but also must be sensitive to the idea that dress and grooming are simply another form of communication. "Clothes make the (wo)man" is not entirely true, but clothing does influence our perceptions and even behavior.

Your clothes and grooming communicate to your students as well. You may remember teachers who wore interesting, kid-oriented pins, outlandishly loud ties, or dramatically out-of-style clothing. You may remember teachers you thought were sharp dressers or the one who looked as though he came directly from bed to school without a taking a shower, shaving, or combing his hair. How did their clothing and grooming make you feel about each of these teachers? How do you think they felt about themselves, their jobs, and students?

Obviously, everyone has personal preferences in dress and grooming, and the only rule we would suggest is to consider what you are communicating by the way you dress. Our point is that you say something about yourself and your students through your personal appearance. In addition to your personal preferences and comfort, you should consider the atmosphere of your school and classroom—or the atmosphere and attitudes about teacher-student relationships you *wish* to promote—and how your appearance may enhance or detract from it.

There may be explicit guidelines or implicit expectations in the school and community where you teach. Some schools have dress codes for faculty as well as students. A friend of ours teaches in a juvenile detention facility where the students have a very strict dress code: they wear identical, orange prison coveralls. Although there is no faculty dress code, the teacher is careful about the model he provides for his students and colleagues. He tries to treat his students respectfully and to communicate the importance of the educational program. He communicates this both verbally and nonverbally, paying particular attention to his clothes. For example, he always wears a tie and freshly ironed clothes because he believes this helps communicate that he cares enough about his students and what they are doing to deliberately dress up for the occasion.

Generally, more formal kinds of relationships are communicated by more formal dress; more relaxed, and informal relationships are communicated by more casual dress. Thus, your appearance can reinforce your other efforts to create a classroom atmosphere.

PARALANGUAGE

Paralanguage, sometimes referred to as *prosody,* is another dimension of classroom communication. It involves the cues or signals provided by changes in voice tone, pitch, and pacing. Everything you say has a particular pattern determined jointly by your words and grammatical structure and by your "attitude" about what you are saying. You communicate different meanings depending on *how* you say something. For example, you emphasize words or phrases by raising tone or pitch or by pausing to slow the pace. Consider the many different ways you could tell your students, "Please return to your desks." You might say, "PLEASE . . . return to your desks!" or "Please . . . return . . . to . . . your . . . desks" or "PLEASE RETURN TO *YOUR* DESKS," with different meanings provided by your variations in volume, pitch, and pauses. Although the words and syntax are identical, each form communicates something different, such as how serious you are. In addition, your posture, the positions of your arms and hands, facial expressions, and eye contact add to the complexity of the message.

Teachers sometimes view children who are "fast talkers" as more intelligent and competent and may encourage some students to talk out by responding to their more frequent and louder verbalizations. They may view quieter students, on the other hand, as uncooperative, unmotivated, or dull and may overlook them. The intonation, stress, and pacing of your own speech also provide messages to your students about your competence and confidence.

Paralanguage influences students' judgments of teachers as well as teachers' judgments of students.

These prosodic features influence our judgments about students—about the appropriateness or inappropriateness of their behavior. For example, if a student reads a passage aloud in an unexpressive voice, you may conclude that the student either does not understand the material or is bored or unmotivated. Or if a student responds to your questions in a way that seems mocking, silly, or belligerent, you will judge and respond to the student accordingly.

CULTURAL COMPATABILITY IN CLASSROOM COMMUNICATION

Cultural background affects how a student fits into the classroom.

Different communication patterns betweeen students and teachers sometimes result in misunderstandings and even conflicts. Roland Tharp (1989), for example, has analyzed the "goodness of fit" between students with diverse cultural backgrounds and four types of classroom variables: social organization, sociolinguistics, cognition, and motivation. Tharp draws his conclusions from a number of studies of the Kamehameha Early Education Program (KEEP) that involved Hawaiian students of Polynesian descent and Navajo students on the Red Rock Reservation in Arizona. **Classroom social organization** refers to how the classroom arrangement affects interaction among students and teachers; **sociolinguistics** involves the courtesies and conventions of classroom conversation; **cognition** refers to expected types of cognitive or intellectual skills; and **motivation** means the ways students are encouraged to participate and achieve. Each of these variables influences student interpretations of classroom activities, their involvement, their behavior, and teachers' judgments of them.

CLASSROOM SOCIAL ORGANIZATION

In a traditional classroom, as you read in Chapter 1, the social organization typically consists of row-and-column seating, whole-class instruction, and a teacher or leader who instructs and evaluates students on the basis of individ-

Emphasis on individual performance is uncomfortable for students from certain cultures.

ual performance. This pattern of social organization is not equally effective for all students (Tharp, 1989). In fact, students from different cultures sometimes find this social organization unfamiliar and uncomfortable. For example, traditional Hawaiian culture encourages peer orientation and high levels of peer assistance, or *inter*dependence among students. Navajo culture, on the other hand, encourages self-sufficiency, or *independence* among students. In each case, there can be a mismatch between the expectations of traditional classroom social organization and students' cultural styles. Unfortunately, teachers sometimes view those mismatches as student problems. They may see Hawaiian students as less attentive to them and to their work and more interested in gaining peer attention. Anglo teachers may see Navajo students, on the other hand, as aloof and uncooperative.

SOCIOLINGUISTICS

Differing teacher and student patterns of conversation may lead to sociolinguistic conflicts. Traditional classrooms rely heavily on specific patterns of verbal communication, both written and oral. As you may recall from our earlier discussion, many teachers use the instruction-response-evaluation (I-R-E) pattern of classroom discourse in group recitation. Teachers ask questions with known (to the teacher) answers and then evaluate the students' responses. One feature of the I-R-E pattern is called *wait-time*, which represents the pause between teacher questions and student responses, and then between student responses and teacher evaluations of the responses. Typically, wait times are brief—often just one to two seconds between the teacher's question and expected student response.

Wait-times, a feature of I-R-E, vary from culture to culture.

Tharp (1989) reported dramatic differences in wait times for native Hawaiian and Navajo students. In both cases, wait-times were different for students than for their teachers. Hawaiian students are taught more interactive communication patterns and tend toward "negative wait-time"—their answers are apt to be very rapid, marked with interruptions and overlapping speech. Non-Hawaiian teachers can perceive this kind of lively verbal exchange as rude and disruptive (Tharp, 1989).

Wait-time patterns for Navajo students are quite different. They are socialized to prefer more patient, turn-taking interchanges, so their wait-times are longer. But this pattern, too, can lead to a mismatch between student behavior and teacher expectations. Teachers who are unfamiliar with this culturally mediated pattern may see their Navajo students as unmotivated, distracted, and resistant to their instruction. They may interrupt students who were pausing by repeating questions or asking other students the same question (Tharp, 1989).

Native American students in Oregon also encountered conflicts between their culture, which stresses collaborative, group activities, and their teachers,

Allowing student movement and cooperative activities can help teachers avoid some behavioral problems.

who stress individualized, competitive activities. Outside of school, Native American children were discouraged from standing out in a group or acting independently. Some of their teachers, however, encouraged individual student performance by directing questions to individual students, making individual assignments, and announcing individual achievements. They believed their students had more behavioral problems than did teachers who fostered cooperative group activities in their classes (Phillips, 1983).

COGNITION

Earlier in this chapter we mentioned how instruction makes use of different cognitive processes. Traditional classroom instruction tends to emphasize verbal and analytic approaches rather than visual and holistic approaches. However, some students are more comfortable with visual and holistic approaches. For example, in the Navajo culture, students are not expected to dissect and discuss stories but to visualize their messages (Tharp, 1989). Thus, Navajo students can have difficulty analyzing specific parts of a story until they have finished reading the entire piece, and their discussions are facilitated by using diagrams and familiar metaphors.

MOTIVATION

Cultural expectations have effects on students' academic motivation.

A student's motivation to succeed academically and to behave appropriately in school is partly a reflection of individual family and cultural expectations. Hawaiian children, for example, are highly peer oriented and are taught not to approach adults unless invited. Consequently, teachers must reestablish their authority each year by forming personal, emotional relationships with their students. Hawaiian students respond best to teachers whom they consider "nice and tough." Effective teachers are warm, nurturant, and socially reinforcing, while being firm, clear, and consistent. Because peer interaction is so important in Hawaiian culture, punishments that remove individual students from their peer group, such as staying in from recess or being separated in the classroom, are especially aversive (Tharp, 1989).

Navajo children, on the other hand, respond to different kinds of motivational processes. Unlike Hawaiian students, they are often content to be alone and so do not find separation from other students as punishing. Furthermore, teachers' efforts to control their behavior with contingent reward or punishment also tend to be ineffective (Tharp, 1989).

Another example of cultural lack of fit in communication patterns is evident in the teacher-student dynamics of inner-city, African-American classrooms (e.g., Foster, 1986; Hanna, 1988; McIntyre, 1993). The "street-corner culture" of urban youth can conflict with school culture: "'Streetwise' youth have learned the language, mannerisms and manipulative/aggressive tactics of the street corner. . . . They use rough behavior and crude and profane language to assert power or confirm a 'manly' image. They learn the subcultural refusal to work, learn, and behave socially" (McIntyre, 1993). Students may engage in verbal and nonverbal behavior in the classroom to trick, confuse, and intimidate others. Their behavior is often intense and peer relationships sensitive, with lots of physical expressiveness and efforts to manipulate one another (Williams, 1981). They often engage in impromptu "dramas" designed to test, verbally tease, and intimidate their white teachers. Teachers who did not understand the cultural nature of the behavior considered it threatening and tried to suppress it. Often their efforts only increased the teacher-student conflict. Rather than trying to suppress these patterns of verbal and nonverbal behavior, teachers could capitalize on their students' performance skills to meet their instructional goals—for example, by having them prepare and perform skits in front of the class (Williams, 1981).

GENDER AND CLASSROOM COMMUNICATION

Teachers' awareness of gender patterns in communication can also help them establish effective classroom communication.

Classroom communication patterns are apparent not only in the goodness of fit between student and teacher cultures but also in gender relationships. In a review of research about the ways teachers interact with boys and girls in classrooms, Flood (1988) identified some notable gender patterns in teacher-student interactions. For example, boys experience *both* more positive and more negative contacts from their teachers. Although girls have a higher *proportion* of positive contacts with their teachers, boys are involved in about $2\frac{1}{2}$ times more disapproving contacts than girls. In addition, teachers tend to call on girls when they sit in front rows, but they call on boys regardless of where they sit. They tend to help boys start assignments and then have them proceed independently, while they provide more continuous help to girls. Also, teachers give girls more attention in reading but less in math (Flood, 1988).

While there might be some legitimate explanations for these gender differences in teacher communication (for instance, boys may receive more disapproving teacher comments because, as a group, they tend to be more verbally assertive and physically active than girls), these explanations also promote self-fulfilling expectations. A teacher's different expectations for boys' and girls' behavior may unwittingly contribute to gender differences in behavior. For example, teachers can inadvertently help form girls' negative beliefs about their abilities in mathematics and science (Eccles, 1989). During the early years of school, boys and girls, on average, perform fairly equally on measures of math and science achievement. However, by the upper elementary grades, girls begin to fall behind boys. By high school, girls' achievement and interest tend to lag far behind boys'.

Parents as well as teachers may communicate different expectations for academic achievement to boys and to girls.

This is due to multiple social learning factors, most notably parents' beliefs and values about their daughters' aptitudes and future roles. Yet teachers too sometimes strengthen these beliefs. Classroom observation studies of interactions between students and teachers in math classes, for example, have found that most students (*both* girls and boys) rarely interacted with teachers (Eccles, 1989). However, a few students, usually boys, monopolized the teacher's attention. These boys were assertive—even aggressive—in commanding their teacher's attention. The teachers reciprocated by frequently calling on the assertive boys while largely ignoring their other students. In math classes where teachers ensured more equitable participation of class members, however, boys and girls had similar views of their abilities (Eccles, 1989).

In studies comparing secondary mathematics classrooms where male and female students have *similar* confidence in their abilities to those where females have *less* confidence, researchers have found some important procedural differences. Classrooms with no gender differences

> were more orderly, had less of both extreme praise and criticism, and were more businesslike. The teacher also maintained tighter control over student-teacher interactions, ensuring equal student participation by calling on everyone, rather than focusing on the small subset of students who regularly raised their hands. In contrast, classrooms marked by sex differences in the students' attitudes were characterized by student-teacher interactions dominated by a few students. Essentially, these teachers were more reactive, focusing their attention primarily on those students who raised their hand or insisted on attention in other ways. Consequently, a running dialogue emerged between the teacher and two or three students, who usually sat in the front of the room and regularly raised their hands. More often than not these "stars" were white males. Other students rarely volunteered and were never called upon to participate. They sat out of the teacher's view, and as long as they did not cause a disturbance or start trouble, they were allowed to be nonparticipants. The latter group of students included both the males for whom the teacher had low expectations and most of the females. (Eccles, 1989, p. 50)

Teaching practices in classes where male and female students performed similarly included (Eccles, 1989):

- Greater use of either cooperative learning or individualized strategies rather than drill,
- Less use of competitive motivational strategies,
- More hands-on learning,
- Emphasis on practical implications,
- More active, open-ended learning situations often involving teams, and
- Career guidance regarding the importance of math/science.

This research about gender differences in students' beliefs about their ability and actual performance has direct implications for the ways classroom communication patterns affect learning and behavior. Students who are left out of classroom discourse, who are perceived by teachers as less competent academically, tend to interact less with their teachers. When they do, the interaction is public, and any difficulties they may have are apparent to everyone. Some students attempt to avoid future embarrassment and shrink from active participation. Others may defend against their feelings of incompetence and inferiority by engaging in distractions, behaving as if they do not care or showing their skills in other arenas, such as clowning or disruption.

FRAMING

Framing is a critical part of the way teachers convey their expectations to students.

An aspect of classroom communication that relates directly to issues of classroom management is the concept of **framing** (Bowers & Flinders, 1990). Framing refers to *how* something is said, as well as to the words themselves. Metacommunications—like the facial expressions, gestures, intonation, and pauses we discussed earlier—provide frameworks for understanding communication. For example, you may tell a student, "You are doing a good job," and your body language, intonation, and facial expressions correspond with your words to communicate your sincerity. When your actions communicate something different than your words, you may be perceived as dishonest or insincere.

Frames are like brackets that provide temporal and spatial cues to the meaning of social interactions like those in classrooms. *Temporal cues* signal the beginning and end of an interchange; *spatial cues* provide visual information about the nature of the interchange. For example, a ringing bell may frame the start and end of a class period. Or you may stand behind your desk, state, "OK, it's time to take out your social studies books," with a sigh and a bored facial and postural demeanor, communicating (or framing) a particular type of communication. You frame a very different type of interaction when you sit crossed-legged on the floor with your students and glance around the group with a smile on your face and an open book in your hands.

Framing has been described in terms of implicitness, dynamism, essentiality, cultural context, and dual influence (Bowers & Flinders, 1990). *Implicitness* means that frames have "taken-for-granted" meanings. It is usually unnecessary to announce a particular frame of reference. For example, a teacher does not need to say, "This is a lecture" or "Now I'm going to read a story and you are going to quietly listen," unless students appear confused about what is going on. Since communication is fluid, frames are also *dynamic*, continuously changing in the process of social interactions. Frames are *essential* to communication, providing a necessary context for understanding what is said. Even if you tried to control your gestures, facial expressions, and intonations, you would be signaling a kind of frame. You would communicate, "I'm not showing any emotion." Framing always occurs in a *cultural context*. That is, the way we use and interpret metacommunications reflects our experiences, both individual and cultural. When we misread someone's communication, it may be due to our failure to recognize different frames of reference. Finally, frames have a *dual influence:* they help us understand messages and establish and maintain social relationships.

No doubt you have participated in this common greeting and response: "How are you?" "Fine, and you?" "Fine, thanks." This interchange rarely provides information about anyone's health, but it does help establish (or frame) a cordial relationship between the participants. In classrooms, as in other social settings, framing helps communicate meaning and establishes and maintains social status distinctions. For example, when teachers use first names when addressing their students but their students refer to them using *Mrs., Ms.,* or *Mr.,* they are also commenting on their relative status.

The important point of this discussion of framing is that *how* you communicate with your students is often more important than *what* you communicate. It is not enough to tell students to respect you, to pay attention, to cooperate with one another, or to be responsible. You communicate those expectations by the ways you "tell" your students these things.

POWER AND SOLIDARITY

When teachers use their superior authority and status as teachers and adults to force or pressure students to conform to their wishes, they are using a *power* frame. When they attempt to influence students by establishing rapport and mutual caring they are using a *solidarity* frame (Bowers & Flinders, 1990). The Classroom Closeup "Using Power and Solidarity to Influence Student Behavior" contrasts the handling of a similar classroom problem by framing it in terms of power or solidarity relationships.

Students generally respond to power-oriented framing only because they *have* to but respond to solidarity framing because they *want* to. Your choice of frame is related to the communication strategies you use, including *self-disclosure, humor,* and *dialogue* (Bowers & Flinders, 1990).

Whether teachers use power-oriented or solidarity-oriented frames depends on the communication strategies they use.

Self-disclosure

Self-disclosure refers to letting students know that you are a real person with a life outside the classroom, and it can take many forms. For example, if you mention personal experiences that are relevant to a topic studied by your class or express self-doubt with comments like, "I'm not sure I've explained this very

Classroom Closeup

Using Power and Solidarity to Influence Student Behavior

Power

Visibly agitated and angry about several students' interruptions, talking out, and giggling during her presentation, Mrs. Johnson shouts to the class:

Mrs. Johnson: All right, I've taken just about as much of your disrespect as I'm going to! Since you don't know how to behave we're going to have a few rules around here. Number one, No talking without permission. I mean it. The next person who interrupts me while I'm talking will be in big trouble. In fact, anyone who does not raise their hand and have my permission to talk before talking will be staying right here in their seat during recess. No ifs, ands, or buts—no excuses. That's right, if you choose to be rude, you'll be in here copying pages from the dictionary. Is there anyone who has trouble understanding this? Good, now let's get back to our work.

Solidarity

Having been interrupted several times by students interrupting, talking out, and giggling, Mrs. Jones calmly addresses her class:

Mrs. Jones: We seem to be having a hard time concentrating on this presentation. Let's stop for a minute and think about our classroom rules. Remember how we agreed to treat one another with respect? Eugene, what is our policy about raising hands before speaking?

Eugene: We should raise our hands before we talk.

Mrs. Jones: Why did we decide this is important? Sammy, you're raising your hand. Why is that important?

Sammy: 'Cause it's not polite to talk when someone else is talking. It bothers other people 'cause they can't hear.

Mrs. Jones: OK, when we interrupt others, some people can't hear. Is that fair to them? Jenny?

Jenny: No. If everybody just talked whenever they wanted, it would just be chaos in here and we'd never learn anything.

Mrs. Jones: Shizuno?

Shizuno: Like Jenny said, we're here to learn, so we need to be able to listen sometimes. Otherwise, we may as well not come to school.

Mrs. Jones: That wouldn't be good. Then you wouldn't learn and there would be no need for teachers. I'd be out of a job! All right, I think we all remember why it's important to not interrupt and to be good listeners. Let's get back to our lesson. ✳

well," you share your fellow humanity with your students. Generally, revealing your humanity encourages rapport with your students just as distancing yourself from students will cause you to rely on power relationships to control behavior.

Humor

Another framing strategy that affects power and solidarity relationships is humor. We have found that when teachers interject humor into their communication, they build rapport and solidarity with their students. This is because humor tends to reverse status relationships, especially when you make yourself the target. Teachers who "can take a joke," who are not threatened by teasing from students, and who are able to see humor in their own and others' behavior express their solidarity with students. As we will see in Chapter 6, however, teachers should avoid sarcasm or humor that comes at the expense of a student. Humor should be funny, and teachers must be sensitive to how students are likely to interpret it.

Dialogue

Dialogue is the mutual interchange of ideas and information. In traditional classrooms, framing of dialogue is mostly between teacher and students. Teachers already know the answers to their questions and expect students to deliver the "correct" answers in a timely manner (short wait-time). However, this is unlike informal conversation outside of classrooms, where communication is shared and turn-taking continuously negotiated. Conversants initiate or change topics of conversation, interrupt, overlap, and digress. In traditional classroom discourse, however, the teacher keeps dialogue on track to its predictable outcome by asking all the questions and evaluating all the students' responses. The teacher exercises total power over the discourse.

There are alternative approaches you can use to frame student-teacher and student-student dialogue, including one-to-one conversations with your students, peer tutoring, and cooperative learning strategies. The cognitive, linguistic, and academic development of culturally and linguistically diverse students has been found to benefit from *instructional conversation* (Tharp & Gallimore, 1989) or *instructional discourse* (Garcia, 1992). Instructional conversations are discussions that focus on ideas or concepts that elicit a high level of student participation. The teacher serves as discussion leader, guiding and pacing without dominating class discussion, by introducing provocative ideas and then encouraging involvement by prodding, challenging, and questioning students (Garcia, 1994). A central feature of these instructional conversations is reducing the didactic, I-R-E pattern of classroom discourse. The teacher facilitates, rather than dominates, discussion. To encourage more interactive dialogue among their students, teachers should develop a "stopping sense": they must *stop* asking all the questions, providing the "correct" responses, evaluating, enforcing rules, and rewarding compliance (Bowers & Flinders, 1990, p. 151).

Although instructional discourse may be especially valuable for culturally and linguistically diverse learners, we think it can be a worthwhile instructional feature in any classroom. Because instructional discourse engages students in the instructional process, they are likely to become active participants in, rather than recipients of, instruction. This student involvement should contribute to a heightened sense of solidarity.

Communicating solidarity with students is usually more helpful to teachers than communicating power over them.

Communicating solidarity with students and letting them know you and they are in this together is usually a more fruitful approach to managing your classroom than relying on your more powerful status to compel students to participate and behave appropriately. This does not mean that you become a buddy to your students. Classrooms are complex, crowded ecosystems where miscommunications will sometimes occur. As the responsible adult—the leader of your classroom environment—you will control the nature of inter-actions. If you attempt to control your students solely by exercising power, you will likely fail. Classroom discourse will be framed as "us versus them" and will generate mutual distrust, with students attempting to undermine your author-ity. If, however, you communicate solidarity with your students through self-disclosure, your sense of humor, and encouragement of dialogue, you will likely frame a "we're-in-this-together" atmosphere that establishes mutual trust and strengthens your authority.

SUMMARY AND REVIEW

In this chapter, we have related issues of classroom management to classroom communication. We identified major forms of communication, including verbal communication, nonverbal communication such as proxemics and kinesics, and paralanguage. We discussed how the culture of the classroom is communicated by its social organization, sociolinguistics, cognition, and mo-tivation patterns. We also examined how teacher-student communication affects gender-related patterns of behavior and achievement. Finally, we dis-cussed the idea of framing to communicate power or solidarity relationships in classrooms.

Although we cannot fully explore all the implications, we have suggested some ways communication is related to classroom problems. Teaching and learning rely on effective communication. The ways you communicate with students will affect the meaning they derive from their classroom experiences. Consequently, teachers must be aware of the significance of students' verbal and nonverbal behavior and of individual and group (sociocultural) differ-ences in communication, and try to provide a good fit between student and classroom patterns.

There are infinite individual and group variations in classroom commu-nication. As a teacher you will not always be aware of how this diversity affects communication and instruction and influences your perceptions and judgments of student behavior. The taken-for-granted aspects of communication are resistant to objective analysis. We are rarely conscious of how culture-bound our own verbal and nonverbal communication is. However, as a teacher you need to be sensitive to, and try to understand, where your students are coming from and their "taken-for-granted" perspectives. You need to examine *your* own taken-for-granted perspectives as well. Only then can you arrange school and classroom environments, adjust academic and behavioral expectations, and use teaching approaches that allow for a better fit between the student and the classroom culture.

REFLECTING ON CHAPTER 2

As a new teacher, Annie will need to attend to different aspects of her communication strategy—although it will take time to analyze the different parts of her style.

- As she begins the year, what are some things she should be thinking about?

- Observe some of your teachers or colleagues. What do you notice in their nonverbal communication patterns? Do they differ? What about their verbal styles? Can you see examples of the communication patterns discussed in this chapter?

- Think about people you feel particularly comfortable or particularly uncomfortable with (family members, roommates, significant others, classmates). Try to analyze what about their interaction patterns causes you to feel that way. Do you think they are aware of these patterns?

Key Terms

verbal and analytic language (p. 40)	level (p. 48)
visual and holistic language (p. 40)	precedence (p. 48)
contextualization (p. 41)	classroom social organization (p. 55)
I-R-E (p. 41)	
metacommunication (p. 44)	sociolinguistics (p. 55)
proxemics (p. 44)	cognition (p. 55)
kinesics (p. 44)	motivation (p. 55)
paralanguage (p. 44)	framing (p. 60)

Building Your Own Knowledge Base: Suggested Readings

Foster, H. (1986). *Ribbin', jivin' and playin' the dozens: The persistent dilemma in our schools.* New York: Ballentine. Describes and identifies verbal interaction patterns of black, inner-city youth to help teachers understand and communicate more effectively.

Garcia, E. (1994). *Understanding and meeting the challenge of student cultural diversity.* Boston: Houghton Mifflin. Identifies and discusses forms of cultural diversity and suggests ways teachers can promote understanding and appreciation of diversity in their classrooms.

Nowicki, S., & Duke, M. P. (1992). *Helping the child who doesn't fit in.* Atlanta, GA: Peachtree Publishers. The authors describe nonverbal communication problems of some students and suggest ways to remedy them.

References

Anderson, E. (1990). *Streetwise: Race, class, and change in an urban community.* Chicago: University of Chicago Press.

Anderson, E. (1994). The code of the streets. *The Atlantic, 273,* 81–94.

Birdwhistle, R. L. (1970). *Kinesics and context: Essays on body motion communication.* Philadelphia: University of Pennsylvania Press.

Bowers, C. A., & Flinders, D. J. (1990). *Responsive teaching: An ecological approach to classroom patterns of language, culture, and thought.* New York: Teachers College Press.

Cazden, C. (1986). Classroom discourse. In W. C. Wittrock (Ed.), *Handbook of research on teaching* (3rd ed.). New York: Macmillan.

Cazden, C. (1988). *Classroom discourse: The language of teaching and learning.* Portsmouth, NH: Heinemann.

Cummins, J. (1989). *Bilingualism and special education.* Clevedon, Engl.: Multilingual Matters.

Eccles, J. S. (1989). Bringing young women to math and science. In M. Crawford & M. Gentry (Eds.), *Gender and thought: Psychological perspectives.* New York: Springer-Verlag.

Eibl-Eibesfeldt, I. (1972). Similarities and differences between cultures in expressive movement. In R. H. Hinde (Ed.), *Non-verbal communication.* Cambridge: Cambridge University Press.

Ekman, P. (1982). *Emotion in the human face.* New York: Cambridge University Press.

Ekman, P., & Friesen, W. V. (1975). *Unmasking the face: A guide to recognizing emotions from facial expressions.* Englewood Cliffs, NJ: Prentice Hall.

Ekman, P., Friesen, W. V., & Ellsworth, P. (1972). *Emotion in the human face: guidelines for research and an integration of findings.* New York: Pergamon.

Flood, C. (1988). Stereotyping and classroom interactions. In A. O'Brien Carelli (Ed.), *Sex equity in education: Reading and strategies.* Springfield, IL: Thomas.

Foster, H. (1986). *Ribbin', jivin' and playin' the dozens: The persistent dilemma in our schools.* New York: Ballentine.

Garcia, E. (1992). Effective instruction for language minority students: The teacher. *Journal of Education, 173,* 130–141.

Garcia, E. (1994). *Understanding and meeting the challenge of student cultural diversity.* Boston: Houghton Mifflin.

Hall, E. (1966). *The hidden dimension.* New York: Doubleday.

Hanna, J. (1988). *Disruptive school behavior: Class, race, and culture.* New York: Holmes and Meier.

Heath, S. B. (1983). *Ways with words: Language, life, and work in communities and classrooms.* Cambridge: Cambridge University Press.

Izard, C. E. (1971). *The face of emotion.* New York: Appleton-Century-Crofts.

Izard, C. E. (1977). *Human emotions.* New York: Plenum Press.

Jourard, S. (1966). An exploratory study of body accessibility. *British Journal of Social and Clinical Psychology, 8,* 39–48.

McDermott, R. P. (1977). Social relations as contexts for learning in school. *Harvard Educational Review, 47,* 198–213.

McIntyre, T. (1993). Teaching urban youth with behavioral disorders. In R. L. Peterson & S. Ishii-Jordan (Eds.), *Multicultural issues in the education of students with behavioral disorders.* Cambridge, MA: Brookline Books.

Nowicki, S., Jr., & Duke, M. P. (1992). *Helping the child who doesn't fit in.* Atlanta, GA: Peachtree Publishers.

Phillips, S. U. (1983). *The invisible culture: Communication in classroom and community on the Warm Springs Indian Reservation.* New York: Longman.

Tharp, R. G. (1989). Psychocultural variables and constants: Effects on teaching and learning in schools. *American Psychologist, 44,* 349–359.

Tharp, R. G., & Gallimore, R. (1989). *Challenging cultural minds.* London: Cambridge University Press.

Walker, D. W., & Leister, C. (1994). Recognition of facial affect cues by adolescents with emotional and behavioral disorders. *Behavioral Disorders, 19,* 269–276.

Williams, M. D. (1981). Observations in Pittsburgh ghetto schools. *Anthropology and Education Quarterly, 12,* 211–220.

Zabel, R. H. (1978). Recognition of emotions in facial expressions by emotionally disturbed children. *Psychology in the Schools, 15,* 119–126.

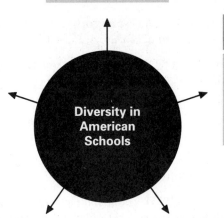

Nature and Nurture/Biophysical Factors

- Heredity and temperament
- Temperamental traits
- Biochemical factors
- Neurological factors
- Nutrition
- Environmental toxins
- Prenatal and later alcohol and drug effects

Sociocultural Factors

- Race
- Ethnic groups
- Cultural groups
- Linguistic differences
- Social status characteristics
- Gender
- Disability

Ecological Factors

Include ALL of the following:
- Biophysical factors
- Learning factors
- Psychosocial factors
- Sociocultural factors

Diversity in American Schools

Psychosocial Factors

- Psychosexual development
- Psychosocial development

Learning Factors

- Classical conditioning
- Operant learning
- Social learning theory

Chapter **3**

Diversity in American Schools

Annie's Journal

OCTOBER: I think I can say, with a small degree of confidence, that I sort of, from time to time, occasionally, have the day-to-day routine of my classroom down. Of course, it changes every day, so I guess that's not an exceptional statement. Actually, now that I see myself emerging from the panic of those first weeks, I find that there are things I didn't have time to worry about that now claim my attention. Like individual kids. Like Terrell in particular. I've been mulling over something that happened yesterday and trying to figure it out. Maybe if I write about it I'll see the problem. This incident didn't really stand out. I mean, it's not like it hasn't happened before. But this time I guess I realized that it *had* happened before—that it was something that happened quite a bit, so I'm trying harder to figure it out.

OK. It was during math, and I was working with Terrell's group. We'd been talking about geometric shapes—reviewing some of the basic ones and adding some new ones. It was pretty relaxed, the kids seemed interested in what we were doing. We were talking about shapes in the room, in advertising logos, or anywhere they could pick them out. I gave them some sheets with different shapes all over them, some even overlapping, and asked them to outline the various shapes in different colors—like circles in red, squares in blue, triangles in green, rectangles purple, polygons black, and so forth. There were several different sheets, so they didn't all have the same one. Well, most kids got started right away—I mean, it wasn't a very hard or stressful or unusual assignment—and I was walking around looking at their work. Then I notice Terrell. He's sitting at his desk with a brown crayon (brown was not one of the colors in my instructions) in his hand looking frantically around at the other kids' papers. I watch for a while, and he picks up first one color and then another, looking around all the time. The thing is, no one near him has the same paper he does. Finally I see him start to do something with the crayon, so I go over and say,

70

"How's it going, Terrell? Any questions?" As I look down at his paper, I see he's scribbled in brown all over it—not outlining anything. He looks at me, scrunches up his paper and stuffs it in his desk, and says, "This is baby work. I'm not doin' it."

Whoa. Confrontation. I know this is where I'm supposed to be cool and calm, but I wanted to say, "Baby work, huh? Well, if it's so simple, how come you're not doing it? Now you get that paper out and do it correctly, or you'll be doing it after school, young man!" That's what I *wanted* to say, but fortunately, I'm a well-trained, nurturing, 90s-type teacher, so I smiled through my clenched teeth and said, "It looks as though you're not ready to do the assignment now, Terrell. Why don't you finish the reading you started and we'll talk about this later?" Pretty good, huh? Actually I did it to stall because I didn't know *what* to do. I know he was being defiant, but I've seen some of this before with him—the looking around before starting an assignment, the unwillingness to ask me how to do it. I'm not sure what's going on. It seems as if there could be lots of explanations for his behavior, but I'm not sure how to decide which one fits. I'm really having trouble getting to know this kid. He doesn't seem interested in much that we do in class, and when I try to draw him out, he just gets quieter. He stares around the room a lot, seems to daydream during discussions, and rarely turns in his homework. I don't know what the deal is—and I'm not really sure who to talk to about it. . . .

I also still have some concerns about Carla. At first, I thought she was just a talker—like from morning until night. But now it's other things too—she's here, there, everywhere. She's not trying to get in trouble, but she's just all over the place. And something is always moving with her—her mouth, her foot, her pencil, her desk, her hands. It seems as though I'm always saying, "Carla, sit still. . . . Carla, be quiet. . . . Carla, sit down." The other kids are picking up on it too, and I don't like the way they seem to imitate *me* in saying those things to her. I've got to think up some more positive approaches to dealing with this.

Speaking of positive approaches, I'm still searching for something that works with Tremaine and Danny. I've separated them in class and put Danny in a group of quiet girls. I thought that would help and was really patting myself on the back when it looked like Danny was getting to be friends with Laura, a pretty, quiet girl who sat next to him. "Hey, Teacher," I thought, "you've got this thing figured out—divide and conquer!" Then the next recess, I see Danny and Tremaine playing tug-of-war . . . with Laura in the middle. They each had one of her arms and seemed to be trying to determine how much force it would take to split the poor girl apart. Needless to say, this did not seem to be a positive experience for Laura. Oh well, at least this job is never dull!

**FOCUS
QUESTIONS**

✳ What questions should a teacher be asking when a student behaves as Terrell does?

✳ What are some possible explanations for Terrell's behavior?

✳ Who should Annie be talking with to get some advice about Terrell's behavior?

✳ What do you think might be going on with students who exhibit behavior like Carla's? Danny's?

✳ Was Annie's intervention with Danny successful?

✳ What might be the next step in dealing with both of these students?

WHAT IS DIVERSITY?

Recently, we encountered triplets who were about six months old and were out with their parents, observing the world. The three girls were dressed alike and looked identical as they rode in a stroller built for three pushed by their father. At first glance their lives seemed identical: same clothes, same parents, identical genetic structure. However, despite their striking similarities, the girls were having somewhat different experiences. The view from the front seat of the stroller was different from the view in the middle or back seat. Each girl was looking in a different direction and was encountering different features of her surroundings. Although they were genetically alike, and their experiences within their families and other environmental contexts were similar, they were *not* identical. As these three girls develop increased mobility to independently explore their worlds, it is likely that their experiences will become even more divergent.

"Diversity" refers to individual as well as group distinctions.

In this chapter, we will treat **diversity** in a broader sense than usual. *Diversity* usually refers to group distinctions based on race, ethnicity, language, socioeconomic status, gender, and (dis)ability. But we believe that diversity also has to do with individual differences: genetic inheritance, temperaments, learned behavior, and developmental levels. Although the many aspects of diversity make the idea of classroom unity seem impossible, we think it is possible. However, it is only possible when you understand and appreciate the diverse natures of your students. In this chapter we will first consider factors that influence individual differences in learning and behavior and then examine factors that affect group differences.

NATURE AND NURTURE

Every person, even an identical triplet, is a unique expression of **nature** and **nurture.** Your mind and your personality (if these can be considered inde-

No two people have precisely the same experiences or are exactly alike.

pendently) are complex combinations of "what you are born with" (nature) and "what you experience" (nurture). Nature consists of biological factors, including the general physical and behavioral characteristics that identify us as human beings, and it also includes the individual physical and behavioral characteristics that reflect our genetic inheritance. Some factors of nature are not yet apparent at birth but become evident only later during development. For example, a child with tall parents may have a genetic predisposition to grow tall but may not reach his or her full stature until late adolescence. Or a child may inherit predispositions to become athletic or mechanical or musical, but those skills emerge only later and are affected by nurture as well as by nature.

Nurture consists of the modifications and changes that occur as the result of your individual experiences with the physical, social, and cultural environment. In a general sense, nurture reflects what you acquire or learn through experience. Nutrition, accident, and illness may affect how tall a child grows; opportunity, learning, and motivation influence whether a child actually develops athletic, mechanical, or musical interests and abilities.

Human beings have certain characteristics that distinguish us from other species, yet each human is also different from every other one. As products of a unique mixture of ancestral genes, human characteristics are expressed uniquely in each person. For example, members of the human species have heads containing brains and other material that are protected by skulls, which are covered by skin. As genetically unique, individuals also have brains of somewhat different sizes, skulls of somewhat different shapes, and skins of somewhat different colors from those of other fellow humans.

Nurture includes all the factors that reflect the influence of life experiences on our development as individuals. Nurture can include even some "biological" factors, such as the effects of nutrition on our physical and cognitive development both before and after we are born. Nurture also includes the myriad of experiences we have interacting with our environments and with our ecosystems— within families and cultural institutions like schools.

Everyone's development is the result of both nurture and nature.

Every individual's development—cognitive, physical, social, and emotional—is the product of interactions between nature *and* nurture. When asked whether nature or nurture has the greater influence on human development, a sage person responded that we might as well ask whether the length or width has a greater influence on the area of a rectangle. The answer is clear: they cannot be considered apart from one another.

To help you understand and appreciate the diversity of your students, we will draw upon several models or perspectives for understanding human behavior—models that focus on *biophysical, learning, psychosocial, sociocultural, gender, (dis)ability,* and *ecological factors.* No single perspective can tell you "everything you always wanted to know" about behavior and learning. Together, however, they should help you understand the "raw material" your students will bring to your classroom.

BIOPHYSICAL FACTORS

Biophysical factors in development are primarily features of nature.

Biophysical factors include influences on behavior that we would consider primarily features of "nature." Every student's learning and behavior are clearly influenced by biological factors, including genetic predispositions, inborn temperamental traits, biochemical make-up, and neurological functioning. Of course, these biophysical factors are not entirely independent from one another but should be viewed as providing different aspects of understanding human behavior. That is, genes are a major determinant of temperamental traits, as well as of biochemical and neurological functioning (see Figure 3.1).

Heredity and Temperament

If you have siblings, do you share any notable physical and behavioral traits with them? Has anyone every commented on similarities in your appearance? Have you noticed similar characteristics in your mannerisms, gestures, or voice in video recordings of yourself? Do you have similar hair color, body frame, height? Many of us have had the experience of recognizing physical resemblances of individuals and their siblings or biological parents. Most children bear some clear physical resemblance to one or both of their biological parents, siblings, and other close relatives.

Not so obviously, children also inherit behavioral traits in the genes they receive from their biological parents—half contributed by the mother, half by

FIGURE 3.1   Biophysical Factors That Influence Behavior

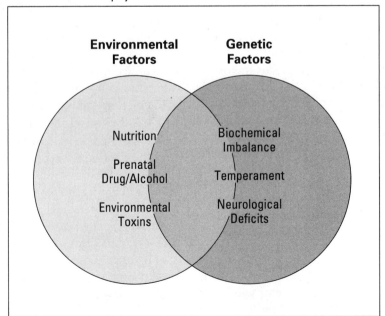

*Children inherit
behavioral as well as
physical traits.*

the father. A student recently told one of us that she had long noticed that she had a different temperament than her adoptive parents and brother. She was excitable and stubborn; they tended to be calm and easy-going. She also saw some of her own traits in her own young daughter. As a young adult, she met her biological mother and siblings for the first time, and she believed they had temperaments similar to her own.

Some behavioral similarities are obvious; others are more subtle. Always, your inherited behavioral characteristics are mediated and modified by your experiences and learning. Behavioral traits that are especially noticeable, as in severely disordered behavior, can have a genetic component. For example, studies of autism (the severe, pervasive disorder that we mentioned in Chapter 2) among identical and fraternal twins indicate that heredity plays a decisive role (Ritvo, Freeman, Mason-Brothers, Mo & Ritvo, 1985). In fact, when one identical twin is autistic, the other twin is also highly likely to have the disorder. Among fraternal twins, however, the likelihood that both twins will have autism is much lower. For other patterns or syndromes of disordered behavior, including schizophrenia, clinical depression, conduct disorders, and attention deficit hyperactive disorders (ADHD), evidence of genetic predisposition is apparent. In fact, genetically close relatives of children with these diagnoses are more likely than the general population to also have the disorders (Rizzo & Zabel, 1988).

Does this mean that heredity is the sole cause of these disordered patterns of behavior? Probably not, since persons who are genetically similar also tend to have similar environments and similar experiences. Even where there is a higher probability for a deviant behavioral pattern (such as autism and schizophrenia) among close relatives, not everyone inherits the disorder. To date, no specific genes or combinations of genes have been identified for most behavioral disorders. Thus, even pronounced and pervasive patterns of disordered behavior are likely the result of multiple and complex influences. A child may inherit a predisposition for certain patterns of behavior, but the person's experiences during the course of development may determine whether the predisposition is promoted or inhibited.

Temperamental Traits

*Temperamental traits
appear to be present at
birth or soon after.*

*Recognizing
temperamental traits
can help teachers
appreciate diversity
among their students.*

Temperamental traits or constitutional factors are individual characteristics that appear to be inborn. That is, they are present at birth, or shortly after, and result from the interaction of genetic, prenatal (intrauterine experiences prior to birth), and perinatal (experiences during birth) factors. Temperamental traits are relatively stable over time, and we often consider them aspects of personality. You can probably identify aspects of your own temperament that you have noticed in one or both of your parents. Recognizing your students' temperamental traits can help you appreciate differences in their learning and behavioral styles.

The existence and persistence of temperamental traits were the subject of the New York Longitudinal Study (Thomas & Chess, 1977, 1984; Thomas, Chess & Birch, 1968), which followed 136 children from birth through age 12. The researchers analyzed a variety of data, including parent and teacher interviews, observations of the children at home and in school, performance on standardized tests, and parenting practices. They reached the following conclusions about temperamental characteristics:

- They can be identified early in a child's life,

- They vary from child to child, and

- They remain relatively stable over time.

The New York Longitudinal Study identified nine relatively stable dimensions of temperament: *activity level, rhythmicity, approach or withdrawal, adaptability, intensity of reaction, threshold of responsiveness, quality of mood, distractibility, attention span,* and *persistence* (see descriptions in Table 3.1). The researchers evaluated their subjects along these dimensions to determine how their temperament traits compared to those of other children.

Using these dimensions of temperament, children can be divided into three distinct groups: *difficult, easy,* and *slow to warm up* (Thomas, Chess & Birch, 1968). *Difficult* children exhibit low rhythmicity, withdrawal, slowness in adapting to change, negative mood, and high intensity of reactions. Their parents find them demanding, stressful in the family, and difficult to manage. Their difficult behavior does not seem to result from particular parenting styles since researchers found no significant differences between parents of difficult and other children. However, over time the demands of dealing with a difficult child often led to conflict and power struggles, especially if the parents had similar "difficult" temperaments.

Children characterized as *easy* tend to have positive moods and low-intensity reactions to stimuli. They are adaptable and approach new situations positively. Their parents, teachers, and others see them as generally pleasant, likeable children who pose few problems for others.

Children considered *slow to warm up* tend to withdraw from interaction with others, adapt slowly to new situations, have relatively low activity levels, and have reaction tendencies and moods that are neither very positive nor negative. They can however, adapt to a variety of situations if allowed to do so at their own pace without pressure.

"Difficult" children experience more stress and conflicts in their ecosystems than "easy" and "slow to warm up" children do.

For educators, a significant finding of the New York Longitudinal Study is the likelihood that children who fit the "difficult" temperament pattern are much more likely than either "easy" or "slow to warm up" children to develop behavioral problems in school. Although this research does not mean that we can reliably predict which infants will later have problems in school, it does indicate that temperamental traits are relatively stable over time and that

TABLE 3.1
Temperamental Traits

Activity level is the relative amount of activity or movement characteristic of a child. Highly active children are described as fidgeting, squirming, wriggling, and grabbing. Low-activity children are described as more placid and quiet.

Rhythmicity refers to degree of regularity in biological functions of sleeping, eating, and elimination. Children with more regular patterns have higher rhythmicity, while those whose eating, sleeping, and elimination habits are less predictable and more irregular are low in rhythmicity.

Approach or withdrawal refers to distinct patterns in responses to novel situations and unfamiliar people. Some children are more inclined to smile at strangers, accept different foods, and explore new toys, while others are more aloof and likely to avoid strangers and resist unfamiliar situations.

Adaptability refers to ability to adjust to different situations. Some children are more flexible and able to adapt to changed circumstances than others, who are distressed by changes and insist on maintaining routines.

Intensity of reaction refers to the strength of responses to environmental stimuli. For example, one child might display a low intensity, barely noticeable response to a loud noise, while another might be startled and scream loudly.

Threshold of responsiveness refers to the intensity of stimuli (such as auditory, visual, or tactile) needed to elicit a response. Some children notice and respond to relatively mild stimuli, while others react only to more pronounced stimuli. Furthermore, children vary in their responsiveness to different kinds of stimuli. A child could have a higher threshold for auditory stimuli, responding only to louder sounds, while having a lower threshold for visual stimuli, readily noticing and reacting to colors, movement, and so on.

Quality of mood refers to a child's affective quality. Some children tend to be more friendly, pleasant, and happy, while others seem to be consistently unfriendly, irritable, and unhappy.

Distractibility refers to a child's capacity to maintain attention to an activity or task. Some children are more easily distracted by external stimuli, while others seem less likely to notice them and maintain their focus.

Attention span and *persistence* are related to distractibility, but refer to the length of time a child can maintain an activity even without external distraction. Some children show greater persistence than others.

Source: Adapted from Thomas and Chess (1977, 1984), Thomas, Chess and Birch (1968).

"difficult" children experience stress and conflict at home, in the neighborhood, and in school.

Behavioral problems develop as the result of conflicts between a child's temperamental traits and environmental conditions (Thomas & Chess, 1984). Parent, teacher, and peer behavior can affect a child's temperament in positive and negative ways. These findings have been extended to different groups, including Australian, French Canadian, Swedish, and Puerto Rican children

Adaptability is one of
the temperamental
traits that can be
identified early in a
child's life.

*(Elyse Lewin Studio Inc./
The Image Bank)*

(Maziade, Cote, Boudreault, Thivierge & Caperaa, 1984; Oberklaid, Prior &
Sanson, 1986; Korn & Gannon, 1983).

Biochemical Factors

*Biochemical factors in
development focus on
chemical processes of the
central nervous system.*

From another perspective, a person's behavior can be seen as the result of
biochemical factors and processes. Your central nervous system transmits messages to and from sensory receptors and the brain. What you see, hear, feel,
smell, and taste is the result of receptors reacting to environmental stimuli and
transmitting neurochemical messages along nerve cells (neurons) to your
brain, where they are sorted and dispatched to the appropriate areas of your
brain. The messages are responded to as perceptions; some produce physical
reactions.

When a pin pricks your finger with sufficient force, something like this
happens: sensory receptors in the finger release neurotransmitters that carry
the information along neurons and across synapses (gaps between neurons)
to the brain. Your brain processes the information ("Ouch! That hurts!") and
sends return messages to the site of the sensory reception ("Quickly withdraw

finger from this painful stimulus"). This process occurs very quickly, and in the case of a pin prick, a reflexive reaction—withdrawing your finger—actually precedes your perception of pain.

Biochemical factors in development are complex and not yet fully understood.

Of course, the processes of biochemical transmission are more complex than our description implies, and these processes are not yet fully understood. There are, for example, individual differences in the amount of sensory stimulation necessary to excite sensory receptors and thus start the process. Also, many neurotransmitters can help transmit messages to and from the brain. Some enhance and others inhibit the transmission and perception of sensory information.

Teachers may expect to have 2 or 3 students with ADD in classes of 20 to 30 students.

A pattern of individual variability in biochemical functioning that you are likely to encounter in your classroom is **attention deficit disorders (ADD)**. ADD may affect as many as 10 percent of elementary age children (Barkley, 1990), with boys outnumbering girls by a ratio of at least three or four to one. If these estimates are correct, you might expect, on average, two or three students with ADD in classes of twenty to thirty students. Some students with ADD are also considered hyperactive, or to have **attention deficit hyperactive disorders (ADHD)**.

Students with ADHD are excessively active, distractible, and impulsive (Barkley, 1990; Zentall, 1993). Characteristics of *excessive activity* include fidgety behavior, frequent motor movements, and difficulty handling sedentary activities like sitting for extended periods of time. Characteristics of *distractibility* are problems paying attention to "important" stimuli (like the teacher and assignments) and distraction by extraneous stimuli such as other students' behavior, sounds, and sights. Characteristics of *impulsivity* include responding too quickly without considering the consequences. For example, a student might do sloppy work with lots of errors, blurt out answers without being called on, talk back, or shove someone who has bumped him or her.

Clearly, when we say a student has ADHD, we are saying that his or her behavior is extreme compared to that of other students of the same age in the same environmental conditions. ADHD behaviors can be a problem in a classroom where students must sit quietly for long periods, pay attention, and concentrate on their academic work and social interactions. We might say there is a "lack of fit" between the expectations of the classroom ecosystem and the activity level of the student.

ADHD is a rather vaguely defined syndrome and reflects both inner characteristics of the student and external behavioral expectations and standards (Reid, Maag & Vasa, 1993; Rizzo & Zabel, 1988). For some students diagnosed as having ADHD, the "problem" is apparent primarily in classroom settings, where they have difficulty adapting, although they may function acceptably elsewhere. Some students with ADHD, however, display behavioral excesses in all their ecosystems.

Our current understanding suggests that it is likely there are multiple causes and contributors to ADHD, including inherited predispositions, expo-

Biochemical factors do seem to play an important role among multiple causes of ADHD.

sure to models of high activity, and even reinforcement for highly active behavior. However, for some children with ADHD, biochemical factors seem to be critical. These children sometimes respond favorably to pharmacological (drug) treatments. Central nervous system stimulants such as Ritalin, Dexedrine, and Cylert seem to reduce activity levels and help some children focus on relevant tasks (Barkley, 1990; Silver, 1990). Although parents and teachers report mostly favorable results for children with ADHD treated with these stimulant medications, some researchers caution that the effects are highly variable from child to child, do not always have academic significance, and entail risks of undesirable side effects (Forness, Swanson, Cantwell, Guthrie & Sena, 1992). Some children may behave restlessly and impulsively because they are anxious or bored, rather than because they have a biochemical imbalance.

The treatment with chemicals that are normally considered stimulants (commonly known as "speed") may seem paradoxical. Why would stimulants help calm a hyperactive child? A plausible, though unproven, explanation is that these medications stimulate the production of *inhibitory* neurotransmitters, thus effectively slowing down transmission of sensory messages to and from the child's brain.

Neurological Factors

Neurological factors in development focus on the influences of the structures of the central nervous system.

While biochemical factors focus on the chemical processes of the central nervous system (CNS), *neurological factors* emphasize the influence of the structures of the CNS. Perhaps an analogy with electrical transmission would be helpful. Consider biochemical factors as analogous to the electric current and neurological factors as analogous to the wires, fuses, and circuit breakers— the structures—through which electricity flows. Damage to the CNS can produce deviations in normal neurological functions. Often called "brain damage," the results of damage to the central nervous system are sometimes obvious as in cerebral palsy, spinal cord injuries, muscular dystrophy, and traumatic brain injuries that may impair muscle control and coordination, speech, emotional, and cognitive functions. Cerebral palsy, for example, results from brain damage due to prenatal or perinatal injuries or illnesses such as anoxia (lack of oxygen) during birth. Of course, even within diagnoses like cerebral palsy, there are variations in the severity and type of involvement.

Damage to the central nervous system can result in learning, behavioral, and emotional problems.

In recent years there has been a greater awareness of the emotional, behavioral, and learning characteristics resulting from traumatic brain injuries (TBI). Approximately 200,000 children experience traumatic brain injuries each year (Humphreys, 1989) from physical abuse, falls, auto accidents, and sports injuries as well as diseases like strokes. These injuries are often difficult to diagnose and treat, especially with a "closed head injury," where there is no skull fracture, but the brain is bruised or otherwise damaged. TBI can result in learning, behavioral, and emotional problems, some of which may become apparent long after the injury. Head injuries that seem mild can have enduring effects on an individual's behavior, personality, and learning, including problems with attention, memory, concentration, fatigue, irritability, and aggressiveness (Allison, 1992).

Even mild forms of neurological dysfunction can include educationally significant behavioral and learning characteristics. For example, when learning disabilities—now the largest classification of educational disabilities—were first described, researchers believed they resulted from *minimal brain damage* (Strauss & Lehtinen, 1947). In the absence of any other explanation for a child's learning problems, people thought that subtle damage to the central nervous system was responsible. The structural damage might be hereditary or from an injury before, during, or after birth or from an illness that included a high, prolonged fever. Early researchers used the term *minimal brain damage* because they did not have technology to actually locate the damage, although they found associated "soft" signs indicative of brain damage such as coordination and perceptual problems.

Today, you will rarely encounter the term *minimal brain damage*. Educators instead use the term *learning disabilities* because it does not imply a specific cause of learning and behavior problems. Learning disabilities, whether relatively mild and specific or more pronounced and general, probably result from many factors, both internal and external (Adelman & Taylor, 1993; Lerner, 1993). Still, it is likely that many students with learning disabilities have some type of neurological dysfunction.

The federal definition of learning disabilities excludes children whose learning problems result from "mental retardation, or emotional disturbance, or environmental, cultural, or economic disadvantage" (*Federal Register,* 1977, p. 65083). In addition to accident, injury, or illness, several types of environmental causes of neurological damage have been identified for learning disabilities, behavior problems, and other disabilities. They include poor nutrition and toxins such as lead poisoning and prenatal exposure to alcohol and drugs. These factors also can influence the learning and behavior of students who may not qualify as disabled.

Damage to the structures of the central nervous system may be due to heredity, injury, or illness.

Poor nutrition and environmental toxins can also damage the central nervous system.

Nutrition

Both prenatal and postnatal nutrition affect physical and cognitive development. Diet influences a pregnant mother's health and resistance to disease and directly influences the growth and development of the fetus. The specific effects of prenatal nutrition are hard to separate from those of diet following birth (as well as other factors). For instance, low birth weight (less than $5\frac{1}{2}$ pounds) can result from genetic or congenital disorders, prematurity, *or* nutritional deficiencies. In addition, low-birth-weight infants may be intellectually delayed and manifest neurological abnormalities (Peterson, 1987).

A newborn's brain contains less than one half of its adult cells and grows rapidly, especially during the first year. After that critical first year, brain growth is primarily in the size of cells and their connections with one another rather than in number of cells. Brain growth continues through adolescence, and different parts of the brain develop at different rates and can be affected by malnutrition. Whereas *prenatal* nutrition can affect development of the cerebral cortex and its processes of learning and integrating sensory motor behavior like speech, *postnatal* nutrition tends to affect the cerebellum, which controls motor coordination and the transmission of electrical impulses between various parts of the body and the brain (Peterson, 1987).

Even for school-age children, nutrition continues to affect the development of the structures and processes of the central nervous system, as well as to influence behavior and learning. Students who are hungry or who have inadequate diets may be frequently sick and may be lethargic, unmotivated, and irritable.

Prenatal and postnatal nutrition affect development of different parts of the brain.

Environmental Toxins

Some children are exposed to environmental toxins that affect their growth and development and can contribute to learning and behavioral problems. Recently, for example, we have become more aware of the detrimental effects of maternal tobacco smoking during pregnancy on fetal development and from *passive smoking* (breathing smoke-filled air) during childhood (Conlon, 1992).

We have also become more aware of the damaging effects of heavy metals in the environment, most notably lead, that can cause disease as well as neurological damage that affects learning and behavior. Ingested in sufficient quantities, lead causes physical deformities, illnesses, and enough neurological damage to produce learning disabilities, mental retardation, and behavioral problems, as well as seizure disorders (U.S. Environmental Protection Agency, 1992).

In many city and household water systems, lead pipes and soldering release lead into drinking water. Although lead-based paints are no longer sold, many older buildings have layers of these paints. Small children sometimes eat the sweet-tasting paint chips that have peeled from walls and ingest lead paint dust from carpets, floors, and window sills as they put fingers, toys, and other objects in their mouths. The soil in yards and playgrounds and in the air, especially near streets and freeways, often has high levels of lead and other metals deposited from gasolines with lead additives that were used in cars until a few years ago.

Passive smoking and ingestion of metals such as lead can cause diseases and neurological damage.

Prenatal and Later Alcohol and Drug Effects

Over the past few years the detrimental and life-long effects of prenatal consumption of alcohol and other drugs have become apparent. Researchers have now convincingly demonstrated what they long suspected—that a preg-

A pregnant mother's consumption of alcohol or other drugs can cause damage in a child's development.

nant mother's use of alcohol, even in relatively small amounts at critical periods of fetal brain development, can produce defects that adversely affect a child's physical, intellectual, and behavioral development. The implications for later learning and behavior problems in your classroom can be tremendous (Vincent et al., 1991).

Fetal Alcohol Syndrome. **Fetal alcohol syndrome (FAS)** is the name for a constellation of physical and cognitive characteristics that can result from a pregnant mother's regular and heavy alcohol consumption during pregnancy. The affected fetus who survives can suffer from

- Small birth weight and delayed physical growth;
- Measurable mental deficits, including IQs in the "mildly retarded" or "borderline" range (between about 65 and 80), delayed language development, below-average performance across academic subjects, and inability to develop abstract thinking skills;
- Distinctive facial features, including small head circumference, a low nasal bridge, epicanthal folds of skin in the inner corner of the eyes, small noses, and upper lips with indistinct philtrum (groove in upper lip); and
- Physical abnormalities, which can include missing or undeveloped limbs, organ malformations, and seizure disorders.

Learning and behavioral problems associated with FAS include perceptual disturbances, short memory, distractibility, and emotional instability. Often these children are considered hyperactive, inattentive, impulsive, and lacking "common sense" (Streissguth & La Due, 1987)—characteristics we earlier discussed as central to ADHD.

Characteristics of FAE are more subtle than those of FAS.

Fetal Alcohol Effects. **Fetal alcohol effects (FAE)** refer to less obvious symptoms that can result from even moderate and occasional alcohol consumption. FAE are harder to diagnose since their manifestations are more subtle than those of FAS, but FAE also involve more children. Possible physical and social characteristics are head and body rocking, clumsiness, difficulty getting along with peers, poor judgment, and an underdeveloped sense of right and wrong. In addition, children with FAE have difficulty with academic tasks such as learning multiplication tables and telling time (Forbes, 1984).

In *The Broken Cord: A Family's Ongoing Struggle with Fetal Alcohol Syndrome* (1989), Michael Dorris writes powerfully about the development of his adopted son, Adam and his gradual discovery that Adam has FAS. The Classroom Closeup "A Struggle with Fetal Alcohol Syndrome" contains a description of Adam's experiences in school.

Prenatal Drug Exposure. **Prenatal drug exposure**—use of illegal drugs, such as heroin, cocaine, and marijuana by pregnant mothers—can have a variety of

Classroom Closeup

A Struggle with Fetal Alcohol Syndrome

"Adam is a delightful boy and a real pleasure to have in my class," commented his third-grade teacher. "Adam is a very loving child. I enjoy working with him," said his fourth-grade instructor. "He's doing *so well* this year! It's hard to believe it's the same youngster," wrote the school principal at the beginning of the fifth grade. All these good men and women were determinedly optimistic. They praised Adam's "progress" in things like map making and social studies, his fondness for reading books, his great interest in art, the leaps he was making in friendships and self-control. They proclaimed his mastery of basic arithmetic, . . . vocabulary, telling time.

The fact was, improvement was hard to come by and even harder to sustain once it had appeared. Reviewing those end-of-the-year teacher reports, it is now clear that in grade after grade Adam was working at the same level on exactly the same tasks. Every year he started fresh, showed promise up to a point, then couldn't take the next step. His learning curve resembled more than anything else one of those carnival strong-man games in which a platform is struck with a weighted mallet and a ball rises up a pole toward a bell. In my son's case, sometimes the bell rang, but then the ball always fell back to earth. He was the little engine that couldn't make it over the mountain, and, in frustration and disappointment, without ever actually saying so, all but a dedicated few eventually stopped thinking that his trip was worth their effort.   (Dorris, 1989, pp. 110–111) ✳

Babies exposed to illegal drugs before birth may have complex cognitive, and social, and behavioral characteristics.

long-term effects on children's health and development, including congenital physical abnormalities, neurobehavioral disorders, and chemical dependence. As many as 10 percent of babies born today have been exposed to some illicit drug (Chasnoff, 1988).

No doubt you are aware of the detrimental effects of crack-cocaine. This relatively cheap and powerful form of cocaine was introduced on the streets in the mid-1980s (Chasnoff, Landress & Barrett, 1990; Keith, MacGregor, Friedell, Rosner, Chasnoff & Sciarra, 1989). Crack-cocaine exposed infants who survive the pregnancy are often addicted at birth and have a low birth weight, small head size, lack of response to caregivers, and disorganized responses to their environments (Hadeed & Siegel, 1989).

Because many crack-cocaine exposed children are now in school, teachers are faced with the complex cognitive, social, and behavioral characteristics and the challenges they present (Bauer, 1991; Toufexis, 1991; Van Dyke & Fox, 1990). Some of these children have mild to moderate mental retardation and significant delays in their educational achievement. In addition, some display chronic and severe patterns of disordered behavior, including aggressive, destructive, noncompliant, disruptive, and hyperactive behavior.

Drug Use Among School Children. The problem with drugs is not limited to those who were vicitimized before they were born, however. There are currently many children, some not yet out of elementary school, who are taking illicit drugs. In many communities, these drugs are more available than in the past, and some children are actively encouraged and pressured by their peers and drug dealers to use drugs. Some communities and schools have more pronounced drug problems than others, but no community or school is immune from drug-related problems. The most common drugs are alcohol, marijuana, and cocaine, which are sometimes considered "gateway" drugs (DuPont, 1984), because they are relatively available and inexpensive and children may think they are harmless and nonaddictive. Some experiment with drugs, some develop patterns of social or recreational usage, others actively seek opportunities for regular drug use, and for others, drugs become a focus of their lives.

Warning signs such as mood swings and deteriorating performance can alert teachers to students' drug use.

In your classroom and school, you may observe evidence of alcohol and other drug use by students. Children who use drugs experience altered moods and behavior depending on the kind, strength, and frequency with which they use them. Possible other warning signs include sudden changes in emotional and behavioral patterns, such as a student's deteriorating school performance, mood swings, depression, irritability, slowed or slurred speech, diminished alertness, weight loss or gain, and frequent lying and stealing (Rizzo & Zabel, 1988). Of course, some students may offer more direct evidence of their drug use by possessing drug paraphernalia, having more money than usual, or even telling you about it.

It is usually impossible to sort out the relative effects of prenatal or postnatal drug and alcohol consumption from other environmental effects on learning and behavior. Use of drugs and alcohol frequently (although not always) goes hand in hand with other conditions that constitute a drug lifestyle, including poor prenatal and postnatal nutrition, inadequate or nonexistent health care, maternal smoking, poverty, unstimulating home environment, and neglect and abuse. Consequently, the relative contributions of each are impossible to factor out, and we face some major challenges to successful intervention.

Other Illnesses and Injuries. The varieties of illnesses and injuries that can affect student behavior and learning are infinite. Although the relationship between health and behavior can be obvious, as when a student is distracted by the pain of scrapes and bruises from a fall on the playground, sometimes it is not so obvious, as when a student has a low-grade fever. In his report on conditions in American schools, Jonathon Kozol describes how poor health really does affect student learning and behavior. See the Classroom Closeup on "Health Conditions in East St. Louis, Illinois and the South Bronx, NY."

Behavioral symptoms of illnesses and injuries may be acute or chronic. That is, they may be fairly pronounced and transient, such as bruises and scrapes, or on-going and persistent, such as chronic headaches, earaches, and

Classroom Closeup

Health Conditions in East St. Louis, Illinois and the South Bronx, New York

East St. Louis . . . has some of the sickest children in America. Of 66 cities in Illinois, East St. Louis ranks first in fetal death, first in premature birth, and third in infant death. Among the negative factors listed by the city's health director are the sewage running in the streets, air that has been fouled by the local plants, the high lead levels noted in the soil, lack of education, crime, dilapidated housing, insufficient health care, unemployment. As in New York City's poorest neighborhoods, dental problems also plague the children here. Although dental problems don't command the instant fears associated with low birth weight,

fetal death or cholera, they do have the consequence of wearing down the stamina of children and defeating their ambitions. Bleeding gums, impacted teeth and rotting teeth are routine matters for the children I have interviewed in the South Bronx. Children get used to feeling constant pain. They go to sleep with it. They go to school with it. Sometimes their teachers are alarmed and try to get them to a clinic. But it's all so slow and heavily encumbered with red tape and waiting lists and missing, lost or cancelled welfare cards, that dental care is often long delayed. Children live for months with pain that grown-ups would find unendurable. The gradual attrition of accepted pain erodes their energy and aspiration.   (Kozol, 1991, pp. 20–21) ✳

---

toothaches. Sometimes we misinterpret illness-related behavior. For example, a student who seems uncooperative, distracted, unmotivated, or grouchy may actually be in pain. Younger children, especially, may not even recognize they are sick, so teachers need to be aware of possible symptoms, adjust their expectations, and seek assistance from the school nurse and parents so students can receive the treatment they need.

Students' behavior problems may be the result of health problems.

Sometimes, a student's apparent behavioral problems are a direct result of physical problems. If you have a student who is inattentive, distractible, and slow to participate, it is possible that hearing or visual impairments are contributing factors. A student who cannot hear or see relevant stimuli in your classroom may display symptoms that look like motivation or behavior problems. Again, your school nurse can help you determine whether your student has a health problem that may affect behavior and can alert the student's parents if necessary.

Medications.   Physician-prescribed medications also affect learning and behavior. In addition to medications prescribed to treat physical illnesses, some students take psychoactive drugs to modify their behavior. These include anticonvulsants to control seizures, antianxiety medications, tranquilizers, and

Teachers are highly likely to have some students who take prescribed medications.

antidepressants. The most common psychoactive medications are the central nervous system stimulants prescribed for hyperactivity that we mentioned earlier. About 500,000 (1 to 2 percent) of elementary students receive stimulant medications (Gadow, 1991), so it is likely that you will sometime have students who receive psychoactive medications.

Drug treatment for learning and behavioral problems is deservedly controversial. Admittedly, medications can help reduce the frequency and intensity of disruptive and aggressive behavior, motor activity, and restlessness, and increase attention and cooperation of some children (e.g., Kavale & Nye, 1984; Halperin, Gittelman, Katz & Struve, 1986). However, medications do not provide total solutions for learning and behavioral problems of students believed to have ADHD or other disorders. It is difficult to determine appropriate dosages, and some children take medication irregularly or cease taking it after a short time. In addition most psychoactive drugs have side effects such as drowsiness, headaches, moodiness, irritability, and talkativeness that influence learning and behavior (Swanson et al., 1992; Forness et al., 1992). Too often, drugs are used in place of thoughtful and systematic adjustments in the environment and in expectations, and for the convenience of adults.

Medications can reduce learning and behavior problems, but they do not solve the problems.

Remember that psychoactive medications alone do not *directly* influence a student's ability to learn, although they can help some students become more receptive learners. Thus, psychoactive medications are best used as part of more comprehensive approaches that stress teaching self-control techniques, academic interventions, individual and family counseling and training.

Doctors often prescribe psychoactive medications to have maximum benefit for students while they are in school. When you have students receiving drug treatment, you may be the most valuable source of information about their effectiveness. You should be alert to the medication's intended behavioral effects and potential side-effects. You should also communicate your observations of changes in student behavior to parents and physicians. As a teacher you are in the unique position of observing a student's behavior and comparing it with classmates' behavior. Your observations can help physicians and parents monitor drug effects.

Teachers are often the best sources of information about a prescribed medication's effectiveness.

As We See It: *The Authors Talk*

Bob: You know, advances in genetics like the Human Genome Project are really going to cause significant debate about the role of inheritance of traits and behaviors.

Mary Kay: I think *debate* may be too mild a word. As research scientists are able to identify more and more genes associated with specific traits or conditions, our whole society is going to have to rethink some things.

Bob: But these discussions should be healthy for society as a whole. We *should* begin to think more carefully about the way we define and value difference and what we mean by those terms.

Mary Kay: But what if we begin to use that information to provide or deny services? What happens when we've identified genes associated with ADHD, with reading problems, with deafness, or with aggressive behavior? Do we do genetic screenings as part of preschool enrollment? Or will we be able to wait and see how nature and nurture interact to produce a human being? Don't we run the risk of a "brave new world" where, between genetic research and psychological medications, everyone has the same vague smile on his or her face?

Bob: I think you're being a bit extreme. The genome research has shown that because a gene is identified with a certain trait or condition doesn't mean we can alter it. And people are already talking about how to get the developing information on genetics into the classroom, so students can begin to understand it at an early age.

Mary Kay: You're right, but I still think our society is in for some hard discussions about how much we really value diversity in development—and whose job it is to make some of these tough decisions.

Bob: I agree. We'll have to be sure that educators continue to be part of these discussions and that the viewpoints of those who work with children and young people are well represented.

Mary Kay: Great. Another committee.

LEARNING FACTORS

Biophysical factors ("nature") interact with experiences ("nurture"), including what children learn through interacting with their environments. From birth, human beings are ideally suited to expand their skills and understandings, to make sense of their environments, and to respond to them. Three explanations of how learning affects behavior are the **classical conditioning, operant learning,** and **social learning** theories (see Table 3.2). Although we cannot explore the details of each theory here, we think you should understand them. They explain how people learn and provide the theoretical underpinning for important instructional approaches and behavioral interventions (referred to collectively as behavior modification) that we discuss in later chapters.

Classical Conditioning

Classical conditioning, sometimes called *respondent* or *association learning* assumes that organisms, including human beings, are programmed to respond

TABLE 3.2
Three Explanations of
How Learning Affects
Behavior

THEORY OF BEHAVIOR	ASSUMPTIONS
Classical conditioning	Human beings and other organisms are programmed to respond reflexively to certain stimuli. Human beings and other organisms may learn to respond to new stimuli as they formerly responded to other stimuli. Some patterns of problem behavior may be learned.
Operant learning	The consequences of behavior teach new behavior and maintain or strengthen existing behavior. Behavior followed by reinforcement is more likely to be repeated. Behavior followed by punishment diminishes. Reinforcement histories profoundly affect classroom behavior.
Social learning	There is a cognitive component to how learning affects behavior. Learning occurs vicariously as people observe others who model the behavior. Patterns of behavior are the result of vicarious learning.

reflexively to certain environmental stimuli. Just as Pavlov's dogs responded to the stimulus of food by salivating, people respond reflexively to certain stimuli. When stimuli occur together (when food is presented together with a ringing bell), stimulus properties may become associated. For example, food and the bell are associated with one another, and we, like Pavlov's dogs, may learn to respond to new stimuli as we formerly responded to other stimuli.

Classical conditioning provides only a limited explanation for the vast amounts of learning that humans accomplish. However, it helps explain how certain patterns of problem behavior, like phobias or "psychosomatic" symptoms, can be learned. For example, a student who has a stressful stimulus, like taking a test might develop a headache, stomachache, back pains, or other physical symptoms that have no physiological basis, yet they are painful and interfere with the student's performance. The student may have *learned* to react this way whenever faced with the stressful experience. In the same way, a student who fails or is rejected at school may become fearful and avoid school.

Operant Learning

Operant learning theory explains how people learn behavior because of its consequences. When you think of operant learning, you may recall B. F. Skinner's experiments with pigeons, which showed how consequences of behavior teach new behavior and maintain or strengthen existing behavior (Skinner, 1974). Behavior that is followed by *reinforcement* is more likely to be repeated, while behavior followed by *punishment* diminishes (your mother understood this principle when she required you to eat your vegetables *before* you got dessert). Reinforcement is defined as consequences that increase the future rate of a behavior; punishment is consequences that reduce the future rate of behavior (Skinner, 1974).

If you consider the many behaviors you engage in each day and their consequences, you will likely find that you mostly seek reinforcement and avoid punishment. When you cannot find contingent reinforcement or punishment, you may be engaging in behavior that has been "conditioned" by past reinforcement. A behavior like brushing teeth, a habitual behavior that most of us perform regularly, is a good example of how operant learning operates. Why do you brush your teeth, if not for its consequences? As a child your parents may have praised (reinforced) you for brushing and scolded (punished) you for not brushing your teeth. Today, you may seek social acceptance (reinforcement) by having sparkling, clean teeth, fresh smelling breath, and avoid social rejection and the discomfort of tooth decay and dental work (punishment).

If you accept this operant learning explanation, you can see how your students' reinforcement histories influence their classroom behavior. For example, a student who has had academic success and has been rewarded with attention, praise, and status is more likely to be academically motivated than one who has been unsuccessful and punished with negative attention, criticism, and low status. Likewise, a student whose bullying behavior has been reinforced by getting his way or by attention, praise, and status from others will more likely use bullying behavior than a child who has been unsuccessful and unrewarded by such behavior.

Operant learning can explain how reinforcement can influence students' behavior.

Operant learning theory acknowledges that the same consequences are not reinforcing or punishing to everyone. Reinforcement, for instance, takes different forms. It may be *primary* (fulfilling basic needs like food) or *secondary* (social approval and acceptance). There are also *intrinsic,* or self-rewarding, consequences like feeling good about your accomplishments. Reinforcement need not be positive—consequences you might consider desirable. For example, your negative attention to some student behavior, in the form of scolding, criticism, or even corporal punishment, can actually reinforce the unwanted behavior. The student might prefer your negative attention to no attention or may derive some satisfaction and peer status from being "bad."

Negative attention from a teacher may be more desirable to a student than no attention.

Once behavior is learned, it is part of a person's behavioral repertoire and does not need to be reinforced every time it is performed (Skinner, 1974). *Intermittent* reinforcement actually produces more stable responses than continuous reinforcement, which is why some problem behaviors, such as arguing or tantrums, may continue even when you ignore or punish them. These behaviors have been reinforced in the past, perhaps by parents and others, and may be intermittently reinforced when students occasionally get their way or gain attention.

Another valuable insight of operant learning theory is the power of reinforcement as opposed to punishment. Aversive, unpleasant consequences, such as spanking, scolding, or exclusion, can suppress behavior. However, the

Punishment may suppress behavior without teaching alternative behavior.

suppression is often only temporary because punishment does not teach alternative, more acceptable behavior. Consequently, more powerful punishments are sometimes needed to suppress the behavior. In fact, the most powerful lesson learned from punishment is to avoid the punisher.

Operant learning theory offers the rather mechanistic view that events and consequences automatically determine behavior. While that assumption may be valid for pigeons, rats, and chimps under laboratory conditions, people in "real-life" situations, such as you and the students in your classroom, are a lot more complex and unpredictable.

Social Learning

Social learning theory (Bandura, 1977, 1986) adds a cognitive component to learning theory that provides the underpinnings for the cognitive behavior modification approaches we will discuss in later chapters. According to social learning theory, most learning occurs *vicariously*. That is, we learn by observing others (parents, siblings, peers, and teachers) who model the behavior. In addition, we vicariously learn behavior portrayed in the media, such as television, radio, magazines, books, movies, and videos. We then cognitively store that learned behavior until we encounter situations where we can use it.

People who serve as models of behavior usually are admirable, older, or more competent than the learner or observer.

Anyone you encounter may serve as a model, although people who are likely to serve as models share certain attributes. They are usually of higher status—they may be older or more competent and have traits that the observer finds desirable. The observer or learner may see the model as having characteristics similar to his or her own. In addition, Bandura's research has shown that children are more likely to imitate modeled behavior that they have seen reinforced.

Examples of behavior learned vicariously are virtually limitless. From infancy, children learn by seeing and hearing others. They acquire behavior as the result of both casual learning and deliberate teaching. Consider how a child learns to use language, for example. Children are exposed to models of parents, siblings, and others who use language. They are also deliberately taught to use language by their parents, teachers, and others who model use of words, grammar, and syntax and encourage and reinforce children for copying their behavior.

Children learn language through exposure to models who use language.

Many patterns of behavior are the result of vicarious learning. Children who have models who are nurturing, cooperative, supportive, friendly, and trusting, for example, will learn these behaviors. Those whose models argue, fight, steal, and lie are likely to learn these behaviors. Under the right conditions—where they think the behavior will be useful and be reinforced—children are likely to perform the behavior they have learned from watching and listening to others.

As we mentioned in Chapter 2, some poor, inner-city African American youth copy patterns of aggressive demeanor and actual violent behavior in their search for respect (Anderson, 1994). These patterns of behavior are transmitted through social learning. Some families display deep-seated bitterness and anger over discrimination and persistent lack of jobs. Anderson refers to "children of the street" who learn physical and verbal aggressiveness from models in their homes and neighborhoods. Children who see anger, verbal disputes, and physical aggression in their street-oriented homes learn that might makes right. Among their peers also, they see that the "violent resolution of disputes, the hitting and cursing, gains reinforcement." Younger children see older children handling their disputes with cursing, abusive talk, and violence. Thus, lessons they learn at home about toughness as a virtue and humility as a fault are reinforced by behavior they encounter in their community (Anderson, 1994).

The so-called decent families, who comprise the majority, tend to accept mainstream values—respect for authority, hard work, self-reliance, cooperation—and try to instill them in their children (Anderson, 1994). However, their children are confronted by oppositional behavior when they step outside their homes. To survive they, too, need to assume a street-oriented demeanor. Although the oppositional behaviors Anderson describes are extreme, they are a fact of life in many inner-city, poor neighborhoods and schools. In all classrooms, of course, you will find students who have learned behavior in their homes and communities that affects their classroom behavior.

We think the most valuable insight offered by social learning theory is the powerful influence of models. Your students will "listen" more closely to what you *do* than to what you say, so you will want to behave in ways you would like your students to imitate. Does this mean you must behave flawlessly at all times? That when the hamster has just died, Amy has thrown up *again,* and the principal has put a note in your mailbox that just says, "See me," you need to be a model of calm and cool decorum? No, because such an expectation would be impossible. What you *can* do is foster a sense of open communication in your classroom that allows you to say, "Whew! There is certainly a lot going on in here today. I think we all need to take a break and do something fun" (or quiet, or silly, or thoughtful—whatever fits the situation). Social learning theory also offers *cognitive behavior modification techniques* that you can use to help your students increase their self-control by modifying their own thoughts and behavior. In Chapters 7 and 8 we discuss some cognitive behavior modification approaches.

PSYCHOSOCIAL FACTORS

Psychosocial theories of behavior identify universal changes that occur in people's lives.

While learning theories view behavior as the result of learning through association, reinforcement, and modeling, psychosocial perspectives emphasize universal changes that occur in the process of normal emotional and social development. Foremost among the psychosocial explanations are those of

Sigmund Freud and Erik Erikson. Both portray individual social-emotional development as a progression through distinct stages that correspond with age levels.

Psychosexual Development

Freud's theories regarding the role of internal, unconscious motivational forces on emotional development are referred to as *psychodynamic* or *psychoanalytic.* Although there is ongoing debate about the validity of many specific features of psychoanalytic theory, much of the Freudian perspective is infused into our everyday beliefs about how and why people behave as they do. One of these beliefs is the assumption that people are not always consciously aware of the underlying motives and feelings that generate their behavior.

The psychosexual theory suggests that children's personalities develop as they interact with other people.

The psychoanalytic perspective suggests and identifies distinct stages of personality development. Children's personalities develop as they progress through several distinct stages. Infants are essentially bundles of self-centered instinctual drives, or the *id,* which Freud considered primarily sexual in nature. In addition to id (the raw, instinctual, self-centered element of personality essential for survival), young children develop an *ego* (a rational sense of self) that mediates between the id and a third element, the *superego* (one's conscience or understanding of right and wrong). Each element of personality develops as the child interacts with significant others, especially parents, during the first few years of life. According to the psychoanalytic theory, a child's personality is fairly well established by the time the child enters school.

The elements of personality—id, ego, and superego—are balanced in a well-adjusted personality. Conversely, a poorly adjusted personality is one in which one element dominates the others. For example, a child who is messy, uncontrolled, and aggressive and shows little concern for others could be seen as expressing more id than superego; an overcontrolled and moralistic child has an overdeveloped superego.

Psychosocial Development

Erikson's theory of psychosocial development follows the sequential stages outlined by Freud but emphasizes *social* and *cultural* forces on personality, rather than sexual drives (Erikson, 1963). Based on case examples of his patients and studies of child-rearing practices in different cultures, Erikson explained personality development as the result of a series of psychosocial crises, each with possible positive or negative outcomes. For example, an infant's interactions with caregivers during the first year of life determine whether the child develops a *basic trust* and optimism or *distrust* and pessimism toward the world. A child who is loved, nurtured, and has basic needs met develops a trusting personality; a child who is neglected and rejected and whose basic needs are unmet develops a mistrusting personality.

The psychosocial theory suggests that children's personalities develop as they experience various developmental crises.

As a teacher, you need to be aware of the level of psycho-social development your students are experiencing.
(Sieplinga/HMS Images/ The Image Bank)

Experiences in later life can change earlier psychosocial development.

Freud's and Erickson's theories offer insights rather than complete explanations.

Erikson believed that each stage builds on and incorporates the earlier stages. A child who does not acquire basic trust during infancy will likely continue to be mistrustful and have difficulty achieving a sense of autonomy, independence, competence, and identity—the positive outcomes of later developmental crises. However, he also believed that subsequent experiences can modify earlier psychosocial development. For example, children who are rejected and neglected as infants may later encounter nurturing, loving people, such as teachers, who help them acquire a more trusting perspective.

Over the years, the ideas of Freud and Erikson have attracted the attention of researchers, theorists, and practitioners who have expanded, revised, critiqued, and disputed some of their assumptions and conclusions. Today, few people accept these theories as complete explanations of social and emotional development, but they do offer insights about child behavior that can can help you understand some human behavior. For example, Freud and Erikson stressed the importance of the *qualitative* changes that occur during a child's development. An infant thinks, feels, and behaves differently than a two-year-old, an eight year-old, an adolescent, or an adult. Older children have not simply accumulated (learned) more behavior, but they actually experience, interpret, and respond to their worlds differently than younger children. As a teacher you need to be aware of your students' developmental levels and establish expectations that are developmentally appropriate. Another important implication for teachers is that individual children vary in their developmental course. Despite general patterns, every child does not develop at the same rate, and some do not progress as far as others.

The psychosocial model stresses the important effect of early experiences on a child's current behavior. A child's feelings and behavior reflect not only present conditions but also past experiences. The psychosocial model also views behavior as the overt expression of underlying feelings. Thus, your students' anger, mistrust, frustration, or depression may have their origins in past and current experiences outside your classroom—in their families and communities. Although students' feelings may be generated elsewhere, they may still influence their behavior in your classroom. A psychodynamic explanation of this process is called *transference*. Students can transfer their feelings for one person, such as one of their parents, to another person, such as a teacher, whom they perceive as safer or a more convenient target. We have found it reasssuring to know that students sometimes express anger toward teachers not because their teachers caused the feelings but because they are more convenient and, perhaps, "safe" targets.

Teachers need to understand that they may be the targets rather than the cause of students' feelings.

The pupil conflict cycle proposed by Long and Duffner (1980) depicts how students transfer various forms of life stress (developmental, economic, psychological, reality) that detrimentally affect their feelings and behavior in the classroom. Stress can negatively affect feelings and produce destructive behavior directed at convenient targets like teachers and classmates. For example, a student may be angry about his parents' harsh, punitive treatment but be fearful of even greater punishment if he were to express anger toward them. In the safer classroom environment, however, the student may express those strong feelings in angry words and actions directed at the teacher and classmates.

When you are unaware that a student's strong feelings have been generated elsewhere and are being *transferred* to you, you may become angry and punitive toward the student. This behavior—called *countertransference*—reinforces the student's anger and elicits more negative behavior. A vicious cycle can result: negative experiences generate negative feelings, which generate negative behaviors, which generate negative reactions from others (like you), which generate more negative feelings, behaviors, and reactions. Your goal should be to recognize the relationship between a student's feelings and behavior, understand the process of transference, and avoid getting caught up in a self-perpetuating conflict cycle that is increasingly difficult to interrupt.

Self-perpetuating cycles of conflict are difficult to break.

SOCIOCULTURAL FACTORS

One of our themes in this book is the importance of recognizing and appreciating student diversity in your classroom. As we noted at the outset of this chapter, our use of *diversity* encompasses a wide range of individual and group characteristics that make every classroom a unique teaching and learning environment. As human beings, all of us need ways of conceptualizing and categorizing ourselves and others as subsets of humanity. "Human beings are perhaps the only species that asks itself: Who, or what, am I? . . . Classification of the human species is an extension of the answer to the who-am-I, or the who-are-we, question" (Webster, 1992, p. 36). In addition to individual characteristics, we consider our similarities and differences according to group distinctions. Group categorizations that are relevant to understanding diversity in classrooms are (1) racial identities, (2) ethnic, cultural, and linguistic classifications, (3) socioeconomic status, (4) gender, and (5) (dis)ability (see Figure 3.2).

We all have characteristics that can be classified according to these categories. How would you define yourself in each of them? Obviously, categories of group descriptors overlap one another, and some of them provide a more meaningful understanding of group distinctions than others. In this book we often speak of racial, ethnic, cultural, and socioeconomic diversity in behavior, habits, beliefs, and values that vary according to the social influences of a group. In this section we look at these ways of considering group differences.

Race, ethnic background, cultural identity, linguistic preference, or *socioeconomic status* are common ways to think of group differences. But what exactly do they mean? Because they are sometimes used interchangeably, some clari-

FIGURE 3.2   A Wide Range of Individual and Group Characteristics Create Diversity

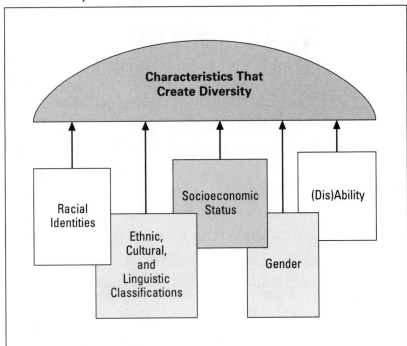

fication is in order. It is important to remember that they are *concepts* that have little objective reality beyond the meaning we give to them.

Racial Identities

Race refers to classifications supposedly made on the basis of certain physical attributes (such as skin color and skeletal features) that a person has in common with others of the same racial classification and with their ancestors. Have you been asked to designate your racial classification on official forms like census counts, job applications, scholarship forms, government reports, and descriptions of research subjects? These classifications have always been arbitrary and are becoming increasingly difficult to justify as individuals from various racial and ethnic groups marry and reproduce (Wright, 1994). Children who are asked to "check the appropriate box" on school and other forms are frequently confused or embarrassed by their inability to determine which is appropriate.

Racial classifications are arbitrary and increasingly difficult to justify.

In the United States we define race differently from most other cultures. According to the Office of Management and Budget, the federal office responsible for determining classifications of racial and ethnic data, there are four general racial groups in the United States: American Indian or Alaskan Indian, Asian or Pacific Islander, black, and white.

Ethnicity can also be broken down into the categories of Hispanic Origin or Not of Hispanic Origin. A majority of the U.S. population—about 78 percent in 1990—is considered white (or Caucasian), generally of European ancestry, although persons whose ancestors are from northern Africa, the Middle East, or south Asia are sometimes included.

Over the last twenty years, there has been a dramatic shift in the racial make-up of the U.S. population, due largely to the greatest immigration into the country since the 1890s and an increasing number of multiracial children. During the 1980s the national population grew 9.8 percent. The number of non-Hispanic whites grew by 6 percent, the number of African Americans grew by 13.2 percent, Native Americans by 37.9 percent, Hispanics by 53 percent, and Asian-Pacific Islanders by 107.8 percent (Hodgkinson, 1992). In the school-age population, the percent of minority students is even higher than in the general population, reaching approximately 30 percent of the total in 1990. Given current trends, 36 percent of the U.S. population will be minority (nonwhite and/or Hispanic) by the year 2000.

Even though the term *race* is commonly used and has an official status, racial categories are extremely broad and increasingly diverse. We might ask, for example, what do Asians have in common, or blacks, or American or Alaskan Indian, Asian or Pacific Islanders, or whites? What particular traits qualify someone for membership in a particular race? How do persons of Japanese, Vietnamese, Chinese, and Laotian ancestry qualify as Asian? Why are some Cubans considered white, others black or Latino or Asian? What makes a person black (or African American) in this country? "According to various estimates, at least seventy-five to more than ninety per cent of the people who now check the Black box could check Multiracial, because of their mixed genetic heritage" (Wright, 1994).

Racial classifications do not constitute homogeneous groups.

Clearly, to speak of any racial classifications as if they constitute a homogeneous group is misguided. The many group and individual variations within these broad classifications make race a highly questionable concept. Although the concepts of ethnicity and culture are also somewhat vague, they seem to offer a more meaningful understanding of group differences because they are groupings based on their members' common experiences, beliefs, values, and patterns of behavior. "Children come to school today with different diets, different religions (there were more Moslems than Episcopalians in the United States in 1991), different individual and group loyalties, different music, different languages" (Hodgkinson, 1992). These differences are better characterized as ethnic or cultural than racial groups.

Ethnic Classifications

Ethnic groups are identifiable populations that are not fully assimilated into the mainstream culture and retain a distinct identity. Ethnic distinctions are based primarily on the geographical, national origin, religious, and linguistic backgrounds of the persons who identify with the particular group. Within the Asian-American population, for example, are many ethnic groups identified according to their common language, country or region of origin, traditions, and history. Asian Americans include such diverse groups as Cambodians, Chinese, Japanese, Hmong, Samoans, Vietnamese, Lao, Pakistani, Indonesian, Filipino, and Thai.

Likewise, there are distinct ethnic groups among Hispanics, most of whom either speak Spanish themselves or have ancestors who spoke Spanish. An exception is the Brazilians, whose language is Portuguese, and some other ethnic groups. Hispanic ethnic groups have ancestral backgrounds in areas of North, South, and Central America (Latin America) that were settled by Spanish conquerors. Mexicans, Argentinians, Cubans, Brazilians, and others may be officially lumped together as Hispanic (or Latino), yet they are more apt to define their ethnicity according to their unique geographical origins, histories, and traditions. To further complicate this classification, Hispanics may be identified in different racial categories. Some Mexicans would be classified American Indian had they been born in the United States; some Cubans are black and others are white; most Argentines are of European origin.

Similar distinctions exist within the classifications of Native American and European American. Many European Americans retain strong ethnic identities as Czechs, Serbs, Poles, Irish, Jews, or Italians, for example. An ethnic group can be diverse. In addition, some members of an ethnic group identify more closely with it than others. For example, some Mexican Americans are recent immigrants to the United States, speak only Spanish, retain Mexican traditions, and have a strong ethnic identity. Other Mexican Americans, however, are descended from families that have lived in the United States for generations, do not speak Spanish, retain few Mexican traditions, and have little ethnic identity.

Cultural Groups

If these concepts of race and ethnicity are not sufficiently confusing, culture offers another way of considering group differences. Culture is "often used in a vague manner and referring to some combination of differences in skin color, country of origin, language, customs, socialization priorities, and sometimes socioeconomic class" (Triandis & Brislin, 1984). For example, within a single ethnic group such as Native American, the Navajo, Sioux, Inuit, Ojibwa, and others have separate cultures based on their distinct languages, geographical origins, traditions, and histories; but even more important, each has a distinct world view or way of thinking.

Cultures are distinguished by the behavior, thinking, and values of the people in the group.

Culture can be seen as a way of life (Klineberg, 1935) or as having an individual personality (Benedict, 1934). In other words, cultures can be distinguished by the kinds of behavior, thinking, and values expressed by the people of the culture.

Today, people usually think of culture in terms of the meanings that are assigned to behavior both by those who are engaging in the behavior and those who are observing and judging it. "Shared meanings" are the knowledge and attitudes toward life of different cultural groups (Szalay & Maday, 1983). When people in different cultural groups are asked to provide free association responses to words like *education, illness, money,* and *problems,* some groups think more alike than others. For example, black and white Americans share more meanings with one another than either group shares with Hispanic Americans (Szalay & Maday, 1983). When people recognize that culture is not just *apparent* distinctions like physical traits, language, or country of origin but the *meanings* attached to those characteristics, they are forced to look beyond the apparent markers of culture. Other factors—such as common history; urban, rural, or suburban background; immigrant, refugee, or several-generation native status; and socioeconomic status—also influence our shared meanings.

Looking beyond apparent distinctions to their meanings is important.

Sensitivity to Ethnic and Cultural Diversity.   We think it is critical for you to be sensitive to the ethnic and cultural diversity of your students, to know about culturally influenced behavior, and to be able to adapt your teaching and classroom management to cultural variations: "Cultural sensitivity is an awareness of the general problems culturally diverse students experience in school because of their cultural differences, how cultural differences influence students' preferred learning styles, how they may cause students to behave in ways that are acceptable in their cultures but not in school, and how these differences may lead students to react in unanticipated ways to behavior management techniques" (Grossman, 1991, p. 23).

How can you become more culturally sensitive? We can't offer a simple, single answer to this question, since your situation, your students, and your own backgrounds vary. You may teach in a school where students and staff represent a variety of ethnic and cultural backgrounds or where most or all students have backgrounds different than your own. You may represent the cultural majority or minority in your school. You may already be familiar with your students' cultural backgrounds, or you may be encountering them for the first time. Even if you and your students share a racial or ethnic heritage, you will not necessarily share a cultural background. Your cultural identity may be middle class, suburban, mainstream; your students may be lower socioeconomic status, inner city, and have a different identity. You may have grown up on a farm in a rural area of the South but teach in an affluent suburb of a large city in the North.

Cultural sensitivity is recognizing that ethnic and cultural variations affect students' behavior.

Teachers can study cultural diversity in their classrooms, schools, and communities.

Cultural sensitivity first means that you recognize ethnic and cultural variations among your students that affect their behavior. It also means that you recognize that *you* represent a particular cultural background and that you and your students may have different backgrounds, values, and identities. The research we cited in Chapter 2 about teacher perceptions of behavior problems in native Hawaiian and Navajo classrooms (Tharp, 1989) is instructive: teachers who are unaware of their students' culturally mediated behavior patterns may mistakenly view them as behavior problems. We think it is essential to study the cultural diversity within your classroom, school, and community by observing and analyzing, asking questions, reading, sharing your own culture, and deliberately fostering cultural understanding and appreciation among your students.

Linguistic Classifications

Linguistic differences are another type of group diversity in many American classrooms. Students whose primary language is not English are a part of classrooms in every state, and teachers must help them to succeed academically and to become fluent in English. Students whose primary language is not English are often referred to as **LEP,** or **limited English proficient** (although the state of Illinois is pioneering the use of the term *PEP—potentially English proficient*—to put a more positive spin on the label). Such students are defined as pupils who because of their inability to speak, read, write and or understand the English language are excluded from effective participation in the educational programs offered by a school district.

A student's inability to effectively communicate or understand the language of instruction can lead to misunderstandings about ability and behavior. If you have LEP students, you will need to be sensitive to their nonverbal behavior and have different ways to communicate what behavior you expect of them. To recent immigrants, especially, much about American school behavior and expectations seems strange and unfamiliar. Aspects of school we take for granted such as standing in line, raising hands, working independently, or even using group bathrooms may seem odd or incomprehensible to newly arrived students. You can help your students by making a determined effort to understand the situation they have come from (refugee, immigrant, or other status) and their educational history (school attended or not, type of educational system). You should initiate an appropriate language assessment (including a home language survey) to help your students make a successful transition.

Socioeconomic Status

How would you describe your socioeconomic status? Social class is a way of characterizing group differences. Americans like to think that the United States has a less rigidly stratified social system than many other countries. Theoretically, it is possible for individuals to move up or down the socioeconomic hierarchy. Economic wealth and education are a primary—though not the only—determinant of social status in this country. In the United States we think of broad stratifications of upper, middle, and lower socioeconomic status (SES), although these can be further broken down into, for example, upper middle class, lower middle class, or under class.

Nearly 20 percent of American children are considered poor.

Nearly 20 percent of American children (12,600,000) are considered poor, and 41 percent of them are in families whose incomes are less than one-half the poverty level (Children's Defense Fund, 1994). In addition, schools for poorer children often receive substantially lower funding than schools for wealthier children (Kozol, 1991), thus exacerbating disparities of educational and socioeconomic opportunity. Socioeconomic distinctions often intersect with racial, ethnic, cultural, and linguistic characteristics, placing some students **at risk** for school problems. *At risk* refers to social factors that make students less likely to attain the necessary skills, knowledge, and attitudes, to graduate from high school, or to function effectively in our society. Factors that can place children at risk include poverty, minority status, unstable home environment, inadequate nutrition and health care, limited English proficiency, and substance abuse.

Poverty is a key factor in placing children at risk; its effects are pervasive, and are associated with other risk conditions. The largest number of poor children in this country are white, but a higher percentage of African-American, Hispanic, and Native American children are poor. For example, about 15 percent of white children, 36 percent of Hispanic children, and 44 percent of black children are poor (Children's Defense Fund, 1994). Within economically disadvantaged populations, there are also higher rates of single parent families, high school drop-outs, unemployment, and crime. Needless to say, these conditions have a tremendous influence on students' learning and behavior in school.

Gender

Learning and behavioral characteristics of boys and girls are generally quite similar, especially during elementary years.

Gender is another educationally significant factor. We are concerned here about *general* group differences between males and females. In general, learning and behavioral characteristics of boys and girls are quite similar, especially during the elementary years, and gender-related characteristics may not be as important as individual or cultural characteristics. Two areas that are relevant for classroom management are gender differences in aggressive behavior and in patterns of intellectual aptitudes.

Aggression. Think back on your experiences in elementary, middle, and secondary school. Do you remember particular students who were aggressive, who talked back to teachers, disrupted classes, or got into fights? Were most of these aggressive classmates boys or girls? No doubt you may have pictured mostly boys, since as a group, boys tend to be more physically and verbally aggressive than girls. Even male infants tend to be more active and irritable than girls, and preschool boys engage in more rough and tumble play and pretend fighting. During elementary years, these differences continue, as boys engage in more physically and verbally aggressive behaviors.

Constitutional factors are likely to be partially responsible for males' tendencies to behave more aggressively than females.

Because a male tendency toward more aggressive behavior appears early in life and across cultures, constitutional factors (genetic, hormonal) are likely at least partially responsible. However, social and psychological factors undoubtedly also play an influential role. From early life, parents and others communicate their expectations about appropriate gender-related behavior. Sociocultural environments tend to encourage, allow, model, and reward more aggressive behavior by boys than girls, who are encouraged to be more nurturing and physically passive. Although there are great individual differences in the gender-socialization experiences of children, it is clear that boys, who may be more prone to aggressive behavior, are also exposed to multiple influences that further encourage it, while girls, less innately aggressive, are also exposed to influences that tend to discourage aggression.

For teachers, gender differences can pose challenges. Although every experienced teacher has encountered girls who are notably aggressive, boys more often come into conflict with teachers, who are often female. In fact, boys are more often publicly criticized and yelled at by their teachers (Eccles & Blumenfeld, 1985). Boys' tendencies toward boisterous, physically active patterns of behavior are especially likely to clash with the regimen of traditional classrooms, with their highly structured, row-and-column seating, controlled recitation, and quiet seatwork. Boys are also much more likely than girls to be considered to have significant emotional or behavioral disorders in school (Rizzo & Zabel, 1988).

Intellectual Abilities.   Another apparent gender difference relates to patterns of intellectual abilities. On average boys tend to do better on tests of mathematical and spatial ability than girls, although there is a wide range of individual difference within each group (Halpern, 1986). Constitutional differences may contribute to gender differences in quantitative skills, but it appears more likely that they result primarily from socialization experiences. Over time, multiple social influences—parents' and teachers' behavior, as well as that of peers, friends, siblings, and the media—shape boys' and girls' beliefs about their aptitudes and values (Eccles, 1989). Although girls and boys perform similarly in math and science during the early years in elementary school, by the upper grades girls begin to express less confidence in their abilities and are less likely to value these subjects as areas of study relevant to their futures. Not surprisingly, in high school girls tend to fall behind boys in math and science.

What is the significance of these kinds of observed gender differences for you? We think that we all must be aware of how our attitudes and beliefs about gender differences can influence classroom communication, instruction, and management. On the one hand, it is important to recognize possible gender differences in behavioral and learning styles. For example, you should not be surprised that many male students engage in more physical activity than many of your female students. On the other hand, as teachers we need to be sensitive about how we may unintentionally confirm expectations about competence and ability that limit student opportunities. For example, when teaching subjects like math and science, you can encourage girls to actively participate and try to reduce the intimidation and lack of relevance many of them feel.

Constitutional differences and socialization experiences may contribute to gender differences in quantitative skills.

(Dis)ability

Teachers can and should expect to have students with identifiable disabilities in their classes.

Since the 1970s, and particularly since passage of federal legislation requiring special education for students with disabilities, there has been a tremendous growth in the number of students considered educationally disabled. You can expect to have students with identified disabilities—some relatively mild, others moderate, and some quite pronounced and severe—in your classes.

Students with disabilities have been traditionally categorized according to educationally significant characteristics they have in common. The following categories are specified in federal legislation:

- Mental retardation,
- Learning disabilities,
- Serious emotional disturbance (emotional and behavioral disorders),
- Visual impairments,
- Hearing impairments,
- Orthopedic disabilities,
- Traumatic brain injury,

- Autism,
- Multiple disabilities,
- Other health impaired, and
- Speech and language disorders.

Most of the special education categories were included in the original legislation, but others (traumatic brain injury and autism) formerly were included under other categories and later became independent categories. For example, autism was considered a type of serious emotional disturbance, then moved to the classification called *other health impaired* until 1990, when it became an independent category. Congress is now considering adding a new category of attention deficit disorders (ADD) or attention deficit hyperactive disorders (ADHD). Currently, some students with ADD are identified as having learning disabilities, emotional and behavioral disorders, or other health impairments, although others who do not fit these categories may receive special education if their condition adversely affects their educational performance.

Federal legislation does not mandate special education services for *gifted and talented* students, although some states consider these students exceptional and require special programs. Even where programs are not legally mandated, some districts and schools identify and provide enriched educational programs for students with exceptionally high ability.

In many ways, these broad classifications of educational (dis)ability have no more validity than the racial classifications we discussed earlier. Like racial classifications, there is considerable diversity within each category (Ysseldyke & Algozzine, 1992). The classifications represent only limited characteristics of a student's functioning, and they often overlap. *Mental retardation,* for example, refers to significantly below normal intellectual capacity for learning and deficiencies in adaptive behavior. However, there is a wide range of learning, behavioral, and physical characteristics among individuals in this category. Students with mental retardation are categorized as mild, moderate, severe, and profound depending on the degree of deviation from norms for intellectual and adaptive functioning. In addition, they may have other disabilities, as well as abilities.

As we stated in Chapter 1, the vast majority of students with disabilities (over 90 percent) have learning disabilities, serious emotional disturbances, speech and language disorders, or mental retardation. Many of these disabilities are considered relatively mild, and the students are usually included in regular educational programs for most of their schooling. Even students with more pronounced disabilities are likely to receive at least part of their education in regular classrooms. However, some students with variant intellectual, learning, behavioral, and physical characteristics receive special education in segregated programs.

Some states do consider gifted and talented students a category of exceptional students.

There is a wide range of learning, behavioral, and physical characteristics among individuals who fit in any disability category.

More and more, even students with pronounced disabilities are likely to receive some of their education in regular classrooms.

Because these separate programs are expensive, lack established evidence of efficacy, and may by their separateness be inherently unequal, there is a movement toward full inclusion of students with disabilities in regular classrooms. With schools now providing greater integration, classroom teachers can no longer look to special education to assume primary responsibility for some students with disabilities. These changes require new attitudes, understandings, and skills, not only to provide direct services in regular classrooms but also to effectively collaborate with colleagues and other service providers to provide appropriate educational programs for all students. In Chapter 9 we will discuss some ways you can work with your school and district support personnel, parents, and other service providers inside and outside of school to meet the educational needs of your students with exceptional needs.

Full inclusion requires new attitudes, understandings, and skills from teachers.

Multiple "Intelligences." In recent years, it has become apparent that our schools have had a limited view of student abilities. Expanding our views of the nature of intelligence can help us understand and accommodate diverse learning characteristics of our students. In *Beyond IQ* (1985) and *The Triarchic Mind* (1986), Robert Sternberg argues that intelligence consists of far more than what is measured by IQ and achievement tests. He proposes that intelligence actually consists of a range of additional behaviors that helps us *apply* knowledge and skills, including how we go about solving problems, how we deal with new or unfamiliar situations, and how we adapt to our environments and try to shape them.

In addition to scholastic or academic intelligence—the types of ability traditionally valued, measured, and rewarded in school—there is also practical intelligence. Practical intelligence reflects the multiple ways individuals can be effective and adapt to situations in their world and includes skills such as identifying and solving problems, allocating time, and working well with other people. About intelligence, Sternberg says, "Stated simply, it is mental self-management" (1986, p. 72). The components of intelligence may be the same for everyone across all cultures, since we all must define and solve problems, deal with new situations, and adapt to and shape our environments. However, both as an individual and a member of a cultural group, you (and each of your students) face different problems, different new situations, and must adapt to and shape different environments. Consequently, what is adaptable thinking for one person in one cultural or situational context is not necessarily the same for another person.

Adaptable thinking differs for people in different cultures or contexts.

Like Sternberg, Howard Gardner (1983, 1991) maintains that our schools traditionally have had a very limited and limiting focus on two general types of intelligence, what he calls "verbal-linguistic" and "mathematical-logical" abilities. The academic curriculum emphasizes these types of skills and measures ability and achievement by assessing students' verbal (reading, writing) and quantitative (arithmetic) skills. Gardner asserts these are just two of at least seven general types of "multiple intelligences." He classifies the intelligences into the following categories:

- Verbal-linguistic,
- Mathematical-logical,
- Musical,
- Spatial,
- Bodily-kinesthetic,
- Interpersonal, and
- Intrapersonal.

According to Gardner, individual intelligence varies across these seven domains. All of us possess and exhibit all kinds of intelligence, although we vary in the amounts and combinations, for "we are a species that has evolved to think in language, to conceptualize in spatial terms, to analyze in musical ways, to compute with logical and mathematical tools, to solve problems using our whole body and parts of our body, to understand other individuals, and to understand ourselves" (Gardner, 1991, p. 81).

When we place little emphasis and value on certain abilities and skills in school, some students are deemed educational failures because their strengths are not in the domains we value. Students who have traditionally excelled are those who are proficient in the verbal-linguistic (reading, writing) and logical-mathematical (mathematics) areas, although they may not be so proficient in areas such as music, art, athletics, social skills, or self-understanding. Further, many students who are successful in school (they get high grades and do well on standardized tests) do not necessarily have real understanding of what they are doing or skill in applying their knowledge (Gardner, 1991).

Students do not all learn and use knowledge in the same ways.

We think that Sternberg's and Gardner's theories of multiple intelligences offer important insights for teachers of diverse learners. All students do not learn and use knowledge in the same ways. Thus multiple approaches for facilitating learning are appropriate to utilize all types of ability. Some behavior problems result from teachers' overlooking and not appreciating their students' multiple intelligences. Often, lack of motivation, frustration, and distraction develop because learning tasks do not draw on and engage a student's particular kinds of intelligence. As a teacher, your goal is to provide opportunities for students to develop their abilities and skills to deal effectively with their environments—both within and beyond your classroom.

ECOLOGICAL FACTORS

In examining individual and group factors affecting student learning and behavior, we have focused on some of the internal substrates of behavior (biophysical and psychosocial) and some more external forces (learning and sociocultural). Although our orientation to classroom management is ecological, this does not diminish the value of understanding how biophysical, behavioral, psychosocial, and sociocultural factors affect student behavior and learning because all these perspectives are incorporated into an ecological perspective.

An ecological orientation recognizes the potential importance of *all* elements of an individual's ecosystem and adds another element to the analysis. Whereas the other models imply that an individual's behavior is the product of *either* biophysical, learning, psychosocial, or sociocultural factors, the ecological perspective asserts that behavior is the product of *all* these factors— much like a fabric woven from multicolored threads. In addition, all of the factors have a *reciprocal influence* on one another. In other words, people are not simply passive respondents to environmental conditions but active participants who help define and form their environments.

All of the factors in an individual's ecosystem have a reciprocal influence on one another.

Consider, for instance, possible interpretations of a student's aggressive behavior (frequent pushing, grabbing, threatening, calling names) in your class. It could be

- A reflection of genetic predisposition, "difficult temperament," biochemical imbalance, or neurological damage (biophysical),
- Learned from aggressive models or reinforced by others (behavioral),
- Displaced acting out of anger toward others (psychosocial), or
- Characteristic of socioeconomic status or cultural acceptance of aggression (sociocultural).

Each, or a combination, of these factors may contribute to the student's aggressive behavior. Often you will not know which factors are most critical. More important, you can have little direct impact on most of these factors outside of your classroom and school. You cannot change a student's temperament, neurochemical balance, reinforcement history, cognitive development, emotional development, prior social development, or sociocultural forces. However, you can *understand* how these kinds of factors affect your students' behavior in the ecosystem of your classroom and school. That understanding should help you choose the most appropriate responses and interventions.

Teachers cannot change certain factors in their students' lives, but they can understand them.

SUMMARY AND REVIEW

In this chapter we explored individual and group diversity in classrooms. We noted the contributions of both nature (biology) and nurture (environment) on student behavior and learning. Although the many factors that contribute to individual and group differences cannot be completely disaggregated from one another, we focused on several influences. We discussed biophysical factors, including genetic, biochemical, neurological, and nutritional factors, as well as the effects of environmental toxins and drugs and alcohol on students' behavior. In addition to individual temperamental traits, we noted some distinct syndromes—including attention deficit disorders, fetal alcohol syndrome and effects, and traumatic brain injuries—that pose special challenges for teachers.

Because students' behavior is also a product of their prior experiences, we also discussed learning and psychosocial factors. Learning theories—classical conditioning, operant learning, and social learning—stress the role of environmental conditions for teaching behavior. Psychosocial perspectives, such as the psychodynamic theories of Freud and Erikson, stress a child's relationships with others during the course of their development, for defining their personalities and behavior.

Finally, we examined the role of sociocultural factors, including racial, ethnic, cultural, gender, or (dis)ability classifications. We discussed how students' membership in sociocultural groups may influence their learning and behavioral characteristics in classrooms.

Appreciating student diversity is not just a passing fancy or a buzzword for the politically correct. Diversity is a reality and, increasingly, a mirror of the United States at large. Old stereotypes, expectations, even commonsense statements are being disproven every day. (Did you know there are more persons who identify themselves as Hispanic in Illinois than there are in New Mexico?) As teachers and educational providers, we can choose to view this situation with alarm and mourn the passing of "the way it used to be," or we can see it as an opportunity to enrich our own lives and the lives of *all* the students that we teach.

The truth is, America and American schools have always been diverse. There have been racial, ethnic, cultural, language, ability, and performance diversities in America since the first immigrants crossed the land bridge from Asia. Diversity is not new. What have changed are our ability and willingness to recognize diversity, to view it as an important part of our educational consideration, and to utilize it to make classrooms growing places for all the teachers and students.

Attempting to view each student in your classroom as an individual should not be seen as a hopeless or frustrating task. The fact is, each student *is* a unique product of nature and nurture, of his or her genetic, developmental, psychosocial, learning, ethnic, cultural, language, gender, socioeconomic, and intellectual characteristics. The old way of attempting to stuff kids into predetermined categories or molds is a much more frustrating and failure-ridden task than taking them as they arrive—and moving on from there. Educators often speak of a goal of life-long learning for all of us. A clear source of instruction and enrichment for those of us who teach is found in our students.

**REFLECTING
ON CHAPTER 3**

As Annie works with the students in her classroom, she will have to balance all these possible aspects of diversity. For instance, as she analyzes the difficulty Terrell is having with the math assignment, she must weigh the various possible options. Does he understand the instructions (language)? Does he have some sensory deficiency (color blindness, visual difficulty)? Does he have a perceptual difficulty? Does he rush impulsively to begin a task before understanding the directions? Does he *hear* the directions? Is he overly anxious about success and failure? Afraid to take home a less than perfect paper? The list could go on.

- What other explanations can you give for Terrell's behavior?

- How should Annie go about finding out which of these explanations may be correct?

- Might there be more than one correct answer—and if so, how would they interact?

- How do you see the nature-nurture debate reflected in current political and educational issues?

Key Terms

diversity (p. 72)
nature (p. 72)
nurture (p. 72)
attention deficit disorders
   (ADD) (p. 79)
attention deficit hyperactive
   disorders (ADHD) (p. 79)

fetal alcohol syndrome (p. 83)
classical conditioning (p. 88)
operant learning theory (p. 88)
social learning theory (p. 88)
limited English proficient (p. 100)
LEP (p. 100)
at-risk (p. 101)

Building Your Own Knowledge Base

Children's Defense Fund. (1994). *The State of America's Children, 1994.* Washington, DC: Children's Defense Fund. This annual report on children and families describes the effects of social, economic, and political conditions on the health, education, financial status, and safety of American children and youth and advocates measures to improve children's lives.

Dorris, M. (1989). *The Broken Cord: A Family's Ongoing Struggle with Fetal Alcohol Syndrome.* New York: Harper & Row. A father writes a personal account of his gradual discovery that his adopted son has FAS, shares research about causes and characteristics, and suggests policy and intervention approaches.

Gardner, H. (1983). *Frames of Mind.* New York: Basic Books. Gardner proposes that human beings are capable of at least seven different forms of intelligence, that individuals vary in the strength of those intelligences and learn in different ways, and that profound educational reforms are necessary.

Kotlowitz, A. (1991). *There Are No Children Here: The Story of Two Boys Growing Up in the Other America.* New York: Anchor Books. A journalist chronicles the difficult and dangerous lives of two brothers, Lafayette and Pharoah, who struggle to survive in a Chicago housing project.

References

Adelman, H. S., & Taylor, L. (1993). *Learning problems and learning disabilities: Moving forward.* Boston: Allyn and Bacon.

Allison, M. (1992). The effects of neurologic injury on the maturing brain. *Headlines, 3,* 2–10.

Anderson, E. (1994). The code of the streets. *The Atlantic, 273,* 80–94.

Bandura, A. (1977). *Social learning theory.* Englewood Cliffs, NJ: Prentice-Hall.

Bandura, A. (1986). *Social foundations of thought and action: A social cognitive theory.* Englewood Cliffs, NJ: Prentice-Hall.

Barkley, R. A. (1990). *Attention deficit hyperactivity disorder: A handbook for diagnosis and treatment.* New York: Guilford.

Bauer, A. M. (1991). Drug and alcohol exposed children: Implications for special education for students identified as behaviorally disordered. *Behavioral Disorders, 17,* 72–79.

Benedict, R. (1934). *Patterns of culture.* Boston: Houghton Mifflin.

Chasnoff, I. J. (1988). Newborn infants with drug withdrawal symptoms. *Pediatrics in Review, 9,* 273–277.

Chasnoff, I. J. , Landress, H. J., & Barrett, M. E. (1990). The prevalence of illicit-drug or alcohol use during pregnancy and discrepancies in mandatory reporting in Pinellas County, Florida. *New England Journal of Medicine, 322,* 1202–1206.

Children's Defense Fund. (1994). *The state of America's children 1994.* Washington, DC: Children's Defense Fund.

Conlon, C. J. (1992). New threats to development: Alcohol, cocaine, and AIDS. In M. L. Batshaw & Y. M. Perret, *Children with disabilities: A medical primer* (3rd ed.) (pp. 111–136). Baltimore, MD: Brookes.

Dorris, M. (1989). *The broken cord: A family's ongoing struggle with fetal alcohol syndrome.* New York: Harper & Row.

DuPont, R. L. (1984). *Getting tough on gateway drugs: A guide for the family.* Washington, DC: American Psychiatric Press.

Eccles, J. S., & Blumenfeld, P. (1985). Classroom experiences and student gender: Are there differences and do they matter? In L. C. Wilkinson & C. Marrett (Eds.), *Gender influences in classroom interaction.* Hillsdale, NJ: Erlbaum.

Eccles, J. S. (1989). Bringing young women to math and science. In M. Crawford & M. Gentry (Eds.), *Gender and thought: Psychological perspectives.* New York: Springer-Verlag.

Erikson, E. (1963). *Childhood and society* (2nd ed.). New York: Norton.

Forbes, R. (1984). Alcohol-related birth defects. *Public Health, 98,* 231–241.

Forness, S. R., Swanson, J. M., Cantwell, D. P., Guthrie, D., & Sena, R. (1992). Response to stimulant medication across six measures of school-related performance in children with ADHD and disruptive behavior. *Behavioral Disorders, 18,* 42–53.

Gadow, K. D. (1991). Psychopharmacological assessment and intervention. In H. L. Swanson (Ed.), *Handbook of assessment of learning disabilities: Theory, research, and practice.* Austin, TX: Pro-Ed.

Gardner, H. (1983). *Frames of mind.* New York: Basic Books.

Gardner, H. (1991). *The unschooled mind: How children think and how schools should teach.* New York: Basic Books.

Grossman, H. (1991). Special education in a diverse society: Improving services for minority and working-class students. *Preventing School Failure, 36,* 19–27.

Hadeed, A. J., & Siegel, S. R. (1989). Maternal cocaine use during pregnancy: Effect on the newborn infant. *Pediatrics, 84,* 205–210.

Halpern, D. F. (1986). *Sex differences in cognitive abilities.* Hillsdale, NJ: Erlbaum.

Halperin, J. M., Gittelman, R., Katz, S., & Struve, F. A. (1986). Relationship between stimulant effect, electroencephalogram, and clinical neurological findings in hyperactive children. *Journal of the American Academy of Child Psychiatry, 25,* 820–825.

Hodgkinson, H. (1992). *A demographic look at tomorrow.* Washington, DC: Center for Demographic Policy, Institute for Educational Leadership.

Humphreys, R. (1989). Patterns of pediatric brain injury. In M. Miner & K. Wagner (Eds.), *Neurotrauma 3—Treatment, rehabilitation and related issues* (pp. 115–126). Stoneham, MA: Butterworths.

Kavale, K., & Nye, C. (1984). The effectiveness of drug treatment for severe behavior disorders: A meta-analysis. *Behavioral Disorders, 9,* 117–130.

Keith, L. G., MacGregor, S., Friedell, S., Rosner, M., Chasnoff, I. J., & Sciarra, J. J. (1989). Substance abuse in pregnant women: Recent experience at the perinatal center for chemical dependence of Northwestern Memorial Hospital. *Obstetrics and Gynecology, 73,* 715–723.

Klineberg, O. (1935). *Race differences.* New York: Harper.

Korn, S. J., & Gannon, S. (1983). Temperament, cultural variation, and behavior disorder in preschool children. *Child Psychiatry and Human Development, 13,* 203–212.

Kozol, J. (1991). *Savage inequalities: Children in America's schools.* New York: HarperCollins.

Lerner, J. (1993). *Learning disabilities: Theories, diagnosis and teaching strategies* (6th ed.). Boston: Houghton Mifflin.

Long, N. J., & Duffner, B. (1980). The stress cycle or the coping cycle? The impact of home and school stresses on pupils' classroom behavior. In N. J. Long, W. C. Morse, & R. G. Newman (Eds.), *Conflict in the classroom* (4th ed.). Belmont, CA: Wadsworth.

Maziade, M., Cote, R., Boudreault, M., Thivierge, J., & Caperaa, P. (1984). The New York longitudinal studies model of temperament: Gender differences and demographic correlates in a French-speaking population. *Journal of the American Academic of Child Psychiatry, 23,* 582–587.

Oberklaid, F., Prior, M., & Sanson, A. (1986). Temperament of preterm versus full-term infants. *Journal of Developmental and Behavioral Pediatrics, 7,* 159–162.

Peterson, N. L. (1987). *Early intervention for handicapped and at-risk children.* Denver: Love.

Reid, R., Maag, J. W., & Vasa, S. F. (1993). Attention deficit hyperactivity disorder as a disability category: A critique. *Exceptional Children, 60,* 198–214.

Ritvo, E. R., Freeman, B. J., Mason-Brothers, A., Mo, A., & Ritvo, A. M. (1985). Concordance for the syndrome of autism in 40 pairs of afflicted twins. *American Journal of Psychiatry, 142,* 74–77.

Rizzo, J. R., & Zabel, R. H. (1988). *Educating children and adolescents with behavioral disorders: An integrative approach.* Boston: Allyn and Bacon.

Silver, L. B. (1992). *Attention-deficit hyperactivity disorder: A clinical guide to diagnosis and treatment.* Washington, DC: American Psychiatric Association.

Skinner, B. F. (1974). *About behaviorism.* New York: Knopf.

Sternberg, R. J. (1985). *Beyond IQ: A triarchic theory of human intelligence.* New York: Irving.

Sternberg, R. J. (1986). *The triarchic mind: A new theory of human intelligence.* New York: Viking.

Strauss, A. A., & Lehtinen, L. (1947). *Psychopathology and education of the brain-injured child.* New York: Grune & Stratton.

Streissguth, A. P., & La Due, R. A. (1987). Fetal alcohol: Teratogenic causes of developmental disabilities. In S. Schroder (Ed.), *Toxic substances and mental retardation* (pp. 1–32). Washington, DC: American Association on Mental Deficiency Monographs.

Szalay, L. B., & Maday, B. (1983). Implicit culture and and psychocultural distance. *American Psychologist, 44,* 349–359.

Tharp, R. G. (1989). Psychocultural variables and constants: Effects on teaching and learning in schools. *American Psychologist, 44,* 349–359.

Thomas, A., & Chess, S. (1977). *Temperament and development.* New York: Brunner/Mazel.

Thomas, A., & Chess, S. (1984). Genesis and evolution of behavioral disorders: From infancy to early adult life. *American Journal of Psychiatry, 141,* 1–9.

Thomas, A., Chess, S., & Birch, H. G. (1968). *Temperament and behavior disorders in children.* New York: New York University Press.

Toufexis, A. (1991). Innocent victims. *Time.*

Triandis, H. C., & Brislin, R. W. (1984). Cross-cultural psychology. *American Psychologist, 39,* 1006–1016.

U.S. Environmental Protection Agency. (1992). *Lead poisoning and your children.* EPA Publication No. 800-B-92-002. Washington, DC: Author.

Van Dyke, D. C., & Fox, A. A. (1990). Fetal drug exposure and its possible implications for learning in the preschool and schoolage population. *Journal of Learning Disabilities, 23,* 160–163.

Vincent, L. J., Paulson, M. K., Cole, C. K., Woodruff, G., & Griffith, D. R. (1991). *Born substance exposed, educationally vulnerable.* Reston, VA: Council for Exceptional Children.

Webster, Y. O. (1992). *The racialization of America.* New York: St. Martin's Press.

Wright, L. (1994). One drop of blood. *The New Yorker, 70,* 46–55.

Ysseldyke, J., & Algozzine, B. (1992). *Introduction to special education* (3rd ed.). Boston: Houghton Mifflin.

Zentall, S. S. (1993). Research on the educational implications of attention deficit hyperactivity disorder. *Exceptional Children, 60,* 143–153.

Orchestrating Successful Classrooms

Part Two, Orchestrating Successful Classrooms, *emphasizes the teacher's role as classroom orchestrater who prepares environments where students are learning, where they are successful, and where there are few disruptions and distractions.*

Chapter 4, **Effective Instructional Approaches,** *describes characteristics of effective schools and effective instruction and points out relevant factors for classroom management.*

Chapter 5, **Preventing Behavioral Problems,** *describes ways to prevent or minimize many classroom behavior problems by preparing and organizing the physical and psychological environment of your classroom, by communicating your expectations for student behavior, and by becoming a withit teacher.*

What Are Effective Classroom and School Ecosystems?

- Establishing safety and order
- Establishing effective leadership
- Instructional focus
- High expectations

Approaches to Cooperative Learning

- The beginning of approaches to cooperative learning
- The Johnson and Johnson approach
- The Slavin approach
- Learning outcomes promoted by cooperative learning
- Peer tutoring
- Variations of peer tutoring

The Science and Art of Teaching

- Meeting individual social and academic needs
- Meeting group social and academic needs

Effective Instructional Approaches

Quality of Instruction

- Teacher enthusiasm
- Structuring lessons
- Clarity, redundancy, and pacing
- Asking questions
- Providing feedback

Quantity of Instruction

- Academic learning time
- Academic engaged time
- High student success rates

Chapter **4**

Effective Instructional Approaches

Annie's Journal

NOVEMBER: Well, O Problem-Solving Journal, I've got a good one for you this time. I really don't know how to handle this situation, and I think I'm not going to be able to just wait it out. Here's the deal. As I've mentioned before, I've really been working to try and establish useful, functioning cooperative groups. It was definitely not as easy as I expected it to be. I made the charts, figured out what the make-up of each group would be, established the teaching objectives, devised the lessons, and felt really organized and on top of things. (I should have known—that feeling usually signals impending disaster....) I started using groups in science and then planned to add math.

Well, first of all, the groups didn't operate too smoothly because the kids weren't used to doing things this way. Oh, they'd been part of cooperative groups before (most of them, anyway), but not exactly the way *I* was doing it. I decided we really needed to work on social skills, like listening to one another, taking turns, being supportive, and so on. We're still working on those things—I think this may take a while. Anyway, we continued with the groups for science, and after about three days of it Nketi came up to me and said he didn't want to be in a group. Yikes! This guy is my science whiz—in fact I think of him as Dr. Science (from that radio routine *Ask Dr. Science*). I asked him to stay with me a few minutes after school so we could talk about it, and he did. He said he didn't want to be in the group because he felt he could learn the material faster and better on his own. He didn't like having to slow down for the other group members, and he wanted to move on faster. I explained to him that there were other skills to be learned here, leadership, helping others, etc., but he wasn't buying it, I could tell. He went home, and I mulled things over. He *is* an extremely bright student—particularly in science and math. His father is a senior scientist (physics) at a big research lab in the city, and his mother is a physician in private practice. I guess Nketi is right—he probably could learn the

material faster on his own. But I think there's more to learning than absorbing facts. I feel it is important for him to be able to discuss the things he's learning, to explain, expand, and generalize the stuff we're doing. His group does have one student who isn't as quick in this area, but she (Tamica) is a good reader and certainly shouldn't be slowing anyone down. The group also includes Rafael, whose first language is Spanish—but he's a really quick learner and his English in terms of conversation is excellent. OK. So I thought about these things and decided to leave the group alone, hoping that Nketi would see my point and come around.

Then today (about a week after this happened) I get a call from Nketi's mother, asking to see me after school. Swell. Two weeks before parent conferences and I need to deal with an upset mom. She came in after school and basically said the same things Nketi did—in fact, it was like hearing an echo. I wonder who thought these phrases up first. She feels he can learn better and faster on his own, she doesn't want him "wasting his time" tutoring slower students (ouch! that says a lot about the esteem she has for teachers), she and her husband see great things in Nketi's future, and he is not to be impeded by less able students. I was stunned!

I really didn't know what to say—but several things that have happened over the last three months suddenly became a bit clearer: like Nketi telling me several times a day that he was really good at science and math, his goofy, almost infantile behavior when he plays with the kids at recess (I wonder how much playing he's done in his ordered life?), and the near-panic in his eyes when he doesn't understand a concept the minute I introduce it. OK, maybe I'm trying to find things to make his parents look like ogres, but it really upset me to have her take such an arrogant attitude about something I'd thought long and hard about. So anyway, now what?

Do I cave in and remove Nketi from his group? Maybe they'd like me to set up a private lab in the bathroom for him—sorry, that wasn't nice— or do I keep him in the group and try to prove my point about other types of learning? I got the feeling that she didn't think anything but total surrender on my part would be acceptable, but I did manage to say that we'd discuss this further when she and her husband (Dr. Mom and Dr. Dad) come in for their regular conference in two weeks.

I guess I'm feeling a little defensive because *I'm* not so sure I'm doing things exactly right. The groups are going more smoothly—the kids seem to be listening and responding better—but there is still a lot of chitchat and doodling. Maybe I *am* wasting their time, although I don't really believe that. Hey! I could change the groups and really set Nketi up. . . . I mean I could put him with Claire, who's so social she'd persuade him to do anything—and Yoshiro, whose logic and persuasive argument could convince him up is down and day is night—and Toby, who'll start telling him some endless story about what's *really* in that beaker or slide. Poor Nketi would be so confused he wouldn't know what hit him! No, I wouldn't do that, but it does show me that I have a lot of bright, gifted, and eccentric kids in this room, and it's my job to come up with instruction that is right for all of them, not just one. Somehow I don't think Nketi's mom will be interested in that philosophy. . . .

FOCUS QUESTIONS

✱ What should a teacher in Annie's situation with Nketi and his parents do next?

✱ Are there further points that she could make to the parents?

✱ Are there things that she should have done before the parent called?

✱ Is use of cooperative groups effective instruction? Why or why not? How can they be explained?

ORCHESTRATING CLASSROOMS

At this point in your formal education you have been exposed to many teachers. You may have had fifty, sixty, or more teachers in elementary, middle, and secondary school alone, not counting people who have taught you outside of school in recreational activities, sports, jobs. If you were to identify your five favorite teachers, past and present, who would they be? What characteristics make them stand out from all the others? What is it about their personalities, teaching styles and approaches, interpersonal skills, knowledge, and communication and management skills that you like? Have you had teachers you really did not care for? What made them your least favorites? Have your favorite teachers also been your best teachers? Did you learn more from them than from others? Have you had teachers whom you liked very much but considered only mediocre teachers? Have you had teachers you did not particularly care for but nevertheless thought were effective? What makes a teacher effective?

While we all can identify teachers we prefer and find more effective than others, it is not always easy to identify the specific characteristics that influence our judgments. In this chapter we will explore features of effective teaching and traits of effective teachers and show how they are integral to effective classroom management. Our hope is that you will be able to relate this discussion of effective teaching to the models you have encountered and begin to develop approaches that will help you become an effective teacher.

Teaching is a complex endeavor. Teaching looks easy in a well-planned, well-organized classroom, where the class appears to run by itself; the teacher coordinates the learning of students, who respect and cooperate with their

Effective teaching and specific teacher traits are integral to effective classroom management.

classmates, and who are generally interested and engaged in their work; and the atmosphere is relaxed yet purposeful, and there is a sense of warmth and caring between teacher and students. However, teaching looks a good deal more complex in a classroom where there is chaos, where a frustrated teacher struggles to establish safety and order, students show little respect for one another, little learning appears to occur, and there is an atmosphere of mutual hostility.

Every day, as a teacher in an elementary, middle, or secondary school, you will engage in hundreds—or perhaps thousands—of interpersonal exchanges with students (Jackson, 1990). These exchanges involve instruction, behavior management, and bureaucratic tasks. Given the number and scope of your daily decisions and actions, you cannot always thoughtfully consider your options for every action. Yet everything you do (or do not do) has some effect on your classroom ecosystem.

Given this complexity, the two major task functions of classroom teachers are to *create order* and *ensure learning* (Doyle, 1986). Of course, creating order and ensuring learning can have quite different meanings for different people. At one end of a continuum, *order* may be established by the teacher's efforts to impose strict routines, explicit procedures, and rules of conduct. At the other end of a continuum, order may be seen as established and maintained by teacher communication and expectations for students to self-manage their behavior. (See Figure 4.1.)

Likewise, *learning* occurs in many ways. Some may see learning as a product of highly structured and directive teaching; others may see it as the result of classroom environments that are conducive to independent learning. Whatever forms they take, order and learning are ultimately inseparable,

Effective teaching often looks easy, but that is far from the case.

Every teacher's countless daily exchanges with students affect the classroom ecosystem.

Teachers' two major tasks are to create order and ensure learning.

FIGURE 4.1   Creating Order in the Classroom

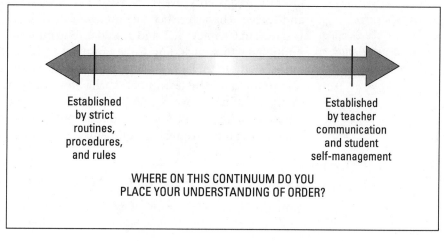

Established by strict routines, procedures, and rules

Established by teacher communication and student self-management

WHERE ON THIS CONTINUUM DO YOU PLACE YOUR UNDERSTANDING OF ORDER?

FIGURE 4.2   Ensuring Learning in the Classroom

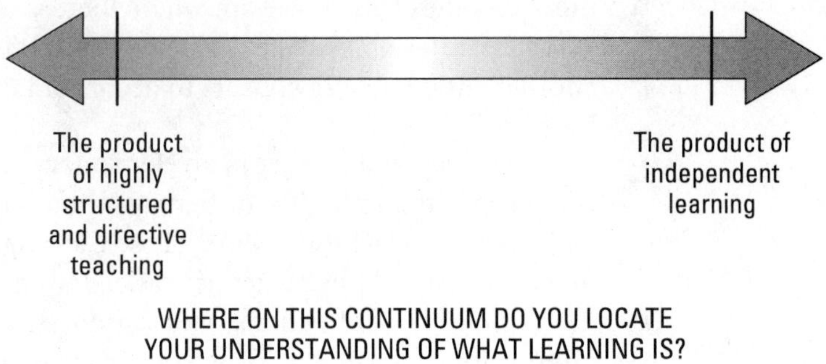

The product
of highly
structured
and directive
teaching

The product of
independent
learning

WHERE ON THIS CONTINUUM DO YOU LOCATE
YOUR UNDERSTANDING OF WHAT LEARNING IS?

so that, in a very real sense, *good classroom management is good teaching* (see Figure 4.2).

In this chapter we examine the part of this symbiotic relationship that represents good teaching. While recognizing that teachers have both management and instructional functions that cannot be disconnected from one another, we focus here on the elements and processes of effective instruction.

WHAT ARE EFFECTIVE CLASSROOM AND SCHOOL ECOSYSTEMS?

As a teacher, you are the critical element in establishing the learning environments of your classroom ecosystem.

Over the past twenty-five years researchers have isolated several specific school and teacher characteristics that are associated with student achievement. As you read in Chapters 1, 2, and 3, student learning and behavior are affected by multiple factors, including some powerful forces outside the classroom and school ecosystems. Still, what happens inside schools and classrooms is clearly important to student learning and behavior. As an individual you may not exert extensive influence over schoolwide features, but you do help determine your school's environment. And, without a doubt, you are the critical element in establishing the learning environments of your own classroom.

ESTABLISHING SAFETY AND ORDER

Your first task is to ensure safety and order in your classroom. Unless your students believe that their schools and classrooms are places where they will encounter little physical and psychological threat and where events occur in fairly predictable ways, they will be unable to focus their attention on learning. Likewise, unless you feel safe and comfortable in your classroom, you will be unable to devote your attention to teaching.

Creating safe environments is not always easy. Most students live in relatively safe homes and neighborhoods and feel safe and comfortable in their schools. For some, however, physical and emotional dangers are ever-present realities in their lives outside of school. For some students, even travel to and from school entails risks. You may exert little influence over these home, neighborhood, and travel safety issues, but it is important to acknowledge their existence, to do whatever is possible to advocate safe transportation and safe environments, and to talk with students about their concerns and fears.

Teachers' awareness and willingness to discuss dangers and fears with students is important.

Inside schools, students can encounter criticism, sarcasm, rejection, frustration and failure, and intimidation by classmates and even by teachers. Almost any living thing that feels threatened seeks to protect itself, and students in school are no exception. Protective strategies can include avoiding school altogether, directing verbal or physical intimidation at others, withdrawing, and aligning with more powerful allies. As a teacher, you may use similar tactics if you feel unsafe in your classroom.

To be an effective teacher, you must create and maintain classrooms that communicate safety and order. You can try to make sure your students are not anxious or alienated and that they do not feel threatened by other students or by their own actions or feelings. You can accomplish this by planning, organizing, and managing your classroom and—most significantly—by modeling self-control, respect, caring, and encouragement.

Why Order *Is* Important

Order is necessary for students' safety and security.

Classroom organization and management skills that ensure safety and order are a prerequisite of effective instruction. Because groups of students are a central feature of classrooms, orderly interaction is necessary for safety and security. An orderly classroom is one where "within acceptable limits the students are *following the program of action necessary for a particular classroom event to be realized in the situation*" (Doyle, 1986, p. 396). Order does *not* mean that classrooms will be rigidly regimented or organized and ordered in the same ways all the time. Order does mean that there are identifiable arrangements of learners, materials, and communication patterns at any given time.

Sometimes your students may be working cooperatively in small groups, sometimes they may be engaged in independent seatwork, sometimes they may be actively performing in large group activities, sometimes they may be attending to demonstrations or lectures, sometimes they may be using computers. Regardless of the types of instructional formats and techniques, orderly procedures are necessary. Order is an integral aspect of effective instruction. It is established through your instructional leadership, maintenance of instructional focus, communication of high expectations, and use of effective instructional methods.

EFFECTIVE LEADERSHIP

Teachers establish classroom leadership in a number of ways. Their styles can be characterized as *autocratic, permissive,* and *democratic,* reflecting the teacher's views of child behavior and classroom management approaches (Dreikurs, Grunwald & Pepper, 1982). Autocratic teachers have a low opinion of human nature and believe that students cannot, or will not, control their own behavior. They believe they must use their authority to control students by determining and enforcing standards of behavior in the classroom. While autocratic teachers may appear to have classrooms that run like clockwork, their reliance on external control ultimately fails to instill in students a sense of personal responsibility or to teach self-management skills.

The approaches used by autocratic teachers do not teach students personal responsibility or self management.

Permissive teachers, on the other hand, have a naively optimistic view of human nature, believing that if left alone, children will make good decisions and behave favorably. Permissive teachers, whose primary goal is to be liked, abdicate their authority and offer little guidance to their students. Frequently these teachers recognize too late that the laissez-faire approach of freedom without responsibility can lead to classroom chaos. Neither the autocratic nor the permissive approach recognizes that in successful classrooms students and teachers must *share* power and responsibility.

The approaches used by permissive teachers often lead to chaos.

Democratic teachers believe that (1) students can develop responsibility and self-control and (2) their role is to teach students these attitudes and skills. Democratic teachers act as leaders who provide opportunities for students to become active participants in their education. They use instructional approaches that establish an orderly and structured environment as well as encourage student involvement and participation. They seek to enhance their students' self-esteem, promote positive interpersonal relationships, and develop mutual respect and caring. Democratic teaching also requires that you communicate respect and caring for your students. It requires skills in listening, protecting, and encouraging students. It involves your deliberate use of classroom management and instructional strategies that motivate your students and ensure high success rates.

Approaches used by democratic teachers are flexible and balance teacher-directed and student-centered learning.

Democratic teachers attempt to balance teacher-directed and student-centered activities (Henley, Ramsey & Algozzine, 1993). They recognize that in some situations and for some purposes, *they* must assume a more directive approach to determining content and activities; in other situations and for other purposes, *students* must assume an active role in determining content and nature of activities. We have found that both teacher-directed and student-centered approaches are needed for effective, meaningful instruction and classroom management.

INSTRUCTIONAL FOCUS

A number of factors, including high expectations for learning and close monitoring of student progress, have been associated with effective schools (see Figure 4.3). Of course, these factors are not independent of one another, but are *inter*dependent and have a cumulative effect on school effectiveness. A single factor like "careful monitoring of student progress" has little meaning in isolation from factors like "high expectations for learning" or "emphasis on academic achievement." Neither does a list of effective school characteristics tell us much about cause-effect relationships. For instance, we do not know whether parent involvement helps create more effective schools or whether more effective schools tend to invite more parent involvement. In the same way, we don't know whether established order and effective discipline are contributors to or outcomes of effective schools. What research does tell us is that the factors listed in Figure 4.3 are *associated with* more effective schools.

Characteristics such as time spent on academic instruction and high expectations for learning are critical features of effective schools. An interesting

FIGURE 4.3   Factors Associated with Effective Schools

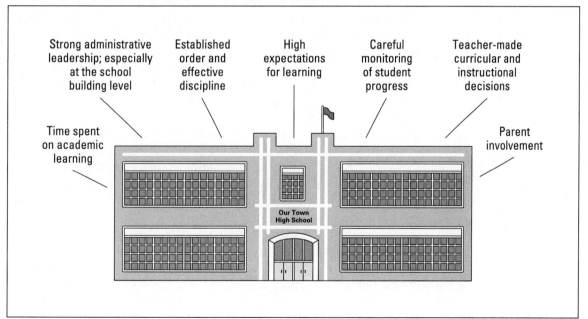

Source: Based on several syntheses of research (e.g., Edmonds, 1981; Elmore et al., 1990; Good & Brophy, 1986; Phi Delta Kappa, 1980; Purkey & Stanley, 1983).

study (Brookover et al., 1979), compared *higher-achieving* schools (defined as schools where students' average achievement scores were above national averages) and *lower-achieving* schools (where average scores were below national averages). Sixty-eight elementary schools were used, with classroom observations and interviews with teachers, principals, and students.

Schools were compared on the basis of similar input characteristics, including size, socioeconomic status and racial make-up of student bodies, teacher-student ratio, and amount of teacher experience. Although these input variables had some effect on student outputs (academic achievement), there were also differences between high- and low-achieving schools in the ways they allocated time. First, in higher-achieving schools, teachers spend *more time on instruction* and allow substantially *less time for independent study* on classroom assignments. Second, teachers in higher-achieving schools spend *less time on material their students have already mastered,* although they spend as much time as needed to teach *new* concepts and skills. Overall, there is more academic interaction between teachers and students in higher-achieving schools (Brookover et al., 1979).

Higher-achieving schools spend more time on instruction than lower-achieving schools.

HIGH EXPECTATIONS

In higher-achieving schools, teachers *expect the vast majority of students to work at grade level and to complete their assignments.* In lower-achieving schools, teachers tend to have lower expectations for student performance. In fact, some students are not really expected to participate in instruction. Teachers in higher-achieving schools also use appropriate rewards for student performance, while many teachers in lower-achieving schools inconsistently and inappropriately reward students, sometimes telling students they have done well even when they have not.

In higher-achieving schools, teachers have high expectations of the students.

In higher-achieving schools, there is more **heterogeneous grouping** (grouping students with different abilities and backgrounds), and students in all groups are expected to make progress. Students in lower-achieving schools, on the other hand, are more likely to be grouped **homogeneously** (together with students who have similar characteristics) for instruction, even though few students seem to benefit from homogeneous grouping.

As we stated earlier, good instruction and good classroom management go hand in hand. It is hard to imagine students learning in environments where instructional goals are obscure, where learning activities are not engaging, where behavior is disorganized and chaotic, and where expected outcomes are uncertain. Learning can and does occur in a variety of instructional arrangements, including large- and small-group recitation, lectures and demonstrations, independent seatwork and homework, individual projects, cooperative group projects and activities, and peer tutoring. Each of these instructional approaches has many permutations. You can effectively utilize different in-

Teachers may choose different instructional approaches depending on their students, the learning tasks, and the goals of instruction.

structional approaches depending on the characteristics of your students, the content of the learning tasks, and the goals of the instruction.

THE SCIENCE AND ART OF TEACHING

You have probably heard the statement that teaching is both an art and a science. Some very effective teachers have had little or no training in pedagogical (teaching) methods. Their approaches are intuitive, or perhaps derived from trial-and-error experiences, rather than the result of formal training in the technology of teaching. Some of the most notable teachers throughout history have also employed very different approaches to instruction. For example, Socrates asked questions to draw understanding and knowledge from his students, Jesus relied on parables to communicate meaning, and Buddha utilized silence to encourage reflection and introspection. Does this mean that the findings of contemporary educational researchers about characteristics of effective teaching are irrelevant? Not at all. Effective teaching will always combine identifiable instructional strategies and intangible elements such as individual teacher personality. (In the above examples, the charismatic force of the individuals was certainly a key to their influence.) Thus, effective teaching approaches are packaged differently by every teacher. The intuitive approaches used by natural teachers have been identified by researchers as well: the Socratic method is represented in questioning and feedback approaches; parables are metaphors, a kind of example and illustration that relate ideas to real life; and silence might be likened to the instructional wait-time that allows students to consider and formulate their responses before answering questions.

Effective teaching combines identifiable instructional strategies and intangible elements.

We agree that effective teachers practice art as well as science. Intuition, creativity, rapport, and strength of personality are important ingredients of effective instruction, but they are rarely sufficient. To be an effective teacher you will also need to be knowledgable about what you are teaching and be able to use a variety of pedagogical skills.

MEETING INDIVIDUAL AND GROUP ACADEMIC AND SOCIAL NEEDS

Educational researchers have learned a good deal about effective instruction by comparing the effects of different teaching approaches on student learning and by observing more effective and less effective teachers. Of course, in any consideration of teaching effectiveness, we have to be clear about what we mean by *effective*. The real question is, "Effective at what?" Although researchers have focused on different measures of effectiveness, in most cases they have used some measure of student academic achievement.

Schools are expected to do many things, and there appears to be no limit to the responsibilities our society places on schools and teachers. However, the central purpose of public schools has always been to help prepare children to be contributing members of our society—to have the necessary knowledge, skills, and values to participate in the economic, social, political, and cultural activities of a democratic society (Cremin, 1961; Dewey, 1916). Student academic achievement is by no means the only measure of teaching effectiveness, nor are students' scores on standardized achievement tests the only measures of academic achievement. However, teaching academic skills certainly represents a major function of schools, and student performance on these outcome measures provides one evaluation of academic learning.

Teachers must meet students' individual needs as well as attend to the general goals of schooling.

In addition to attending to the general goals of schooling, you must focus on the individual needs of your students. As we saw in the last chapter, a range of individual differences in physical, cognitive, emotional, and social developmental levels exists in every elementary, middle, and high school classroom. In addition, family, socioeconomic, community, and cultural factors affect every student's academic performance and behavior.

QUANTITY OF INSTRUCTION

Academic performance is also related to the amount or quantity of instruction that students receive. Time allocated for instruction, the amount of time students are actively engaged in instruction, and the success rates they experience during instruction can affect learning outcomes.

Certain kinds of teacher behavior are likely to produce higher student academic performance (Berliner, 1988; Brophy & Good, 1986; Good & Brophy, 1986, 1991; Rosenshine & Stevens, 1986). **Process-product studies** examine how specific instructional behaviors (or processes) result in specific learning outcomes (or products). The general findings appear to be independent of other student and school characteristics. In fact, teacher behaviors associated with maximum learning gains for students in general also are effective for students with disabilities in mainstream classes (Larrivee, 1989) and students with economic disadvantages (Crawford, 1989).

We should mention that most of these studies have focused on teaching that follows explicit steps, as in the teaching of *facts*, or teaching that presents a general skill that can be applied to other problems and situations. Examples of teaching facts include grammar, vocabulary, and arithmetic. Examples of skills include mathematical computations, blending sounds in decoding, and map reading. These teaching procedures may not be as applicable to teaching higher-level cognitive skills. For example, they are more appropriate for teaching vocabulary in a story than comprehension of the ideas and concepts in the story.

ACADEMIC LEARNING TIME

There is a strong link between student achievement and the quantity and pacing of instruction.

There is a strong link between student achievement and **academic learning time (ALT)**—the *quantity* and *pacing* of instruction. Thus, student learning appears directly related both to the opportunity to learn material and the speed at which it is taught. Not surprisingly, more time spent in learning activities generally correlates with greater academic achievement. Student achievement increases when teachers (1) expect their students to master the curriculum and (2) ensure that most school time is allocated to curriculum-relevant activities.

ACADEMIC ENGAGED TIME

For instructional time to be effective, students need to be actively paying attention and participating.

It is not simply allocated instructional time, but, more important, the amount of time that students are actually engaged in learning that determines learning outcomes. A teacher may allot time to academic activities, but students may not be actively attending and participating. **Academic engaged time (AET)** varies from class to class, from school to school, and, of course, from student to student. Rates of student engagement depend on a number of specific teaching skills related to organizing and managing an efficient learning environment. Teaching skills that tend to promote engagement are

- Preparing the classroom well,
- Developing rules and procedures early in the school year,
- Spending little time getting organized,
- Dealing with inattentive or resistant behavior briefly and in an orderly manner,
- Running academic activities smoothly,
- Pacing lessons smoothly,
- Offering a variety and an appropriate level of challenge in assignments,
- Using consistent procedures to ensure student accountability for learning and follow-up of independent seatwork,
- Establishing clearly when and how students can get assistance with their work, and
- Planning activities for when individual work is finished.

Students learn most efficiently when they are engaged in activities that are appropriate to their developmental and achievement levels, the subject matter, the student-teacher ratio, and the teacher's instructional and management skills. An effective teacher first must ensure that the *curricular content is neither*

Content should be neither too hard nor too easy, and pace should allow the students to succeed.

too simple nor too hard and that the *pace of instruction allows students to make continuous progress*, with *relatively high student success rates* and *relatively little frustration and failure.*

HIGH STUDENT SUCCESS RATES

Student success rates are directly related to academic performance. When students are able to choose their own activities freely, they tend to select those that offer moderate challenges (Deci & Ryan, 1985). Not surprisingly, students avoid activities where they often fail as well as those that are so routine that they offer no challenge. Students make their greatest academic gains when their success rate is between 75 and 100 percent. That is, during instruction, students should be able to successfully answer or complete at least 75 percent of teachers' questions or problems; during follow-up independent practice of those skills, even higher success rates (90–100 percent) are desirable. High levels of successful performance are important because they reinforce student performance and also ensure that students are *not* learning incorrect information, concepts, and skills.

Students are more engaged when actively instructed by teachers or when participating in cooperative learning groups and tutoring arrangements.

Students tend to be more engaged and achieve more when they are actively instructed or supervised by their teachers than when they are working independently. In **active instruction** the teacher personally presents information and skills to individual students, to small groups, or to the whole class and then gives the students opportunities to participate in recitations and practice the skills with appropriate feedback. Active instruction also occurs in cooperative learning groups and peer tutoring arrangements, where students assume both teacher and learner roles.

QUALITY OF INSTRUCTION

Several teacher behaviors that affect student achievement relate to the quality of instruction. These qualitative behaviors include teacher enthusiasm; lesson structure; clarity, redundancy, and pacing; questioning strategies; and feedback.

TEACHER ENTHUSIASM

We cannot overstate the influence of teacher enthusiasm on student engagement in learning. When you are excited about a topic or activity, you contagiously excite and motivate your students. Think again about those effective teachers you remember. You probably remember them as enthusiastic and excited about their subjects, as students have described their "good" teachers

Classroom Closeup

What Students Say About Good Teachers

Students tell me that a good teacher is deeply interested in the students and in the material being taught. They also say that such a teacher frequently conducts class discussions and does not lecture very much. Almost all of them say that a good teacher relates to them on their level; the teacher does not place herself above them, and they are comfortable talking with her. They also tell me that a good teacher does not threaten or punish and that they have little respect for teachers who do . . . Students tell me they appreciate teachers who make an effort to be entertaining. To maintain student interest month after month in potentially boring courses, good lead-teachers try to inject humor, variety, and drama into the lessons. (Glasser, 1990, pp. 66–67) ✳

to William Glasser (see the Classroom Closeup "What Students Say About Good Teachers)."

Several specific kinds of teacher behavior that can communicate enthusiasm include the following (Rosenshine, 1970):

- Rapid speech,
- Frequent movement,
- Use of gestures and facial expressions,
- Variations in voice,
- Use of eye contact,
- Relaxed appearance,
- Lots of questions, and
- Frequent feedback and praise.

Teacher behavior that communicates enthusiasm attracts students' attention and reduces boredom.

These kinds of behaviors tend to attract and maintain student attention to the learning activity. They also reduce boredom and opportunities for distraction.

Meeting the Competition for Attention

As you know, teachers encounter a great deal of competition for students' attention. Most of your students will have watched a lot of television, some for thousands of hours. Many spend more time watching TV than they spend in school. In a sense, teachers must compete for the attention of students who are accustomed to being entertained. TV shows are characterized by short-term segments, frequent changes, and active visual and auditory stimuli. Most shows (especially those for children) are limited to half-hour formats that are further broken down for commercial breaks. Shows (and commercials) are designed to attract and hold viewers' short-term attention. You'll see rapid-fire visual and auditory stimulation intended to grab and maintain viewers' attention even in educational programs such as Sesame Street and other shows produced by the Children's Television Workshop.

Teachers are not limited to thirty-second sound bites or fancy technology.

While you cannot compete with the production budgets and technology available to television, you must recognize that your students are accustomed to high-stimulation experiences that do not require sustained attention and elicit only passive responses. As a teacher, though, you do have other advantages—opportunities for effective instruction are not limited to thirty-second sound bites and sophisticated technology. One instructional advantage is your direct involvement that allows you to adapt and modify how you teach according to individual student behavior. For example, you can determine how well your students understand instructional activities by their attention, responses to your questions, and nonverbal behavior. In turn, you can use features of teacher enthusiasm (eye contact, movement, gestures and facial expressions, proxemics, pacing and quality of your voice, questions, praise and feedback) to make instructional adjustments that help involve your students.

Expressing Genuine Enthusiasm

Of course, students must perceive your enthusiasm as genuine. It must reflect your personality and interests, and your behavior must be appropriate to the instructional activity and content. This means your speech should not be so rapid that students cannot keep pace, and your movement around the room should not confuse and distract. Your gestures, facial expressions, and variations in voice should be relevant to the content. Simply raising or lowering the volume or changing the pitch of your voice in ways that are irrelevant to the communication, for example, distracts and confuses students. You can even overdo eye contact, which tends to be an arousing stimulus, to the point of producing discomfort.

Enthusiasm and praise should be genuine.

You should also use praise cautiously. Praise is effective when it is provided contingently for specific performance but is ineffective when it is overused and not tied to specific accomplishments (Brophy, 1981). We will discuss systematic approaches to individual and group reinforcement in Chapters 7 and 8. Despite these qualifications, you should recognize the components of enthusiasm and try to incorporate them into your teaching.

LESSON STRUCTURE

In addition to showing enthusiasm, there are several ways you can structure lessons so they will contribute to student learning. Drawing on a body of research on effective instructional methodology, Rosenshine and Stevens (1986) derived the following six fundamental instructional functions:

1. Review and check previous day's work (and reteach, if necessary),

2. Present new content or skills,

3. Guide student practice,

4. Provide feedback and correctives (and reteach, if necessary),

5. Allow independent student practice, and

6. Give weekly and monthly reviews.

The components of structuring lessons help teachers solve the problems of helping students remember information and skills.

By following these steps, you can help your students understand relationships between new information and skills and those that they have previously learned. These steps also help students remember the new information and skills you are teaching.

CLARITY, REDUNDANCY, AND PACING

Clarity, redundancy, and *pacing* are related to quality of instruction. Teachers who use *examples* and *analogies* more adequately clarify the information or skills they are teaching than teachers who do not. A teacher who is presenting the concept of cities, states, and nations, for example, may refer to specific, recognizable examples (the students' own city, state, nation) and then have students identify other examples. Or, in teaching geometric shapes, a teacher may use analogies: "A cylinder is like a soda can or this waste basket," and "A cube is shaped like a file cabinet or a box."

Some redundancy, or repetition, in reviewing general rules, procedures, and concepts also contributes to academic achievement. Redundancy does not mean that teachers repeat the same task or information over and over. Rather, it involves having students apply the same rules to different tasks, so that they generalize information or skills.

Pacing of instruction is also a key to effective instruction. Generally, when you move rapidly through material, you are likely to maintain your students' attention. At the elementary level, especially, students tend to learn better when their teacher's presentations are relatively short and interspersed with opportunities for practice. While you will generally want to avoid lengthy wait-times, maintaining a pace that exceeds the ability of most students to understand the material is also undesirable, since you may lose some students along the way.

QUESTIONING STRATEGIES

You can use questioning strategies to actively involve your students and to obtain feedback about their understanding and performance. Student responses to questions also inform you about your instructional effectiveness. Effective teachers try to ask questions clearly. They ask one question at a time to avoid confusion, and they provide adequate time for students to respond.

Although we cannot suggest hard and fast rules for appropriate response wait-times, different types of questions demand different amounts of time for student responses. For example, drill types of questions (e.g., multiplication facts, spelling of words) should elicit automatic responses and short response times, while more complex questions requiring students to apply abstract concepts need more time. Also, as we discussed in Chapter 2, it is important for teachers to be sensitive to individual and cultural variations in wait-time.

Once again, when you do question students, look for mostly correct responses. When students have difficulty answering your questions, they may not understand the material, they may not understand your questions, or they may be making careless mistakes. When this happens, you will likely need to reteach the concepts or skills.

Of course, not all questions have right or wrong answers. For instance, different yet plausible interpretations of poetry and prose should be encouraged. You might ask questions like, "What do you think the author means in this passage?" or "How does this passage make you feel?" or "Have you ever had experiences like this?" These questions encourage students to draw on their personal experiences and make their own judgments. Sometimes you want students to recognize ambiguities and differences of opinion. In these cases you would not want to be the arbiter of right and wrong ideas, feelings, or values because you could stifle your students' thinking and discussion. Just as *you* need to be a problem solver, so you want your students to develop the skills to become problem solvers too.

Questions that ask students to recognize ambiguities and differences of opinion can help them become problem solvers.

There are even some experiences that are best left alone. All learning experiences do not need public discussion and analysis. For example, sometimes the best thing you can do after reading a wonderful story is to just close the book and allow a little time for your students to think about it.

PROVIDING FEEDBACK

Overtly acknowledging correct responses is helpful, but excessive praise may not always be necessary.

You should overtly acknowledge correct responses (nodding or saying "OK," "Right," or "Yes," for example). Sometimes it is helpful to reiterate correct responses to reinforce them for other students: "Yes, seven times six is forty-two." Normally, you need not excessively and publicly praise students' correct responses unless the question or task has been especially challenging or the student is anxious or dependent and seems to need the reassurance.

In the case of incorrect responses, whether they result from a student's lack of understanding or from a technical error, you should clearly indicate that the answer is incorrect and then rephrase the question, perhaps providing cues to the correct response. Sometimes it is helpful to offer the correct response together with an explanation that enables the respondent and other students to understand: "No, remember our rule: '*I* before *e*, except after *c*.' *Receive* is spelled *r-e-c-e-i-v-e*."

Seatwork and Homework

Independent seatwork and homework are usually part of instruction in elementary, middle, and secondary classrooms. They should be used during or after instruction to provide opportunities for students to practice and apply what they are learning. Effective teachers avoid using assignments just to keep students occupied and attempt to make their assignments interesting, varied, and challenging enough to motivate their students to complete them. Of course, you will need to clearly explain independent work using examples before your students begin their work. Also, because students usually do seatwork and homework independently, they should have very high success rates. You certainly do not want your students to practice a skill incorrectly! A near 100 percent correct performance on completed seatwork and homework should indicate your instruction was effective.

Circulating among students as they do seatwork to monitor progress and give help is an effective approach.

In-class seatwork usually is most effective when you circulate through the group, monitoring your students' progress and helping students as needed. As a general rule, you should keep individual help brief, so you can maintain a focus on the group as a whole. If many students need help with their seatwork, you probably should reteach the material to those who are having difficulty. Whether independent work is completed in class or outside, your students need to know that you hold them accountable for their work and will provide feedback about their performance. Timing is important. You should monitor student work, evaluate assignments, and provide feedback about performance as soon as possible.

EFFECTIVE TEACHING AND EFFECTIVE CLASSROOM MANAGEMENT

One misconception that might emerge from our discussion of effective teaching is that it is simply the automatic application of the skills we discussed above. Nothing could be further from the truth. Effective teaching is more than isolated teaching techniques. Effective teaching is an art in which you as teacher put teaching techniques together in creative ways that draw on your skills and personality, that meet your students' individual and group characteristics, that are appropriate for the content and skills you are teaching, and that you have adapted to the unique environmental conditions of your classroom ecosystem. Teaching is always an interactive process, with students and teachers interacting within complex ecosystems of classrooms, schools, communities, and cultures. In this context, students' interpretations of the meaning of what you say and do is critical to their learning. "Good instruction" and "good classroom management" overlap, and teachers' actions speak louder than their words

(Anderson, Evertson & Emmer, 1980). In a study of more successful and less successful managers in third-grade classrooms, for instance,

> Teachers who were better managers demonstrated many behaviours that probably were conveying purposefulness and seriousness about school learning to the students. In so doing, they were providing a rationale for expected performance—telling the students why it was important that they co-operate and stay involved in school tasks. In contrast, teachers who were less good managers often behaved in ways that may have communicated a lack of clear purpose and a feeling that "going through the motions" was adequate, that filling in the time with acceptable activities was the most important objective each day. (Anderson, Evertson & Emmer, 1980, p. 346)

Another possible misconception from our discussion of effective teaching is that teachers who use these approaches are cold, distant technicians. Again, we have found that just the opposite is true. There is no evidence that systematic instruction entails an overbearing manner or that it results in poorer student attitudes about themselves or about school. Instead, teachers in formal classrooms today are warm, flexible, task-oriented, and determined that students will learn (Rosenshine & Stevens, 1986, pp. 380–381):

> Better managers established classrooms with routines and procedures that insured that instruction and learning took top priority, and that the students were informed about their responsibilities for performing the work, as well as about the importance of the work to the teacher. The better managers were not stern task-masters who rule by the clock. Instead, their classrooms were very congenial and pleasant, but definitely oriented toward learning academic content. (Anderson, Evertson & Emmer, 1980, p. 347).

Although definitely oriented toward teaching academic content, better classroom managers were also congenial and pleasant. The key message from research in this area is that effective classroom management is effective teaching.

As We See It: *The Authors Talk*

Mary Kay: I have a concern about all the information we're presenting here on various effective teaching practices.

Bob: What is that?

Mary Kay: I'm concerned about the research that indicates new teachers are more likely to teach the way *they've* been taught in elementary, middle, and secondary school (modeling)—or like their student teaching supervisor— than to actually use the strategies they've learned at college. They spend all this time learning new techniques and methods, but they tend to teach in the ways they remember from their own school days. I know that was true for me. I spent my first year of teaching (third grade) trying to remember what my third-grade teacher, Mrs. Killian, had done fourteen years before.

Bob: I remember doing that too. A lot of what I did in my first classroom (sixth grade) had to do with my memories of Mrs. Zacovek, my sixth-grade teacher. Maybe in addition to the information on teaching strategies, we need to remind new teachers that you don't become a good teacher in the time between graduation and your first job. Learning to be an effective teacher is a time-consuming process.

Mary Kay: Right. Knowing a number of strategies for effective teaching doesn't mean that you use them all the first week. Teachers need to add to their repertoire of skills gradually, building on what they know and trying new things as they seem appropriate.

Bob: It doesn't hurt to have had a good third-grade teacher, either.

APPROACHES TO COOPERATIVE LEARNING

A major challenge for you will be designing and maintaining environments that will accommodate individual and group differences and enhance the achievement of *all* your students. Students differ in their learning styles and rates, but too often traditional instructional approaches have presented the same material in the same ways and at the same rate to all students in a classroom. Although some students do progress in the one-size-fits-all approach, many—including those with learning and behavior problems and limited English proficiency—are likely to fail. Their frustration, boredom, and diminished self-esteem are likely to produce behavior that is conducive neither to their own academic performance nor to that of others in their classrooms.

Traditional classroom procedures have tended to emphasize competitive arrangements, with students essentially pitted against one another. Special education programming, on the other hand, has tended toward the opposite extreme, emphasizing individualized instruction, which often limits interaction and interdependence among students. Group instruction, a feature of most classrooms, does not always facilitate learning for all the members of the group or ensure that each participates. Both competitive and individualized instructional approaches have limitations in classrooms with diverse learners.

Cooperative learning can boost academic achievement, socialization, and self-esteem.

Cooperative learning approaches can be used across a wide range of curricular areas and can simultaneously benefit academic achievement, socialization, and self-esteem. Cooperative learning provides instructional formats that facilitate small groups of students working together rather than inde-

Cooperative learning
teaches skills in
interdependency
and group decision
making.
(Paul Conklin/Photo Edit)

pendently or competitively. Furthermore, compared to competitive and individualized instructional approaches, cooperative learning teaches skills in interdependency that can better prepare students for real-life conditions necessary for effective functioning in families, workplaces, and communities.

THE BEGINNINGS OF APPROACHES TO COOPERATIVE LEARNING

The origins of these contemporary approaches to cooperative learning go back at least to the beginning of this century. One of the foremost educators of the twentieth century, John Dewey, advocated classrooms as laboratories of experiential learning that would utilize democratic procedures. In place of traditional didactic instruction, where the teacher is expert and dispenses all knowledge and skills, Dewey urged teachers to form small, problem-solving groups of students in their classrooms to search for their own answers (1916). He believed that through regular interaction students would learn skills in cooperating, sharing, and taking responsibility that they could apply later in life.

Dewey urged teachers to form small, problem-solving groups of students rather than rely on didactic instruction.

More recently, several research teams—including Elliott Aronson and colleagues at the University of Texas, David Johnson and Roger Johnson at the University of Minnesota, Shlomo Sharan at Tel Aviv University, and Robert Slavin at Johns Hopkins University—have promoted cooperative learning applications. These teams have developed cooperative learning strategies, researched their application and efficacy, and offered training in cooperative learning to thousands of educators. While there are some differences in their approaches to cooperative learning, they share the following features:

- Students work on academic materials in teams,

- Teams consist of heterogeneous learners (that is they are ability, gender, and ethnically mixed), and

- Rewards are for the group, rather than for individuals.

Cooperative learning approaches are especially appropriate in classrooms with diverse learners.

Given these features, cooperative learning approaches are especially appropriate for classrooms with diverse learners. These learning approaches accomplish the multiple purposes of strengthening academic performance while teaching cooperative social skills, building self-esteem, and promoting mutual understanding among students. Compared to traditional instructional approaches, cooperative learning has been effective in increasing achievement and acceptance of students who have often been served outside regular classrooms in compensatory, remedial, and special education programs (e.g., Johnson, Rynders, Johnson, Schmidt & Haider, 1979; Slavin, 1989). In the following material, we will focus on the Johnson and Johnson and the Slavin approaches because they are the most widely used cooperative learning programs.

THE JOHNSON AND JOHNSON APPROACH

According to Roger Johnson and David Johnson, cooperative learning involves small, heterogeneous groups. Although traditional classrooms have often utilized groups, these groups have tended to be homogeneous; group members have shared similar, rather than different, characteristics. For example, some elementary teachers divide their classes into low, middle, and high reading groups. Unfortunately, such homogeneous groups provide limited opportunities for students either to learn from, or to teach one another. The result can be social and academic stratification within classrooms that appears to emphasize rather than reduce those differences. Ability grouping that begins as early as kindergarten can have long-lasting effects on teacher expectations, on student self-esteem, and on academic achievement (Rist, 1970).

Homogeneous ability grouping emphasizes differences and affects students' self-esteem and academic achievement.

Promoting Positive Interdependence

In the Johnson and Johnson approach to cooperative learning, students serve as learning resources for one another. Because the performance of individual group members depends on other group members, *positive interdependence* develops among group members. Positive interdependence is established by

- Determining mutual goals to make sure that all group members learn the material,
- Arranging face-to-face interactions through activities like oral summarizing, giving and receiving explanations, and elaborating,
- Stressing and assessing individual learning within the group by individual examination or selecting individuals to answer or report for the entire group,
- Teaching communication, leadership, decision-making, and conflict management skills that enable groups to function effectively,
- Providing time and procedures for students to analyze their group's functioning and use of social skills, together with teacher or student observer feedback, and
- Providing group rewards when all group members achieve according to preset criteria rather than by comparison with others.

The Teacher's Role

In the Johnson and Johnson approach to cooperative learning, the teacher acts as a consultant to the groups, rather than the sole source of learning. The teacher's role contains elements of direct instruction that we outlined earlier. That is, you specify expectations, deliberately teach skills, monitor and provide feedback to students, and evaluate their performance. Elements of the teacher's role in cooperative learning are

1. *Specifying expected behaviors*, making it clear that you expect everyone to listen, contribute, help, and encourage others to participate (you clarify rules and procedures for staying with the group, sharing, asking questions, and volume of voice),

2. *Teaching collaborative skills* (e.g., praising, summarizing, encouraging, asking for help, checking for understanding) by defining, explaining each skill, and having students practice them with feedback,

3. *Arranging and monitoring interactions* among group members, circulating among your groups to determine if members understand their assignments, and providing feedback and reinforcement for appropriate use of group skills,

4. *Providing assistance* to your students by clarifying, reteaching, and elaborating on tasks as needed and suggesting procedures for working effectively together,

5. *Evaluating* (testing) how well your students complete the assignments and guiding their evaluation of their group-processing skills, and

6. *Providing recognition* of individual and group effort and achievement.

Cooperative Learning Strategies

The Johnsons have described numerous cooperative learning activities that can be used depending on the curricular goals and content. Although we can describe only a few strategies here, you will find others in their publications (see our suggestions in Building Your Own Knowledge Base at the end of this chapter).

Jigsaw is especially appropriate for teaching social studies, literature, and other subjects where material is in narrative form.

Jigsaw. Jigsaw is a cooperative learning activity that is also used in other cooperative learning programs. This approach is especially appropriate for teaching subjects like social studies, literature, and areas of science where material is in narrative form and where concepts, rather than skills, are the learning goals. In *Jigsaw,* each student in a group of three or four reads and studies part of a selection, such as a story, and then teaches what he or she has learned to the other members of the group. Each student then quizzes group members to ensure they also understand.

Cooperative Reading Groups. In cooperative reading groups one individual is assigned to be the *reader,* another the *recorder,* and a third the *checker.* The students write several answers to each question and indicate the best response. All members of the group must certify that they understand and agree on the correct answers.

Problem Solvers. This strategy involves giving each group a problem to solve. The group determines what each member will contribute to completing the problem. For example, to practice multiplication problems, one student could write down the problem, a second could complete the calculation, while a third could write down the answers. Students rotate responsibilities throughout their group, so that each member practices each skill. Since you hold all members of the group responsible for knowing how to do the problems, they help one another by instructing and correcting one another.

Writing-Response Groups. Writing response groups have students read and respond to the written work of the members of their group. For example, you might ask students to mark what they like with stars, mark what they do not understand with question marks, and then discuss the paper with the writer. Next, you might ask them to mark spelling, grammatical, punctuation, and other problems and discuss them with the writer. Finally, you can have group members proofread the final draft and point out any errors that need to be corrected.

Group Reports. In group reports students jointly research a topic. You assign each student a responsibility for checking different sources and sharing information. Then each student writes part of the report.

THE SLAVIN APPROACH

There are similarities between the cooperative learning approaches suggested by the Johnsons and those developed and studied by Slavin and his colleagues. Slavin's *Student Team Learning* (STL) and *Teams-Games-Tournament* (TGT) emphasize team goals and team recognition when all team members achieve learning objectives. Competition among the cooperative groups is an added feature. The key elements of STL and TGT are heterogeneous teams, team rewards, individual accountability within the group, and equal opportunities for success for each team member.

Heterogeneous teams involve learning groups of four students. The teacher carefully forms the groups to assure a mixture of student abilities, performance levels, gender, and ethnicity. The particular mix depends on the characteristics of your students and your social and learning goals.

Team rewards are certificates or other rewards for achieving a weekly criterion. However, teams do not win rewards at the expense of other teams that lose. All (or none) of the teams may reach the criterion, since each team's success depends on the individual learning of *all* its members—individual accountability. Slavin believes this emphasis helps focus team members on tutoring one another to make sure everyone is ready for a quiz or other assessment of individual performance that students must take without help from their teammates.

Equal opportunities to succeed mean that individual students contribute to their teams by *improving* their past performance rather than by having their performance compared to that of others. Thus, whether they are high, average, or low achievers, students contribute to their teams by demonstrating individual progress.

Slavin and his associates have extensively described and implemented several general types of Student Team Learning. *Student Teams–Achievement Divisions (STAD)*, *Teams-Games-Tournament (TGT)*, and *Jigsaw II* are methods that you can adapt to a variety of subjects and grade levels. We describe STAD, TGT, and Jigsaw II below, but for more detailed descriptions and examples of application you should see resources listed in Building Your Own Knowledge Base at the end of the chapter.

Student Teams-Achievement Divisions (STAD)

STAD is most appropriate for teaching subjects that have well-defined objectives with single right answers, such as mathematical computation, spelling, grammar, science facts, and map skills. STAD has been used across a wide range of grade levels in a variety of classroom settings. It is intended to encourage students to help one another master the skills you present by offering team rewards for group achievement.

STAD uses four-member teams formatted to include diverse student characteristics such as gender; ethnic and cultural backgrounds; and academic,

High, average, and low achievers contribute to team success through individual progress.

Teachers can adapt several types of team learning to a variety of subjects and grade levels.

STAD is especially appropriate for teaching subjects that have well-defined objectives with single right answers.

social, and communication skills. The team may work together or in pairs tutoring, comparing answers, discussing, and quizzing one another to help team members learn the material. In most cases you will use your own curricular lessons and materials with STAD.

A complete cycle of STAD activities consists of several steps and typically requires three to five class periods. First you present a lesson. Next you have students work in their groups, making sure every member of the team masters the lesson. Then you test students individually (and independently) on the material. You compare individual scores with each student's previous average scores, and award points when they match or surpass their past performance. Each team receives the total of individual points earned by their group, and you may also provide group certificates or other rewards.

Teams-Games-Tournament (TGT)

TGT also employs teacher presentations and teamwork but instead of weekly tests, uses tournaments or competitions between teams to earn points. Students compete at three-person tournament tables with members of other teams who have similar past performances in the subject area. You can keep competition even by changing students' tables each week based on their previous performance. The winner at each table contributes points to his or her team, regardless of whether it is a high-, medium-, or low-achieving table. Again, you can present certificates or other kinds of recognition and rewards to high-achieving teams.

TGT can excite, motivate, and engage even reluctant students.

The use of competitions in TGT is intended to add an element of excitement to the cooperative group activities. Teamwork is promoted as teammates help prepare one another for the games by studying worksheets and explaining work to one another. We have seen these team competitions motivate and engage even highly reluctant students in a youth detention facility.

Jigsaw II

While both STAD and TGT follow some type of teacher instruction, Jigsaw II begins with students reading some form of narrative or descriptive material, such as a story, a chapter in a textbook, or a biography. You then assign parts of the material (e.g., chapters, units, or sections) to individual team members, who must respond to Expert Sheets of questions regarding what they have read. When finished, individual members of each team meet with the members of other teams who are responsible for the same material—an Expert Group—to discuss what they have learned about their topics. They rejoin their teams and take turns teaching their teammates what they have learned. In the last step of Jigsaw II, students take individual quizzes covering *all* the topics studied by their group. The teacher computes individual improvement scores, like the team scores in STAD, and recognizes high scoring teams with certificates.

LEARNING OUTCOMES PROMOTED BY COOPERATIVE LEARNING

Cooperative learning is effective in promoting academic performance, teaching and enhancing social skills and intergroup relations, and improving individual self-esteem. Cooperative learning is especially valuable for promoting learning and social interaction for students—including mildly disabled and at-risk students—who often are left behind academically and left out socially in competitive learning structures (Johnson, Rynders, Johnson, Schmidt & Haider, 1979; Slavin, Karweit & Madden, 1989). Among the established outcomes of cooperative learning are

- Higher academic achievement for high-, average-, and low-achieving students in urban, rural, and suburban schools,

- Improved ability to view situations from others' perspectives,

- More positive, accepting, and supportive relationships with peers, regardless of gender, ethnic, social class, or (dis)ability conditions,

- More positive attitudes toward teachers and other school personnel, toward learning and subject matter, and toward school generally,

- Higher self-esteem, and

- More academic time on-task, less disruptive behavior, improved attitudes, and greater skills for collaboration with others.

Many resources—publications, training materials, and workshops—are available to teachers interested in utilizing cooperative learning in their classrooms. Several are listed in Building Your Own Knowledge Base.

PEER TUTORING

Another successful approach for teaching diverse learners is peer tutoring (Slavin, Karweit & Madden, 1989), which teachers can use in combination with the cooperative learning strategies discussed above. Peer tutoring involves placing a student who has mastered a particular skill in a one-to-one relationship with another student who has yet to master that skill. Although tutors may be specially trained teachers, paraprofessionals, or adult volunteers, you can also train your students as peer tutors.

As we have emphasized throughout earlier chapters, in all classrooms individual students vary in their learning abilities and skills. They arrive in school with different backgrounds and experiences, and they require different types and amounts of instruction to master the same skills. This is true even where there is academic tracking, with students placed in classes with other students who have similar background and learning characteristics. Despite the individual differences among your students, however, you will rarely find opportunities to provide *individual* instruction for twenty or more students. Peer tutoring offers a means for you to accommodate and even take advantage of your students' individual differences in one-to-one or small group arrangements.

Peer tutors can benefit academically as much or more than the students they tutor.

Peer tutoring can be beneficial for academic skills, communication skills, and interpersonal relationships for both tutors and learners. You may have heard it said, "The best way to learn is to teach," and, in fact, tutors can benefit academically as much or more than the students they tutor (Jenkins & Jenkins, 1981). After all, tutors study the material several times—during their initial learning, during review, when preparing to teach, and while teaching another student. In addition to possible academic benefits, tutors also practice positive interaction skills, can develop a greater sense of responsibility, and experience satisfaction from helping another student. Thus, the tutoring arrangement can help foster a climate of kindness within the peer culture of the school (Strayhorn, Strain & Walker, 1993).

VARIATIONS OF PEER TUTORING

Three variations of peer tutoring are *interschool, intergrade,* and *within class.* Interschool programs typically involve older students, perhaps from a middle school or high school, paired with elementary students. Intergrade programs pair students in upper grades with students in lower grades, sometimes on a schoolwide basis. Within-class models pair more advanced and less advanced students from the same class.

The logistics of scheduling interschool, and even intergrade, programs are more complex than within-class programs and require careful planning and collaboration among teachers and administrators. Generally, for interschool and intergrade programs to work well, someone must be responsible to coordinate the program, to conduct meetings and training sessions for tutors, and to arrange tutoring schedules. Within-class models are more feasible for most teachers to implement independently. The potential benefits of peer tutoring will not increase automatically. You will first need to carefully train your tutors. The Classroom Closeup "Peer Tutoring Task Analysis" contains a task analysis of the various activities involved in the seemingly simple task of one student reading a story to another.

Guidelines for Developing a Peer Tutoring Program

The following guidelines can help you develop a peer tutoring program:

Peer tutors are usually—but not always—academically more able, upper-grade students.

1. *Tutors should have at least adequate skills in the material to be taught.* Generally, you should select average- or high-performing students to tutor those with less developed skills. Thus, more academically able, upper-grade students who can complete much of their own work independently are potential tutors for less advanced and lower-grade pupils. However, sometimes you may use lower-performing students to tutor students who

Classroom Closeup

Peer Tutoring Task Analysis

Tutors must introduce the activity to the child and engage the child's participation rather than just starting reading out of the blue. They must read in an enthusiastic tone, emphasizing the important words of each sentence rather than using a monotone. They must hold the book so that the listener can see the pictures rather than holding it upside down or at a great distance relative to the young child. They need to reinforce rather than punish the child's utterances about the story. They should use differential attention by sitting silently and waiting if the child's attention wanders momentarily. They should chat with the child and discontinue the reading if the child's attention wanders for a longer period of time. . . . They should use a tone of approval to announce the end of the story so as to reinforce the child for attending. Similar sets of skills are taught for conversing with the young child and for dramatic play as well as for specific tutoring activities aimed at teaching reading, writing, and mathematics. (Strayhorn, Strain & Walker, 1993, p. 20) ✴

are much younger or less skilled than themselves. In some learning activities, such as drill-like tasks (e. g., practicing spelling words or math facts), students with similar skills can tutor one another.

Even students who are "problems" may be dependable, sensitive, and caring when they tutor others.

2. In addition to age, grade, and ability, *some interpersonal skills are important for tutors.* The most effective tutors might be described as "dependable, sensitive, and caring." However, sometimes the process of tutoring brings out these characteristics in students who might not otherwise display them, including students who are considered problems. Just as your cooperative learning groups are comprised of heterogeneous learners, you can deliberately select peer tutoring pairs that encourage interaction, communication, and understanding across cultural, ethnic, socioeconomic, (dis)ability, and gender groups.

3. *Tutoring should be regularly and carefully scheduled.* Tutoring sessions should be part of your established routines and scheduled so that neither tutors nor learners miss presentations, demonstrations, and discussions that cause them to fall behind in other work.

4. *Tutors must be trained, and tutoring must be carefully monitored.* Trainees must know the purpose of the program and their responsibilities, including time commitment, confidentiality, reliability, and positive concern for their learning partners. You should also require tutors to maintain the quality of their own academic work. You will need to teach them how to collect data on their instruction (e.g., amount of material covered, percentage of correct responses) and how to record data so you can readily

monitor student progress. You also need to instruct tutors in the specific skills to be taught by modeling teaching skills for them. In addition, tutors need to know how to offer appropriate feedback, keep lessons on task, and reward good effort by their tutees.

5. It is important to *provide feedback, encouragement, support, and recognition to tutors.* You can recognize your tutors' contributions in a variety of ways, including verbal feedback, certificates, notes sent home to parents, and recognition in school newsletters.

Peer tutoring can help you meet the diverse academic, communication, and social needs of your students. It is an instructional approach you may use to supplement other forms of instruction with your class as a whole or for selected pairs of students in your class.

SUMMARY AND REVIEW

Good teaching is evident when students are motivated and engaged by their learning tasks, when they are learning meaningful ideas and skills, and when learning occurs in safe and orderly environments. While there is no single prescription for good teaching, we hope the characteristics of effective instruction we have examined in this chapter offer guidance for procedures that enhance your instruction and that you can adapt to individual learner, teacher, and setting characteristics. Most important, though, you must be aware of the powerful model you provide for your students. When you are purposeful, organized, enthusiastic, and caring in your teaching, you are likely to motivate your students to be purposeful, organized, enthusiastic, and caring learners.

As we stated at the outset of this chapter, "good teaching is good classroom management." The instructional approaches we have discussed here are primarily focused on academic instruction, yet they influence your students' attitudes, feelings, and behavior as well. For some approaches, such as cooperative learning and peer tutoring, learning interpersonal skills such as caring, sharing, and cooperating are implicit. In the next two chapters we will shift our attention to approaches that have direct impact on your students' behavior.

REFLECTING ON CHAPTER 4

Refer back to the beginning of this chapter and the questions we asked about the teachers you remember. Discuss those questions with your classmates and see if any themes emerge.

- Do most of you have similar memories of your early teachers?

- Do the same traits show up in different people and settings? or do preferences vary?

- Sit down and write a letter to the teacher or teachers you remember most positively. Tell them why you have such positive thoughts and thank them.

- Discuss candidly your experiences with cooperative learning groups. Most students have participated in this type of instruction in secondary school or in college or university classes. How did you feel about this form of instruction? Strengths? Weaknesses?

- What does Annie's experience tell you about introducing different techniques in the classroom? There has been much more public scrutiny of educational methodology recently, from cooperative learning, to whole language, to effective educational methods, to sex education. How can teachers prepare for and respond to such inquiry and criticism?

Key Terms

heterogeneous grouping (p. 126)
homogeneous grouping (p. 126)
process-product studies (p. 128)
academic learning time (ALT) (p. 129)

academic engaged time (AET) (p. 129)
active instruction (p. 130)
cooperative learning (p. 137)

Building Your Own Knowledge Base

Glasser, W. (1990). *The quality school: Managing students without coercion.* New York: Harper & Row. Glasser argues that effective teachers are effective managers and proposes ways teachers can lead and motivate their students.

Good, T., & Brophy, J. (1991). *Looking in classrooms* (5th ed.). New York: Harper & Row. The authors provide many ideas about effective teaching and classroom life.

Johnson, D., & Johnson, R. (1989). *Cooperation and competition: Theory and research.* Edina, MN: Interaction Book; (1987). *Learning together and alone: Cooperative, competitive, and individualistic learning* (2nd ed.). Englewood Cliffs, NJ: Prentice-Hall. The Johnson brothers offer a philosophical and research basis for cooperative learning and describe ways teachers can use it to enhance academic and social skills.

Kagan, S. (1989). *Cooperative learning: Resources for teachers.* San Juan Capistrano, CA: Resources for Teachers. Practical applications of cooperative learning across subject areas and age/grade levels as well as classroom management methods that utilize cooperative learning.

Slavin, R. E. (1990). *Cooperative learning: Theory, research, and practice.* Englewood Cliffs, NJ: Prentice-Hall. Slavin provides an overview of his approach to cooperative learning, including applications and suggestions provided by classroom teachers who use cooperative approaches.

References

Anderson, L., Evertson, C., & Emmer, E. (1980). Dimensions in classroom management derived from recent research. *Journal of Curriculum Studies, 12,* 343–346.

Berliner, D. C. (1988). The half-full glass: A review of research on teaching. In E. L. Meyen, G. A. Vergason & R. J. Whelan (Eds.), *Effective instructional strategies for exceptional children.* Denver: Love.

Brookover, W. B., Beady, C., Flood, P., Schweitzer, J., & Wisenbaker, J. (1979). *School systems and student achievement: Schools can make a difference.* New York: Praeger.

Brophy, J. (1981). Teacher praise: A functional analysis. *Review of Educational Research, 51,* 5–32.

Brophy, J., & Good, T. L. (1986). Teacher behavior and student achievement. In M. C. Wittrock (Ed.), *Handbook of research on teaching* (3rd ed.). New York: MacMillan.

Crawford, J. (1989). Instructional activities related to achievement gain in Chapter 1 classes. In R. E. Slavin, N. L. Karweit & N. A. Madden (Eds.), *Effective programs for students at risk* (pp. 264–290). Boston: Allyn and Bacon.

Cremin, L. (1961). *The transformation of the school.* New York: Vintage Books.

Deci, E. L., & Ryan, R. M. (1985). *Intrinsic motivation and self-determination in human behavior.* New York: Plenum Press.

Dewey, J. (1916). *Democracy and education: An introduction to the philosophy of education.* New York: Macmillan.

Doyle, W. (1986). Classroom organization and management. In M. C. Wittrock (Ed.), *Handbook of research on teaching* (3rd ed.). (pp. 392–431). New York: MacMillan.

Dreikurs, R., Grunwald, B., & Pepper, F. (1982). *Maintaining sanity in the classroom.* New York: Harper & Row.

Edmonds, R. R. (1981). Making public schools effective. *Social Policy, 12,* 28–32.

Elmore, R. F., & Associates. (1990). *Restructuring schools: The next generation of educational reform.* San Francisco: Jossey-Bass.

Glasser, W. (1990). *The quality school: Managing students without coercion.* New York: Harper & Row.

Good, T. L., & Brophy, J. (1986). School effects. In M. C. Wittrock (Ed.), *Handbook of research on teaching* (3rd ed.) (pp. 570–602). New York: MacMillan.

Good, T. L., & Brophy, J. E. (1991). *Looking in classrooms* (5th ed.). New York: HarperCollins.

Henley, M., Ramsey, R. S., & Algozzine, R. (1993). *Characteristics of and strategies for teaching students with mild disabilities.* Boston: Allyn and Bacon.

Jackson, P. W. (1990). *Life in classrooms.* New York: Holt, Rinehart and Winston.

Jenkins, J. R., & Jenkins, L. M. (1981). *Cross age and peer tutoring: Help for children with learning problems.* Reston, VA: Council for Exceptional Children.

Johnson, D. W., & Johnson, R. T. (1987). *Learning together and alone: Cooperative, competitive, and individualistic learning* (2nd ed.). Englewood Cliffs, NJ: Prentice-Hall.

Johnson, D. W., & Johnson, R. T. (1989). *Cooperation and competition: Theory and research.* Edina, MN: Interaction Book.

Johnson, R. T., Rynders, J., Johnson, D. W., Schmidt, B., & Haider, S. (1979). Interaction between handicapped and nonhandicapped teenagers as a function of situational goal structuring: Implications for mainstreaming. *American Educational Research Journal, 16,* 161–167.

Kagan, S. (1988). *Cooperative learning: Resources for teachers.* Riverside, CA: University of California.

Larrivee, B. (1989). Effective strategies for academically handicapped students in the regular classroom. In R. E. Slavin, N. L. Karweit & N. A. Madden (Eds.), *Effective programs for students at risk* (pp. 291–319). Boston: Allyn and Bacon.

Phi Delta Kappa (1980). *Why do some urban schools succeed?* Bloomington, IN: Phi Delta Kappa.

Purkey, W. W., & Stanley, P. H. (1983). *Invitational teaching, learning, and living.* Washington, DC: National Education Association.

Rist, R. (1970). Student social class and teacher expectations: The self-fulfilling prophecy in ghetto education. *Harvard Educational Review, 40,* 411–451.

Rosenshine, B. (1970). Enthusiastic teaching: A research review. *School Review, 78,* 499–512.

Rosenshine, B., & Stevens, R. (1986). Teaching functions. In M. C. Wittrock (Ed.), *Handbook of research on teaching* (3rd ed.) (pp. 375–391). New York: MacMillan.

Slavin, R. E. (1989). Comprehensive cooperative learning models for heterogeneous classrooms. *The Pointer, 33,* 12–19.

Slavin, R. E. (1990). *Cooperative learning: Theory, research, and practice.* Englewood Cliffs, NJ: Prentice-Hall.

Slavin, R. E., Karweit, N. L., & Madden, N. A. (1989). *Effective programs for students at risk.* Boston: Allyn and Bacon.

Strayhorn, J. M., Jr., Strain, P. S., & Walker, H. M. (1993). The case for interaction skills training in the context of tutoring as a preventive mental health intervention in schools. *Behavioral Disorders, 19,* 11–26.

Building a Foundation for Effective Classroom Management

• Preparing for school to start
• Arranging the physical environment

Preventing Behavioral Problems

Monitoring Student Behavior and Dealing With Problems

• Group focus
• Momentum
• Smoothness
• Overlapping
• Withitness
• Variety and challenge

Becoming a *Withit* Teacher

• Determining rules and procedures
• Seeing classrooms and schools from students' perspectives
• Monitoring students' work
• Analyzing and communicating expectations

Chapter 5

Preventing Behavioral Problems

Annie's Journal

DECEMBER MIDYEAR EVALUATION (EXCERPTS)

Ms. Annie Harris   Observations on 9/15, 10/20, 11/8, and 12/5
Madison School   Conducted by Alice Wright, Principal
Grade Four

Classroom Environment

Your classroom is warm and welcoming and seems to be a place where students would be comfortable. Your use of student work is obvious and certainly provides recognition and encouragement for student productivity. I particularly like your Poetry Corner, where a new poem appears weekly for students to read and enjoy—and respond to with work of their own. The Mystery Question posted on your door has stumped me on several occasions, and I know this provokes lively discussion in your classroom as well as some others! I know you have tried several different room arrangements for your students, and such experimentation is a good idea, as long as it doesn't disrupt the students too much. Your current seating pattern does seem to be successful during your group work times, but I notice that several students have to turn all the way around in their desks to see the board. This may not be a problem if you don't use the east board very much or if the students who have to move are not unduly hampered by such a situation, but you might observe carefully to ensure that this is the case.

In my initial observations, I was somewhat concerned about the noise level in your classroom. While I am certainly not a proponent of silent classrooms, teachers must be aware of the level of sound in their rooms and make sure that it is not audible to others in the building. At times, as I walk by your room, I can hear quite a bit of commotion, and you need to be sure that such noise is the result of active learning, not misbehavior. As I have observed in your room, I do notice students moving around a lot, discussing, and assisting one another. These are all marks of an active and involved class, and I commend you for it. First-year teachers often become overly concerned with control issues and are uncomfortable with even an appropriate level of sound coming from their rooms. I certainly don't want you to take my remarks as a directive to lower the level just for the sake of silence. Just continue to monitor each activity and be certain that the talking and exchanging of information is germane to the task at hand.

All in all, I find your classroom to be a welcoming setting where it is easy to see active learning and genuine interest in the subject matter.

Academic Objectives

In the areas of literature and social studies you are doing a particularly outstanding job. Your students are engaged and excited by what they are learning, and you have managed to show connections between what they are reading and what is going on in their lives. Bravo! I am certain that your strengths in these areas will make you a leader in our school, and I plan to call on you to assist others and to work with your team in building everyone's skills in these areas of relevance and motivation. Your students' writing is, for the most part, excellent. You have a real knack for inspiring them to write about what they know. You may need to spend more time on the mechanics of writing with some of the less skilled students. It is certainly not too early to begin stressing some patterns in terms of paragraphs, topic sentences, etc.

You might consider trying to bring some of the variety you infuse into your social studies teaching into other aspects of your curriculum. Each time I have observed your class, you seem to be following the same patterns in spelling and, to some extent, in math. You seem to do the same things in these areas on the same day of the week. As the year progresses, I can see students becoming bored with what they know will happen in these areas. Consider varying your approach—get away from so much drill and practice in these areas—and I think you'll see interest increasing.

As I look over your daily lesson plans, you seem well organized and consistent. Your notations in the margins as you go through the day are very helpful to you, I'm sure.

You might want to consider making more use of the computer lab—your students could benefit from such experience—and of the media center. As you know, Mr. Baker feels that the media center should be a daily resource for all students and teachers, and he is happy to assist with a unit or research experience. Why don't you talk with him about how he can assist your students with your next social studies unit?

Classroom Management

As I have indicated above, your students seem to be enthusiastic and excited about learning, and this speaks well of your classroom management techniques. You are generally positive and supportive. I know you have been concerned about a couple of your students, and I would like to address those concerns specifically. Danny and Tremaine have been exhibiting more and more aggressive behavior, both in your classroom and in other areas of the school, such as the playground, the bus, and the lunchroom. We have talked about methods of dealing with this behavior, and I know you have been trying different options in the classroom. I think the time has come to ask for more assistance, so I suggest you request a meeting of the Teacher Assistance Team to discuss this situation. As you know, you need to fill out the request form, giving your perception of the problem, and I'll arrange a time for the team to get together. I think for this situation, we should include Dr. Fox (school psychologist), Mr. Wood (special education), Ms. Cohen (social work), and Mr. Ramirez (fifth grade). These professionals have all shown great interest and skill in dealing with students whose behavior is challenging, and I think they would be useful people for you to know. Let's see if this kind of intervention will stop the problems we've been experiencing.

Again, I would stress that your classroom management techniques seem to be working quite well for this group. As I observe your class, I see you attending well to the various parts of the room, including students in the task at hand with words and looks, and generally creating a positive environment. Occasionally I have observed you ignoring a potential disruption a bit too long, but I think you will develop a sense for when to wait and when to step in. I would also encourage you to begin keeping a log, specifically relating to incidents concerning Danny and Tremaine. You may find it helpful to identify exactly when certain incidents take place, and such information also will be helpful to the Teacher Assistance Team. We need to be more active in involving both boys' parents in this situation, too. I have not spoken with you about parent conferences. Did these parents come? We'll talk more about this later.

FOCUS QUESTIONS

* How do you think Annie will feel about this report? How might other new teachers feel about it?

* Do Ms. Wright's comments seem helpful? Which ones are not helpful to a new teacher?

* What should Annie do to improve her reports—or should she do anything?

BUILDING A FOUNDATION FOR EFFECTIVE CLASSROOM MANAGEMENT

With careful planning and preparation, you can create learning environments that are conducive to your students' intellectual, emotional, and social growth. You can prevent, or at least reduce, the likelihood of many behavioral problems that can interfere with your students' progress. In Chapter 4 we focused on the direct effect of teachers' academic and behavioral expectations on student performance as well as on the importance of establishing an orderly, safe environment for improved performance. We also discussed conclusions of recent research on effective schools and effective teaching. This research shows how a teacher's control over several factors—including curriculum content, allocation of time, enthusiasm, pacing of instruction, grouping of students, and types of instructional activities—directly influences student motivation, academic achievement, and social behavior.

Planning is key to effective classroom management.

In this chapter we expand our discussion to consider ways you can design classroom environments to enhance learning and minimize behavioral problems. Effective, experienced teachers know that planning and preparation are keys to classroom management. What you do even before students arrive in your classroom and during the first days and weeks of school is critical to establishing a positive learning environment that can set the tone for the rest of the year.

Preparing to manage a classroom might be likened to designing and building a house. We may pay most of our attention to location, size, number and arrangement of rooms, decorating, and furniture, and we may ignore the relatively unglamorous foundation. After all, most people do not notice the foundation and may be unaware of its role in ensuring the stability and integrity of the entire structure. However, without a secure foundation, a house will eventually sag, leak, crack, and in time even collapse. A poor foundation requires continuous patching up or even major renovation. The required repairs can be costly and inconvenient for those living in the house.

Preventing behavioral problems is easier than correcting them.

When we as teachers think of classroom management, we may focus on disciplinary strategies to deal with problem behavior. Such problems sometimes develop because we have not laid an adequate foundation. It is almost always easier to prevent problems than to correct them. The ideas in this chapter should help you build the foundations of effective classroom organization and management. We examine ways of determining expectations for student behavior, arranging physical space, establishing rules and routines, developing schedules, and managing transitions. We also discuss some specific teacher behaviors that will help you discourage deviant student behavior.

PREPARING FOR SCHOOL TO START

Some of the most important work you can do occurs *before* the first day of school. You probably will need to spend several productive days in your school and classroom ecosystem before your students arrive, especially if you are new to the school or the grade level or have a new role and responsibilities.

A primary use for this time is to become acclimated to your environment—to become familiar and comfortable with the physical setting of the school and classroom. When you move into a new apartment or home, you study room sizes, shapes, and configurations. You consider how your furniture, appliances, and other equipment might fit in existing spaces and how you could arrange and store things efficiently and conveniently. You are interested in the flow of traffic through the living space. You also think about how to decorate your new living space to create a comfortable environment to help you and others feel at home. In a similar way you can study and arrange the physical and psychological environment of your classroom. You can become alert to "the behavioral map" (Evertson & Emmer, 1982) of your classroom and school and see them from your students' perspectives. Although there is not a set order to this process, there are several elements of the school and classroom environment for you to explore and then prepare.

Become Familiar with the Physical Environment

Ecosystems in a school can include the hallways, gym, lunchroom, and supply rooms among others.

One of your first goals should be to become familiar with the physical environment of the school and classroom. If you are new to the school, you probably will have been given at least a cursory guided tour by the principal, but you also can do some systematic exploring on your own. Think about the ecosystems of the school. These can include the hallways, gym, lunch room, music and art rooms, library-media center, playground, assembly halls, and supply rooms for books, instructional materials, and media equipment (e.g., overhead projectors, video equipment, computer hardware and software). You will need to plan procedures and schedules for using these places and resources.

Learn the Roles and Responsibilities of Colleagues

Even considering traffic patterns to and from different places in school helps build a strong foundation for classroom management.

Meet your colleagues and visit their offices. They will provide services to you and your students, including special education resource programs, compensatory programs (at-risk, Title I, ESL). Visit the offices of the principal, nurse, psychologists, social workers, counselors, custodians, and others who are available in your building. As you meet these colleagues, ask them about their services and resources and think about how you and your students might be involved with them. Consider traffic patterns to and from other locations, how behavioral expectations in each setting might vary, and what procedures might help you access and use these resources effectively.

Learn About School and District Procedures and Services

Most schools have handbooks outlining services and personnel within the school and district and detailing school and district policies related to educational philosophies, procedures, and discipline. Read them, and if you have questions, ask your principal or other appropriate colleagues for clarification.

Times when groups of students are moving between locations can have a high probability of problem behavior.

Students routinely use hallways, playgrounds, cafeterias, media centers, bus-loading areas, and bathrooms. There are usually school rules and procedures concerning behavior in these areas. Be clear what these are so you can discuss them with your students early in the year. Transitions, especially those requiring the class to move to another location, tend to involve more problem behavior, such as pushing and running. The class should discuss ahead of time why they should not be excessively noisy.

Every school also requires certain housekeeping or administrative tasks, such as collecting lunch counts, taking attendance, and distributing notices and school newsletters to parents. The teacher is responsible for these efforts at the classroom level and must schedule them and plan how to handle them efficiently. Your students can assume some of these responsibilities. You could appoint two-person teams, for example, to collect and record morning lunch counts and deliver them to the office, freeing you to handle other responsibilities. In Chapter 6, we discuss how other classroom tasks can involve students in their own classroom ecosystem to help develop individual responsibility and skills and to contribute to the common good of the class and school.

ARRANGING THE PHYSICAL ENVIRONMENT

A classroom's physical environment has a strong effect on student behavior.

You have considerable control over the arrangement and decor of the classroom. The size and shape, lighting, ventilation, types and numbers of desks, tables, equipment, and general condition of the room may be givens, but you still have a good deal of latitude in how you arrange them and define the classroom environment. Although you will make changes later, before your students arrive you need to decide on the arrangements that will best support your instructional goals and activities, especially at the beginning of the year.

The organization and accessibility of storage space for supplies and equipment can add or detract from efficient transitions from one activity to another. Arrangement of classroom furniture can impede or facilitate movement, so you will want to consider desirable traffic patterns.

The physical environment of a classroom has a tremendous effect on student behavior. As we stressed in Chapter 2, how you arrange your classroom will likely communicate more about your expectations than your words. Consider, for example, how rows and columns of student desks facing a teacher's desk at the front of the room communicate different expectations and encourage different kinds of interactions than clusters of four desks facing one

The physical
environment of your
classroom helps
communicate your
attitude toward
learning.
(Elizabeth Crews/
Stock Boston)

*Teachers' attention to
their classrooms'
appearance affects both
students' and teachers'
attitudes.*

another with your desk in the center of the room. The rows and columns configuration works well for large-group instruction and recitation. Since everyone is facing you, this arrangement makes it easier to teach the whole class while keeping students from talking with each other. The small clusters of student desks, on the other hand, tend to promote small, interactive group work since students are facing one another. However, this may make it more difficult for students to pay attention to you.

The physical environment of your classroom will also communicate your attitudes. Some classrooms are visually interesting and upbeat because of how the furniture is arranged and how the wall spaces, bulletin boards, and windows are decorated. Others are drab, uninviting spaces with little visual appeal. Remember Jonathan Kozol's description of the two classrooms in Chapter 1? While you must not overwhelm students with visual distractions, you do want to design an appealing and comfortable setting. If nothing else, your obvious attention to room arrangement and decor communicates to students that you care about your mutual living and learning space and that you have deliberately arranged it with them in mind. Remember, too, that *you* inhabit the classroom with your students. Its ambience and comfort will affect your attitudes and behavior as well as theirs.

Careful arrangement of the classroom also facilitates learning and minimizes disruption.

Every teacher wants to arrange the classroom to facilitate learning and minimize disruptions. Physical arrangements can promote your objectives or undermine them. For example, visual and physical accessibility are essential to student learning and classroom management. If you can't see some of your students, you may not know when they are not paying attention (or when they are paying attention to a distraction). If crowded conditions keep you from circulating to some areas of your room, you may be unable to interfere quietly with the disruptive behavior of two students without calling the entire group's attention to it.

Here are four guidelines for creating a good arrangement of the physical features of the classroom (Emmer et al., 1989):

- Avoid congestion in high traffic areas such as near doorways, the teacher's desk, pencil sharpeners, and storage areas that are regularly used. Separate high-traffic areas.

- Make sure you can easily see all of your students so you can monitor their activities and prevent disruptions and distractions.

- Arrange your regularly used teaching materials and supplies so you can get them easily and store them away as efficiently as possible without disrupting your teaching.

- Use seating arrangements that allow all students to see the chalkboard, overhead projector, video or film screens, and demonstrations on desks and tables.

Other features of the physical arrangement of your classroom that you will want to pay attention to include wall space, floor space, equipment and supply areas, and learning centers.

Wall Space

Wall space is at a premium in most classrooms and may consist of windows, chalkboards, bulletin boards, book cases, and cabinets, as well as bare surfaces. You can use these areas to support instruction by providing visual information to students. Chalkboards generally are used for temporary displays such as a daily quotation or mystery message, steps in math problems, daily assignments, or individual or group exercise practice. Bulletin boards are useful for more permanent displays. You might use bulletin boards to display information related to what you are teaching and periodically change the displays to correspond with changes in the curriculum. A bulletin board is also a place to post classroom rules, to recognize student academic work and art projects, and to highlight such things as birthdays or special student interests.

Creative use of wall space involves use of chalkboards, bulletin boards, book cases, cabinets, and bare surfaces.

Try to prepare several bulletin boards and bare wall spaces before your students arrive in order to communicate that you have put care and planning into the classroom. Although you will not have student work to display at the beginning of the school year, it is an effective use for bulletin boards and other wall space as well as a good way of recognizing exemplary or improved performance. As the school year progresses, you can involve your students more directly in planning and preparing these displays.

Floor Space

You should arrange your classroom floor space to reflect the kinds of activities that will take place and the kinds and locations of your equipment. Every classroom will have some constraints on furniture (desks, computer terminals, special equipment for children with disabilities, tables, file cabinets, book shelves, storage cabinets) and usable floor space. Some areas are rigidly defined because there are windows, doorways, electrical outlets, and sinks that are permanent fixtures.

The most important consideration in arranging floor space is accessibility for interaction and efficiency of movement.

In most classrooms there are individual desks where students spend much of the instructional time and where they store some of their books and supplies. Although you may arrange the desks in a variety of configurations, the most important consideration is accessibility during instruction. Typically at least some instruction will involve your interaction with the group as a whole. For these times, it is essential that students are able to face the instructional area where you and the chalkboard or overhead screen are located. Students should be able to see, hear, and participate comfortably in the instructional activity. Especially during individual seatwork and smaller group activities, you will want to circulate through the classroom, monitoring and providing assistance to students. As previously mentioned, it is also essential for you to be able to monitor all the students easily during group instruction and activities to determine their interest, involvement, and understanding.

Overcrowding can encourage deviant behavior, so you will want to study likely traffic patterns to determine how to arrange the furniture for accessibility and to avoid congestion. Think how students will get from their desks to group working areas, to storage areas, and to your desk. Before students arrive, arrange the furniture and then cognitively walk through the daily schedule from both your perspective and the students' to see how well the arrangement will facilitate efficient, comfortable movement and to determine the changes that will be needed each day. Of course, you will make additional changes after your students arrive.

Arrangement of floor space should be flexible to elicit different types of behavior and enhance different kinds of instructional activities.

Remember that different seating designs elicit different types of behavior. For example, face-to-face, side-by-side seating at tables and at desk clusters tends to encourage more nonverbal, verbal, and sometimes, physical interaction among students. For some instructional activities (group discussions, cooperative learning, peer tutoring), you want to encourage communication among students. For other kinds of activity, such as individual seatwork and whole-group instruction, you want to encourage students to pay attention and keep distractions at a minimum.

Where you put your desk also depends on how you plan to use it. If your desk is the place from which you provide whole-group instruction, then you need to place it where all your students can easily see it. If you plan to work with individuals and small groups at your desk, you need to ensure adequate space for you and your students to stand, sit, and move to and from their work stations and to place instructional materials on the desk. If you plan to use your desk minimally as a work area or instructional base, you can move it to a less prominent area of the classroom. Of course, you may plan to use several arrangements for different instructional and activity goals (see Figures 5.1, 5.2, and 5.3). If so, you will want to establish orderly, efficient procedures for changing those configurations. Figure 5.1 shows a traditional classroom arrangement with all of the students desks facing the front of the room. In the arrangement shown in Figure 5.2, students sit in small groups that enhance cooperative learning. In Figure 5.3, the classroom arrangement is organized around content-area interest centers.

FIGURE 5.1 Traditional Classroom Arrangement

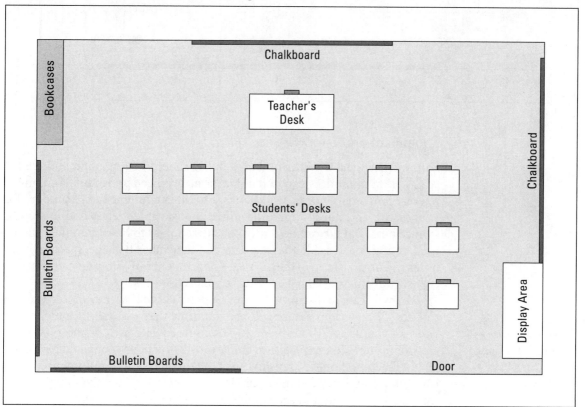

FIGURE 5.2   Small-Group Classroom Arrangement

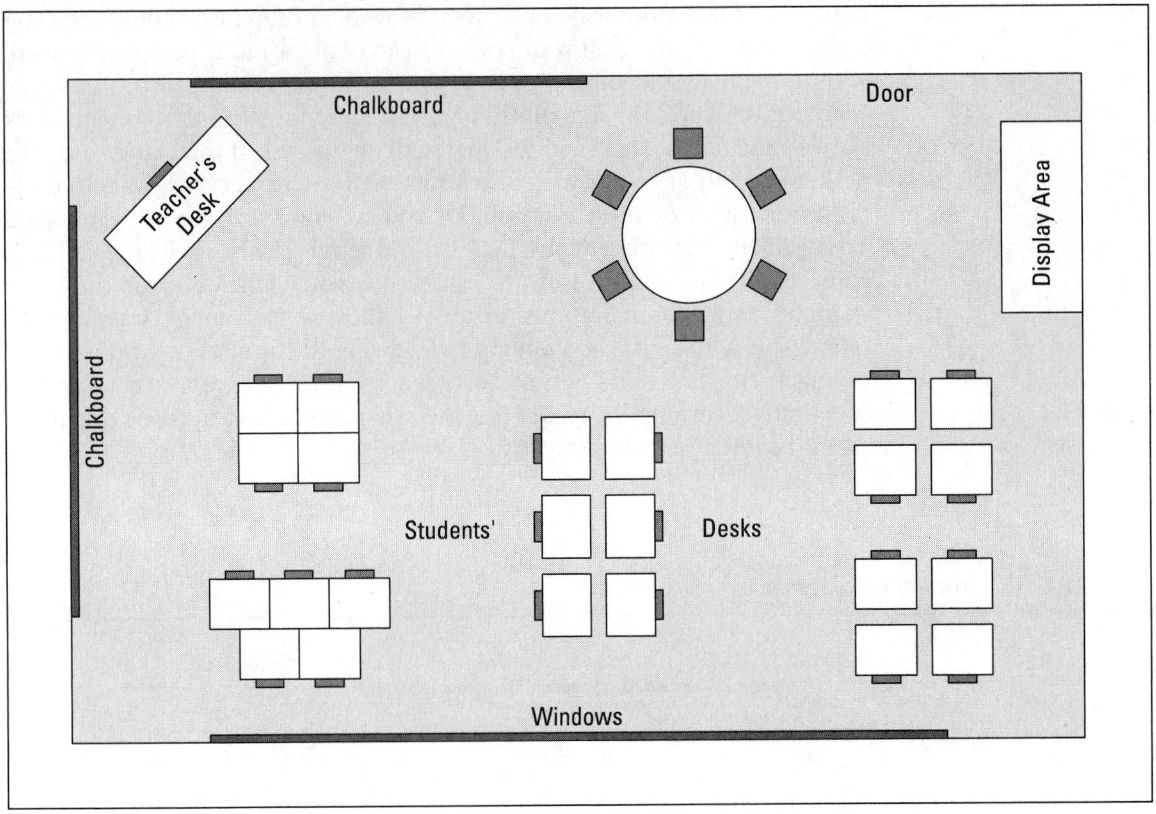

Equipment and Supply Areas

Your instructional equipment and supplies should be organized and readily accessible to minimize delay and distraction. Overhead projectors, computers, reference materials, books, workbooks, and other equipment and supplies for science, art, and music should be stored on available shelves and in closets, storage bins, and file cabinets with consideration as to how often they will be used and how accessible they need to be. Remember that the appearance of order and organization in the physical environment can communicate that you expect your students to behave in an organized way.

You will want to discuss with your students about how they should use and care for all classroom equipment the first time they use the equipment, and you can repeat the procedures at early subsequent uses. Some objects in classrooms tend to invite misuse and create distractions (Long and Newman, 1976). Teachers should be sensitive to ways that objects and equipment (props) can distract students and invite careless and destructive use. You might cover musical instruments and art supplies and communicate procedures for using equipment like computers and aquariums.

Some objects, such as musical instruments, need to be stored carefully.

FIGURE 5.3   Content-Area Interest Centers

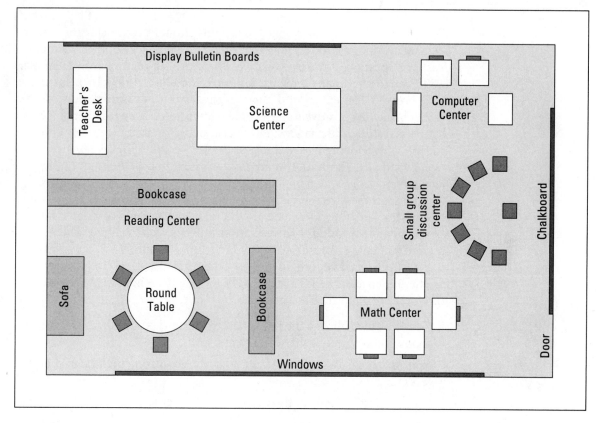

Learning Centers

Many teachers use special activity centers for individuals or small groups of students. These often include equipment such as computers, audiotape players and headphones, art supplies, science equipment, reading materials, games, or programmed materials. When you arrange these areas, be aware of visibility and accessibility and determine procedures for use and care of materials and equipment.

As we discussed earlier and as you've seen in Annie's journal, even with careful planning, there is no way for you to prevent all possible behavior problems in your classroom since not all behavior problems are the direct result of the classroom ecosystem. Nevertheless, there are a number of ways you can avoid contributing to unproductive, disruptive behavior and can create environments that minimize problems. Attention to how the physical and psychological environment communicates expectations and attitudes and influences behavior will help you avoid many problems.

Teachers can solve some behavioral problems before they start by carefully making decisions about the physical and psychological environment.

BECOMING A *WITHIT* TEACHER

We think some of the most valuable insights about effective classroom management are derived from studies at the Research and Development Center for Teacher Education at the University of Texas (Anderson, Evertson & Emmer, 1980; Evertson, Emmer, Clements, Sanford & Worsham, 1989). In their studies, they observed elementary and junior high classes to determine how specific teacher behaviors positively affect student attention and engagement in learning, reduce student deviancy and off-task behavior, and ultimately enhance student achievement. The findings of the University of Texas research team strongly support the notion that *effective instruction and effective classroom management go hand in hand.*

Although these researchers do not claim that the characteristics of more effective teachers they identified are the sole determinants of greater student achievement, they found positive relationships between specific teacher behaviors and student performance. Based on their observations and case studies of "more effective classroom managers," they identified several strategies of effective managers that are relevant to beginning the school year. For example, they found that effective teachers

- Are skilled at analyzing the important tasks of orienting students to expectations at the outset of the school year,

- Explicitly teach classroom procedures and rules during the first days and weeks,

- View the classroom from their students' perspective, and

- Closely monitor student behavior and deal with behavioral problems as they occur.

The following section elaborates ways you can make use of these characteristics.

ANALYZING AND COMMUNICATING EXPECTATIONS

It is important for teachers to have optimistic, positive expectations for students.

As we pointed out in earlier chapters, teacher expectations exert a powerful influence on student behavior. Students tend to live up to (or sometimes, unfortunately, *down to*) your expectations, so it is important to communicate optimistic, positive expectations to your students. You will communicate these behavioral expectations in several ways, including the models you provide, your verbal and nonverbal communication, the way you structure your schedule and arrange your classroom environments, and your method of establishing rules and procedures. Effective classroom managers understand developmentally appropriate behavior and are clear about how they expect their students to behave in different classroom settings and tasks.

In a typical elementary classroom a variety of subjects are taught, using different instructional strategies, grouping arrangements, and settings within and outside of the classroom. Individuals and groups of students move in and out of the room to other areas and activities in the school. In secondary schools and some middle schools it is likely that students will change classrooms and teachers every hour or period. Some behavioral expectations for students, such as treating one another with respect, may be relevant across all settings. Others, such as procedures during cooperative learning groups or for individual seatwork, may be dramatically different from activity to activity. You will have to determine what your behavioral expectations will be for each activity and how you will communicate them in each of these situations.

Teachers have to decide what their behavioral expectations are for each activity and plan how to communicate them.

DETERMINING RULES AND PROCEDURES

Classroom rules and procedures are a means of formalizing some behavioral expectations and should be discussed early in the school year. Effective classroom managers do not keep their students guessing but explicitly define expectations *with* their students. Sometimes they implicitly communicate their expectations in spoken or written guidelines—delineated rules and procedures. Sometimes they communicate their expectations non-verbally through gestures and facial expressions or implicitly by the ways they arrange their classrooms and schedule activities.

Every textbook on classroom management suggests that teachers establish rules of conduct and communicate them to students early and often. There are few classrooms that do not have their lists of rules prominently displayed—sometimes above the heads of students who blatantly ignore them. If rules are such a good idea and so often implemented, why do we still have problem behavior in schools? We think it is not just a matter of teachers telling students what they ought and ought not to do—it is an unusual student who actually thinks it is all right to hit, push, take someone else's things, or be rude and disrespectful—but a matter of making sure students understand and are committed to the rules. Simply stating the rules that were defined and written by the teacher has little effect.

The whole class—students and adults—should work together to establish rules.

Classroom rules are best devised by *all* those who have a stake in their maintenance—the teacher, students, aides, and anyone else regularly involved in the classroom. Establishing rules at the beginning of the year should be a whole-class activity, with you serving as the leader or facilitator, asking for definitions and clarifications. You can frame the rule-development process by asking students why rules are important and how they will benefit the class as a whole. Teachers who involve their students in establishing classroom rules and procedures usually find the students are concerned with fairness, equity, and consistency. Regardless of age, most students recognize that rules and procedures are necessary for groups to function smoothly.

As you discuss class rules and procedures, designated students can write them using their own words where everyone can see them. When you believe everyone is clear about the meaning and rationale of each rule, your class can vote on them. You can then post the agreed-upon rules on a wall or bulletin board. The clear advantage of involving students in determining class rules is that *they* assume responsibility for following their rules. You are not imposing and enforcing your own rules of conduct, but the group as a whole is deciding how it wants to be treated and how its members will treat one another. The process itself should reduce the need for rules. When infractions occur, you are able to say, "I thought we agreed this was important for our classroom this year. Have you changed your mind about that?" This response is clearly preferable to, "You broke my class rule. I told you not to do that."

In the early part of the school year you can periodically highlight the posted rules and discuss them. You might ask, "Are these still the rules that we need in our class? Are there others we could add that we don't have? Do we need all of these?" Rules may be added and deleted as you and your students see a need. Discussion of rules and classroom expectations is crucial to the ongoing life of the class as a whole. Students who feel no stake in the way the classroom is governed will not feel constrained to abide by the rules anyway. Time you spend on the important social skill of group governance is time you will save intervening later to change problem behavior.

During the school year, rules may be added or dropped as needed.

As students define and discuss rules, they may sometimes come up with some that you think are unnecessary, irrelevant, or even wrong, but as long as they do not promote negative behavior or cause problems, we suggest keeping student ideas in the list and letting the *students* discover their flaws. You might consider using a book like Denys Cazet's *Never spit on your shoes* (1990) to add humor as students begin thinking of rules. This delightful book (designed for younger children but enjoyable for anyone who has ever been in school) is about the first day of first grade. The class includes Raymond, who makes the suggestion 'Never spit on your shoes' when the class is discussing rules. Self-governance and management are learning experiences for students and teachers alike, and viewing them as a critical part of the total curriculum and school experience should lead to a more integrated and relevant classroom ecology. In the Classroom Closeup "Guidelines for Establishing Class Rules of Conduct" we have listed several guidelines for establishing class rules.

Procedures, like rules of conduct, let students know what is expected of them. They are routines that encourage group processes, promote efficient use of time, and reduce the uncertainty and anxiety students experience when they are unclear about what is expected of them. Just as with rules of conduct, you can let your students participate in determining classroom procedures while you provide instruction and guided practice during the first days of the school year. For each activity and transition between activities, you should consider the goals and purposes of the activity, ask students for ideas about procedures

Students can participate in developing procedures as well as rules.

Classroom Closeup

Guidelines for Establishing Class Rules of Conduct

1. Remember that the process of determining rules is as important as the rules themselves.

2. Rules should be positive statements of how students *will* behave rather than how they *will not* behave.
3. Keep the rules simple.
4. Use students' own words as much as possible.
5. Keep the number of rules small. ✱

to help the class function, establish these, and then clarify the procedures that have been determined. If the activity involves moving from one subject to another, for example, students need to know where to put their completed work, what supplies and materials they will need for the next activity, and where they should be.

You can begin establishing some procedures the first day of school. These procedures can include lining up, using the pencil sharpener, arranging desks and tables, using the bathroom and drinking fountain, and passing in the halls. You can discuss the need for the procedures the first time an activity occurs and then verbally rehearse and reinforce the procedures until they are routine. Some procedures apply to specific irregularly occurring events, such as using the school library or media center, and you can clarify these as they are scheduled. You can post some procedures, written as steps or illustrated by pictures, at appropriate locations to serve as a reference for students. The Classroom Closeup "Using the Computer" contains procedures for using the computers in an intermediate-level classroom.

You don't want more detailed routines and procedures than absolutely necessary. Schools and classrooms can easily become overregulated and regimented in the name of "orderly procedure." Discussing with your students the reasons for and history behind certain ways of doing things is a worthwhile activity. Students are more likely to adhere to routines and procedures willingly if they see their purpose and help determine them. After all, school is one of the only places in a person's life where one needs permission to go to the bathroom!

Schedules can be helpful to students by providing consistent markers about how a day, week, term, or even a year is spent.

Many teachers find it helpful during the first few days of the school year to have a poster, bulletin board, or chalkboard of the daily and weekly general schedule. At the secondary level, you can prepare a course syllabus that shows the schedule of topics, dates for assignments, projects, and tests, and other course information for longer periods—an entire term or even a year. Whether you post or print the schedule, you can refer to it as your class progresses and

Classroom Closeup

Using the Computer

Steps for Starting

1. Sign in and record your start up time on the *Computer Log.*
2. Load your disk.
3. When your disk appears on the screen, double click on it.
4. Find your file, and double click.
5. Begin your work.

Steps for Ending

1. To save your work, click on *Save* or *Save As* (add name) from the *File* menu.
2. To delete, click on the little box.
3. Click on the little box again to clear screen.
4. Go to the *File* menu. Click on *Quit.*
5. After the message shows on screen, turn off the computer.
6. Record your time on the Computer Log. ✳

your students begin to internalize the schedule. Your students' awareness of where they are in the temporal scheme adds security to their lives, and, in an era when other time markers (such as mealtimes and bedtimes) are often erratic, school times can provide consistent markers about how the day is spent. In addition to posted schedules, many teachers begin each day (or class period at the secondary level) with a brief review of the previous day (or hour), followed by an overview of the day ahead, noting any variations in the usual routines and alerting students to special occurrences (an all-school assembly, visitors).

In most classes, some students have schedules that vary from the general schedule of the group. Students may leave your classroom to participate in band, art, music, or physical education classes. They may have appointments with special education resource teachers, speech therapists, physical therapists, school psychologists, counselors, or social workers. They may be part of a compensatory reading or math program or receive English as a second language (ESL) instruction. Some of your students may regularly go to other teachers or classes for instruction in some academic areas. In addition, other students may join your class for instruction and other activities.

Given the multiple programs and support services in schools, it is a challenge to ensure everyone is where he or she needs to be, that students come and go on time, and that disruptions for other students are minimal. To help you keep track of these variations, you will need a master daily and weekly schedule. You might build this into your lesson plans or prepare it separately. Students who have regular variations in the usual schedule can post a card on a corner of their desk or in their notebook to help them keep track of their own time.

Having a master daily and weekly schedule built into lesson plans or kept separately is helpful.

MONITORING STUDENT WORK

Assessment, or monitoring students' work and evaluating their performance, is another aspect of classroom management. Teachers' evaluations provide feedback to students about their performance as well as records of that performance. In most cases, teachers provide both **summative evaluations** in the form of grades and **formative evaluations** (evidence of progress toward goals) for their students. Of course, grades are often used as evidence of student performance. Teachers usually maintain grade records in gradebooks or on computers and periodically summarize and report them to students and parents as indications of student academic performance. Grade report cards sometimes include teacher ratings of citizenship or social behavior.

Spread-sheet programs can help teachers maintain records and figure grades.

If your grades are to be valid measures of student performance, you will need to maintain careful, accurate records. Although some teachers record and calculate student grades by hand, if you have many students, this can take a good deal of time. Elementary classes typically contain twenty to thirty-five students working in several curricular areas. At the middle school and high school levels a teacher may have that many students in a single class and have five or six classes per day. In each curricular area, students produce individual and group products in the form of daily assignments, tests, and projects, generating a tremendous amount of material to evaluate and record. Fortunately, computer spread-sheet programs that simplify maintaining records and figuring grades are available. Using these programs you can assign different weightings to grades, maintain ongoing averages of student performance, and quickly tabulate term grades.

Using Authentic Assessment

Although numerical or letter grades often are used to represent student performance, they provide only indirect evidence of performance. A letter grade or percent tells us (or students and parents) nothing directly about *what* or *how* a student is learning. In place of grades, many teachers are attempting what is called **authentic assessment** (see Chapter 1 for our discussion of outcomes-based education).

Portfolios can help students learn to critically evaluate their own work and the work of others.

Some teachers find **portfolio assessment** a meaningful way to evaluate their students' work. Portfolios are collections of materials assembled over time that enable students to demonstrate their knowledge and skills. Portfolios contain representative student work that can serve both summative and formative evaluation purposes. They include the tangible evidence of students' work and can help students learn to critically evaluate their own and others' efforts. Materials may include *artifacts* (representative samples of performance or products), *reproductions* (copies of work), and *attestations* (confirmations of student performance or products by the teacher or other knowledgable witnesses). A valuable feature of portfolio assessment is involving students in the evaluation process. By documenting their learning experiences, students learn to evaluate their own work.

In *The Unschooled Mind,* Howard Gardner (1991) advocates the use of "process-folios" to "capture the steps and phases through which students pass in the course of developing a project, product, or work of art" (p. 240). The processes of learning, as much as the products, are included in process-folios. When completed, they include the student's initial brainstorming efforts, early drafts and critiques, journal entries of experiences during projects, drafts of the work, and critiques by peers, teachers, other experts, and by students themselves. More than just storage containers of completed work, process-folios can encourage ongoing dialogue between students and teachers, other students, parents, and outside experts (Gardner, 1991).

Preparing portfolios can help students learn valuable skills, but they are time consuming.

While students can learn valuable skills from portfolio preparation and portfolios may offer more meaningful assessment of student performance than grades, they have some limitations, as well. Portfolio assessment can be time-consuming since you must determine the kinds of documentation that are relevant to particular learning experiences and then teach your students to recognize and judge the quality of that evidence. Even though students are responsible for assembling and presenting their portfolios, it is likely that you will find portfolio assessment more time consuming than traditional grading. You will need to develop your portfolio system, teach your students to document and evaluate their work, oversee the process, review and evaluate materials, and provide opportunities for students to share their portfolios with others. In addition, you may need to spend time teaching students, parents, and even colleagues about this kind of assessment. You may also need to translate portfolio evidence into grades, when they are required by your school.

Despite these qualifications, the portfolio-assessment process can be well worth the time for both you and the student. It forces you both to critically examine and understand the goals and objectives of learning experiences and to establish standards of performance. As a beginning teacher you may want to use portfolio assessment for projects in areas where it seems most meaningful, adding it to other areas as your time and energy permit.

SEEING THE CLASSROOM AND SCHOOL FROM THE STUDENT'S PERSPECTIVE

Effective classroom managers are able to predict aspects of the school and classroom environment and procedures that might confuse their students. Before students arrive, we suggest that you put yourself in your students' shoes. Try sitting in several student desks in different locations of the room, placing yourself at approximately the height level of the students in your classes. Check for sight lines, distracting visual blocks, or potential trouble spots, such as a desk that is too close to the hamster cage or one that directly faces a window

Sitting in students' desks can help teachers see potential trouble spots.

to the playground. Spend some time putting yourself in your students' places— "Does this room look friendly, inviting, exciting, interesting, a place I would want to spend time? Is the lighting as clear as possible, is the teacher's desk accessible, are traffic patterns as open as they can be, especially if students with disabilities are a part of the class?" These considerations should help you prepare a welcoming, barrier-free environment that promotes rather than inhibits behavior conducive to learning.

MONITORING STUDENT BEHAVIOR AND DEALING WITH PROBLEMS

Despite your careful planning, preparation, determination, and communication of your expectations in classroom rules and procedures, student (mis)behavior that interferes with their own and others' learning and with your instructional goals will sometimes occur. Effective teachers are effective monitors of their students' behavior, are aware of misbehavior, and quickly deal with problems as they occur (Evertson et al., 1989). In the rest of this chapter we elaborate on the importance of your awareness of individual behavior and preventative management approaches.

There are, fortunately, use of specific actions that you can take to minimize the detrimental effects of such misbehavior. More than twenty-five years ago Jacob Kounin (1970) and his colleagues studied effective group management techniques across a variety of classroom settings. Kounin's analyses of filmed observations of student-teacher interactions during group recitation and individual seatwork revealed several distinct teacher behaviors that produce a high rate of student work involvement and low rates of deviancy as well as some teacher behaviors that actually encourage distraction and deviancy. Kounin named these effective and ineffective classroom communication and management techniques

- Withitness,
- Overlapping,
- Smoothness,
- Momentum and slowdowns,
- Maintaining group focus, and
- Avoiding satiation with variety and challenging activities.

Each group management technique involves a type of teacher behavior that prevents or minimizes off-task and disruptive student behavior—particularly those that may escalate or become contagious and spread to other students.

WITHITNESS

Mild behavior problems such as daydreaming and giggling can grow into more serious problems.

Withitness means being aware of what is going on in your class *and* communicating to students that you are aware. Withitness is what is sometimes referred to as having eyes in the back of your head. Too often a teacher does not notice or intervene to stop a relatively mild problem behavior (e.g., daydreaming, whispering, giggling, working on the wrong page) until it escalates into a more serious problem, directly or indirectly involving other students.

Sometimes teachers make *timing* mistakes. For example, two students may start whispering, but the teacher may not attempt to stop the behavior until several others join them. Or the teacher does not notice that a student inadvertently started working on the wrong page of an assignment until the student has fallen far behind the rest of the group. In each of these cases, a minor annoyance has grown or has spread to more students, making it more difficult to deal with.

Teachers can use body language to nip potential behavior problems in the bud.

Sometimes deviancy increases in seriousness before a teacher attempts to correct it. For example, one student may whisper to a second student, who laughs and pokes him and is, in turn, poked back. Then both students giggle, push, and poke each other, attracting the attention of students around them before the teacher intervenes. As a *withit* teacher, you would be aware of the potential distraction of the initial whispering and giggling and nip it in the bud before it became a crisis that endangered the participants and distracted the others in the class. For example, you could move closer to the offending students, catch their eyes when they glance toward you, and signal your awareness and disapproval of their behavior by simply shaking your head.

OVERLAPPING

Overlapping refers to a teacher's ability to deal with more than one activity at a time. Do you remember the discussion in Chapter 1 of classrooms as *multidimensional* environments where many activities occur simultaneously? Teachers who are effective overlappers communicate their attention to simultaneous activities by talking and using nonverbal signals and simple looks. For example, you may be working with a reading group while you simultaneously monitor and redirect the attention of some other students doing individual seatwork. You try to do this without being distracted from your reading group or allowing them to be distracted:

> The teacher is working with a reading group and Mary is reading aloud. John and Richard, sitting in the seatwork region, are talking loudly. The teacher looks at John and Richard and at almost the same time says, "Mary, continue reading, I'm listening," then says, "John and Richard, I can hear you talk. Now turn around and do your seatwork." (Kounin, 1970, p. 83)

Another form of overlapping involves the handling of *bring-ins.* For example, you are working with the above group, and another student, Josh, who is working independently, approaches and asks a question. You glance briefly at Josh but continue listening to the group member who is reading. After a few seconds, you quietly tell him, "Wait a minute," and return to listening to the oral reading until you can efficiently answer his question. Depending on established procedures in your class, other options for dealing with the interruption are to direct Josh verbally ("Josh, go back to your desk until I can help you") or nonverbally (shake your head at Josh and point back toward his desk or glance at him while using a wait hand gesture and continuing to attend to the oral reading). Or you may place a hand on Josh's shoulder, indicating you acknowledge his presence, but he needs to wait until you can speak with him. In each of these examples, you acknowledge the interrupting student but do not allow the ongoing activity to be disrupted.

Ineffective Overlapping

Ineffective overlapping occurs when a teacher is distracted by the behaviors of individual students, as when the teacher hears John and Richard talking and abruptly leaves the reading group to deal with it, or stops the oral reading and loudly tells the boys to stop talking and get back to work, or is totally immersed in the reading activity and is apparently unaware that the boys are off task. Overlapping may sound impossible to do at first, but as you and your students get to know one another, routines are established, and you develop relatively unobtrusive signal systems, it becomes more manageable.

SMOOTHNESS

There are group management techniques that reflect how teachers can smoothly initiate, sustain, and terminate activities (Kounin, 1970). As you remember from earlier discussions, there are many changes in individual and group activities in a classroom each day, sometimes even within a class each hour. This is a feature of classroom life that can overwhelm inexperienced (and even some experienced) teachers. Some changes require students to move from one area of the classroom to another, in and out of the classroom, or to and from other areas of the school. Others involve movement from one type of activity to another. Effective classroom managers ensure that these changes occur as smoothly as possible and that a proper amount of momentum is maintained. You can achieve **smoothness** in managing these transitions by avoiding *jerkiness, flip-flopping,* and *stimulus boundedness*—teacher behaviors that distract students from involvement in learning activities (Kounin, 1970).

Jerkiness is characterized by abrupt changes from one activity to the next. For example, a teacher may be working with a small group while other students are working independently at their desks. When a member of the reading group finishes reading, the teacher says, "Good job, Maria. You may all return to your desks." Then, without pausing, the teacher instructs the entire class, "Everyone take out your math books and turn to page 85." A smoother way of handling this transition would be to alert students ahead of time about the approaching transition ("You should be finishing your assignments in the next five minutes before we move on to math").

Abrupt interruptions of a group activity will prevent smoothness.

Jerkiness is also characterized by *thrusts*—a teacher's abrupt interruptions of a group activity by interjecting a statement, an instruction, or a question, without regard for the students' readiness for it (Kounin, 1970). For example, during a teacher-led class discussion of a story, when students are raising their hands to answer content questions, the teacher remembers a change in the afternoon schedule and abruptly says, "Oh, we won't be going to the library today until 2:15. OK, Jayne, what happened after the hurricane?" No doubt neither Jayne nor the other students will be able to readily shift attention from discussion of hurricanes to the library and back to hurricanes.

Another form of jerkiness is *dangles,* which involve directing student attention to an activity but then leaving them dangling. For example, students may be checking their answers to a math assignment by reading their answers in sequence. The teacher calls on Robert, saying, "Robert, your turn," but before he responds, asks, "Does anyone know if the volleyballs were returned to the gym after recess?" A *truncation* is an extended dangle where the learning activity is never resumed. For example, the teacher who has left Robert dangling might become focused on the volleyball situation, continuing, "Leah and Jean, will you go check with Ms. Tyler to see if the volleyballs are in the gym? Class, we have to remember to return everything we use. How do you think we can remember better?" While procedures for handling gym equipment may be needed, the teacher's interruption distracts students from their math studies and will make it difficult to reorient. The volleyball issue should be discussed at a more appropriate time.

Flip-Flopping

Flip-flops occur when a teacher starts students on one activity and then interferes with their pursuing it by introducing distractions. For example, after instructing the class to turn to page 85 in their math books and beginning an explanation of the exercise, the teacher might say, "Oh, everyone should pass their corrected homework to the front of the room," or "How many of you brought back those questionnaires about the open house we sent home yesterday?" These kinds of flip-flops distract and disrupt students.

Stimulus Boundedness

A teacher who is *stimulus bound* is easily distracted from the relevant learning activity and thus distracts the students as well. For instance, during a group art project, a teacher finds a backpack on the floor and asks, "Whose backpack is this? Where are we supposed to keep our backpacks? If we leave things like this in the aisle someone is going to trip over it."

Each of these examples of teachers interfering with student concentration may seem like exaggerated illustrations of poor teaching practice. Still, you have probably had similar situations in your own schooling. The point is that it is not only other students but sometimes even teachers themselves who interrupt, confuse, and distract students. When this happens, student involvement in the learning activities is undermined. When students are distracted and sense that their teacher is confused and disorganized, they tend to feel confused and disorganized themselves, which makes it harder to bring them back on-task. This is why we think it is important to be aware of these poor teaching behaviors and try to avoid them.

Even experienced teachers need to avoid interrupting, confusing, and distracting their students.

MOMENTUM

Another general category of teacher behavior, **momentum,** refers to the pacing of group activities. Effective classroom managers are careful to move neither too quickly nor too slowly through an activity and to be aware of student behavior that indicates the pace is appropriate (Kounin, 1970). Maintaining group movement is easiest to see in its absence. Two ways teachers can impede group momentum are *overdwelling* and *group fragmentation.*

Teachers can learn to recognize student behavior that indicates whether the pace is too fast or too slow.

Overdwelling

Overdwelling means giving more attention to a behavior or incident than is necessary. For example, when a teacher provides excessively detailed or redundant directions or preaches or nags students beyond what is needed to make the point, the teacher is overdwelling. To avoid interfering with the momentum of your group, keep your instructions as simple as possible (Kounin, 1970).

Group Fragmentation

Group fragmentation can also hinder group momentum. An example of group fragmentation is providing the same directions several times to individual students rather than once to the group as a whole. For example, instead of saying, "Everyone in computer group 3 may now go to the computer center," a teacher might say, "Carlos, you may move to the computer center. Henri, you may go to the computer center. Ellen, you may move to the computer center."

GROUP FOCUS

Two ways teachers can maintain group focus on instruction are group alerting and accountability (Kounin, 1970). **Group alerting** means the degree to which you are able to involve nonparticipating students in group tasks and maintain their attention. Teachers can have both positive and negative effects on group alerting, as you can see in the Classroom Closeup "Group Alerting to Help Students Participate." There are times, of course, when you may decide to use one of these techniques—for instance, students who are afraid of speaking in front of the class may do better if they know ahead of time that they will be called on to answer a certain question. Students with learning disabilities that involve difficulty processing oral questions may be reassured if they know when and what they will have to respond to.

Accountability means making students responsible for their performance. Some ways you can ensure student accountability are asking them to have their seatwork available for you to see while you circulate through the group, having students recite in unison, and asking for a show of hands of those who are ready before beginning a task.

VARIETY AND CHALLENGE

Repetitive tasks are likely to result in students' becoming bored or exhausted.

Effective group managers ensure that their students do not become *satiated* by an activity (Kounin, 1970). That is, they sustain their students' interest and motivation to participate by minimizing boring repetitive tasks. Too often students are assigned worksheets or exercises that require many more repeti-

---

Classroom Closeup

Group Alerting to Help Students Participate

Positive methods of group alerting provide cues that
- Create suspense before selecting a reciter ("All right, I'd like to see who knows . . ."),
- Keep students in suspense by calling on students randomly,
- Intersperse individual responses with verbal and nonverbal group responses ("Raise your hands if you think . . ."),
- Alert nonparticipators that they could be called on ("I haven't heard from some of you, so you should all be ready when I call on you"), and

- Include novel, enticing material (high-attention-value props).

Negative group-alerting cues tend to reduce group involvement and should be avoided. They include:
- Changing the focus of teacher attention from the group to an individual, so that other students are ignored,
- Selecting a reciter before asking the question, so other students know they are not accountable, and
- Having students recite or participate in a predetermined sequence, such as calling on students in alphabetical order or moving sequentially up and down the rows, so that some students need not pay attention before or after their turns. ✳

tions than are necessary for mastery of the skill. Certainly, some repetitive practice is necessary for students to learn to perform some skills automatically (e.g., math computations), but redundant practice can lead to satiation. Many of us have looked forward to Thanksgiving dinner with its roast turkey and trimmings. The dinner is delicious (although we may eat too much). In the following days there are plenty of leftovers, which are at first appealing, then just OK, and after several days, barely palatable. Even initially attractive experiences can become mundane or even unattractive as they are repeated.

Even interesting activities and experiences can become dull if repeated too often.

As we noted in Chapter 4, students are most engaged in learning when they experience a high level of success in moderately challenging tasks. Remember that nonchallenging exercises repeated *ad nauseum* bore students and can generate distaste for the activity itself. Students may think, "I hate math," when what they really hate is the unchallenging, repetitious computation.

Unfortunately, students' feelings about boring activities often generalize to the teacher who requires them. Not only do they see the task, activity, or subject as boring, but they also see the teacher as boring. When satiated and bored, some students look for opportunities to break the monotony in more interesting, stimulating activities. It should be no surprise that some of these activities take the form of distractions and disruptions that might have been avoided.

If students see certain tasks as boring, they may start to see the teacher as boring too.

You can decrease the likelihood your students will become satiated when you employ a *variety* of activities and classroom processes. Areas to consider include variations in the following:

- *Content* or *subject matter;*
- *Types of activity:* seatwork, group recitation, cooperative groups, peer tutoring, computer use, independent reading, scientific experiments;
- *Types of presentations:* demonstrating, reading aloud, quizzing, leading singing, circulating, checking work;
- *Use of materials and props:* pencils, paper, books, maps, charts, overhead transparencies, poster displays;
- *Group configuration:* entire class, subgroups, individuals;
- *Student roles:* passive or active listening, reciting aloud (individually or as part of group), doing an activity as a group, determining their own pace, selecting activities from a menu, working on group projects.

Generally, you can increase your students' motivation when you communicate your own enthusiasm, involvement, and curiosity about the activity. You can *challenge* students by showing genuine enthusiasm, by making statements about the attractiveness of an activity ("I think this is one of the more exciting points"), or indicating that it will be challenging ("This next question is *really* tricky, so be very careful!").

When teachers are not interested or even communicate that topics or activities will *not* be interesting, students are not apt to be interested either.

If teachers communicate that tasks are dull and boring, those expectations are likely to be fulfilled.

Consider, for instance, how you would respond to these teacher comments: "Now, I know it's hard to make U.S. history very interesting for most students," or, "My students in the past have always hated this term paper assignment, but they have learned a lot from it." If your teacher made these comments, would they pique your interest in U.S. history or make you eager to get started on the term paper? Unlikely. Expectations are often fulfilled.

The way you present learning activities helps frame your students' expectations. How could you reframe the statements above to stimulate, rather than stifle, student interest and enthusiasm? You might say something like, "The history of our country is fascinating; there are so many interesting stories and events that can help you understand how we have become the people and the country we are today," and "In the past my students have thought the term paper assignment was really challenging; they learned a lot about doing research and writing, and they became experts on their topic."

Of course, even the most enthusiastic teachers may not stimulate interest in every student. And most teachers have trouble mustering much enthusiasm themselves about certain topics and actitivies in their curriculum. Some topics and activities are simply not as intrinsically appealing as others. Still, when you frame learning activities in a positive way, when you try to communicate what is interesting and challenging about them, and when you display your own interest and enthusiasm, your students will more likely become engaged themselves.

As We See It: *The Authors Talk*

Bob: I think this issue of teacher enthusiasm is really critical—but I know everyone can't be completely enthusiastic and motivated about every subject every day . . .

Mary Kay: True. But maybe people can learn to *pretend* to be enthusiastic. I think a lot of good teaching is acting. Teachers are on stage every day and the audience comes to know them well—so they have to be very good.

Bob: You mean teachers should fake interest in their topics? That doesn't sound like very good advice.

Mary Kay: Not fake it—but cultivate those signs of enthusiasm, like relating personal experiences or stories connected with the topic or doing unexpected things to demonstrate a concept or point.

Bob: You mean like the day Mr. Baker demonstrated the concept of tool use to his sixth-grade class by putting a marble in his nose, then removing the marble by pushing on the side of his nose with a pencil?

Mary Kay: Yes. Or the science teacher who finished a discussion of terminal velocity by telling the kids about an air show he attended where someone's parachute didn't open . . . or Robin Williams reciting "O Captain, My Captain" standing on his desk in the movie, *Dead Poet's Society.*

Bob: Showing enthusiasm needn't mean jumping up and down and getting wildly excited. Presenting information in a new way can show enthusiasm too.

Mary Kay: We probably shouldn't recommend that marble business, although it was certainly memorable. . . .

SUMMARY AND REVIEW

In this chapter we have examined a number of ways you can prevent student behavior problems in your classroom while maintaining student engagement and focus on instructional tasks. Most of the approaches do not directly address problem behavior, but they do lay the foundation for conditions that will reduce the chances that problems will occur.

Of course, even with good planning, a thoughtfully arranged physical environment, careful communication, established and monitored rules and procedures, withitness, and enthusiasm, you will not prevent every problem. In the next chapter we begin to look at approaches to help you deal with group and individual behavior problems when they do occur.

REFLECTING ON CHAPTER 5

Annie's principal seems to see her as a withit and caring teacher. That may have something to do with the school and environment in which Annie is teaching. The principal's report provided here is more complete than those done in many schools, but it is the sort of document that can be of real help to a beginning teacher.

- What aspects of the report indicate Annie's withitness?
- How does Annie appear to have set up her classroom so that it is welcoming and does not cause behavior problems?
- What else could Annie do to create a useful environment?
- Talk with your classmates about teachers you have had in the past or that you have now that you consider motivating. What do they do to keep your interest? Are their styles similar or are they different? Can you adapt some of their characteristics for your own teaching?

Key Terms

assessment (p. 171)   overlapping (p. 174)
summative evaluation (p. 171)   smoothness (p. 175)

formative evaluation (p. 171) momentum (p. 177)
authentic assessment (p. 171) group alerting (p. 177)
portfolio assessment (p. 171) accountability (p. 178)
withitness (p. 174)

Building Your Own Knowledge Base

Emmer, E. T. et al. (1989). *Classroom management for secondary teachers* (2nd ed.). Englewood Cliffs, NJ: Prentice-Hall; Evertson, C. et al. (1989). *Classroom management for elementary teachers* (2nd ed.). Englewood Cliffs, NJ: Prentice-Hall. These two books are valuable resources that suggest ways teachers can arrange their classrooms, develop rules and procedures, organize and manage instruction, and deal with many other aspects of classroom management.

Kounin, J. (1970). *Discipline and group management in classrooms.* New York: Holt, Rinehart & Winston. Kounin provides descriptions and examples of specific teacher behaviors, like *withitness* and *maintaining smoothness and momentum* that increase student involvement in learning and decrease deviant behavior.

Ohanian, S. (1994). *Who's in charge? A teacher speaks her mind.* Portsmouth, NH: Heinemann. A compilation of thoughtful and challenging essays on a variety of topics, written by an accomplished teacher, who argues that the key to classroom management is engaging students in meaningful learning.

References

Anderson, L., Evertson, C., & Emmer, E. (1980). Dimensions in classroom management derived from recent research. *Journal of Curriculum Studies, 12,* 343–346.

Cazet, D. (1990). *Never spit on your shoes.* New York: Orchard Books.

Emmer, E. T., Evertson, C. M., Sanford, J. P., Clements, B. S., & Worsham, M. E. (1989). *Classroom management for secondary teachers* (2d ed.). Englewood Cliffs, NJ: Prentice-Hall.

Evertson, C., & Emmer, E. (1982). Effective management at the beginning of the school year in junior high classes. *Journal of Educational Psychology, 74,* 485–498.

Evertson, C. M., Emmer, E. T., Clements, B. S., Sanford, J. P., & Worsham, M. E. (1989). *Classroom management for elementary teachers* (2nd ed.). Englewood Cliffs, NJ: Prentice-Hall.

Gardner, H. (1991). *The unschooled mind: How children think and how schools should teach.* New York: Basic Books.

Kounin, J. (1970). *Discipline and group management in classrooms.* New York: Holt, Rinehart & Winston.

Long, N. J., & Newman, R. G. (1976). Managing surface behavior of children in school. In N. J. Long, W. C. Morse & R. G. Newman (Eds.), *Conflict in the classroom: The education of children with problems* (3rd ed.). Belmont, CA: Wadsworth.

Ohanian, S. (1994). *Who's in charge? A teacher speaks her mind.* Portsmouth, NH: Heinemann.

Managing Individual and Group Behavior

Part Three, Managing Individual and Group Behavior, *presents specific strategies for dealing effectively with behavior problems that occur despite the approaches discussed in earlier chapters.*

Chapter 6, **Dealing with Problem Behavior,** *discusses relatively straightforward techniques for interfering with surface behaviors—common and mild forms of disturbing and distracting student behavior. Chapters 7 and 8 discuss interventions for handling more persistent and pronounced problem behavior.*

Chapter 7, **Intervening with Individuals,** *describes strategies for dealing with problem behavior in individual students, including individual contingency management, contracting, mediation essays, self-management, counseling, and time-out. Chapter 7 also suggests procedures for handling crisis situations like fights or arguments.*

Chapter 8, **Intervening with Groups,** *focuses on interventions to improve the behavior of your entire class or subgroups within it, including class meetings, affective education approaches, group contingency management, token economies, and social skills training.*

Choices for Dealing
with Behavior Problems

• Permitting
• Tolerating
• Interfering
• Preventing
• Modifying physical
  arrangements
• Regrouping

Dealing with
Problem
Behavior

Ecological Analysis
of Behavior Problems

• Cost/benefit
  considerations in
  interventions

Chapter 6

Dealing with Problem Behavior

Annie's Journal

JANUARY: A new year . . . a new beginning? Do I need a new beginning? I'm half way through my first year and where have I gotten so far? OK— first of all, survival. I'm still here. I know some people who haven't made it this far, even in my own school. A teacher who started with me—Tracy— taught sixth grade and didn't make it past November. I feel kind of bad about that. I mean, I didn't really do anything to help her. She seemed really distant and I never got to know her. She didn't come to any of the new-teacher events the district put on . . . never joined in the Friday afternoon gluttony sessions that Frank and Jan and Charlotte and I sometimes indulge in. I didn't even see her at any of the inservice presentations. I heard she just walked into Dr. Wright's office and quit one day. So anyway, I guess that's a point in my favor: I'm still here!

I got my midyear report in December, just before break. Great timing. At first I was really upset—my class is *not* too noisy—it's *active learning*— but the more I read it, the better I felt (about some things). I'm glad she likes my literature and social studies planning—and I guess I have to admit that my spelling activities *are* a bit repetitive (there I go, relying on my own fourth-grade experience). I'm really upset about the Danny and Tremaine section. The *last* thing I want to do is convene a meeting and stand up in front of all those successful teachers and support people and say, "Um, I'm, like, this new teacher? and, um, I, like, can't deal with two ten-year-old boys in my class? and I was, um, wondering what I should do?" Great. A real professional moment for me. Perhaps I should arrange to have it videotaped. I'm getting sidetracked, though (Danny and Tremaine do have a tendency to do that to me). My purpose here was to list the things I feel good about so far and the things that I want to work on for the rest of this year.

Good things first (I'm no dummy). (1) I'm still here. (2) I like being here (most of the time). (3) The room looks great—good visual environment, lots of student-made stuff on the walls, a fairly good organizational pattern. (4) I feel creative and fairly confident in my literature and social studies teaching. (5) I know at least *something* about each of my kids. (6) I've gotten a lot of help from Gloria (the ESL teacher), and I'm increasing my skills in working with Lupe and Rafael. (7) Carla is accomplishing more work than she was. She still talks all the time, but sometimes I can interfere with her chatter with just a look. (That's progress, isn't it? I mean, I was just telling her to be quiet about eighty-four times a day.) (8) Matt, who seemed to be basically uninterested in what I had to teach, is now writing stories almost every day. (9) Renita has stopped crying every recess—or at least reduced it to about once a week. (10) Marion Partridge, the third-grade teacher across the hall who hasn't spoken to me yet when she didn't *have* to, actually smiled a little before she slammed her door closed yesterday (it was probably a facial tic, but I'm searching here). All in all, a fair record of success.

OK. Now for the need to section. I had ten good things, so I can't have more than ten bad ones . . . otherwise I'd be here all night. Why is it always so much easier to find things that need changing than things that are going well? I need to remember that as I think about the kids. I wonder if I say as many positive things as negative or neutral ones. . . . I should count sometime. Here are the things I need to do. (1) Be more creative and interesting in spelling assignments. (2) Find more nonpaper and pencil ways to work in math. (3) Spend more time in the teacher's lounge. (That sounds funny, but I often eat lunch at my desk to catch up on things, and I think it's making me look antisocial—shades of Tracy.) (4) Find more time for Lee—she alternates between boisterous acting out and real sadness—and figure out what's going on. (5) Do something about the Rolandria-Tamica twosome. I was so glad to have Rolandria (just moved here this year) find a friend that I didn't notice until right before break how they seemed to be excluding everyone else—whispering, talking all the time, giggling at other people's expense, not attending as much as they should. (6) Do something about Aaron's daydreaming. He doesn't get started on assignments until everyone else is about halfway through. (7) Find *something* that interests Justin. (8) Pack Danny and Tremaine in a large cardboard box and ship them to Pittsburgh (just kidding). (9) Have more contact with the parents. (10) Lose ten pounds (my annual resolution). OK. Not such an impossible list. I could probably even accomplish most of those things by May (except number ten). I feel better just writing them down. I think perhaps I'll have the kids do this on Monday—make a list of things they feel they have accomplished this year and another list of things they'd like to do by May. Should be interesting.

✱ What techniques do you think Annie has used to accomplish her
successes?

✱ What suggestions would you give a new teacher for trying to work with
Lee? Rolandria and Tamica? Aaron? Justin? Danny and Tremaine?
Marion Partridge?

✱ Make some notes of your ideas before you read the chapter and compare them to your thoughts after you read it.

CHOICES FOR DEALING WITH BEHAVIOR PROBLEMS

To be an effective classroom manager, is it enough to be a *withit* teacher? Is it
sufficient that you understand the ecological nature of classrooms, communicate effectively with your students, appreciate their individual and group
differences, practice sound instructional approaches, and skillfully prevent
problems? We believe that although these kinds of understandings and skills
are necessary for successful classroom management, they are rarely sufficient.
(No doubt you guessed we had more to say about classroom management,
since you have read only half the book.)

Even experienced, master teachers encounter behavior that interferes with
the smooth functioning of their classroom ecosystems. In any group there is
the possibility (or, more likely, the probability) of disruptions and distractions.
In most cases they are relatively minor, passing disturbances that involve
limited numbers of students. However, as we mentioned in Chapter 5, if
teachers don't deal with them effectively, even minor disturbances can develop
into more serious, chronic problems. Disruptions and distractions may quickly
involve and affect more students and become more difficult to change. Your
immediate goals for dealing with minor behavior problems should be to limit
contagion and **escalation,** to interfere with the spread of problems from one
or a few students to others (contagion), and to prevent minor problems from
developing into major ones (escalation) that are more resistant to change.

When you are confronted with student behavior that does not match
established expectations, you actually have several choices. Sometimes modifying the physical environment of a classroom, like making distracting materials less available or rearranging groups of students, can reduce undesirable
behavior. At other times, something else is needed. Imagine, for example, the
ways you might respond to the scenario described in the Classroom Closeup
"Raymond's Distractibility."

If you were Mr. Nigro, you could respond to Raymond's behavior in a
number of ways, and you would have to decide how supportive, directive, or
intrusive you should be. You might consider your choices along a continuum
from less intrusive to more intrusive responses—from permitting, to tolerat-

Classroom Closeup

Raymond's Distractibility

Raymond is a student in Mr. Nigro's second period, eighth grade, general science class. He is a bundle of energy and activity, squirming at his desk, sitting first on one leg and then the other, drumming on his desk with his pencil or fingers. His desk is a mess, with frayed and crumpled papers stuck in his books and spilling out of his backpack onto the floor. He is fairly attentive when Mr. Nigro is teaching the whole class. He seems interested, participates, and eagerly volunteers answers to Mr. Nigro's questions. Sometimes he seems too eager, as he vigorously waves his hand, calls Mr. Nigro's name, and blurts out answers to questions.

Each day, Mr. Nigro allots some time for students to work on their assignments. He uses this time to correct student work, to pre-pare for his next class, and to help students who come to his desk for help with their work. Most of the students finish their homework assignments during this time and may read, relax, or visit quietly with one another for the few minutes remaining in the period. Raymond, however, rarely finishes his work in class or at home. Instead, during this time he leans far out of his desk whispering to other students, looking around the room trying to catch other students' attention, and making faces at them. He sometimes leaves his seat, ostensibly either to help or get help from other students on his assignment. This usually involves some giggling and even good-natured scuffling. Mr. Nigro's impression is that Raymond is actually talking about something other than the assignment, wasting time, and distracting other students. ✳

ing, to preventing, to interfering (see Figure 6.1). Part of your responsibilty as a problem solver is to choose the intervention approach that best fits the behavior problem you are facing.

PERMITTING

As we suggested in Chapter 5, clearly establishing expectations for academic performance, social behavior, and classroom procedures can often produce beneficial long-term outcomes. Often, however, teachers, parents, and other adults are quick to tell children what they should *not* do but fail to tell them what they *should* do. When a student like Raymond fails to meet his teacher's behavioral expectations, his behavior is not necessarily a willful act of defiance; he may simply be uncertain about Mr. Nigro's expectations.

You need to be sure your students know what you expect, both positively and negatively. Although most of your students may seem to implicitly understand your expectations, others, like Raymond, may be uncertain. For these students, you will need to explicitly communicate your expectations about

Your students need to be clear about your expectations.

FIGURE 6.1   Intervention Continuum

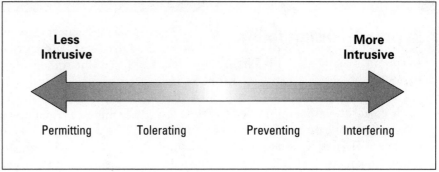

what is acceptable and what is not. For example, Mr. Nigro could tell Raymond, "You must stay at your desk and talk only with permission until you have finished your work. After you both finish your assignments, you may quietly visit with John." By permitting Raymond to visit with his friend once work has been completed, Mr. Nigro is clearly showing him how to achieve his goal of interacting during class.

TOLERATING

There are some types of behavior that you may decide are best tolerated or ignored. You are aware of them, but you deliberately decide to do nothing to change them. In other words, you may tolerate behavior that reflects a student's developmental level or behavior that is symptomatic of an illness or disorder. This does not mean that you endorse the behavior, but you recognize that it is either unreasonable to expect the behavior to change or not worth the effort. For example, you might have a student who obsessively chews on her fingernails. Although her nail biting bothers you, it does not seem to disturb other students or interfere with the student's performance, involvement, or peer acceptance. You know that this kind of habitual, self-stimulating behavior would be difficult for you to change, and it is not significantly interfering with the student's life or others' lives, so you decide your best course is to tolerate it.

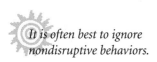
It is often best to ignore nondisruptive behaviors.

Given different kinds of information about the same type of behavior, however, you might decide that you cannot simply tolerate nail biting, but must do something about it. For example, if your student's fingers are bleeding and other students express their dislike for the behavior and avoid interacting with her, you might decide the behavior should not be tolerated. In this case, you might talk with the student's parents, perhaps involving your school nurse, to develop a plan to change the troubling behavior.

Some disturbing behaviors, like sniffling, coughing, and throat clearing, are due to physical ailments like colds or allergies. These kinds disturbances go with the classroom ecosystem. Fortunately, they usually pass. Although there is little you can do to change them, you can alleviate them by, for example, having tissues available and asking students to cover their mouths when they cough or sneeze.

You may have students with disabilities who behave in unfamiliar ways in your classroom.

As more students with behavioral, mental, and physical disabilities are educated in regular classrooms, it is likely that you will have some students who behave in ways that are symptomatic of their disorders. As you recall from Chapter 3, students with autism often engage in ritualized (or stereotypic) movements like hand-flapping or finger-flicking and echolalic speech, and students with Tourette's disorder engage in motor and vocal tics. With appropriate kinds of support and accomodations, some students with conditions like autism and Tourette's disorder may be able to function in your classroom, even though their unfamiliar and unusual behavior may distract and disturb others.

If you have students who exhibit behavior patterns that are symptomatic of behavioral, cognitive, or physical disorders, it is likely they are beyond their (and *your*) control. In most cases, these behaviors do not directly affect other students, although they may initially attract attention because they are unfamiliar and unusual. To lessen your students' fears and reactions to disability-related behaviors in new students, you should prepare them by describing the kinds of behavior they will likely see and asking for their understanding and tolerance. In most cases, even when the behavior is unfamiliar and bizarre, your other students will become accustomed to it and not be distracted or disturbed by it. Of course, the model you provide will influence your students' understanding and acceptance.

In our earlier scenario, Mr. Nigro might consider tolerating Raymond's behavior. Raymond's constant shifting around in his desk, disorganization and messiness, attention-seeking from peers, and distractibility may be somewhat extreme, but not unusual for a thirteen-year-old boy. If his behavior is pronounced and occurs across settings, he may have an attention deficit disorder. However, Raymond's behavior does not seem too distracting to other students or to Mr. Nigro. As long as his movement is generally contained to his personal space and his messiness does not spill over into other areas, his teacher may decide not to attempt to modify them at this time. Instead, Mr. Nigro could look for any evidence of self-control, order, and neatness and quietly offer Raymond support and encouragement for any improvement that he shows.

PREVENTING

In the last chapter we emphasized how your attention to classroom rules and procedures, arrangement of the physical environment, and consistency could help prevent behavior problems. Students are very influenced by your *withit-*

How teachers behave can keep misbehavior from spreading.

ness, overlapping, maintaining smoothness and momentum, and *seatwork variety and challenge.* These behaviors also minimize **contagion,** the spread of deviant behavior thoughout the group.

The importance of minimizing contagion is well established (Kounin, 1970). Teacher reactions to student misbehavior produce ripple effects throughout a classroom, affecting not only the misbehaving students but also the observing students (Kounin, 1970). There are three types of **admonishments** teachers can use to get students to cease their misbehavior: *clarity, firmness,* and *roughness.*

Clarity, Firmness, and Roughness

Three teacher tactics for stopping misbehavior are clarity, firmness, and roughness.

Clarity involves naming the misbehaving student ("Gloria . . ."), specifying the misbehavior ("I hear you humming . . ."), and explaining why it is unacceptable ("and it's really distracting us"). **Firmness** communicates that you will not tolerate the behavior ("Franklin and Wesley, you may not run in the hallway"), and **roughness** contains threats or punishment ("Michael, you have lost five minutes of recess for leaving your group").

Clarity benefits the students who are watching.

Firmness benefits only misbehaving students.

Roughness upsets other students.

Although all three types of teacher admonishments may stop the misbehavior of participating students, clarity benefits observing students. Clarifying admonishments tend to increase conformity by *other* students. Firmness, however, tends to affect the behavior of only those students who are misbehaving. The most aversive form of teacher admonishment, roughness, actually has the least beneficial effect on other students' behavior, and it tends to upset them.

If you wish to stop misbehavior *and* minimize contagion within the group, your most fruitful approach will be to use the three steps of clarifying:

1. Name the misbehaver,

2. Specify the misbehavior, and

3. State why it is unacceptable.

Try to avoid making the clarification seem like a condemnation of the student: "Gloria, your ear-splitting, off-key humming is giving me a headache!" Instead, simply identify the misbehavior and explain as objectively as possible why it unacceptable. In reference to the scenario involving Raymond, Mr. Nigro could use a clarifying admonition. For example, he might state, "Raymond, you're out of your seat. You are not getting your work done, and you're not letting John finish his, either. You need to stay in your seat."

INTERFERING

Permitting, tolerating, and preventing are legitimate approaches for dealing with minor behavior problems. However, you must sometimes deal with

Sometimes teachers need to intervene directly when a student misbehaves.

student behavior that demands more direct interference. Sometimes the behavior is too disruptive and distracting to other students; sometimes the participants are missing important learning opportunities; or sometimes the behavior is threatening, dangerous, or destructive.

Fortunately, there are some relatively straightforward methods you can use to handle misbehavior. No doubt teachers have used interfering techniques since they have taught groups of students. Professionals have written about these techniques, recognized as some of the most effective and efficient methods of managing student misbehavior, for the last forty years. (See, for example, Redl & Wineman, 1952; Redl & Wattenberg, 1959; Jones & Jones, 1990; Long & Newman, 1976; Rizzo & Zabel, 1988; and Walker & Shea, 1991.)

Surface behaviors are forms of classroom misbehavior.

Redl and Wineman called their methods "techniques for the antiseptic manipulation of surface behavior." **Surface behaviors** are distracting and disruptive forms of classroom behavior, such as talking out, not paying attention, not getting started, misusing equipment and materials, disregarding classroom rules and procedures, and arguing. Although you might not initially consider these behaviors severe problems, they tend to develop into more complex problems (escalation) that involve more students (contagion) if you do not interfere with them.

Antiseptic manipulations are teacher techniques to stop misbehavior and keep it from spreading.

Antiseptic manipulation means that the techniques are intended to interfere with the problem behaviors while minimizing their spread. The techniques help keep the entire group moving along smoothly but are not intended as long-term solutions for serious and chronic behavioral and emotional disorders.

The appeal of these techniques is that you can readily learn and use them in a wide variety of situations. They are simple, common-sense strategies that do not require extensive training or planning yet are among the most effective behavior-management strategies you can use. The techniques for interfering with surface behavior fall into three categories: **planned ignoring, nonverbal interference,** and **communicating and building relationships** (see Table 6.1).

Planned Ignoring

Planning not to pay attention to a problem behavior is called **extinction.**

Planned ignoring, sometimes called **extinction,** is deliberately not responding to problem behavior. As we noted in our discussion of operant learning and social learning theories in Chapter 3, much human behavior can be characterized as attention-seeking. In one way or another, most of us want other people to pay attention to us. In a classroom, students seek attention and status from their teachers and classmates through academic achievement, leadership and social skills, and conformity. They may measure their success by the approval they receive (or the disapproval they avoid) from teachers and peers. Although students generally seek positive attention, some may have either failed to get this approval for appropriate behavior or received more attention and status from misbehavior.

TABLE 6.1
Techniques for
Interfering with
Behavior Problems in
Your Classroom
Ecosystem

INTERFERING TECHNIQUE	WHAT IT IS	WHEN YOU MIGHT USE IT
Planned ignoring	Deliberately not responding to problem behavior	When a student is seeking attention for behavior that you disapprove of
Nonverbal interfering	Discouraging problem behavior with • Signal interference (facial expressions, eye contact, gestures) • Proximity control (moving closer to a student) • Touch control (gently calming a student or redirecting him or her with touch)	When planned ignoring has not interfered with problem behaviors
Communicating and building relationships	Using humor Providing extra affection Helping students overcome hurdles Helping students interpret experiences Building common interests	Almost all of the time in your classroom ecosystem; especially helpful in defusing tension and in engaging and motivating students

Negative attention can sometimes reinforce misbehavior.

One of the interesting features of social reinforcement is that it does not always take the form of approval. Even behavior that elicits disapproval may be attention-seeking. (A friend of ours calls these "teacher-torture behaviors": humming, tapping pencils, tipping desks.) For example, one of your students belches loudly and her classmates respond with laughter and comments. You, too, may respond with a scowl or verbal reprimand ("Please mind your manners"). Despite your disapproval, you may have helped reinforce the behavior. By reacting to the student's belching, you run the risk of calling even more attention to it and possibly starting an argument that leads to a power struggle. Given the reaction of her peers, your student already has them on her side. Unless this is a persistent behavior that is significantly disturbing other students, you may decide not to respond, since any reaction may unintentionally reinforce the behavior.

In some situations, the teacher must intervene.

Although there are some situations for which a teacher's planned ignoring is appropriate, it does not work as well for other behaviors and situations. For example, ignoring students who are daydreaming, sleeping, or actively chatting is unlikely to diminish those behaviors since they are sustained by reinforcement from other sources. Nor can you ignore behavior that is dangerous, threatening, and disruptive or that is likely to escalate and spread. Also, some students will try harder to get your attention when you ignore them. They may repeat the behavior or engage in it more vigorously until it is no longer possible for you to ignore it. Another limitation of planned ignoring is that despite your efforts to ignore the behavior, other students may support it or try it themselves when they see peer reactions to their classmate's behavior.

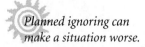

Planned ignoring can make a situation worse.

Planned ignoring sometimes actually exacerbates a problem. You may, in effect, teach students that you respond to their behavior only when it occurs repeatedly or is especially pronounced. Or you may reinforce the behavior by only occasionally responding to it.

Generally, planned ignoring is effective when you are confident that others in the classroom environment will also ignore the behavior. In some cases, you can enlist your other students' cooperation and even provide incentives for their efforts to ignore another student's troubling behavior.

Nonverbal Interference with Misbehavior

If planned ignoring is not sufficient to interfere with problem behaviors, there are several nonverbal approaches to consider. **Signal interference, proximity control,** and **touch control** are three forms of nonverbal teacher behavior that subtly communicate your awareness of misbehavior and interfere with it without calling attention to it.

You can make a gesture to stop misbehavior without interrupting class activity.

Signal Interference. You can use forms of nonverbal communication like facial expressions, eye contact, and gestures to communicate that a certain behavior is unacceptable. You may "give the evil eye," point briefly, or shake your head or finger toward a student to communicate that you are aware and disapprove. These don't interrupt the flow of an activity or call attention to the problem behavior. For example, most of your students are working quietly at their desks, but one student's rocking movements are making an annoying squeaking noise. Instead of calling her name, you try to catch her eye and silently mouth, "Shh." By not drawing more attention to the disturbing behavior, you interfere with it without introducing more disruption.

If a student engages frequently in an annoying behavior, you may need to talk quietly with the student to arrange a signal system that will help him or her manage the behavior. You might say something like, "I know you probably aren't aware of it, but it is really distracting when you hum while we're trying to work. What if I look at you and pull my ear when I hear you starting to hum? That will be our sign that you need to stop humming." This technique will, of course, ensure that the student will try out the system several times the first day or so, but by providing the attention the student needs without making it a negative or hostile situation, you may avoid more problems later.

Moving near students can stop some misbehavior.

Proximity Control. One of the most effective interfering techniques you can use is proximity control. This technique simply involves moving closer to students to reduce their distraction or to interrupt their misbehavior. Simply standing next to some students seems to have a calming effect. Many teachers find that frequently circulating through their rooms, monitoring student behavior and performance, and redirecting students when necessary are effective ways to interfere with potentially troublesome behavior and keep students engaged.

Signal interference will quickly become a part of your behavioral repertoire.

(Junebug Clark/ Photo Researchers)

Proximity control can be subtle and usually does not call other students' attention to deviant behavior. Of course, proximity control does not always require that *you* move. Arranging where students sit and who they sit with are forms of proximity control. For instance, you might place students who are more distractible closer to you and independent learners further away. Be careful about moving performing students to a place where the class can see them more easily, though, since this provides an even larger audience. The key to containing some misbehavior is to determine the student's goal and interfere with it. If a student's goal seems to be drawing attention to himself or herself and away from the relevant activities, try to place the student where that is difficult to achieve, where you can readily monitor the behavior, and where the class can't easily see him or her.

You should always be aware of the influence of your proximity on student behavior and position yourself in strategic locations. For example, experienced teachers recognize the importance of standing in or near the doorway as students come and go. Transitions that involve group movement and crowding are times when arguments, scuffling, shoving, and pushing are more likely to occur. These events are usually accidental, although some students deliberately find opportunities for misbehaving during these times. Your presence can inhibit these collisions as well as smooth transitions from one activity or place to another.

Standing near trouble spots can help students behave better.

We're not suggesting that you use your physical presence like a prison guard, sternly overseeing every student movement in order to quickly stifle any difficulties. Rather, your verbal and nonverbal contact should subtly communicate expectations for positive behavior. Teachers who seem anchored to a desk or who stay in limited areas of the room communicate their insecurity, and when students sense their teacher is insecure they will be too.

Proximity control and signal interference would probably interfere with the behavior of a student like Raymond, whom we described earlier (see the Closeup box "Raymond's Distractibilty"). Raymond doesn't seem to be seeking attention from his classmates or his teacher. Mr. Nigro could move Raymond closer to his own desk or position himself closer to Raymond. As his students work independently, Mr. Nigro may need to circulate, monitoring Raymond and his other students. In addition, he could nonverbally communicate with Raymond—using eye contact, a head shake, or a scowl—when Raymond appears to be about to leave his desk or to talk with other students.

Touch Control. You can sometimes use touch control with proximity to calm a student by placing your hand on the student's shoulder. In some cases, you may redirect a student to another area by placing your hands on the student's shoulders and guiding him or her in the right direction. For example, if a student interrupts you while you are working with another student, you might gently turn the student around and direct him or her back to his or her desk.

Teachers must be very careful in touching students.

There are many reasons why touch control must be used with caution. Some students are uncomfortable being touched by an adult and may misinterpret the teacher's intentions. Students who are already angry or frustrated may interpret your hand on their shoulder as an attempt to restrain or punish. They may flinch, respond verbally, or push your hand away. Some students have experienced physical or sexual abuse and are understandably sensitive about adults touching them. There are also cultural variations in students' comfort with being touched by a teacher. It is essential to be sensitive to the verbal and nonverbal cues students provide about receptivity to being touched. If you sense they are at all uncomfortable or you feel uncomfortable, this is a clear signal that touch control is inappropriate.

*Teachers should **never** hurt students.*

Under *no* circumstances should teachers touch students in ways that cause physical discomfort (e.g., grabbing, shaking, pinching, or hitting). Not only are these *physically aversive* techniques professionally and ethically (and often legally) unacceptable, they also produce highly undesirable responses on the part of students and teachers alike. Instead of calming the student, corporal punishments intensify strong emotions. They can also communicate to both the recipient and students who witness the event that the teacher is out of control and has inadequately dealt with the situation. Physically aversive responses also provide an undesirable model of self-control and conflict resolution. They communicate that might makes right, hardly a lesson you want your students to learn.

You may sometimes need to physically restrain a student.

Occasionally, you may encounter a situation where *physical restraint* seems to be your only recourse, such as in a rapidly escalating fight in which students are hurting one another or when a student who seems out of control is destroying property. Fortunately, these situations are rare in most classrooms. The likelihood of your needing to deal with student fighting or property destruction depends on many factors, including prevailing attitudes and behavior patterns in the neighborhood and school environments. We believe that the approaches you are learning in this book will enable you to prevent and interfere with most behavior problems before they reach crisis proportions.

Teachers should not use physical restraint unless they have to.

Although there are techniques of physical restraint that emphasize non-punitive, nondamaging restraint coupled with verbal deescalation strategies, physical restraint *always* entails some risk of injury to you and to the restrained students. Even with training, teachers should physically restrain individuals only as a last resort in crisis situations to stop a physical assault, self injury, or damage to valuable property or equipment. If such a crisis situation does develop, you should follow procedures discussed in "Handling Crisis Situations" (Chapter 7).

As We See It: *The Authors Talk*

Bob: The use of physical restraint is an issue I'm becoming concerned about.

Mary Kay: You mean physical punishment or physically restraining a student?

Bob: Physical punishment has no place in schools, and I don't think many people are arguing for it, but many districts have become interested in physical restraint programs. Some districts have even considered having all of their teachers trained in these procedures, not just the ones working with violent or unusually aggressive kids.

Mary Kay: And you don't think that's a good idea? It seems logical that if teachers know how to use physical restraint appropriately, there will be less damage.

Bob: That may be true for some schools, but what concerns me is that once you've been trained to do something, you're more likely to use it. So if we train large numbers of teachers to use physical restraint and we don't provide training about how to keep kids from ever *needing* physical restraint, we'll have people turning to intrusive intervention even more often. This may cause violent behavior to escalate even more.

Mary Kay: It may also give people a false sense of security. Using physical restraint techniques should be a last resort—and particularly with large, violent, or armed students, a teacher could get hurt. I guess we need to be sure that these techniques are only a small part of a teacher's repertoire of interventions.

Bob: It may also be important for us to examine why we are even considering such interventions in school. Twenty years ago, we would have laughed at the notion that teachers needed such skills, but we're not laughing now.

Mary Kay: Doesn't make you too optimistic about the next twenty years, does it?

Communicating and Building Relationships

We consider the surface management techniques that strengthen communication and build relationships between teachers and students very important. These techniques include using *humor*, providing extra *affection*, helping students *overcome hurdles*, helping them *interpret experiences*, and *building common interests*.

Using Humor to Strengthen Communciation. You can often defuse (or decontaminate) tense situations with humor. In events that you and your students might otherwise find threatening, your sense of humor communicates simultaneously control and comfort to students who are distressed and to students who are observing the interchange. One caveat to using humor, however, is that it should never come at a student's expense. Sarcasm and putdowns may relieve group tension, but they also diminish a student's self-esteem and status. A student who is the target of a teacher's joke often tries to save face by retaliating with putdowns and sarcasm directed back at the teacher. Also, teachers should avoid using humor when it is inappropriate. Some situations are simply not very funny, and you will not want to treat them lightly.

Humor can calm and comfort upset students.

As we noted in Chapter 2, humor helps communicate your humanness to students and helps build rapport and an atmosphere of solidarity in your classroom. It shows that you enjoy interacting with your students and that you can share good times. Humor not only lightens tension, but motivates and engages students. The scene described by Tracy Kidder in the Closeup box "Using Humor to Engage and Motivate Students" illustrates how teacher Chris Zajak used humor to bring her math class out of the doldrums.

Humor can also help motivate students.

Using Hypodermic Affection. Due to events that happen outside of the school or beyond your classroom, you will have students come to class depressed, tired, anxious, or angry. Troubles at home or with the peer group may weigh heavily on a child's feelings and behavior. Although you may not know the

Classroom Closeup

Using Humor to Engage and Motivate Students

It was a Wednesday morning, the dead middle of a week in late fall. . . . The day was overcast. Jimmy's skin looked gray under fluorescent light. He lay with his head down on his desk, shifting his stick-like forearms around under his cheek as if rearranging a pillow. The usually high-spirited Manny gazed open-mouthed toward the window. Felipe had slid halfway down the back of his chair and scowled at his lap. "You can't make me do it. I'm not going to do anything unless you give me more attention," Felipe seemed to be saying to her. . . . Robert was dismantling another pen. Soon he'd have ink all over his hands and his pants. . . . Horace was trying to do his homework now, by copying from Margaret's. At least he seemed awake. Jorge's eyes were shut, literally shut. He had told his homeroom teacher, who had told the story in the Teachers' Room, that he'd get even by not doing any work this year, and she couldn't make him, because his mother didn't care. . . .

Chris had seen progress in this group. They would start long division fairly soon. But today even the well-behaved ones, such as Margaret, looked sleepy. . . .

Chris considered telling them she couldn't teach *celery,* but the eyes that were open and looking at her seemed to say that they didn't want to hear it all from her again. . . . They did not want to hear that Mrs. Zajac couldn't drill holes in their heads and pour in information, that they had to help, which meant, first of all, paying attention. Jimmy yawned. He didn't even bother to cover his mouth. . . . She'd try something different. An old trick might work.

Chris turned and wrote on the board:

$$296$$
$$\underline{x78}$$

"All right, Jimmy, you go to the board."

Jimmy rose slowly, twisting his mouth. He slouched up to the green board and stared at the problem.

Chris sat down in Jimmy's seat. "I want you to pretend you're the teacher, and you're going to show me how to multiply, and I don't know how." So saying, and in one abandoned movement, Chris collapsed on Jimmy's desk, one cheek landing flat on the pale brown plastic top and her arms hanging lifelessly over the sides.

A child giggled.

"Gonna get my attention first, Jimmy?" called Mrs. Zajac.

Several children giggled. Jorge's eyes opened, and he grinned. All around the little room, heads lifted. Chris's mouth sagged open. Her tongue protruded. Her head lay on the desk top. Up at the board, Jimmy made a low, monotonic sound, which was his laugh.

Abruptly, Chris sat up. "Okay, Jimmy," she called. "I'm awake now. What do I do first? Seven times six is. . . ."

Jimmy was shaking his head.

"No? Why can't I multiply seven times six first?" she said and she pouted.

There was a little more light in the room now. It came from smiles. The top group had all lifted their eyes from their papers. Judith smiled at Mrs. Zajac from across the room.

Jimmy got through the first step, and Chris turned around in Jimmy's chair and said to Manny, "You're next. You're a teacher, too."

"*Diablo!*" Manny looked up toward the ceiling.

Chris climbed into Manny's seat as he sauntered to the board.

"I'm gonna give you a hard time, like you give me," Chris called at Manny's back. She looked around at the other children. They were all looking at her. "When you sit in this seat, see, you've got to sit like this." She let her shoulders and her jaw droop, and she stared at the window.

"Look out in space!" declared Felipe.

"Look out in space," she agreed.

The clock over the closets jumped and rested, jumped and rested. The smell of pencil shavings was thick in the air. Giggles came from all sides.

"Boy, do I have a lot of friends helping me out! Now who wants to teach Mrs. Zajac?"

"Me!" cried most of the class in unison.

Crying "No!" and "No way!" at Chris's wrong answers and "Yes!" when the child at the board corrected her and she turned to the others to ask if the correction was right, the low group found their way to the end of the problem. Arising from the last child's chair she had occupied, her black hair slightly infused with the new redness in her cheeks, her skirt rustling, she turned back into Mrs. Zajac. "Okay, thank you. Now that I know how to do it, I hope you know how to do it. I'm going to put examples on the board," she said. "You are going to work on them." (Kidder, 1989, pp. 41–44) ✳

source of the problem and often have no means of directly helping the student resolve it, you can be sensitive to your students' nonverbal cues and provide **hypodermic affection** to lessen their negative feelings and draw them back into your class. This kind of response isn't always easy since students' strong feelings tend to discourage involvement. *Hypodermic affection* is extra attention, such as a smile, a pat on the shoulder, a wink, kind words, or verbal acknowledgment of a child's feelings ("You look a little down today," "Let's see a smile," "Do you want to talk later?"). It communicates your awareness of and concern about the students' feelings. Knowing that you are aware of their discouragement or distraction and that you are concerned often enables a student to feel better and, at least temporarily, to refocus on relevant classroom activity.

Letting students know that you are aware of their troubles can encourage them.

Unfortunately, communication of emotions or affect seems to be missing in many classrooms. Based on observations in more than a thousand classrooms, John Goodlad (1984) reported that "affect—either positive or negative—was virtually absent. What we observed could only be described as neutral, or perhaps 'flat' " (p. 467). As we saw in Chapter 2, expression of feelings is fundamental to classroom communication. Like using humor, letting your students know that you care about them and like them helps build rapport and gain your students' trust. When you reduce the social distance between you and your students and communicate caring and concern (as in Kidder's description of the math class), you let your students know you are sensitive to their needs. They, in turn, will more likely respond to yours.

Letting students know you care about them helps them trust you.

Helping students start a task can encourage them to complete it.

Helping Overcome Hurdles.   Sometimes students need an extra boost to get them started on an activity or assignment. You can offer help getting over a hurdle or obstacle in a number of ways, such as briefly reviewing the procedures or steps for some task ("Remember how we did this regrouping yesterday? First, we . . .") or making sure a student is on the right page, has the necessary materials, or can complete the first problem. Your help at the outset of an activity will often provide sufficient impetus for a reluctant student to become engaged in the activity. When you help students complete the first problem or two, you not only provide a model to follow that will lessen their chances of becoming frustrated, but you also reduce the possibility that you will have to help them catch up later.

Teachers can help students avoid misunderstandings by explaining what happened.

Helping Interpret Experiences.   You can sometimes avoid potential crises by interpretating a student's experience. Small disputes among students can escalate into larger conflicts when the participants misunderstand a sequence of events or mistake the intentions of one another. In these cases, you can be the trusted individual who offers an objective evaluation of what has happened, an interpretation that corrects student misinterpretations. The Classroom Closeup "Interpretation as Interference" contains an example.

Classroom Closeup

Interpretation as Interference

Two sixth-grade students, Kip and Jonathan, have clashing personalities. Although they have been in the same class together for the past two years, they do not get along well. Kip is big, athletic, and self-confident, but he often teases and makes fun of Jonathan, who is small, as well as somewhat immature and anxious. When Jonathan thinks Kip is picking on him, he whines and complains loudly to their teacher, Mrs. Larrison. This history of mutual dislike and distrust colors all of their interactions: Kip easily adopts the role of persecutor, and Jonathan assumes the role of helpless victim.

Mrs. Larrison recognizes the animosity between the two boys and attempts to defuse it. She has talked with them, both together and individually, and Kip is beginning to lessen his verbal attacks on Jonathan.

One day, as students are coming into the room and taking off their coats and gloves, Kip has trouble pulling his arm from his coat sleeve. He jerks his arm, which pops out of his sleeve, bumping into Jonathan's back. Jonathan, who is holding in one hand a terrarium he has made as a class project, loses his balance and drops the terrarium, which crashes to the floor. Mrs. Larrison immediately intercedes between Kip and Jonathan, she assures Jonathan that Kip's bumping was an accident and that she will make sure he can build another terrarium. She asks Kip to join her in helping Jonathan clean up the mess and to salvage as much of the terrarium's contents as possible. ✳

Teachers help build trusting relationships with their students when they share their interests.

Building Common Interests. There are many ways to build positive relationships with your students simply by expressing interest in them. Fostering common interests includes noting accomplishments ("I hear you hit a home run at recess today," "You're keeping your desk very neat these days"), remarking positively about changes in physical appearance ("Your haircut looks great!" or "Those new glasses are really classy"), or sharing a student's interests in hobbies, pets, musical groups, athletic teams, and so on. When you deliberately try to learn about your students' lives and interests and communicate your interest, you will build mutually trusting relationships.

Sometimes even inconspicuous teacher behavior has a substantial impact on student-teacher relationships. The Classroom Closeup "Winning Friends and Influencing Students" describes how one teacher builds relationships with his students.

Looking at students, smiling, and using their names show that you like them.

The key ingredients for communicating effectively and building trusting relationships with students are making eye contact, smiling, using students' names, and quietly exchanging everyday pleasantries (Nichols, 1992). These

Classroom Closeup

Winning Friends and Influencing Students

Years ago, I taught in a program staffed by our children's psychiatric hospital and operated in a public junior high school. Our students registered typical complaints about the boringness or hardness or unfairness of various mainstream teachers, but one teacher escaped their criticism, the science teacher, Mr. Moeller. They thought he was great. When I looked at the homework they brought from his class, it did not appear to be especially stimulating nor geared to their individual learning abilities, nor did the students express any strong interest in the particular science they were studying. New to that school, I guessed that Mr. Moeller might be especially good-looking, young, with-it, but when I identified who he was I saw him to be middle-aged, balding, neither fit looking nor a snappy dresser. I pressed

my questions, got a lot more "I don't know . . . he's just nice" answers, but finally this description: "Well, whenever I go by him in the hall between classes, he always says, 'Hi, Nick,'" so I checked the scene between classes. The rule in that school was that teachers were to be in their doorways between bells, watching students pass. A walk down the halls revealed teachers standing in pairs or alone, arms crossed, faces watchful, true standard bearers of the need for quiet and order in the halls. Mr. Moeller, by contrast, relaxed against his doorjamb and said such things as "Hi" or "How's it going?" or he nodded, or he just smiled. As time went on and I spent more time in classes, I never discovered anything more remarkably charismatic or reinforcing about Mr. Moeller than that he was relaxed, looked at kids when they talked, smiled easily, used their names frequently, and spoke pleasantly. (Nichols, 1992, p. 5) ✳

kinds of behavior communicate involvement, caring, and liking. They also model social skills you would like your students to use with one another.

MODIFYING PHYSICAL ARRANGEMENTS

In Chapter 5, we stressed the importance of arranging the physical environment of your classroom to promote efficiency and reduce distraction. Three forms of handling surface behavior—limiting space and tools, **regrouping,** and **antiseptic bouncing**—refer to ways you can adjust the classroom environment to reduce problem behavior.

Limiting Space and Tools

Some items, like weapons, toys, and food, are not allowed or are restricted in school.

Teachers need to be aware of the seductive properties of some objects found in classrooms. Some students have difficulty controlling their impulses and seem to be always getting into things. Inappropriate use of space and tools can escalate into more serious behavior management problems. Some objects seem to invite student distraction from learning activities or can even be hazardous. School and class rules usually prohibit contraband, or objects that are potentially dangerous (knives, slingshots), illegal (guns, drugs), or highly distracting (toys, sports equipment, food). Other rules may restrict student access to them under prescribed conditions. For example, if you have a general rule forbidding toys or candy in the classroom, they could be put in a secure drawer and returned as the student leaves for the day.

Students sometimes misuse ordinary classroom objects like rulers or musical instruments.

Students sometimes misuse materials and equipment that have legitimate uses in instruction and other activities. Scissors, art supplies, musical instruments, aquariums, gerbil cages (and gerbils), sports and playground equipment, and nearly any other kind of object or material found in a classroom might be used inappropriately. However, some things seem to stimulate more creative uses than others. For instance, your students may need rulers to take measurements for a science experiment, but some may discover that the rulers also make excellent foils for fencing matches.

It is usually wise to consider the ways objects might be inappropriately used by your students. You may want to restrict access to some that you think are most likely to be misused and make sure they are put away when they are not needed. For especially fragile and costly equipment, such as computers, audiovisual instruments, class pets and plants, and individual and group projects, you can establish procedures for use and handling. As we suggested in Chapter 4, students are most responsive to rules and procedures when they participate in determining them. Students then have a clear understanding of the benefit of rules and procedures and are stakeholders in them.

Students should not be allowed to go into each other's desks or lockers.

Generally, we think it is a good policy to make students' desks and lockers off-limits to other students. Given the minimal opportunities for privacy in most classrooms, students should have some personal space. Students are more apt to argue over whose pencil or paper it is if they share supplies. Also, some students rely on using others' materials instead of bringing and taking care of their own. Rather than allowing a lot of borrowing among students, you may make available materials like pencils and paper, that students regularly use. If necessary, you can devise a self-monitoring system, such as placing a name card in a box next to the supplies, to keep track of articles as students check out and return them.

We recommend always keeping your valuable personal property, such as jewelry, money, and credit cards, in a secure place. You can lock items like a purse, billfold, and keys in a desk or file drawer to avoid the risk of theft. If students bring money or other valuable possessions to school, you will probably want to put those in a safe place until they are needed or the student is leaving. It is easier to take simple precautions than to deal with the consequences of lost possessions and feelings of broken trust that result from a missing possession.

Teachers should lock up their valuables.

Teachers should put students' valuables in a safe place.

Regrouping

In Chapter 4 we stressed how seating and grouping arrangements also affect behavior. You may have students who like sitting next to one another but who also like to talk, pass notes, or otherwise interact in ways that distract them and other students. Sometimes physical proximity creates opportunities for teasing or other kinds of mutual aggravation. Teachers sometimes persist with a seating arrangement, attempting to suppress the disruption, when the troubling situation could be handled by regrouping.

Regrouping can involve simply rearranging seating or changing the makeup of a group—physically relocating students by moving them apart from one another (or perhaps closer to you) to reduce their opportunities for disturbing interactions. Sometimes a particular mix of students stimulates misbehavior. Alone or with others they behave appropriately, but together there is a synergistic effect: the students seem to set one another off, acting silly, teasing, arguing. You can remove them from a contagion-prone group and place them in a different group where they are surrounded by students who are less likely to be affected. As we mentioned earlier, when you plan group activities, you should always consider the compatibility and volatility of different group constellations.

Teachers can move students who are disruptive together apart or into other groups.

Antiseptic Bouncing

Another form of regrouping is called *antiseptic bouncing.* There are several situations where you may want to *bounce* (remove) a student *antiseptically* (nonpunitively) from a group or activity. When the group threatens, intimidates, or scapegoats an individual student, when a student is instigating a group commotion, or when a student is being drawn into the contagion of the group, you can bounce the student. You might move the student to another area of

Sometimes a teacher may remove a student from a group or activity without punishing him or her.

your classroom or assign a classroom chore that will remove the student from a bad situation. For example, your student Henri shows signs of frustration while doing some math problems. He is scowling, shuffling his feet, crumpling his paper, and angrily talking to himself. You offer help, but he's not ready to accept it. You decide that he could benefit by a short break, so you ask him to deliver a note to the secretary in the school office. Your note simply says, "Henri needs to cool down. Please keep him in the office for three or four minutes and then send him back with a note to me." Not only do you give Henri a break from frustration, but he is able to perform a service that builds his self-esteem.

ECOLOGICAL ANALYSIS OF PROBLEM BEHAVIOR

We wish we could say that these techniques for managing surface behavior will *always* effectively interfere with *every* problem behavior you may encounter. We have found that these straightforward, efficient methods often can prevent problems from growing and spreading. However, no single technique for handling surface behaviors will work all the time and with every problem behavior. Based on the characteristics of each situation, you will always have to judge which techniques are likely to succeed.

Sometimes the techniques we described in this chapter are not enough to help a problem behavior.

Some students will resist your efforts to interfere and redirect them. In some cases, the persistence and severity of problem behaviors will demand more intensive interventions than the techniques for antiseptic manipulation. The following chapters focus on interventions directed at changing more pronounced and chronic behavior problems. When your preparation, prevention, interference, and other efforts are insufficient to modify troublesome behavior, you will need to consider other strategies.

An ecological behavior analysis can help you understand troublesome behavior.

The first step in this process is to study the behavior in the context in which it occurs. We have frequently referred to two themes in our approach to creative classroom management: the *classroom as an ecosystem* and the *teacher as problem solver*. These themes are combined in an **ecological behavior analysis,** a procedure that can help you identify key information about causes, contributors, and possible solutions. An ecological analysis helps you study a troubling behavior by answering a series of questions, similar to those a reporter asks when writing a news story. First you describe the problem behavior, and then you answer the following questions:

- Where does it occur?
- When does it occur?
- How often does it occur?
- Under what conditions does it occur?
- How does it affect other aspects of the classroom and school environment?

The Classroom Closeup "Ecological Analysis of Classroom Problem Behavior" contains an example of the kinds of information that you could uncover using this approach.

An ecological analysis can help you decide whether and how to intervene in a troubling student behavior.

An ecological analysis not only helps you learn more about the behavior and its relationship to the classroom ecosystem, but it also can help you develop a rationale for intervening. It helps you determine whether the behavior might benefit from a change in your expectations and whether it might respond to modifications in the classroom ecosystem. It can also give you clues as to whether you will need a fairly simple or more intensive intervention plan and whether you will need assistance from others.

COST-BENEFIT CONSIDERATIONS IN INTERVENTIONS

The costs and benefits of interventions can vary greatly.

An ecological analysis can reveal problems that involve your entire class, certain subgroups within the class, or individual students that require more concentrated, deliberate interventions. Even with this information, your course of action is not always clear. There may be several possible solutions that are dictated partly by the information you obtain from the ecological analysis and partly by evaluating the costs and benefits of various interventions. Some interventions are relatively low cost; they entail relatively little time and effort, additional resources, and assistance. However, some interventions make more demands on student time and effort and interfere with your normal classroom procedure. Not only do the costs of interventions vary, but so do the benefits or probable desirable outcomes to students, the program, and you. Some interventions offer the likelihood of only negligible change, while others may result in substantial change.

A teacher must consider whether a particular intervention is worth its cost.

Experienced classroom teachers weigh the relative costs and benefits of the interventions they use to deal with student behavior problems (Wood, 1991). Teachers deliberately choose the intensity and intrusiveness of interventions that match the challenges of a specific type of problem. Teacher tolerance for problem behavior depends partly on the type of behavior. Teachers generally have less tolerance with acting out and aggressive, defiant behavior than for socially immature or physically disturbing forms of behavior.

Effective classroom management involves coordinating a variety of intervention strategies, which can be categorized into four general groups: *communication, support, teaching,* and *control interventions* (Wood, 1991):

- *Communication interventions* establish tasks and expectations for class members and clarify rewards and penalties for behavior. Delineating classroom expectations, rules, and procedures fits in this category.

- *Support interventions* encourage desirable or appropriate behavior and build a sense of well-being. Teacher attention, use of cooperative groups, peer tutoring, and fun activities are supportive strategies.

Classroom Closeup

Ecological Analysis of Classroom Problem Behavior

Student: Jason   Teacher: Ms. Johnson
Time: 4th period   Activity: Freshman English

What is the problem behavior?

Jason has trouble keeping his hands off other students. He grabs, pushes, hangs on, and sometimes even punches other students (usually other boys) on the arm. He also picks up anything on desks when he walks by, then laughs and tosses it back to the owners when they react. He engages in these behaviors when he enters and leaves my room as well as during class. Other teachers tell me they see the same behavior in their classes. Some students complain to me, but most tell him directly to stop (often angrily saying things like, "Stop it!" or "Lay off, Jason!"), push him away, or even punch him. He acts as though it is funny, laughs or smirks, and then pouts when students complain or I tell him to stop. He usually argues "I was just kidding" or "He pushed me first." The other students don't think Jason's behavior is funny. Jason is the smallest boy in the class. Academically, he does above average work, but he's also the most immature and socially rejected student in my class. The other kids are annoyed by his behavior and don't hide their dislike of Jason.

Where does it occur?

In the hallways, the classroom—anywhere in the school when Jason is in a group.

When does it occur?

I see it especially during transitions between classes as Jason and others students are coming to, entering, and leaving the classroom, while they are waiting to begin work on group projects, or while they are waiting for the class to gather after they've finished.

How often does it occur?

Two or three times a week students come to my fourth-period English class complaining about Jason's hallway behavior. I suspect the behavior happens more often, but some students don't say anything and deal with it themselves. I see the behavior at least once each day during my class. Sometimes I have to deal with the behavior three or four times during a single class.

Under what conditions does it occur?

It seems to happen most often during transitions and group times when there is a lot of student movement and crowding and a less apparent structure.

How do you feel about the problem?

I'm getting tired of hearing constant complaints about Jason and having my class disrupted. I'm feeling increasingly angry at Jason, frustrated that he persists in this behavior despite my corrections. Rather than improve in response to his classmates' and my responses, Jason's behavior seems to be getting worse. ✳

There are several groups of intervention strategies.

- *Teaching interventions* involve deliberate instruction of desirable social behavior and include approaches such as counseling, self-recording and self-monitoring, and social skills training.

- *Control interventions* stop problem behavior and redirect students back to learning when communication, support, and teaching interventions do not work.

There are intervention choices within each of these categories that are relatively less or more costly both to students and teachers. Although the costs of implementing any intervention depend on the teacher and situation, there is some consensus on relative intervention costs. In Wood's study, over one hundred classroom teachers rated the degree to which they would use more than sixty different interventions. Table 6.2 contains a list of interventions with the classroom teachers' average ratings of the cost of each intervention. Of course, the ratings may not reflect your own judgments. You might consider some that were rated too low and others too high, depending on your familiarity with the intervention and its suitabilty to your classroom.

TABLE 6.2
Costs of Behavior Management Interventions

COMMUNICATION STRATEGIES
1   Structure space, communicating expectations about the use of the physical environment.   Structure schedules, communicating expectations about the use of time.   Structure expectations linking behavior and rewards: "If you choose to do this, you will receive this reward."   Define relationships between unacceptable behavior and sanctions: "If you choose to do this . . . you will be penalized this way."   Establish classroom rules and routines.   Model appropriate behavior for students.   Conduct daily opening sessions to get the group organized for the day (may have a higher cost if your group is very disorganized).
2   Discuss with students the meaning or value of what is to be learned. Solicit and respect a student perspective.   Communicate regularly with students through conversations, notes, journals.   Communicate regularly with parents through notes, phone conversations, conferences.
3   Discuss, clarify, or negotiate goals and objectives with individual students.   Contract with individual students or the group.
4   Conduct closing review sessions: "How did your day go?"
5   Conduct problem-solving sessions focused on specific issues.   Provide group counseling.   Provide individual counseling.

TABLE 6.2
Continued

STRATEGIES FOR SUPPORTING DESIRABLE BEHAVIOR

1
Give attention (remember to give attention only to the behavior you want to maintain or increase).
Verbally cue or prompt.
Verbally praise a student who is behaving appropriately.
Verbally encourage appropriate behavior.
Give grades and other recognition for achievement.
Set up "Because you're you" events.

2
Accommodate individual instructional needs by grouping.
Organize peer tutoring assistance.
Organize cooperative groups.
Reward using an individualized token or point system (individual student).
Reward using group-contingent reward system (also a control strategy).

3
Involve parents in administration of contingent reward system.
Organize and administer group-contingent reward system.

4
Reward using individualized tokens/points system (entire group).
Organize and administer tokens/points system for group.

5
Accommodate individual instructional needs by fully individualizing tasks and instruction.

STRATEGIES FOR TEACHING DESIRABLE BEHAVIOR

3
Teach self-monitoring, recording, evaluating, and rewarding skills.
Provide affective education.

4
Directly teach needed social skills.

STRATEGIES FOR CONTROLLING PROBLEM BEHAVIOR

1
Remind the student of expectations and rules being violated.
Change the student's place in classroom.
Use gesture or signal alert.
Move closer to the student (proximity control).

2
Contact parents to discuss the student's behavior.
Restructure classroom environment.
Verbally confront student about inappropriate behavior.
Apply restitution or overcorrection procedure.
Use verbal humor.
Touch the student with positive intent.

TABLE 6.2
Continued

Reinforce another student who is behaving appropriately to remind the first student of expectations (also a support strategy for the student whose behavior is appropriate).

Reward appropriate behavior using group-contingent reward system (also a support strategy for students whose behavior is appropriate).

Permit problem behavior to occur with the expectation that the student will soon return to appropriate behavior.

Promise a reward for a return to appropriate behavior.

3
Change task assigned to student.
Conduct tension-release activities.
Administer verbal reprimand.
Refer for suspension.
Assign to detention or in-school suspension.
Send student to school office.

4
Conduct group meeting focused on problem behavior that has just occurred.
Supervise time-out at place.
Supervise time-out at special place in classroom.
Apply response cost procedure.
Conduct individual interview focused on problem behavior that has just occurred (life space interview).
Take away problem objects owned or in use by the student.

5
Verbally threaten student with loss of privileges.
Supervise isolation time-out for student.
Call parents to come to school to take student home.

Note: Numbers indicate cost weights from low (1) to high (5).

Source: Wood (1991). Reprinted with permission of the Helen Dwight Reid Educational Foundation. Published by Heldref Publications, 1319 Eighteenth St., N.W., Washington, D.C. 20036-1802. Copyright © 1991.

Some interventions take a lot of time and interfere with your regular classroom program.

Generally, you can consider intervention 1, 2, and 3 reasonable approaches for teachers in regular classrooms. However, interventions 4 and 5 typically entail substantially higher costs in time, effort, resources, support, and interference with the ongoing program. For example, communication interventions, such as "structuring space," "discussing with students the meaning or value of what is to be learned," and "contracting with individual students or the group" are legitimate, regular classroom interventions. However, "conducting closing review sessions" and "providing group counseling" are more costly interventions that require more effort and resources than many classroom teachers are willing to make.

Does this mean that you will not use any of the more costly interventions with students in your classroom? Probably not, especially since more students

Sometimes you may need specialists to help with or take over costly interventions.

with emotional and behavioral disorders are being educated in regular classrooms. What it probably does mean is that other support personnel, such as special education teachers, psychologists, and social workers, may be needed to assist you and, in some cases, to assume primary responsibility for implementing more costly interventions. In Chapter 9, we will discuss the roles and responsibilities of these support personnel and suggest some collaborative approaches.

As you can see from the interventions listed in Table 6.2, we have already considered many of the less costly interventions here and in earlier chapters. As we move on to consider more complex, costly interventions for individuals and groups of students, we want you to be aware that they generally require larger investments of your energy and time. They will likely have more pervasive effects on your classroom ecosystem, and they may also require assistance and support from others. However, these more costly interventions may be necessary to meet individual or group behavioral needs in your classroom, and their benefits in terms of improved behavior and learning may be well worth your investment.

Costly interventions can take a great deal of time and energy.

SUMMARY AND REVIEW

In this chapter, we have looked at techniques you can use to deal with surface behaviors—relatively mild, transient behavior problems. Your choices include permitting, tolerating, and preventing. We also examined a number of relatively simple, straightforward techniques for interfering with surface behavior that do not require intensive understanding of the behavior, elaborate planning, or special resources and assistance.

In most cases the approaches we have discussed in this chapter will help you interfere, at least temporarily, with behavior that distracts your students and hinders their progress. For behavior that is more persistent or pronounced, however, you will need to use more complex, coordinated efforts. In the next two chapters we will present some approaches for intervening with individuals and groups that go beyond merely interfering with problem behavior. While some of the interventions are directed at solving specific problems of individuals and groups of students, others are not intended to solve problems so much as to help students develop more adaptive emotional, social, and academic skills.

REFLECTING ON CHAPTER 6

Annie has been thinking over her first semester and reflecting on what has gone well and what needs to be done next. As she thinks about individual students, she is ready to move on to more specific interventions for them. Given her time and resources, what is the cost-benefit ratio for the interventions you think she should be trying?

We briefly discussed a teacher's use of touch. Discussions of hugging, touching, or patting didn't appear in the literature of a few years ago. Now, however, due to the spate of court cases and publicity surrounding the use of touch by educators and others, teachers must be clearly cautioned.

We heard an interview with a day-care provider on National Public Radio who stated that she did not allow any of the people working for her to touch the children in their care. If a child fell and was hurt (and these children were preschool age), the helpers gave only verbal comfort. A classroom teacher frequently must soothe an injured or upset child, comfort a child who doesn't feel well , or just be a source of emotional support. Doing this while evaluating how that support will be perceived is difficult.

Discuss this issue with your classmates. What kinds of lines if any need to be drawn? Sould teachers resolve never to touch a child in any way? Should there be district policies? What kind of message does such a situation convey to children? How are we going to deal with this?

Key Terms

contagion (p. 190)
escalation (p. 190)
admonishments (p. 194)
clarity (p. 194)
firmness (p. 194)
roughness (p. 194)
surface behaviors (p. 195)
antiseptic manipulation (p. 195)
planned ignoring (p. 195)
nonverbal interference (p. 195)

communicating and building
  relationships (p. 195)
extinction (p. 195)
signal interference (p. 197)
proximity control (p. 197)
touch control (p. 197)
hypodermic affection (p. 203)
regrouping (p. 206)
antiseptic bouncing (p. 206)
ecological behavior analysis (p. 208)

Building Your Own Knowledge Base: Suggested Readings

Goodlad, J. (1984). *A place called school: Prospects for the future.* New York: McGraw-Hill. An examination of the realities of public schooling. Its purposes in a democratic society and how those purposes can be met.

Redl, F., & Wineman, D. (1952). *Controls from within: Techniques for the treatment of the aggressive child.* New York: Free Press. Based on their work with predelinquent children, the authors describe how the physical arrangement, the routines, and atmosphere affect behavior and suggest "techniques for antiseptic manipulation of surface behavior."

References

Goodlad, J. (1984). *A place called school: Prospects for the future.* New York: McGraw-Hill.

Jones, V. F., & Jones, L. S. (1990). *Responsible classroom discipline* (3rd ed.). Boston: Allyn and Bacon.

Kidder, T. (1989). *Among schoolchildren.* Boston: Houghton Mifflin.

Kounin, J. S. (1970). *Discipline and group management in classrooms.* New York: Holt, Rinehart & Winston.

Long, N. J., & Newman, R. G. (1976). Managing surface behavior of children in school. In N. J. Long, W. C. Morse & R. G. Newman (Eds.), *Conflict in the classroom: The education of children with problems* (3rd ed.). Belmont, CA: Wadsworth.

Nichols, P. (1992). The curriculum of control: Twelve reasons for it, some arguments against it. *Beyond Behavior, 3,* 5–11.

Redl, F., & Wattenberg, W. W. (1959). *Mental hygiene in teaching* (2nd ed.). New York: Harcourt Brace Jovanovich.

Redl, F., & Wineman, D. (1952). *Controls from within: Techniques for the treatment of the aggressive child.* New York: Free Press.

Rizzo, J. R., & Zabel, R. H. (1988). *Educating children and adolescents with behavioral disorders: An integrative approach.* Boston: Allyn and Bacon.

Walker, J. E., & Shea, T. M. (1991). *Behavior management: A practical approach for educators* (5th ed.). New York: Macmillan.

Wood, F. H. (1991). Cost/benefit considerations in managing the behavior of students with emotional/behavioral disorders. *Preventing School Failure, 35,* 17–23.

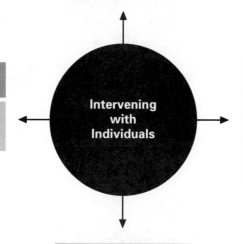

Developing a Rationale for Intervening

- Select intervention methods
- Evaluate intervention effectiveness
- Communicate intervention outcomes
- Reducing dependence on extrinsic reinforcement

Counseling Strategies – Life-Space Interviews

- Life space interviews
- Handling crisis situations

Intervening with Individuals

Promoting Self-Management

- Contingency contracting
- Using mediation essays
- Self-monitoring, evaluation, and reinforcement

Individual Contingency Management

- Using A-B-C analysis
- Using praise and criticism
- Developing individual contingency management plans

Chapter 7

Intervening with Individuals

Annie's Journal

FEBRUARY: All I can say is, thank goodness this is a short month. I suppose I could blame the weather, or the letdown from holiday times, or the stars, or the phases of the moon, but I don't really think any of those things are the cause of this most recent disaster. Is that too strong a word? I don't think so. I'm still shaken and this happened last week.

Actually, I'm not sure *what* happened. We were out at recess—I was concentrating on keeping my feet warm and talking to Lee and Tamica, and all of a sudden I hear this ROAR from the other side of the playground. I look up and it's Danny—this time without his partner in crime—sitting on top of someone I don't recognize and pounding him into the ground. There are kids gathered around, people screaming, teachers running in their direction—the whole nightmare. I get over there as Mrs. Garcelon is trying to pull Danny off the other kid—he's struggling and flailing and kicking—and his fist connects with her head. Her glasses go flying, there is a collective gasp from the kids watching, and she retreats, clutching her jaw. I take advantage of the momentary freeze and get both arms around Danny and pull him off the kid under him, who is not in my class and is bleeding from his nose. I've *never* felt like that. I wasn't the kind of kid that got in fights. I wasn't even the kind of kid that liked to gather around and watch. I was the one running for the teacher. That's what I wanted to do this time, except now I *am* the teacher and I'm supposed to know what to do. But I didn't.

Anyway, one of the other teachers helped Mrs. Garcelon into the building, one of the kids picked up her glasses, the bloody nose boy's teacher scraped him up and took him inside, the kids dispersed (at least some of them), and I just stood there hanging onto Danny with both arms. He had calmed down a little bit, but he was panting and trying to pull away, and I just held on tighter. Finally, I got hold of his shoulders, turned him around to face me and yelled in his face, "*Danny!* What do you think you're *doing?*

Why is it *always* you? Can't you *ever* do anything right?" Looking back, I don't know why I said that. I mean, it certainly wasn't going to help, and I really didn't expect an answer. I was just so scared and upset and angry I had to say something. Danny just looked down at the ground. But he did stop struggling.

We walked back into the school, me hanging onto Danny's arm, the other kids trailing behind, and as we got in the door, I realized we would have to walk by most of the other intermediate classes going back into their rooms. Of course, everyone was talking and pointing at Danny and looking at me, probably wondering if I was going to tear him limb from limb (the thought had entered my mind). Danny walked along, chin stuck out, not looking at anyone. We made it back to the classroom, and I told everyone to sit down. Now what? I was still taking deep breaths trying to get my heart rate down, the kids were all whispering and talking, Danny was in his chair glaring at everyone. I had to deal with this. Then the intercom came on "Ms. Harris, will you please bring Danny to the office? Now. Thank you."

Swell. It seemed that this was going to be taken out of my hands. I looked at Danny, and (surprisingly) he came to me and we started down the hall. All of a sudden, I had this shift of emotion. A minute ago I was so angry at him, I could have smacked him myself. He looked to me like the typical bully—the big bad kid—get him out of my class, the sooner the better. Now, as we walked down the hall in silence, he seemed suddenly smaller, younger—not a threat, but a ten-year-old boy in trouble, and one who was about to go into a *very* uncomfortable situation. I still don't know what happened on the playground, but what if it wasn't all Danny's fault? What if that other kid said something, or hit him first or . . . I don't know. And he didn't mean to hit Mrs. Garcelon. She just got in the way of a flying punch. Will anyone know that? Will anyone care? On the other hand, what if that other kid was really hurt? What if Mrs. Garcelon was hurt? What would they do to Danny? How much of this was *my* fault? Should I have been watching him more closely? Have I ignored too many aggressive incidents in class? Should I have made more efforts to contact Danny's mom? Should I have referred him before this? Did I ever send in the teacher liability insurance form? As we walked down the hall, I could feel myself getting smaller and smaller, kind of like Alice after she ate the mushroom in *Through the Looking Glass*. I felt as though Danny and I were *both* heading for a bad time and, frankly, I was scared. I put my arm around Danny's shoulders and gave him a squeeze, as much for myself as for him. Danny stiffened, looked at me, and moved a little closer. Then he started to cry.

✳ What do you think a new teacher could have done to prevent the incident on the playground?

✳ How might a teacher change the behavior of a student like Danny before it caused a serious problem?

✳ Do you think Mrs. Garcelon responded to the incident appropriately or not? Why?

✳ What do you think are the appropriate and necessary follow-up steps for this incident?

INTERVENTION WITH INDIVIDUALS IN YOUR CLASSROOM

Each of your students is unique, with different backgrounds, skills, and interests.

Although your classroom will be comprised of groups of students and much of the interaction and instruction will occur in group contexts, those groups are made up of individuals. As we have stressed, teachers must always recognize the individual differences among their students. Your classroom will be a heterogeneous collection of biologically, temperamentally, experientially, and culturally diverse individuals. Your students will not all learn in the same ways, will not have the same aptitudes and skills, the same interests and motivations, and the same types of support and encouragement from their families and communities. They will not all perceive their school experiences in the same ways. Your students' individual personalities, aptitudes, and backgrounds will differ as will their daily experiences in and out of school.

Students sometimes come to school with backgrounds and experiences that make it hard for them to behave

You can accommodate some of these individual differences using the group-oriented interventions we will examine in Chapter 8. But many situations will arise where you will need to consider and employ interventions that focus on the needs of individuals. Students can experience stresses in their lives outside of school—in their families, peer relationships, and communities—that affect their attitudes, behavior, and ability to perform in school. Traumatic experiences at home, such as illness, family conflict, abuse, divorce, and financial crises, for example, can result in distraction, lack of motivation, withdrawal and depression, and verbal and physical aggression. Sometimes reactions to environmental stresses pass quickly, and your students respond to your effort to provide a supportive, nurturing classroom environment. However, some individuals' problems are so chronic and pronounced that they present special challenges.

Including students with behavioral disorders in regular classrooms can present a teacher with special challenges.

Also, as more students who have emotional and behavioral disorders are included in regular classrooms, you can expect to have students whose behavior is at times intense and somewhat unpredictable, who have difficulty understanding and controlling their feelings and behavior, and who sometimes cross the boundaries of acceptable conduct. For these students, behavioral problems are more extreme, chronic, and resistant to change.

Just as your class is made up of individuals, your interventions will often have to address individual needs.
(David Young-Wolff/ Photo Edit)

Sometimes, despite good classroom management, a teacher needs to intervene directly with a student.

Certainly, the classroom management approaches we have studied in earlier chapters—creating safe, orderly, and predictable environments; communicating caring, acceptance, and high expectations; engaging students in active learning; preventing and managing surface behavior problems—are all part of creating classrooms that are conducive to individual growth. Such approaches are not always enough, however, and you will sometimes need to intervene directly with individual students. In some cases, such as integrating students with emotional and behavioral disorders, you should receive assistance and support from specialists. However, their assistance will usually occur in collaborative arrangements where *you*, as classroom teacher, retain primary responsibility for educating students and implementing interventions.

The interventions for individuals included in this chapter are consistent with our belief that as a classroom teacher you are responsible for educating *all* of your students by helping them become responsible, confident, competent individuals. Thus, we are including approaches that are oriented not only toward externally controlling student behavior but also toward encouraging and teaching self-awareness, self-management, and self-control.

INDIVIDUAL CONTINGENCY MANAGEMENT

Teachers can arrange consequences to help modify a student's behavior.

Contingency management refers to ways you can systematically arrange consequences to modify student behavior. As you remember from Chapter 3, behaviorists consider that most behavior is *learned* from both the antecedents and the consequences of the behavior. *Antecedents* are events or conditions preceding behavior that encourage the behavior. They are sometimes called *stimulus conditions* or *cues*. For example, when you state, "I'd like your attention," you are providing a verbal cue or antecedent that encourages your students to look at you. Another example of an antecedent stimulus is one student poking another, who angrily responds, "Stop it!" In addition to verbal behavior, features of the physical environment of your classroom and the routines, rules, and procedures we discussed earlier are some of the many antecedent, stimulus, conditions that can influence your students' behavior.

Behaviorists believe that most behavior is learned.

Consequences affect whether or not a behavior is repeated.

As we also discussed in Chapter 3, consequences are events or conditions that *follow* behavior and affect whether or not the behavior is repeated. *Reinforcing consequences* increase future performance of the behavior, while *punishing consequences* decrease it. For example, if Janell burps loudly and students sitting around her giggle, she burps again even longer and louder. We could consider Janell's burping to be reinforced by her peers' giggling (granted, Janell may also have compelling internal, physical reasons for burping). If Willy offers a comment during a class discussion and another student states, "That's dumb," and the teacher responds, "No, you're way off track, Willy," he will likely *de*crease participation in later discussions. We could conclude that Willy's participation in the discussion was punished.

What we see resulting from other people's behavior affects our behavior too.

Frequently, we experience reinforcement and punishment *vicariously*—by observing others. When we observe others' behavior and its consequences, we learn to modify our own (Bandura, 1977). We remember the vicarious experiences and use them later when they seem to fit our own experiences. For example, when Kerri observes Janell's reinforcement for burping, at an opportune time, she engages in the behavior herself. Likewise, other students who observe their classmates' and teacher's criticism (punishment) of Willy's contribution to the class discussion might learn to suppress their own participation. Willy's experience generalizes not only to other situations in his own life, but also to students who observed: they may also learn not to participate in order to avoid being punished by their peers and teacher.

USING AN A-B-C ANALYSIS

A first step in dealing with a problem behavior is to look at what happened before and after.

When you confront problem behavior that does not respond to the surface management techniques we discussed in Chapter 6, your first step could be to conduct an **antecedent-behavior-consequence (A-B-C) analysis.** An A-B-C analysis isolates the events and conditions that precede and follow behavior to determine their relationships. Consider, for example, identifying the antecedents, behaviors, and consequences for Jason's pushing, grabbing, and punching behavior described in our Ecological Behavior Analysis Guide in the last chapter. Here is an A-B-C analysis of Jason's behavior:

A-B-C Analysis of Jason's Pushing, Grabbing, and Punching

* *Antecedents:* entering or leaving class, crowded conditions, unstructured activity
* *Behavior:* pushing, grabbing, punching classmates, picking things up from other students' desks
* *Consequences:* students complain, threaten, push, grab, and punch Jason; teacher admonishes Jason to stop

The purpose of an A-B-C analysis is to give you a clearer understanding of how your students' behavior is affected by conditions in the immediate classroom environment. In Jason's case, you can see that his disturbing behavior occurs under specific antecedent conditions: lack of structure and crowding with lots of movement through the halls and classroom. Likewise, you can identify specific consequences that follow his troubling behavior: critical comments and reactions from his classmates and teacher.

The atmosphere and conditions of a classroom affect a student's behavior.

With information about antecedents and consequences of troublesome behavior, you will have a clearer picture of classroom conditions you could modify that might change the behavior. In our earlier discussions of the importance of communicating with students, preparing your classroom, effectively instructing, preventing, and interfering with surface behavior, we suggested how learning and behavior are influenced by antecedent conditions. The atmosphere and structure of your classroom ecosystem communicate your expectations and can promote appropriate behavior. Given the A-B-C information about Jason, what changes would you suggest that Ms. Johnson make in antecedent conditions to diminish his problem behavior? How, for instance, could she modify traffic patterns in the hallway and classroom? How might she communicate other ways for Jason to interact with his peers?

A wrong use of behavior modification can encourage misbehavior.

Behaviorists have helped teachers become aware of how they sometimes use behavior modification techniques ineffectively and unsystematically. Teachers may sometimes unintentionally strengthen undesirable student behavior when they intend to diminish the behavior (Walker & Buckley, 1972). For example, giving negative attention to problem behavior, such as telling a child to sit down or be quiet or making a stern face sometimes actually reinforces disturbing behavior like talking out, inattention, tantrums, and showing off.

The A-B-C analysis of Jason's behavior indicates that Ms. Johnson and Jason's classmates are both providing consequences that unintentionally reinforce his behavior. Although they dislike his behavior and no doubt intend their critical responses to reduce his pushing, grabbing, and punching, their attention seems to have exactly the opposite effect. Jason's behavior is getting worse, rather than better.

Without examining antecedents and consequences, you will probably be unaware of how environmental contingencies affect behavior. When you clarify relationships between a problem behavior and its antecedents and consequences using an A-B-C analysis, however, you can decide how to modify these antecedents and consequences to change the behavior.

USING PRAISE AND CRITICISM

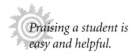
Praising a student is easy and helpful.

The adage "You can catch more flies with honey than with vinegar" has many classroom applications. The hundreds of daily interactions in your classroom include your verbal and nonverbal feedback to students about how they are doing academically and behaviorally. Teacher praise—as you may recall from Chapter 4—is one form of feedback that has received a lot of attention, both critical and favorable. Praise is defined as verbalized approval of student behavior. Teacher praise is the most efficient form of reinforcement you have at your disposal, and it is inexpensive. There is a plentiful supply, it is readily available, and it can be easily dispensed.

There are many ways to praise a student.

On the surface, teacher praise appears to be the perfect form of reinforcement, and in many cases it is indeed a powerful influence on student behavior and self-esteem. As a rule of thumb, we suggest that each day you find something to praise about *every* student. Praise takes many forms, including written and verbal comments about academic performance and positive comments about behavior or appearance. Praise not only provides your students with positive feedback but also helps you notice their positive behavior and accomplishments. For most students, of course, you can easily find opportunities to recognize their accomplishments. For a few, it may be harder to discover behavior you can praise. However, when you deliberately notice and praise student accomplishments, rather than emphasize shortcomings, your classroom atmosphere is likely to become more optimistic and upbeat.

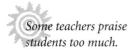
Some teachers praise students too much.

However, teacher praise as well as tangible rewards may be overused in classrooms (Deci & Ryan, 1985; Kohn, 1993, 1994). Even when rewards modify behavior, students may feel manipulated; when students do not receive expected rewards, they may feel punished. Furthermore, critics charge that praise and other external rewards diminish intrinsic motivation. Students who formerly behaved in a certain way because they found it intrinsically satisfying and motivating learn to expect external reinforcement. Students also may

Critics say that praise can make students less self-motivated.

conclude that the behavior is unappealing or difficult if it requires external rewards.

Legitimate Uses of Praise and Other Rewards

We think you should heed these criticisms of using praise and other rewards to influence student behavior. Certainly you should avoid lavishly praising behavior that students already perform. And as you offer praise and encouragement, you should be careful not to give students exaggerated opinions of their accomplishments. Still, there are legitimate uses of praise. For example, you will likely have students who are not always motivated to achieve, to participate, or even to cooperate. They may lack confidence in their competence, or they may receive more attention and reinforcement for disruptive, distracting behavior. These students may need your attention and assurance.

Some students really need praise.

There are many situations in which you can praise and reward student behavior in ways that do not undercut intrinsic motivation or create reward-dependent students. Of course, your praise must be sincere and offered for specific, real accomplishments. You certainly don't want to become a robot with glazed eyes and a fixed smile, repeating, "Good job . . . good job . . . good job . . ." over and over again (see the Classroom Closeup "Guidelines for the Effective Use of Praise").

As We See It: *The Authors Talk*

Mary Kay: Nice section on praise, Bob. Well written, clearly organized, and very informative.

Bob: Well, thank you! I found your contributions to be insightful, appropriate, and most enlightening. I think this project is coming along very well.

Mary Kay: So do I. The cooperative nature of this venture is really satisfying.

Bob: I agree. (To be continued . . . see page 229)

Criticism

Not surprisingly, praise appears to have more long-lasting influence on behavior than criticism or negative feedback. Most of us prefer to be around people who speak positively about our accomplishments. Parents and teachers often overuse criticism to modify the behavior of children and adolescents. The outcomes are predictably poor. A teacher's criticism may temporarily halt or interrupt undesired behavior, but it offers no instruction about alternative, more desirable ways to behave. When students repeatedly hear critical comments from authority figures (like teachers), they come to believe that the criticisms are valid. In addition, criticism makes students embarrassed, angry

Criticism doesn't teach people how to behave.

Classroom Closeup

Guidelines for the Effective Use of Praise

- It is delivered contingent on performance of the behavior rather than randomly.
- It refers to the specific accomplishment rather than a global positive reaction.
- It shows the teacher's clear attention to the specific accomplishment rather than simple conforming behavior.
- It rewards attainment of specified criteria rather than simple participation.
- It provides information about the value of the accomplishment.
- It orients students to their *own* behavior rather than comparing with and competing with others.
- It uses students' *own* prior accomplishments rather than those of peers to describe present accomplishments.

- It recognizes noteworthy effort and difficulty of the task.
- It attributes success to effort and ability rather than to luck or ease of task.
- It fosters student belief that their efforts were directed toward developing skills rather than pleasing the teacher or receiving rewards.
- It focuses student attention on their task-relevant behavior rather than on the teacher as an authority.
- It is provided *after* the performance rather than intruding during the learning process and distracting student attention from the task.

Using these guidelines, you will be able to praise students in ways that will likely reinforce their performance and behavior. Students will sense your sincerity, recognize their accomplishments as real, and be motivated toward further approval and accomplishment (Brophy, 1981). ✴

---

at the critic, and sometimes feel like retaliating. To save face, criticized students defend themselves by arguing, sulking, and deliberately not complying with the teacher. Since criticism and other aversive consequences tend to have the immediate effect of reducing undesired behavior—they seem to work—teachers (as well as parents and others who use criticism) are reinforced for using them. Unfortunately, the behavior doesn't stop for long.

Does this mean that you should never criticize student behavior? Probably not. There will be situations in which you need to stop behavior that is disruptive, distracting, or potentially damaging to persons or property. In these situations, "soft reprimands" (O'Leary, Kaufman, Kass & Drabman, 1970) seem to work best. If possible, you should approach the misbehaving student, gain eye contact, quietly name the misbehavior, briefly explain why it is a problem, and instruct the student to cease the behavior.

When you need to criticize a student's behavior, do it gently and specifically.

As with students who break rules, students who misbehave are rarely unaware of what they are doing. Rather, they may be unaware of the consequences, unaware of alternative ways in which they might gain attention, or unaware that they are jeopardizing their grades or their standing in the

Students may not understand the consequences of their misbehavior.

classroom. We have all heard exasperated teachers or parents say something like, "Arthur, I've told you a thousand times not to do that." Well, if the teacher has indeed told Arthur a thousand times not to do that and he is still doing it, telling him one more time is not likely to have much effect. Arthur knows what we wish he'd stop doing. Something else is missing—the motivation *not* to perform the behavior or the awareness of alternative ways of achieving the same result.

Criticism can make everyone notice the misbehavior.

Frequent verbal criticism has another unfortunate consequence: it calls everyone's attention to the very behavior you are trying to stop. You should try to avoid calling more attention to misbehavior than necessary because it creates further distraction and disruption besides embarrassing the offenders.

As We See It: *The Authors Talk, Continued*

Bob: That last section is too wordy—it needs to be written more clearly and with more examples.

Mary Kay: Oh? Would you be referring to *my* section on criticism?

Bob: Yes. It doesn't read well—too dry and stuffy.

Mary Kay: I see. Perhaps *you'd* like to write that section, since you know so much about the topic. Dry and stuffy are usually *your* department.

Bob: Is that so? Well, maybe I should just finish this chapter myself if that's what you want.

Mary Kay: Maybe you should—in fact, maybe you should just finish this whole *project* yourself.

Bob: Fine!

Mary Kay: Fine!

(We definitely prefer the working conditions of the first to the second dialogue, although we must admit to occasionally lapsing into the critical mode. Maybe those occasional lapses are a necessary reminder of how much more pleasant it is to work in a supportive atmosphere.)

INDIVIDUAL CONTINGENCY MANAGEMENT PLAN DEVELOPMENT

An **individual contingency management plan** is a method of externally controlling and modifying a student's behavior by deliberately manipulating consequences. You can use contingency management in regular classrooms when a student's behavior significantly interferes with his or her own progress *and* when other, less intrusive efforts to deal with the behavior have proven ineffective. Some students do not respond to approaches that are appropriate and effective with most students. When your efforts to encourage a student's intrinsic motivation to participate and cooperate in the classroom have not worked, individual contingency management is an option.

Contingency management focuses on increasing desirable behavior by systematically altering the consequences of behavior. *Contingent* means that a specific consequence depends upon a specific behavior. For example, you might want to increase behavior that contributes to school involvement and academic performance, such as the amount of time a student works on task. You might want to decrease other behavior, such as the number of days a student skips school. Or you might want to directly increase social behavior, like participating in the group, sharing, and cooperating; you might want to decrease behavior like arguing, interrupting, and fighting.

High-probability behavior (higher preference, higher frequency) can be used to increase low-probability behavior (lower preference, lower frequency) (Premack, 1959). Sometimes referred to as *Grandma's Rule* ("First you eat your vegetables, then you can have your dessert"), the Premack Principle uses potential reinforcers that already exist in an environment. For example, a parent might require a child to finish household chores before going out to play; a teacher could require that a student finish an assignment before playing a computer game. Naturally occurring rewards (going outside, playing a computer game) are made contingent on the desired behavior (household chores, assignments).

Some teachers and critics of behavior modification (again, Kohn, 1993, 1994) consider this kind of deliberate application of contingencies a form of bribery because it offers extrinsic incentives to students who are not intrinsically motivated to engage in some behavior. While contingency management does offer extrinsic rewards, remember that much human behavior is motivated at least in part by extrinsic consequences. For example would you, or could you, work for intrinsic rewards only? You like teaching, but you also like being paid to teach. In fact, without the extrinsic rewards you would probably not be able to be a professional teacher. In addition to the potential intrinsic rewards of teaching, such as your satisfaction from seeing students learn and develop, some aspects of the job, such as grading papers and maintaining records, are not so appealing. Still, they are important tasks and necessary to your teaching job, so you extrinsically reward yourself when you complete them by working on an interesting curricular project, taking a break, having a snack, going for a walk, or whatever you find rewarding.

As we emphasized in Chapter 4, classroom activities that offer the elements of challenge, curiosity, control, and fantasy tend to be intrinsically or self-rewarding for students (Lepper & Hodell, 1989). As much as possible, you should to try to structure classroom activities that provide at least moderate challenges to students, engage their curiosity, allow them some control over learning

Sometimes teachers need to set up specific consequences to teach students to change specific behaviors.

A teacher can tell a student to finish a task before playing.

It is normal to need some external reward for working.

Some activities are interesting and inherently rewarding.

conditions, and stimulate their imagination. You also need to be sure that students are capable of performing the activities.

Use the following steps to develop and implement an individual contingency management plan:

- Select target behavior.
- Observe and record baseline data.
- Develop a rationale for intervening.
- Select intervention methods.
- Implement the intervention.
- Evaluate intervention effectiveness.
- Communicate intervention outcomes.
- Reduce dependence on extrinsic reinforcers.

Students need to be involved in a contingency management plan.

Even though contingency management utilizes extrinsic motivation, you should try to involve participating students in the intervention process as much as possible. When you make the process a joint effort between you and the student, you diminish manipulation. Often your students can help choose and define the target behavior, collect baseline data, and discuss the reasons for changing their behavior. As the intervention moves into the implementation stage, you can involve your students in collecting and charting data and judging the effectiveness of the intervention.

SELECT TARGET BEHAVIOR

You should choose a target behavior that can be changed.

Selecting a target behavior can be relatively easy when you have a single, obvious, and pressing problem. Usually, however, you will have several potential target behaviors. When this is the case, you and your student may choose those that your A-B-C analysis indicates are strongly influenced by factors in the classroom environment and that you believe could be changed. If you are successful with relatively easy behaviors, you can extend the intervention to other behaviors.

Before you try to change the target behavior, you will need to know its preintervention status so you can understand the size or severity of the behavior and be able later to determine how well your interventions work. You will need to observe and collect baseline data.

OBSERVE AND RECORD BASELINE DATA

You need to know how often a student is misbehaving to be able to tell whether your intervention is working.

Baseline data usually are recorded as *frequency, rate,* or *duration,* depending on the nature of the target behavior. Frequency is the number of times a behavior occurs. For example, you may want to know the number of times a student is late for class, swears, touches other students, or leaves his or her desk without permission.

Rate measures frequency of behavior over time, such as the number of times the behavior occurs every period, day, or week. For example, over several observations, you might find that Tyrone talks out an average of twenty times during fifty-minute class periods. You can calculate his talk-out rate as follows:

$$\text{Rate} = \frac{\text{Number of talk-outs}}{\text{Number of minutes}} = \frac{20}{50} = 0.4 \text{ talk-outs per minute}$$

You need to know how the student's behavior compares to peer behavior.

Tyrone's rate of talking out is 0.4 per minute (20/50 = 0.4). Of course, knowing the rate of his talking out by itself does not tell you very much. You will usually want to determine if .4 talk-outs per minute is a high, low, or average talk-out rate for your class. Consequently, you will need to know the rate of talking out by *other* students in your class. In our discussion of observation techniques below, we will suggest strategies that will enable you to compare a student's behavior with his or her classmates'.

You may want to know how long a behavior lasts.

For some kinds of behavior, such as tantrums, a third type of measure, duration, may be more meaningful. For example, you might be interested in how long a student works independently before she acts discouraged and quits. Or you may have a student who has tantrums. Her rate of tantrums is low—just one per day—but the rate is not your major concern. Some tantrums last only a minute or two; others continue for as long as thirty to forty minutes. In this situation, duration would be a better measure than frequency or rate.

A variation of the duration measure is called *latency*—the length of delay between the beginning of an activity and an individual student's active involvement in it. For example, your concern about Mike is the amount of time before he begins working. He looks around the room, whispers to classmates, sharpens his pencil, and fiddles with objects on his desk and in his backpack and pockets. You usually have to prompt him several times before he begins assignments. As a result, he is falling far behind in his work, rarely finishes it within the allotted time, bothers other students, and demands a lot of your attention.

Baseline Data

Baseline data show you the basic facts of a misbehavior, such as the number of incomplete assignments.

Baseline data help you to determine the nature and size of behavior as well as to provide a benchmark against which to measure your efforts to change it. Although there are complicated and sophisticated data collection and analysis techniques, you can usually devise one that provides accurate, useful information efficiently. Often you already have baseline data in the form of routinely collected records (e.g., records of absences, tardies, grades, or referrals to the office). Assume, for example, that your student Lin consistently does not bring completed homework to school. You already have baseline data in your records of complete and incomplete assignments. You might use the past two weeks as a baseline period and discover that Lin has completed only 20 percent of her assignments (two of ten daily assignments = 20 percent) during that period. You may be concerned about the quality of Howard's performance in spelling and determine that his average score on the last five weekly tests is 45 percent. Or, according to your records, Travis has been late for school fourteen mornings over the last twenty days (14/20 = 70 percent). Each of these types of routinely collected information could serve as baseline data.

Direct Observation

Sometimes you need to carefully watch a target behavior to record baseline data.

Sometimes you will be concerned about a target behavior for which you have no existing records or measures. If so, you will need to systematically observe and record baseline data. Baseball player and philosopher Yogi Berra has been credited with saying, "You can observe a lot just by watching." While his statement sounds like a truism, Yogi probably watches baseball very carefully, informed by his considerable knowledge of the game. When you formally observe behavior in your classroom, as opposed to just watching or listening, you do more than just watch. You deliberately use structured formats that are informed by your knowledge of the behavior and contexts in which it occurs.

You can select or adapt observation formats to meet your specific needs. If you are uncertain about an appropriate procedure or need help observing, members of your school's teacher assistance team, special educators, and school psychologists should be able to help. Three types of observation that teachers find especially useful for collecting baseline data as well as for monitoring behavior change are called *diary descriptions, specimen records,* and *time samples.*

A diary can be a useful tool for recording behavior.

A *diary description,* or *daily log,* involves simply recording interesting or problematic behaviors regularly. One student may frequently cry and express feelings of being rejected by other students; another may sleep during class; a third may barely begin assignments, then scribble, draw on, and tear them up; and a fourth may get into noisy arguments and shoving matches over use of materials and equipment, place in line, etc. Maintaining a daily log can help you collect information for the ecological and A-B-C analyses. A diary also gives you an ongoing record of important events. Some teachers simply record the times and situations of significant behaviors in a notebook or in a daily planner.

Daily logs or diaries are impressionistic, though. They are often general descriptions of behavioral incidents (tantrums, arguments, withdrawal) rather than specific measurements. They tend to focus on exciting, unusual, or interesting incidents and are not a complete record. Also, by the time you are free to record events—the end of the day or class period—you may have forgotten details or the original event may have become colored by subsequent events. Despite these limitations, however, a diary can be a useful method for you to describe, study, and follow student behavior over time.

A type of observation that does include direct descriptions of behavior is the *specimen record* or *narrative record*. This procedure can help you separate behavioral description and your interpretation or judgments about a student's behavior. In a specimen record you record *everything* the student does and says (and everything anyone else says and does that involves the student) during a specified period of time. The purpose of a specimen record is to give you a complete and objective record of the student's behavior during that time. You attempt to record literally everything the subject does and says during the specified time. Length of each observation depends on the amount of time you need to record the incident or activity as well as feasibility—the amount of time you or another observer can continuously observe—but specimen record observations are typically at least a few minutes long.

To ensure objectivity and completeness—the key features of specimen records—try to avoid interpreting, judging, labeling, and speculating about the student's motives, covert behavior, and feelings. Interpretations, judgments, and labels often represent the observer's preconceived notions and feelings about behavior more than an accurate record of the behavior itself. In addition, the observer should avoid pseudodescriptive accounts of behavior and record dialogue in its entirety. Table 7.1 shows examples of poorly written interpretations of behavior followed by more objective behavioral descriptions appropriate for a specimen record.

A carefully recorded specimen record observation should provide complete, accurate, relatively unbiased behavioral data. An obvious limitation of specimen records is that they require the total attention of the observer, something you can seldom afford as a classroom teacher. Consequently, you

A specimen record gives an objective description of student behavior.

Specimen records should be objective and complete; teachers should not interpret or judge.

Teachers usually need another adult to take over their class while they observe.

TABLE 7.1
Poor and Better Behavioral Descriptions in a Specimen Record Observation

	POOR	**BETTER**
Motives	She was trying to get Marlene's attention.	She tapped Marlene's shoulder four times.
Feelings	She was embarrassed by the comment.	She looked down at the floor and her face turned red.
Covert behavior	He was daydreaming.	He stared at the bulletin board with a blank expression on his face.
Labels	His tone of voice was really obnoxious.	He answered, "No, why should I?"
Pseudodescription	She glared at Billy for a long time.	She glared at Billy for 15 seconds.
Dialogue	He said he didn't want to do his work.	He said, "This stuff is dumb. Nobody could do this."

will usually need to call on someone else (school psychologist, administrator, paraprofessional, or coteacher) to either conduct the observations or supervise the class while you observe.

Time samples are forms of direct observation that involve directly recording specific behaviors during specified units of time. There are many possible formats, and you will need to select or adapt a procedure that meets your needs. First, you need to select and define the behaviors you want to observe. For example, if your target behavior is Peter being out of his seat, how will you operationally define *out of seat*? You could start by defining *in-seat* behavior. Does this mean staying at his assigned desk or in a specified chair? Does it include being at whatever place you expect Peter to be during an activity? Will an *out-of-seat* incident be recorded only if Peter is totally away from his seat or if he is simply leaning far away while maintaining some contact with his seat? Although these considerations may seem picky, if you are going to have accurate behavioral data, you will need to be specific about exactly what you are observing before you begin.

Your second task is determining times and settings that are *relevant* and *representative* of the behavior you are interested in studying. For example, if the target behavior is Joey's disruptive behavior during music, music class would be the relevant time to observe his behavior. You should also observe under typical conditions—observing Joey when there is a substitute teacher might not be the same as when he is with the regular music teacher.

Your third step in designing a time sampling observation procedure is determining observational periods and intervals. Will you observe for one minute, five minutes, twenty minutes, or some other period of time? Will you break these periods into five-, ten-, or thirty-second observation intervals? We cannot give you hard and fast rules about the total length of each observation or its intervals—that depends on the behavior and the context. As a general rule, however, we suggest that you keep the intervals quite short—just long enough for you to judge if the target behaviors occur. Teachers often find that ten seconds is about right for observing and recording behavior. When intervals are longer than ten seconds, the behavior may occur more than once per interval, making it difficult to count.

You will need to observe at several predetermined times during the observational period (such as the ten minutes of independent seatwork following instruction). You can do other things—circulate through the room, monitor student work, respond to questions, provide individual help—while you collect observational data.

For example, you might be interested in Raylene's off-task behavior because she often looks around the room, tries to get others' attention, and does not finish her work. You could momentarily observe Raylene's behavior for three to four seconds about once each minute and record her off-task behavior on a simple form (such as in Figure 7.1) that you carry on a clipboard. Each time you see Raylene off task you would place a checkmark in the appropriate

Time samples are direct recordings of a target behavior for a specific length of time.

The target behavior needs to be very clearly defined.

You should use relevant time periods and settings for your observation.

You must choose for how long and at what intervals you will observe.

FIGURE 7.1   Sample Observation Form for Off-Task Behavior

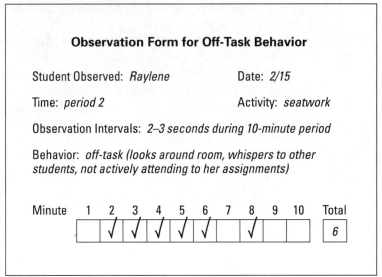

box. Using this format, you could calculate daily percentages of off-task behavior. After several observations, you could calculate her average off-task rate to determine a base rate.

You can extend the time sampling format to simultaneously observe one or more behaviors of a target student *and* peers (see Figure 7.2). To help you determine whether there is a need to intervene, you often need to know how your target student's behavior compares with that of classmates. Using the same procedures as for your target student, you can observe peers involved in the same activities and settings during the same period of time. First, observe and record your target student's behavior; then immediately afterwards observe and record the same behavior for the peers. If you find that your target's behavior is significantly different from the peer behavior, you may be justified in intervening. Although you could also use this peer-comparison feature when continuously recording, a momentary sampling schedule is usually more efficient.

In the example shown in Figure 7.2, ten observations of two behaviors (noise and off-task movement) were scheduled during a thirty-minute period. Ten-second observations of Brian and a classmate were recorded at the beginning of each three-minute interval. As you can see, Brian made noise during 60 percent (6/10) of the intervals and was engaged in off-task movement during 50 percent (5/10) of the intervals. His comparison peer made noise just once and engaged in off-task movement twice. From these data, you can figure *discrepancy ratios*. In this case Brian made noise six times as often as his

You can observe other students to compare their behavior with the target student's.

FIGURE 7.2   Sample Observation Form for Target Student and Peers

Observation Form for Target Student and Peers

Name: *Brian*   Date: *1/22*

Beginning Time: *2:10*   Ending Time: *2:40*

Behavior Codes: *N = noise (talking, humming, whispering)
O = off-task movement (leaning away from or
out of chair, drumming on desk*

												Totals
Target	N O	N	N O	O	O N	N	O	O	N			N = 6 O = 5
Peers			O N			O						N = 1 O = 2

classmate (60/10 = 6:1 ratio) and off-task movements 2.5 times more often (50/20 = 2.5:1 ratio). If several observations over several days yield a similar pattern, you could conclude that Brian's behavior is off task and that he is making noise substantially more than his peer.

You can compute discrepancy ratios with other kinds of data as well. In the earlier example involving Lin, your records might show that, on average, other students in your class completed 80 percent of their homework assignments during the baseline period, compared to Lin's 20 percent completion rate. The discrepancy ratio is 1:4 (20 percent/80 percent = 1:4).

Again, we can offer no hard and fast rules about how much baseline data you need. Sometimes you will see consistent patterns from one observation to the next. Other times, however, you may observe fluctuations. If this is happens, you will want to consider situational factors that may affect the behavior.

A RATIONALE FOR INTERVENING

After collecting baseline data, you can develop a rationale (or justification) for intervening. The *quantitative* baseline data you have collected help you decide whether you should try to intervene, but your rationale also requires *qualitative* judgments about the importance of changing the behavior. Typically, teachers are concerned about behavior that is deficient or excessive. Either the student engages in less of the behavior than the teacher believes is appro-

Teachers should consider how important it is to change a certain behavior.

priate *or* the student engages in more of the behavior than the teacher believes is appropriate.

In cases where a student's *behavior is deficient or inadequate* (too few positive statements directed at others, too small a percentage of work completed, or too little time on task), you might decide it is important to increase the behavior. When the *behavior is excessive* (too often out of seat, too much talking, too much time wasted before starting assignments), you may want to decrease it. Knowing how your target student's behavior compared to peer(s) helps you develop a rationale. You at least have a relevant norm group with which to compare your target's behavior. We suggest the following guideline: When a student's excessive behavior is at least two times more than peer behavior, or a deficient behavior is less than one half that of peers, an individual intervention *may* be justified.

When a student's misbehavior happens twice as often as peers' you might want to intervene.

Clearly, a discrepancy in the frequency, rate, or duration of problem behavior should not be your only rationale for modifying behavior. You also need to judge the importance of the behavior by asking questions such as, "Is the behavior sufficiently important to merit special intervention?" "Is it reasonable to expect a change in behavior?" and "Is the behavior likely to respond to the external consequences available to me?" You might conclude, for example, that it *is* important that your students practice independently what they are learning by doing homework. You know that Lin could do the assignments. She is able to do similar work in class, and the amount seems reasonable—other students complete most of their homework. However, despite talking with Lin about the importance of doing her work, encouraging her performance in school, writing notes, and calling her home, she rarely completes it.

Teachers should consider whether they can change the behavior with the available resources.

You can involve students in developing a rationale for changing their behavior, explaining your concerns, describing the behavior, sharing baseline data, asking for their views, and soliciting a commitment to change. This is the goal setting part of the process. You and the student together identify the behavior to be changed and the reason for doing so. Frequently, being aware of a problem and knowing your concern about it help motivate a student to change. Sometimes, however, awareness and concern are not enough, and your student needs the external support offered by a contingency plan to achieve the change.

You should work with the student to decide which behavior should change and why.

SELECT INTERVENTION METHODS

Students should share in negotiations about an intervention plan.

Although you should have ideas about what features the intervention plan should include, you can often let the student share some negotiations about it. It is especially important to select consequences that will result in the desired behavioral changes.

Many of the tasks and behaviors we expect of students—such as sitting for long periods at an assigned desk, speaking only with permission, or calculating pages of long-division problems—are not in and of themselves intrinsically motivating, yet we believe they are important or necessary to accomplish our educational goals. Consequently, using effective instructional approaches and being enthusiastic are essential. Still, even apparently high-interest activities and an enthusiastic teacher do not motivate all students all the time. Other motivators compete for your students' attention and involvement too. Chatting with friends may be more interesting than listening to you read a story or completing a group project; sleeping may be more attractive than doing seatwork; making funny faces for classmates may be more appealing than paying attention to the teacher.

Teachers sometimes need to offer students rewards.

To maintain social order in your classroom and school and to ensure that students master your classroom and school curriculum, you will sometimes need to offer extrinsic motivators. Certainly, there is no need to reward behavior that students engage in routinely without reinforcement, and such reinforcement may actually undermine their intrinsic motivation. However, we believe it is not unreasonable to reward students for behavior they would not otherwise perform.

Selecting positive reinforcers is critical, and the possibilities for reinforcers are virtually unlimited. You might consider potential reinforcers according to whether the student tends to respond to more extrinsic or intrinsic rewards. Reinforcers fall along a continuum from more extrinsic (external) to more intrinsic (internal) forms as shown in Figure 7.3.

Tangible Reinforcers

Some rewards are tangible.

Tangible reinforcers include objects like toys, stickers, pencils, and trinkets as well as *edibles* like candy, chips, fruit snacks, and meals. Reinforcing activities include preferred events and privileges like classroom jobs, use of computers or tape players, games, group leadership, or free reading time.

FIGURE 7.3   A Continuum of Reinforcers

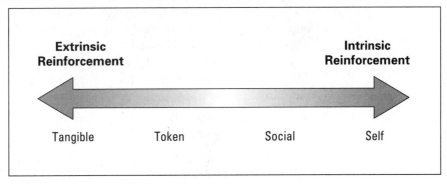

Extrinsic Reinforcement   **Intrinsic Reinforcement**

Tangible   Token   Social   Self

Token Reinforcers

Tokens can be traded for tangible or activity rewards.

Contingency management often uses *token reinforcers*. It is generally more efficient and less disruptive to classroom routines to provide tokens (symbolic rewards with an assigned value) that can later be traded for tangible or activity reinforcers.

Tokens can take many forms, including checkmarks, points, colored ribbons or paper strips, play money, and stickers you have given a specific value to, much like money. Depending on students' ages, your choices of course will vary. You can award tokens to students when they perform the desired behaviors, or at predetermined times (every fifteen minutes or at the end of the period), depending on the nature of the target behavior and your ability to dispense tokens. For example, you could award a token for each math problem correctly completed or for every assignment completed according to a predetermined performance standard (perhaps, at least 90 percent correct). You might establish random times to check if the student is engaging in behavior such as on task or at seat or at work and dispense tokens for these behaviors. If you are trying to increase the amount of time a student stays at her desk, for instance, you could observe the student at irregular intervals six times each hour. When the student is at her desk during at least five of the six observations, she receives a token checkmark.

Giving the reward as soon as possible after the desired behavior helps the student associate the behavior with the reinforcement.

Of course, it's necessary for students to make connections between their behavior and its consequences. To help them associate behavior and reinforcement, you should award tokens as soon as possible *following* the desired behavior. Obviously, if you provide reinforcement *before* they perform the behavior, the contingent relationship may not be learned—there may be no incentive to engage in the behavior.

Social Reinforcers

Social reinforcers are powerful and include verbal and nonverbal attention.

Social reinforcers are among the most powerful and efficient forms of reinforcent at your disposal. They include verbal and nonverbal attention and approval from others, most notably you. You can use verbal expressions of approval ("That's right," "You're doing a good job paying attention," "I like to see you raising your hand"), nonverbal expressions (smile, nod, laugh, thumbs up, wink), proximity (standing or sitting next to student), and physical contact (shaking hands, pat on the back). Teachers use many forms of social reinforcement, including awards and certificates of accomplishment, notes to parents, verbal recognition in front of the group, and special jobs and responsibilities in the classroom and school.

Self-Reinforcement

Self-reinforcement usually refers to good thoughts or feelings individuals have about themselves. Since it is an intrinsic form of reinforcement it is not often used contingently. Think, for example, of a challenging activity you have done particularly well. Do you remember feeling good about your performance or thinking positively about your accomplishment? Even without social approval or recognition, you rewarded yourself for a job well done. You can help students learn to self-reinforce behavior by offering social, token, and tangible confirmations of their achievements. In Chapter 8, we describe social skills programs that systematically teach self-monitoring and self-evaluation skills that can help develop self-reinforcement skills.

You can help students learn to feel satisfied with what they have done.

The best ways to determine potential reinforcers are to observe what students do when they are free to choose their activities and to ask them what objects and activities they enjoy. If you observe the student reading magazines, eating candy, playing board games, or listening to music, those activities might be contingent rewards. Your students are the experts on what they find rewarding and sometimes suggest possibilities you might not have considered. When we asked one student what he would work toward as a reinforcer, he asked if he could help the janitor clean the school—certainly not an activity on *most* lists of rewards.

Rewards must be valuable enough to students to affect their behavior.

Reinforcers must have sufficient value to students to affect their behavior. Table 7.2 contains lists of potentially reinforcing objects and activities for primary, intermediate, and secondary levels. This is by no means a comprehensive listing, nor are certain kinds of reinforcers limited to specific age levels (even older students sometimes enjoy food rewards). Our list simply suggests some possibilities that most teachers could provide. Creativity and whimsy have their place in determining reinforcers. Unusual or offbeat choices are often the most fun—decorating a student's desk with little Christmas lights, trading desks with the student for a day, wrapping a surprise package for the student, allowing the student to take the gerbil home for the weekend—these all are possibilities that go beyond the usual menu of reinforcers.

Unusual rewards can be fun.

You can make lists of rewards or fill a drawer with activity tickets and small prizes.

Many teachers provide a *menu* of potential backup reinforcers and allow students to choose from it. You can stock a cupboard or a drawer with objects and tickets for activities that have assigned values. As in the group token economies described in our next chapter, students may choose to buy relatively inexpensive items on a short term or daily basis or may save their tokens to purchase more costly items. Do not be surprised, however, if some students save points and accumulate great totals. Although they have no intrinsic value, points often become something to treasure (perhaps a measure of self-esteem?), and some students have trouble parting with them.

You can negotiate with a student how much a certain behavior is worth.

After you have selected reinforcers, you can *negotiate* reasonable values, or payoff ratios. For example, if Carlos chooses listening to audiotapes as his reinforcement for staying with his group during social studies, you and he might negotiate that he could earn one point for each ten-minute interval. You could agree that when Carlos earns four points he may listen to a tape of his choice for the following five minutes.

TABLE 7.2
Potentially Reinforcing
Objects and Activities

ACTIVITIES	OBJECTS
Primary grades	
Perform classroom jobs	Stickers
Be a line leader	Stamps
Get learning center time	Special badges
Have extra recess or computer time	Pencils, markers, crayons
Be a teacher helper	Book awards
Eat lunch with teacher	Certificates
Read a story with friend	Note pads
Assemble puzzles	Play money
Play board games	Small toys, trinkets
Use clay, colored pencils	Coloring books
Play with blocks, Legos	Special desk decorations
Intermediate grades	
Sit by friend	Gum, candy, chips
Visit teacher's house	Computer time
Listen to audiotapes	Behavior chart
Make bulletin board	Sports cards
Care for class pets, plants	Art supplies
Choose free-time activity	Comics, sports, and teen magazines
Have independent reading time	Felt pens, markers, notebooks,
Operate A/V equipment	stationery
Pass out or collect materials	
Secondary grades	
Listen to radio or tapes	Most of the above, adapted to student's
Work in computer lab	age level
Be allowed to go home early	Coupons for food
Have reduced assignments	Audiotapes, CDs
Visit with friends	
Have study time for other classes	
Choose free-time activity	
Play games	
Have lunch with principal	

You can use tokens for groups and classes as well.

Token systems are not only for individuals. In the next chapter, we will show how you can develop group, and even classwide, token economies to promote behavior that contributes to your class as a whole. If you have several students who could benefit from the external support offered by a contingency management program, you might implement several individual interventions, with each student's plan focusing on different target behaviors, reinforcers, and payoff ratios. You might even implement several individual contingency plans alongside a class-wide token economy.

Implementation

The first four steps of the individual contingency management plan—identifying target behaviors, observing and recording baseline data, developing a rationale for intervening, and selecting intervention methods—provide the basis for your intervention. They involve collecting information and using it to make decisions (problem solving) about your course of action for persistent and pronounced behavior problems. You are now ready to implement the individual contingency management plan. This may require some additional arrangements, such as coordinating teacher and staff involvement, adjusting routines and schedules, obtaining any necessary materials (e.g., tokens, backup reinforcers), and monitoring the results of the intervention.

EVALUATE INTERVENTION EFFECTIVENESS

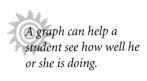

You need to plan how you will evaluate your intervention plan.

You will need to evaluate the effectiveness of individual contingency management plans. Your evaluation procedure need not be complex. Usually you can simply extend the methods you used to collect baseline data. Returning to Lin's case, for example, you could continue to record her homework completions on a daily basis and determine the number and percentage she completes each week. If you use tokens, you can record the number of tokens she earned during each unit of time (period, hour, day). A weekly record card (Figure 7.4) is one possibility for tabulating this kind of data.

COMMUNICATE INTERVENTION OUTCOMES

A graph can help a student see how well he or she is doing.

Graphing behavior changes gives you a helpful reference regarding the student's progress and shows the student what he or she has accomplished. Successful interventions show increases in the behavior you are trying to increase and decreases in behavior you are trying to decrease. If the behavior does not change in the desired direction, or improves for only a short time and then levels off, or ceases altogether your graph tells you that some features of the intervention are not working. The student may not find the consequences sufficiently reinforcing or may have become satiated. If this happens you will need to modify your plan—perhaps change the type or frequency of reinforcement.

Two Evaluation Approaches

Two commonly used evaluation approaches are the **reversal** and the **multiple baseline designs.** The reversal (or ABAB) design involves collecting and charting target behavior during the following phases of your intervention:

- *Baseline phase:* preintervention, or *A* phase
- *Intervention phase:* treatment, or *B* phase
- *Return to baseline phase: A2*
- *Reinstated intervention phase: B2*
- *Postcheck phase*

FIGURE 7.4   Weekly Report Card

Weekly Record Card

Student: *Lin*

1 = Assignment completed
0 = Assignment not completed

Schedule	Mon.	Tues.	Wed.	Thurs.	Fri.	Total
Reading	1	0	1	1	1	4
Language arts	1	0	1	1	1	4
Social studies	0	0	0	1	1	2
Music/P.E.	1	1	1	1	1	5
Math	0	0	1	1	1	3
Science	0	0	1	1	0	2
Daily total:	3	1	5	6	5	20

Number earned:	20
Number spent:	−12
Remaining:	8
Balance forward:	+ 6
New total:	14

Compare the data you collect during each phase. A graphical representation of Lin's progress, for example, might look like Figure 7.5.

What can you conclude about the effectiveness of the intervention based on the graphed behavior in Figure 7.5? During three weeks of baseline (phase A), Lin completed 0, 8, and 4 of her assignments. During the three weeks of intervention (phase B), she completed 15, 20, and 25 assignments. When the intervention was discontinued for one week (phase A2—return to baseline conditions), Lin's completions fell to 10. When the intervention was reinstated (B2), however, they increased to 25 and 27. Periodic postchecks in weeks 12 and 15, show that Lin's homework completion rate had stabilized at a high

FIGURE 7.5 Reversal Design

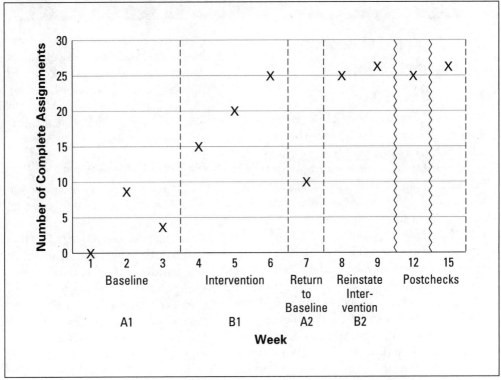

<table>
<tr><td></td><td>Baseline</td><td>Intervention</td><td>Return to Baseline</td><td>Reinstate Intervention</td><td>Postchecks</td></tr>
<tr><td></td><td>A1</td><td>B1</td><td>A2</td><td>B2</td><td></td></tr>
</table>

Week

The reversal design can help you tell whether or not the intervention is working.

Many students are as motivated by the graphs as by the rewards.

A multiple baseline design records several behaviors of one student or one behavior of several students.

level, 25 and 27. Data like these from a reversal evaluation design indicate that the intervention was effective. Lin rarely completed her assignments (about 10 percent) prior to intervention, but as the graph shows, following the intervention she was completing nearly all of her assignments.

Of course, graphing behavioral change helps you determine the effectiveness of an individual contingency management plan. In addition, the graphs can be sources of reinforcement for the students. Most students like to see their progress charted and may be motivated as much by the graphs as they are by the backup reinforcers they are earning. Often you can teach them to record and graph their own behavior. Self-monitoring, self-recording, and self-evaluating are integral to self-management and should be the ultimate goal of your individual contingency management plan.

In addition to the reversal design, you may sometimes use multiple baseline designs to record several different behaviors of one student or a single behavior of several students who are involved in similar contingency management plans. The Classroom Closeup "An Individual Contingency Management Plan" provides an example of how a teacher uses the multiple baseline

Classroom Closeup

An Individual Contingency Management Plan

Target Behaviors

Daniel is a six-year-old in kindergarten who disrupts his class with aggressive behavior, talking out, and inappropriate touching. The aggressive behavior includes grabbing, pushing, kicking, and hitting other students or his teacher, Mrs. Williams, when he is required to participate in an activity or when he tries to take something from others.

Daniel also talks out in a disruptive way. For example, when entering the room he often shouts something like, "Hey, you, I'm here!" in a loud, shrill voice. He speaks loudly without permission during instruction and quiet times, interrupting Mrs. Williams and other students. Several times during a class discussion, he has started loudly singing and dancing to a popular country tune, "Achy Breaky Heart."

Daniel's third problem is inappropriate touching. He grabs other students' arms or legs and hangs on. He also hugs unreceptive classmates. During group-time, while sitting on the floor, he pats or rubs students sitting nearby. The students try to move away and complain to Mrs. Williams.

Rationale for Intervening

Daniel's aggression, talking out, and inappropriate touching are disrupting the class, interfering with his acceptance by other students, and demanding an inordinate amount of attention from Mrs. Williams, who has nineteen other students in her class. Mrs. Williams is increasingly frustrated and angered by Daniel's behavior. She is also afraid he may seriously hurt someone. After consulting the school social worker and Daniel's mother, who expresses concern about his behavior and sees similar behavior at home, Mrs. Williams decides to design an individual contingency management plan.

Method of Data Collection

Given her continuous involvement with the class, Mrs. Williams needs a method to record the three target behaviors efficiently, yet accurately. She decides to record each occurrence of the three behaviors during the three and one-half hours Daniel is in her room each day. Using a grocery counter with four windows, she simply counts each behavior as it occurs. Each window can record up to nine incidents. Based on her informal observations, only talk-outs regularly exceed nine incidents per day, so she can use the fourth window to record additional talk-outs.

Baseline Data

During a five-day baseline period, Mrs. Williams records the following daily average numbers of the three target behaviors:

* Aggressive behaviors = 3.4
* Inappropriate vocalizations = 10.9
* Inappropriate touching = 3.8.

Mrs. Williams decides that Daniel's aggressive behavior is the most important to diminish first because it most directly affects others.

Reinforcement

Based on information from Daniel's mother that he really likes the rubber stamps of animal shapes she uses on students' work, Mrs.

Williams makes a special elephant-shaped note with seven boxes (one for each half hour of the day) that Daniel can take home each day to report his positive behavior.

Intervention Procedures

Mrs. Williams finds an opportunity to talk quietly with Daniel. She describes his aggressive behaviors and explains how his behavior makes it difficult for other children to be friends with him.

She shows Daniel the elephant note and explains that he can earn special animal stamps for not hurting others. She tells him he can keep the note and that each half hour he does not hurt someone he will be able to place a stamp on it. Daniel expresses enthusiasm for the plan. At the beginning of each day, Mrs. Williams gives Daniel an elephant note, briefly reminds him of the contingent stamps, and offers encouragement.

Method of Evaluation

Mrs. Williams uses a multiple baseline design, starting with aggressive behavior. During the first five days, Daniel engages in just three incidents of aggression—two on the first day and one on the second. This is a rate of 0.4 per day ($2/5 = 0.4$) compared to his rate of 3.4 during baseline. Mrs. Williams notices some improvement in Daniel's inappropriate vocalizations and touching during this phase, even though they are not yet the target behaviors. They decrease to an average of 8 vocalizations and 2.5 touches per day. She assumes this is a *halo effect* due to the attention they are giving to Daniel's aggressive behavior.

Given the reduction of Daniel's aggressive behavior, Mrs. Williams adds the second behavior, inappropriate vocalizations, to Daniel's contingency plan. She again meets briefly with him, describes the behavior, and explains that he will now be able to also have a lion-shaped note and earn stamps on it *and* the elephant note each half hour.

Over the next five days, Daniel's average number of inappropriate vocalizations drops to an average of 2.4 per day. His inappropriate touching continues at a rate of 3.1 touches per day during this phase of the intervention.

During the third five-day phase, Mrs. Williams adds inappropriate touching to the contingency plan, giving a buffalo note for his stamps. During this phase she observes Daniel inappropriately touching other students only five times—an average of one per day.

During the three five-day phases of the intervention, Daniel's problem behaviors nearly disappeared. His inappropriate vocalizations and touching began to decline even before Mrs. Williams formally added them to the intervention. Although the intervention required relatively little investment (a grocery counter, construction paper notes, and stamps), it was sufficient to motivate Daniel to change his behavior. Instead of expending a lot of time and effort interfering with his disturbing behavior, Mrs. Williams was able to focus on rewarding him for appropriate behavior.

Everyone in the classroom benefitted from the contingency management plan. The class atmosphere improved, Daniel was better accepted by his classmates, and Mrs. Williams was able to devote more time and effort to all of her students. In addition, Daniel's mother expressed her pleasure with Daniel's improved behavior and noted improvements at home as well. She said he was now coming home happy and eager to share his accomplishments. ✳

design to monitor change in three problem behaviors in an individual contingency management plan.

Although you cannot expect every contingency management plan to work as well as Mrs. Williams's interventions with Daniel, they can be effective when you carefully plan and implement them. Mrs. Williams invested time in her intervention, but it was probably less time and less emotional distress than she would have spent without an intervention plan.

REDUCE DEPENDENCY ON EXTRINSIC REINFORCERS

Students should not be rewarded for what they are already doing.

As we stressed earlier, there is no reason to offer contingent reinforcement if students already perform without it, nor should you provide more reinforcement than necessary to accomplish desirable behavior changes. When you do use contingency management, you should build in procedures to help maintain improvements over time and to encourage self-management. Two methods for reducing dependency on extrinsic reinforcement are called **fading** and **thinning**.

Fading

Fading helps students reinforce their own performance and stop depending on external rewards.

Fading refers to gradually reducing the student's dependance on extrinsic reinforcement by moving from extrinsic to intrinsic reinforcers. You can fade reinforcers by pairing more intrinsic with more extrinsic forms of reinforcement. For example, when you award tangible or token reinforcement, you can pair it with social reinforcement by verbally acknowledging the student's performance ("Carlos, you really helped by staying with your group today"). Eventually, your support and approval (social reinforcement) should be sufficient reinforcement for Carlos to stay with his group. Your ultimate goal may be for Carlos to internalize your verbal feedback and reinforce his own behavior.

Thinning

Thinning is reducing how often a student is rewarded.

Thinning means gradually reducing the frequency (or schedule) of reinforcement. Once behavior has been learned, it is usually not necessary to reinforce it every time it occurs. In fact, behavior is strengthened when it is intermittently reinforced (Bandura, 1977). For example, when Carlos stays with his group when he receives contingent token rewards, you can thin the reinforcement schedule. Instead of providing reinforcement at the end of each period, you might provide reinforcement on a two-period, then three-period, and eventually a daily schedule.

Response Cost

Some teachers use a procedure called **response cost** in their contingency management plans. Response cost is a fine in which students lose previously earned reinforcement, usually tokens, when they either do not perform the target behavior or engage in a specifically proscribed behavior. For example, Carlos might *lose* tokens for breaking certain class rules. We think you should usually avoid using response cost, since it seems inherently unfair to take something away that someone has already earned. Consider, for example, how you would feel if you missed a class. You would not expect to receive credit for work completed during the missed class, but should you also lose credit for work you had completed earlier?

As with any punishing consequence, response cost also has possible undesirable side effects. Carlos is likely to feel angry toward the punisher (you) for taking away something he has earned. If you do use response cost, make sure you carefully specify behavior that can result in fines. Also, make sure that students do not lose more points or other reinforcers than they have earned, or else they may feel they have nothing more to lose and become unmotivated. In most cases, it is better simply to provide no reinforcement for misbehavior than to take away rewards that have already been earned.

Negative Reinforcement

Negative reinforcement is another form of contingency management that has its limitations. Negative reinforcement is usually expressed in threats of aversive consequences to increase behavior. For example, you might say, "You cannot go to lunch until you finish your assignment." If you are nagging or criticizing a student's behavior to get the student to increase some behavior so you will stop nagging, you are using negative reinforcement. As with punishment, negative reinforcement has undesirable side effects, such as creating student antagonism toward the teacher. Also, when you use punishment and negative reinforcement, you provide a model that you probably do not want your students to imitate.

Archaic Management Interventions

Perhaps we should say a word here about some archaic management interventions that still seem to be in use, despite their limited effectiveness. Punishments such as copying pages from a dictionary, writing sentences on the chalkboard, doing pushups, or running laps are not appropriate for several reasons.

When teachers use punishments that resemble schoolwork, they definitely send the wrong message to students. If students are made to copy from the dictionary, they will find it difficult to see reference works as important tools

Teachers can send a wrong message to students when they use punishments that are like schoolwork.

Teachers can send a wrong message to students when they use punishments that are like schoolwork.

Students need time to run around.

Sometimes children need to be removed from a group or to lose privileges.

they may want to use. If they are made to copy endless sentences, writing itself becomes punishing. Taking away recess, breaks, or free time may also backfire. For many students, a time to run, play, relax, and let off steam is crucial to their continued ability to concentrate during the school day. A student who loses these opportunities or, even worse, is made to work while others play and relax, not only learns a negative view of school but also continues to stockpile energy that may be discharged in the classroom.

Having made these statements, we also need to mention exceptions. A child who hurts other children during recess may need to be removed from the group. A student who provokes arguments and intimidates other students during breaks could lose the privilege of future breaks. One excellent teacher we know assigns long, convoluted sentences for misbehaving students to write that introduce humor as well as new vocabulary. Keep in mind that the last thing you want is for your students to view their work, and school, as aversive. Punishing strategies generally produce little improvement. They may make the punisher feel better for a short time, but even that is generally short-lived.

SELF-MANAGEMENT

Both contingency contracting and mediation essays are ways you can promote students' self-management skills by increasing their awareness of problems and devising alternatives. You can also help students learn to manage their own behavior using the cognitive-behavioral strategies of self-monitoring, self-evaluation, and self-reinforcement.

CONTINGENCY CONTRACTING

Some contracts are formal, some informal, and some implicit.

Contracts are an application of contingency management that can help your students develop greater self-control. As in the real world, contracts are reciprocal agreements between two or more individuals that establish the conditions for exchanging services and goods. Contracts may be formal, informal, or implicit. When you are hired as a teacher, for example, you sign a *formal contract* with your school district that explicitly states mutual expectations about your salary and the number of days you will work. In addition, there are usually *informal contractual agreements* you discuss with your employers regarding instructional materials, supplies, support services, and your professional behavior. Beyond that, you and your colleagues have unspoken, *implicit expectations* about how you will treat one another. For instance, you expect your building administrator and fellow teachers to be supportive and to treat you respectfully. Your employers have implicit expectations for you as well.

A classroom contract is a negotiated agreement between a student and a teacher on how a certain behavior will change.

In classroom applications, contracts are negotiated arrangements involving teachers and students that specify behavior, how it will change, and what contingencies will be associated with the behavior change. While many arrangements with your students are either implicit (your mutual understanding of appropriate behavior) and informal (discussion of behavior expectations), you sometimes may need to explicitly formalize and specify expectations and consequences with individual students.

The following are elements of contingency contracts (Homme et al., 1969):

- Specification of target behavior,
- Performance criteria (how much, how often, what quality),
- Reinforcements and payoff ratio between behavior and rewards,
- Time when rewards will be provided,
- Bonuses for near perfect performance,
- Penalties for breaking the contract (optional),
- Methods to determine if criteria are met.

Figure 7.6 contains a sample contract identifying these elements.

FIGURE 7.6   Sample Contingency Contract

```
                         CONTRACT

Be it understood that

Carla agrees to remain at her group table during Social
Studies. Each day Carla does this she will receive 20
extra points to be used to purchase activities during
Fabulous Friday time.

If Carla does not leave her seat at all during the
week, she will be Teacher Assistant next week.

If Carla leaves the Social Studies group more than
three times during the week, she will not participate
in Fabulous Friday time.

We, the undersigned, understand and agree to the condi-
tions of this contract.


Signed: _____    Date: _____

Signed: _____    Date: _____

Witness: _____    Date: _____
```

Negotiating is an important part of making a contract.

When you use contracting to help students change behavior, you must first determine the level of participation they can reasonably assume. For younger students and students without prior experience with contracts, formal, written contracts seem to work best. As teacher-manager, you will make most decisions about target behaviors, rewards, and methods of monitoring and evaluating performance. When your students have had prior contracting experience and understand the procedure, they can play more active roles in negotiating target behavior, rewards, performance criteria, and monitoring and evaluating their performance. A key ingredient of contracting is active discussion and negotiation among the participants. Unless all parties agree to the conditions of the agreement, the contract will fail.

Some contracts can involve three people.

Contracting is not limited to two-party agreements. In some instances, three-party agreements (you and two students; you, another teacher, and a student; you, a student, and a parent) are more appropriate. For example, you, a student, and her parent could jointly agree to change the student's behavior in school, together specifying the behavior and performance criteria. Your role could be monitoring the behavior, the student could provide daily self-evaluations, and the parent might provide reinforcement at home.

Contracts can help a student learn to manage his or her own behavior.

With contracts, you help your students learn skills in self-management. They learn to recognize and monitor their own behavior, to negotiate, and most important, to assume responsibility for changing their behavior. Contracting reduces the element of teacher control that is more evident in other forms of contingency management. Since students actively participate in negotiating a contract, *they* decide what they are willing to do. Consequently, contracting places responsibility for change squarely on the student's shoulders. If they choose to not meet the agreed upon criteria, it is their decision, and they simply do not reap the rewards.

MEDIATION ESSAYS

Mediation essays help students understand what they have done wrong and what they should do to change their behavior.

A **mediation essay** is a kind of cognitive behavior modification that helps students think about their misbehavior and learn strategies for changing it. Mediation essays can be used with a variety of behaviors, settings, and student developmental levels (Morrow & Morrow, 1985). The strategy is straightforward. Students simply answer four questions on a sheet of paper: What did I do wrong?, Why shouldn't I do this?, What should I do?, and What will happen if . . . ?

After a student answers the four questions, you can give him or her feedback. Figure 7.7 contains an example of a mediation essay. If the student does not have the reading or writing skills to respond independently, you can read the questions and have the student dictate answers for you to write down. The student can then copy the answers and read them aloud to you.

FIGURE 7.7
Sample Mediation
Essay

What did I do wrong? I yelled at Ms. Francis on the playground, and I called her a name I shouldn't have.

Why shouldn't I do this? It made Ms. Francis real mad, and I got sent to the office. When I call people bad names, it makes them mad too, and then everybody is mad. And it gets me in trouble.

What should I do? I should tell Ms. Francis I'm sorry, and I shouldn't use that word anymore. I should find other ways to show that I'm angry.

What will happen if . . . ? If I do this again, I'll get sent to the office again and have to write another essay, and Dr. Wright will call my mom. Also, I will be showing that I still don't know how to control myself.

At first glance, mediation essays may appear to violate our previous caution about using academic work as punishment. However, the difference between writing such an essay and copying sentences or pages from a dictionary is that mediation essays can lead to self-knowledge about the behavior. They force the student to analyze his or her own misbehavior, to describe why it is a problem, and to plan ways to change it. As with contracting, the responsibility to judge and correct the behavior is the student's rather than yours. Initially, of course, you might get a lot of dutiful responses. Students will write what they think you want to hear—something along the lines of ". . . and I'll never ever do this again for as long as I live and I'll be a good person and I will behave." This is when you point out that no one is perfect, that we all make mistakes, and that setting a goal of never repeating a misbehavior is possibly unrealistic. You can then discuss alternative behaviors and realistic goal setting.

SELF-MONITORING, EVALUATION, AND REINFORCEMENT

Recording their own behavior encourages some students to change.

Self-monitoring has students observe and record their behavior. For example, one student may record every time she brings her books to class, another student, the number of times he contributes to group discussion. Students can also graph their behavior to see how it changes. Often, when students record and chart their behavior they become more aware of it and more motivated to change it.

As an extension of self-monitoring, you can teach your students to self-evaluate their behavior by monitoring and recording it over time. Reversal and multiple baseline procedures, for example, can help students see how their behavior has changed. You can also ask them to verbally evaluate their behavior based on the data they have collected. For example, a student may refer to his chart and be able to tell you, "I had all my supplies for 80 percent of my classes today, compared to only 50 percent last week."

Seeing evidence of behavioral improvement in graphs can also reinforce student behavior. When they see they have done well, they can reward themselves for achieving a predetermined level of performance. A student might say, "I did a good job preparing for class today" and choose a sticker to place on a performance chart.

Students can reward themselves for doing well.

COUNSELING STRATEGIES—LIFE SPACE INTERVIEWING

Although they should be rare occurrences, crises such as arguments, fights, and tantrums can occur in classrooms. Crisis experiences are events you will try to avoid because of the physical and emotional risks for both participating and observing students. When emotions are high, there are also risks to the teacher who intervenes.

Teachers need to stay calm during a crisis.

In a behavioral crisis, your first goal is to calm emotions and minimize damage. Your second goal may be to use the crisis as a learning opportunity, an experience that will help students handle frustration and anger. We think it is easier to handle a crisis if you view it as a problem to solve or a task to deal with rather than as a personal affront or threat to your authority. Admittedly, that is easier said than done, but when you are facing an angry student and your own adrenaline is pumping, an important first step is to remove your own anger from the situation. The following approaches provide a framework for dealing with these situations in a less volatile atmosphere.

LIFE SPACE INTERVIEWS

Life space interviews are counseling approaches for dealing with the intense emotions involved in crisis situations (Long & Wood, 1991; Morse, 1963, 1980). Sometimes students bring feelings of anger, frustration, and bitterness that have been generated elsewhere into your classroom, where they are directed at convenient targets—you and other students. Some students have learned from models or prior experience that arguing, fighting, and tantrums work—that they achieve desired ends. Or they may not have learned more effective ways of coping with anger and frustration. In addition, classrooms produce the inevitable tensions of interacting in crowded group contexts. There are multiple opportunities for accidents, misunderstood motives, and hurt feelings.

When a crisis does occur, your first goal should be to handle it antiseptically, minimizing infection and contagion. Emotional first aid and the clinical exploitation of life events are two forms of life space interviews that help students

- Acquire a better understanding of how their feelings have contributed to critical incidents,
- Develop motivation to change behavior,
- Learn strategies to deal with their feelings and behavior in the future, and
- Acquire greater trust in adults.

In both procedures, you (or another trained adult) serve as a mediator, or interviewer, to help the participants work through the event.

Emotional First Aid

Emotional first aid gives emotionally overwrought students an opportunity to discharge strong emotions so they can regain composure and resume involvement in the class. Too often, in our eagerness to return students who are angry, frustrated, embarrassed, and hurt to the program, we ignore or suppress their strong feelings. However, without opportunities to express those feelings, students are less able to regain control. The result can be continuing crisis, sometimes with the student transferring his or her feelings onto the teacher, who becomes the focus of the student's anger and frustration.

When students have been upset, they need a chance to talk about their feelings.

Emotional first aid involves lending a sympathetic ear, communicating to upset students your awareness of their strong feelings, while offering emotional support and reassurance. Statements such as, "I can understand how you think that is unfair" or "You're angry, but we'll work this out" acknowledge the student's feelings. You can also refer to routines and procedures that can communicate safety and security. For example, you could remind a student, "We have rules about how we treat one another" or "I can help you deal with this." You can also offer emotional first aid by umpiring disputes between students, interpreting events that may have been misinterpreted ("John didn't mean to bump your desk. He tripped on Rita's backpack"). When you use emotional first aid, you are essentially expressing empathy for the student. You recognize the student's feelings, without approving them. Sometimes, you may follow up emotional first aid with a clinical exploitation of the crisis.

Teachers can give emotional first aid by letting the student know they understand.

Clinical Exploitation of Life Events

The purpose of a clinical exploitation of life events is to guide students toward a better understanding of their feelings, help them recognize relationships between their feelings and behavior, develop values about their behavior, and

Teachers can help students understand their feelings and behaviors.

Talking about a crisis can help the teacher and student understand what happened.

The teacher can help the student understand how he or she was really feeling.

The teacher can help the student think of ways to deal with a similar situation in the future.

learn new behaviors that are more productive and acceptable. Because the clinical exploitation of life events requires the interviewer's total involvement, you must be free of other classroom responsibilities if you are to conduct the interview. The interviewer—whether a classroom teacher, a counselor, a social worker, an administrator, or other trained adult—follows six sequential steps with different types of questioning included in each (Long & Wood, 1991):

Step 1, Focusing on the incident, is the critical first step. The interviewer begins by expressing support and understanding as described in emotional first aid. Interviewer statements like "You looked very upset" or "That was a bad situation, but we'll work on it" help the student focus on the crisis incident. Although the interview should occur while the incident is still clear in the student's memory, it should begin only after the student has regained some composure and ability to talk about what happened.

Step 2, Providing an opportunity to talk about the incident, helps clarify the student's and your understanding. This step has been called "getting the geography of the situation" because it involves asking who, what, where, when, and how types of questions. "Where were you when Lars threw the book?" or "Right after you picked it up, what did you do?" or "Can I summarize what you just said?" are used to clarify exactly what happened.

Step 3, Finding the central issue, involves exploring the student's perceptions and the feelings aroused by the crisis event. Because students are not always aware of the relationships between their feelings and behavior, you may need to point to physical signs of their emotions, such as trembling, flushed appearance, facial expressions, or muscle tension. This can help students develop a vocabulary of feelings—putting names on their emotions so they can verbalize them ("You say you weren't angry at Truman, but you called him a jerk and shook your fist at him. How do you think this means you felt?" or "How did you ask her if you could help?"). During this step, you also solicit the student's perceptions of the incident ("So you think they always pick on you. What is another time this has happened?") and other times and places the student has had similar feelings and experiences ("Did you feel the same way yesterday when William dropped your coat?"). Throughout this step the interviewer should avoid rushing to conclusions before he or she has a full picture of the event.

Step 4, Choosing a solution based on values, involves asking the student to generate possible ways of dealing with similar situations in the future. You should ask the student for answers that reflect a belief that he or she can handle it more effectively ("You've suggested two ways of asking for help. Which do you think would work best?" or "Do you think you can wait for your turn tomorrow?"). The key to solutions that are likely to work is the student's valuing them and believing they will work.

Step 5, Planning for success, involves helping the student anticipate likely reactions from others and then considering and rehearsing approaches for implementing the chosen solution. "If you follow the steps we've talked about, how do you think Raphael and Gloria will react?" or "How will you apologize to Ms. Rizzo?" are the kinds of questions that can help prepare the student to follow the interview.

Step 6, Getting ready to resume activities, is preparing the student to reenter the ongoing activity. Supportive comments like "OK. It's 10:15 now. What do you need so you can join your group?" or "I'll write a note to Mr. Nelson telling him that we've talked about this and that you will finish your work here after school" can help smooth students' reentry into the program.

Obviously, students involved in a crisis must trust the interviewer if this procedure is to succeed. The following are guidelines for communicating care and trust (Long & Wood, 1991):

The student may need help getting back into the school schedule.

- *Nonverbal body language.* Use eye contact, relaxed posture, physical proximity, and facial expressions to convey interest and support.

It is important for a student who is in a crisis to be able to trust the interviewer.

- *Verbal style.* Use concrete words, minimize own talk, use time lines to help organize events, generalize using third-person form, limit references to yourself and negative statements.

- *Relationships.* Use active listening, communicate respect, interest, self-control; convey optimism and competence; avoid value judgments and counteraggression.

Interviewers must show the student that they understand and care.

We think that the most important interviewer trait is communication of *empathy,* or objective caring. Life space interviewers must be able to communicate to the student that they understand and care about their feelings, that they want to help develop solutions, and that they will support the student's efforts.

The clinical exploitation of life events is time- and energy-consuming. It is not a strategy you would use for every behavioral problem, but for crisis events that have not responded to less intense interventions, it sometimes produces long-term benefits. Keep in mind that a student who has learned to control or understand his or her anger and emotions has learned one of the most valuable skills possible.

CRISIS SITUATIONS

Life space intervention can help establish communication with students *following* a crisis, but what do you do in the midst of a crisis event, such as a student screaming obscenities, throwing objects, damaging materials and equipment, threatening, or actually attacking others? First, let's hope you are rarely, if ever, faced with such situations, and that your instructional and preventative approaches lessen the likelihood of such incidents. Crises involving serious physical danger are unusual in most classrooms. Still, students sometimes react irrationally to events, transfer their anger and aggression from another setting to your classroom, or are affected by drug or alcohol use.

We would be presumptuous to offer a single formula for handling crises because each one is unique in the circumstances leading up to it, the characteristics of the persons involved, their relationships with one another and with you, the setting conditions, and the types of assistance you have available. A careful ecological analysis of the factors we described in Chapter 6 that are involved following a crisis (what, where, when, how often, under what conditions, and feelings) may help you deal with future crises. But what will you do during the crisis?

It is critical for teachers to keep their tempers when students are out of control.

The most important, and most difficult challenge is to *maintain your self-control* despite student behavior that may include threats, obscenities, throwing and breaking objects, and even physical assaults on other students or you or themselves. It is not easy to keep self-control under crisis conditions. Angry threats tend to incite angry responses, and physical aggression tends to elicit counteraggressive behavior. Try to remember that reacting to an out-of-control student with similar behavior only escalates the situation and provides a model who is also out of control. As we said earlier, viewing the situation as a problem to be solved rather than as a personal attack may help you to marshal your thoughts and resources.

Tell the upset student what the consequences of his or her behavior will be.

Send for help if you need it.

Don't physically confront the student even if he or she leaves the room.

Attempt to follow this sequence: First, *firmly state the behavior and its consequences.* For example, "Jeremy, you may not run around the room knocking things off the desks. If you don't sit down, you will have to leave the room with me." If the student does not respond to your instructions, *send another student or another adult (if available) for assistance.* Where there has been a history of crisis events involving particular students, you can make prior arrangements with colleagues, such as counselors, special educators, and administrators, to provide assistance.

If the student appears determined to leave the room, it's best to stand aside to avoid a physical confrontation. You can then immediately report to the school office that the student has left your classroom. If the student remains out of control in your room and you believe he or she poses an immediate physical threat to himself or herself or to other students, you should direct the rest of your class to leave the room and to go to a specified location. If another teacher or an aide is available, that person should accompany the class and either return or send assistance.

If the rest of your students are physically threatened, tell them to leave.

Stay with the upset student and give him or her space.

In most cases, you should remain with the out-of-control student and calmly attempt to establish communication and to deescalate the crisis. Again, since physical proximity is emotionally arousing, try to give the student space and avoid blocking the path to the door. You can make comments and questions about the student's emotional state, such as those used for emotional first aid ("You're obviously very upset. How can I help?"). If the student seems likely to strike out or throw objects, you should maintain a safe distance, both to lessen the possibility of injury and to avoid threatening the student by your proximity.

Use physical restraint only if you really need to.

As we mentioned in a Chapter 6, we think it's usually wise to avoid using physical restraint unless the student is actively assaulting others (including you), hurting himself or herself, or an assault is imminent. Many schools and districts are offering training in techniques of physical restraint. However, even when you're trained, you should physically restrain a student only as a last resort. Physical contact during a crisis dramatically increases the risk of injury to the student and to you.

Make sure your physical restraint does not hurt the student.

If restraint is your only option, it should be nonpunitive, should not inflict pain, and should minimize potential injury. You can firmly grasp the student's hands or arms or hold his or her wrists from behind while calmly directing the student to regain self-control ("You're all right . . . Let's calm down"). Once the student has calmed down, as shown by more relaxed muscles, more coherent speech, less struggling, and is able to indicate that he or she has regained control, you should release the student and accompany him or her to an appropriate setting away from the crisis environment.

There need to be consequences for students who lose control.

There should be specific consequences for a major crisis event, such as not returning to the class or being suspended. In most schools, the event requires a formal report and discussion by other school personnel, the participating students, and the students' parents to determine consequences and to develop a plan to prevent a future crisis. Mediation essays or life space interviews might be part of the follow-up activities to devise ways to minimize future occurrences.

Fights, major arguments, and tantrums affect everyone in your classroom. In addition to intervening with the students who are directly involved in such an event, you must also attend to the anxieties and concerns of your other students. You should lead a brief class discussion to assure them that their classmate is being helped and that your usual program can continue. This discussion can help your students express their feelings, understand what happened, see what roles they may have played in it, and think about how it could be handled in the future. You should also commend them for being helpful and behaving appropriately during the crisis. Although it may be difficult, you should try to display a calm demeanor during your discussion.

After a crisis, the teacher should talk with the other students.

A classroom crisis directly or indirectly threatens a teacher's sense of authority and control over classroom events. Consequently, we think it is important for you to talk about it with colleagues, analyzing the antecedents and consequences, so you can plan ways to prevent or alleviate future crises.

Teachers can help students learn from crisis situations.

Although we all would like to avoid situations involving intense anger, frustration, and even violence, the sources of students' feelings and behaviors are sometimes beyond your control. Crisis events can erupt so quickly that you do not have the opportunity to stop them. In a certain sense, a behavioral crisis need not be a totally negative experience. You might use it as an opportunity to help the participants learn to recognize, understand, and deal with their strong feelings and the feelings they create in others. In our next chapter, you will learn about ways to help *all* of your students appreciate relationships between emotions and behavior to develop effective and acceptable self management skills.

SUMMARY AND REVIEW

In this chapter we have considered various methods of intervening with individual students whose behavior is challenging. While we generally see our students as part of a larger group, sometimes individuals must be considered alone, and their behavior addressed in a one-to-one fashion. There are many ways to intervene with individual students, but you should first consider the antecedents, consequences, and ecological causes and effects of the behavior. The quick fix or simplistic solution is not productive over time.

It is also important to actively include the student in an individual contingency management plan. Behavior management is not something you can impose on students without their knowledge or involvement. To succeed in any intervention effort, both parties must be clear about the target behavior, the data collection process, and the desired results.

The time it takes to negotiate, design, and implement individual behavioral plans may seem daunting. After all, your day is already crowded with academic and social responsibilities. Dealing with troublesome behavior, however, is a critical step in creating a healthy classroom environment. In fact, the time you spend dealing with problem behavior is some of the most important learning time for your students. We have all known people with excellent academic or job-related skills who are ultimately unsuccessful in their work because their social skills—their ability to control their emotions or to deal with other people—are so poor. If you are serious about preparing your students to be successful, contributing members of society, it is critical that you pay attention to their interactive abilities and behavior.

REFLECTING ON CHAPTER 7

We've discussed many forms of individual intervention in this chapter. Which ones do you think Annie should try with Danny? In fact, referring back to to Annie's journal, what do you think might happen in the principal's office?

- Assign the roles of Annie, Dr. Wright (principal), Danny, and Mrs. Garcelon to members of your group and role play what happened in Dr. Wright's office.

- Using the suggestions for specific observation, observe a child in a classroom (or in a fast-food restaurant, at home, or on the playground). What specific information did you find?

- Make a list of your own personal reinforcers. What do you find particularly reinforces your behavior? Is your list different from others in your group?

Key Terms

contingency management (p. 224)
antecedent-behavior-consequence
  (A-B-C) analysis (p. 225)
individual contingency management
  plan (p. 229)
reversal design (p. 243)
multiple baseline design (p. 243)

fading (p. 248)
thinning (p. 248)
response cost (p. 249)
negative reinforcement (p. 249)
contracts (p. 250)
mediation essays (p. 252)
life space interviews (p. 254)

Building Your Own Knowledge Base

Kerr, M. M., & Nelson, C. M. (1989). *Strategies for managing behavior problems in the classroom* (2nd ed.). Columbus, OH: Merrill. Kerr and Nelson discuss and describe behavioral methods for modifying problem behaviors.

Kohn, A. (1993). *Punished by rewards: The trouble with gold stars, incentive plans, A's, praise, and other bribes.* Boston: Houghton Mifflin. Kohn questions the usefulness of reward systems in school and on the job.

Long, N. J., & Wood, M. M. (1991). *Life space intervention: Talking with children and youth in crisis.* Austin, TX: PRO-ED. Describes a number of ways to use life space interviews and provides examples.

References

Bandura, A. (1977). *Social learning theory.* Englewood Cliffs, NJ: Prentice-Hall.

Brophy, J. E. (1981). Teacher praise: A functional analysis. *Review of Educational Research, 51,* 5–32.

Deci, E. L., & Ryan, R. M. (1985). *Intrinsic motivation and self-determination in human behavior.* New York: Plenum Press.

Homme, L., Csanyi, A. P., Gonzales, M. A., & Rechs, J. R. (1969). *How to use contingency management in the classroom.* Champaign, IL: Research Press.

Kerr, M. M., & Nelson, C. M. (1989). *Strategies for managing behavior problems in the classroom* (2nd ed.). Columbus, OH: Merrill, Kerr and Nelson.

Kohn, A. (1994). *Punished by rewards: The trouble with gold stars, incentive plans, A's, praise, and other bribes.* Boston: Houghton Mifflin.

Kohn, A. (1994). Punished by rewards: A rejoinder. *Beyond Behavior, 5,* 4–6.

Lepper, M. R., & Hodell, M. (1989). Intrinsic motivation in the classroom. In C. Ames and R. Ames (Eds.), *Research on motivation in education* (vol. 3). New York: Academic Press.

Long, N. J., & Wood, M. M. (1991). *Life space intervention: Talking with children and youth in crisis.* Austin, TX: PRO-ED.

Morrow, L. W., & Morrow, S. A. (1985). Use of verbal medication procedure to reduce talking-out behavior. *Teaching: Behaviorally Disordered Youth, 23–28.*

Morse, W. C. (1963). Working paper: Training teachers in life space interviewing. *American Journal of Orthopsychiatry, 28,* 888–891.

Morse, W. C. (1980). Worksheet on life space interviewing for teachers. In N. J. Long, R. G. Newman & W. C. Morse, (Eds.), *Conflict in the classroom: The education of emotionally disturbed children* (4th ed.). Belmont, CA: Wadsworth.

O'Leary, K. D., Kaufman, K. F., Kass, R. E., & Drabman, R. S. (1970). The effects of loud and soft reprimands on the behavior of disruptive students. *Exceptional Children, 37,* 145–155.

Premack, D. (1959). Toward empirical behavior laws: I. Positive reinforcement. *Psychological Review, 66,* 291–333.

Walker, H., & Buckley, N. (1972). Programming generalization and maintenance of treatment effects across time and across settings. *Journal of Applied Behavior Analysis, 5,* 209–224.

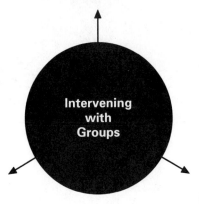

Group Cognitive Affective Approaches

- Affective education techniques
- The Arts
- Exercise and relaxation
- Bibliotherapy
- Peer mediation

Intervening with Groups

Group Behavior Modification

- Group contingency management
- Token economies
- Level systems
- Time-out

Behaviorally Oriented Approaches to Group Interventions

- Social skills training programs
- Turtle technique
- Think aloud

Chapter 8

Intervening with Groups

Annie's Journal

MARCH: OK. I'm good. Yes, I am good. I am a teacher—maybe I'm a good teacher—hey, maybe I'm a *great* teacher. Maybe I'll be a psychologist or a psychiatrist or a *famous* teacher. I really did something right today—had one of those experiences that we used to describe in classes as *peak*. We're talking top of the mountain here. All right, it wasn't all my doing—in fact it was mostly due to the kids. Sometimes they just blow me away. I mean, I go along thinking they rank somewhere between little monsters and big monsters, and then we have a day like today, and I am simply flabbergasted. I want to get this down on paper while it's still fresh in my mind, because I know that there are going to be a lot of days I need to have some evidence that things can go well in my classroom.

Now that I think about it, I can't really take credit for planning what happened—it was more like a "fortuitous confluence of events" (good to know I can think in vocabulary that goes beyond the third grade—I was beginning to wonder . . .). For several weeks now we've been having class meetings right before lunch, where we discuss lots of different things—sometimes current events, sometimes what's going on in our class, sometimes planning things. They've worked pretty well on the whole. I do have to be careful about the dynamics—like Nketi trying to provide a solution before the topic has even been defined, or Lee not saying much of anything at all, or Carla who has something to say on every subject, whether she's thought about it or not. We don't always solve the situations we talk about, but at least we get some discussion going. We certainly haven't been using this time to discuss anything very heavy—I mean, who gets to use the computer during free time is one of the most controversial topics so far.

The other thing I've been doing more often is telling them stories. I had this professor in college who said that every teacher ought to know at least three good stories that could be told well and with no props, stories you could pull out in an emergency or at a time when you just needed to get the group together. I thought about one of my three stories one day and told it to the kids just to fill some time. It was a fairy tale, *The White Snake,* and they really liked it! I was kind of amazed since they seem a little old for fairy tales, but they really listened. So I started learning some other stories and telling them from time to time—sometimes in social studies, sometimes during reading—anytime that it seemed appropriate. Since we're studying the Southwest, I've been telling some Native American stories and they really like that. Last week, I told a story called *A Heart Full of Turquoise,* a Pueblo story I found in a book by Joe Hill. It's about a village that's in trouble with a bad giant who comes and wants to eat first their grain, then their fruit, then their children. They create a good giant who goes out to take care of the bad one (the kids love this part), but after a really interesting battle where the bad giant is killed, the townspeople all gather around to heal the dead giant. The story isn't over until they've helped the bad giant to be good by replacing the pine needles and pitch in his heart with turquoise. The kids liked the story a lot, so I've told it twice now.

OK. Now to what happened today. We were having a meeting, talking about how things were going in our classroom—no big deal, just a general review of the past couple of days, and Idamys raises her hand. She's a really thoughtful kid who doesn't talk a lot, but isn't particularly shy or anything. I call on her and she says, "I've been thinking about that story you told us about the good and bad giants and how the people weren't through until they had fixed the bad giant's heart. And I've been thinking about how that's kind of like Danny and our class." Silence. Danny leans back in his chair, folds his arms across his chest, and smirks at Tremaine next to him. But Tremaine is looking at Idamys and so is everyone else. My palms start to sweat (as they do at any *mention* of Danny), and I wonder where this is going. I mean, we've never used this time to talk about an *individual,* and I certainly don't want this to turn into a gripe session about Danny—we'd be here all year! But I figure that sometimes you've got to risk a little— seize the moment—so I said, "Go on, Idamys—I'm not sure I know what you mean."

She looked at me and said, "Well, we all get mad when Danny is mean, and we tell you or we yell at him . . . but we don't do anything to make him good—like it's not our job." I'm not making this up—she really said that. Wow! Now what? Do I continue this? It turned out I didn't have a choice. Carla chimed in, "Yeah, like the people in the story had to fix the whole problem or it would just come back again."

At this point Danny, probably worrying that someone was about to suggest cutting out his heart and replacing it with turquoise, said, "I don't need fixin'—so you can just forget that." But, amazingly enough, he wasn't angry. He wasn't yelling, or hitting, or hurting—he just said it. Then Matt, who is sort of a friend of Danny's—at least sometimes, said, "Well, not exactly *fix*, you know . . . just sort of, well, not just be mad. Maybe we need to not just get mad when you're mean but do nice stuff too." Nice stuff too. What a concept. I'd been trying to get this particular message across since Day One.

Well, the kids continued to talk, suggesting not getting angry right away when something goes wrong with Danny, talking about ways to make him feel more a part of things, and Danny just sat there. He didn't look upset or mad—actually, he looked kind of interested. I guess if he's always trying to be the center of attention with his negative behavior, maybe getting all this attention in a positive way wasn't so hard on him. I probably had my mouth hanging open. I mean, here was this group of kids, sitting in a circle, discussing the behavior of one of their classmates and their own responsibility like a group of short social workers! I don't think they came up with any new principles of behavior intervention, but they *talked* about it, they were calm and serious and concerned, and Danny heard it all. I kept trying to imagine what was going on in his head, and I really couldn't, but at least he didn't lash out. He listened, even made a few comments on how he feels when he gets mad and how he hates to have people make fun of him.

Mostly I just listened, maybe made a few comments. It didn't last too long—ten minutes—and then we went to lunch. But I really felt good. I felt like such a . . . I don't know, a *facilitator*. And I was so proud of them. They were terrific. I have no illusions that my problems with Danny are over. I'm beginning to think those problems are so big that they are beyond my reach and that of my wonderful class. But to hear them try like that to reason and think, to share and be concerned . . . I had a glimpse of what they might be like as adults, and I was really proud. Even though Danny is not going to be able to change his personality overnight—or to control his anger all the time—for a while today he experienced *good* attention, the concern of his peers, and saw that other people worry about him. What a concept. What a day. What a job!

FOCUS QUESTIONS

✴ What risks was Annie taking? What could have gone wrong and what would she have had to do about it?

✴ Could Annie have planned for what happened? How could she have set up the situation if she had wanted to?

✴ What kinds of follow-up should she provide? Is this a one-time happening or can she provide activities to extend it?

✴ What conditions in Annie's classroom made this event possible?

GROUPS AS A FEATURE OF CLASSROOM ECOSYSTEMS

In our first chapter, we identified groups as a pervasive and influential feature of the classroom ecosystem (Jackson, 1990). Teacher-led recitation with the entire class or smaller groups, large and small group discussions, and cooperative learning teams all utilize groups for instruction. Even when your students are involved in individual activities, these activities occur in the context of groups.

In the last chapter, we looked at approaches you can use to intervene with persistent and pronounced problem behavior of individual students. Sometimes, however, your concern will be the behavior of groups of students or even your entire class. In this chapter, we turn our attention to ways you can intervene directly to deal with group problems. These strategies go beyond simply minimizing student distractions and disturbances or interfering with misbehavior. They include approaches to encourage cooperation, teach communication skills, enhance individual and group esteem, and ensure more positive social interaction among your students.

Some group interventions will take a lot of your time.

The group interventions we will look at in this chapter generally require a greater investment of your time and energy for planning and implementation than the interventions we've already discussed. In fact, they will likely require modifications in your usual classroom routines. In some cases you may need to prepare and use special materials and involve colleagues and support persons in your intervention efforts. Consequently, like the approaches in the last chapter, these group interventions are relatively high cost. They are also, however, potentially high return strategies because learning better ways of living and working together is critically important for your students. Increasingly, our society and the work force are turning to group problem-solving: task groups, Total Quality Management systems, and other collaborative approaches require an ability to function as a group member. Consequently, teaching, practicing, and implementing group participation skills is a legitimate and valuable use of your class time. The group interventions in this chapter include both **cognitive-affective approaches** and **behavioral approaches**.

Being able to work well in a group is one of the most important things a student can learn.

Cognitive-affective approaches focus on improving the ways students think (cognitive) and feel (affective) about themselves and others and are based on the assumption that a person's thoughts and feelings influence his or her behavior. Group cognitive-affective approaches sometimes use class meetings to discuss issues relevant to the functioning of the class as a whole. They also use the arts, exercise, and relaxation techniques to promote self-understanding, self-control, and improved interpersonal relations.

In Chapter 3 we referred to theories of multiple intelligences proposed by Howard Gardner and Robert Sternberg. As you recall, they offer an expanded view of cognitive, affective, and social abilities. In addition to *linguistic* and *mathematical* skills, for example, Gardner identifies five other kinds of intelligence: *kinesthetic* (dance, drama, creative movement, sports, games, exercise); *visual/spatial* (art, design, architecture); *musical* (appreciating and performing vocal and instrumental music); *interpersonal* (understanding and interacting with others, verbal and nonverbal communication, managing conflict); and *intrapersonal* (self-understanding, self esteem, expressing emotions). In this chapter we include some suggestions for developing your students' skills in these areas. There are also excellent resources to help teachers across grade levels and curricular areas include strategies and activities to enhance students' multiple intelligence (see Building Your Own Background Knowledge).

Behavioral approaches focus directly on improving the ways group members treat one another. In the last chapter, you learned how to use applied behavior analysis approaches such as individual contingency management plans and contracting to help individual students change their behavior. In this chapter we will look at some ways you can use contingency management and behaviorally oriented interventions, such as token economies and social skills training, with groups to promote more cooperative, acceptable social behavior in your classroom.

GROUP COGNITIVE-AFFECTIVE APPROACHES

CLASS MEETINGS

It is important for students to feel that their ideas matter.

The class meeting is a good place for students to express their ideas and concerns.

When people believe that their interests and ideas are considered and valued and have an impact on their group, they are more likely to behave as stakeholders in the group. Being a stakeholder means assuming ownership or responsibility for behavior. This is as true for students in classrooms as for teachers in schools. To become stakeholders in schools, students need to become active participants in their classes. In earlier chapters we showed how your communication with students and the design and stucture of your classroom ecosystem should help students feel they are stakeholders. Class meetings offer a format for sharing ideas and interests in structured group discussions that should help students feel they are stakeholders. These class meetings involve students in making decisions about the operation of their classroom and the ways they will treat one another.

Students can help decide how the classroom will run and how they will treat each other.

There are many books that stress the importance of helping students develop responsible decision-making skills (see William Glasser's *Reality Therapy*, 1965; *Schools Without Failure*, 1969; *Control Theory*, 1986; and *The Quality School*, 1990). Drawing on the work of Rudolph Dreikurs (1968; Dreikurs, Grunwald & Pepper, 1982), Glasser contends that student apathy and misbehavior reflect their feelings of powerlessness. Students are often excluded from decisions that affect what and how they are taught and how their classrooms

When you have class meetings, remember to let the students do the talking.
(Billy Barnes/ Stock Boston)

Students behave better when they feel that their opinions count.

are run. However, when students play an integral role in those decisions, they are more enthusiastic participants.

Consider, for example, how some students are highly motivated to participate in extracurricular activities like sports and clubs—arenas where student control is more obvious. To encourage student involvement in their classrooms, Glasser says we need to meet several student needs:

- To belong to a larger community and to be valued by their group
- To have power to make decisions and take responsibility
- To feel self-reliant and in control of their destiny
- To have fun and experience joy and satisfaction in their accomplishments

Class meetings can help your students meet all of these needs. Three types of meetings are *social problem solving, open-ended,* and *diagnostic* (Glasser, 1969). In each of these, you (or another adult) serve as convenor and facilitator, but avoid dominating discussions and being judgmental. The purpose of class meetings is to allow students *to share their ideas and concerns, to generate solutions to problems,* and *to make commitments to change.*

Social Problem-Solving Meetings

Typical conditions in elementary, middle, or secondary classrooms consist of twenty or more diverse individuals living and working together in relatively crowded conditions. The possibilities for social problems reflecting everything from minor disagreements to outright conflicts are enormous. Social problem-solving meetings provide opportunities for students to identify, discuss, and generate solutions to group problems.

In social problem-solving meetings the group focuses on a problem or concern that affects the class as a whole rather than on problems of individual students. If two students have a dispute that does not involve or affect others, it is probably not appropriate for group consideration and need not be addressed in the class meeting. However, if similar disputes involving other students are common, the problem may be appropriate for group consideration. You and/or members of your class may wish to have the group understand a problem and share in solving it. For example, if only a few students are helping put away supplies and clean up after art activities or if some students are consistently excluded from group activities, these may be problems that the class should discuss.

Problem-solving meetings follow several sequential steps. The first step is to ask students to describe the problem to make sure that everyone understands it. Some teachers use a suggestion box, where students can submit descriptions of group problems they would like to have the class talk about. Next, you ask members of the class to offer their own views of the problem. The group then brainstorms possible solutions for dealing with it. Finally, the group decides what to do and makes a commitment to doing it. As the teacher and leader, you must carefully moderate social problem-solving meetings, encouraging the students to share concerns and design solutions. Your role is primarily to keep the discussion focused on the chosen topic and to ensure that fault-finding and punishment are not solutions. It is often difficult to avoid rushing in with *your* solutions and providing your adult wisdom to set things on the right track, but it is critical to avoid doing this. The purpose of a class meeting is for the students to do the thinking, problem solving, and brainstorming, not for the adult to provide his or her answers. See the Classroom Closeup "Guidelines for Class Meetings" for suggestions on holding class meetings.

Open-Ended Meetings

Open-ended meetings offer students a chance to share information, concerns, and interests. Many of the affective education programs discussed in the following section use an open-ended meeting format for group discussion of ideas and feelings. In open-ended meetings, students (or you) select topics that are interesting or thought-provoking to the whole class. Students might bring a treasured book, an interesting object, or an experience to share with the rest of the class. You can have students independently complete question sheets about themselves and use these as the basis for group sharing and discussion. You can use open-ended meetings to help your students learn more about their classmates (numbers and ages of siblings, places they have lived or visited, favorite foods, hobbies, interests, sports, etc.). You can have the group practice

In social problem-solving meetings students work to resolve group problems.

The teacher needs to make sure that blaming someone is not the answer to a problem.

The teacher should let the students do as much of the problem solving as possible.

In open-ended meetings students can share their interests and learn more about each other.

Classroom Closeup

Guidelines for Class Meetings

Class meetings use a variety of formats. The following guidelines concerning scheduling, physical arrangements, length, and procedures should help you use them successfully:

- *Schedule class meetings at regular times.* We think meetings work best when they happen several times a week at predetermined times. When you regularly allot time for meetings, your students consider them part of the usual classroom routine and are more comfortable with them. Only a small proportion of your class meetings should be for problem solving; most should be open-ended or diagnostic.

- You *encourage communication by having students sit in tight circles* where they face one another. (It's hard to talk to the back of someone's head.) You may need to rearrange desks and tables for effective meetings.

- *Vary the length of meetings according to the topic and involvement of participants.* Generally, shorter meetings (five to fifteen minutes) work best in the primary grades, and somewhat longer meetings (ten to fifteen minutes) in the upper elementary grades. At the secondary level, meetings might be longer if the topic is worth it and the students are involved and interested enough.

There is no hard and fast rule on the ideal length of a class meeting. As facilitator, try to maintain a pace that keeps the group focused on the topic. When students start looking tired or bored you will know the group has either used up its interest in the topic or that you need to ask questions or find another way to get students involved.

- *Develop procedures to ensure that your class meetings are orderly and productive.* During initial meetings, you can discuss and ask the group to agree on a few ground rules and procedures that will help the meetings run smoothly. Rules should specify who has the floor, how students should behave ("no put downs," "be an active listener"), how long each participant is allowed to speak, and consequences for those who break the rules. For example, in some groups the facilitator hands a symbolic object, such as a gavel, to someone who wants to speak, either in the order in which students ask or randomly. Whoever has the floor may not be interrupted, although there may be a predetermined time limit. If a few students dominate meetings, you can encourage others to participate and ensure that everyone who wants to speak has a chance. Students who get on a sidetrack will need you to help them refocus on the topic. ✳

brainstorming and consensus skills by making a list of potential field trips, discussing the desirability and feasibility of each possibility, and narrowing the choices. Or you can center the meetings around themes the class is studying by arranging preliminary activities to stimulate student thinking. You might, for example, combine an English unit discussing Orwell's *Animal Farm* with a creative thinking activity on "What would happen if . . . we elected a president for life?" and a class meeting on how decisions are made in the classroom. Individual students can be featured in "Just because you're you" types of activities. For example, the class can shower the individual with positive descriptors ("hard worker," "helpful," "strong," "good sense of humor") and examples ("She sorted the paints for the whole class"; "He helped Willie go the nurse's office"; "Maria carried all the books back to the library").

Open-ended meetings offer opportunities for your students to recognize and appreciate their own and others' beliefs and values. Values-clarification activities on a variety of subjects are especially suitable for secondary level students, but some of them can be adapted to elementary classes as well (Harmin, Kirschenbaum & Simon, 1973). Values clarification topics describe scenarios in which there is no single best course of action, but participants make choices and defend them. One scenario, for example, briefly describes ten people with different attributes who are on a sinking ship. The only lifeboat has room for six people. The students discuss which people they would put on the lifeboat and the reasons for their choices. While discussions like these do not promote a particular set of values, they can help students recognize their own values, develop arguments to support them, and understand that others may operate from different values.

Character education is another topic that may be dealt with in class meetings. These discussion topics often center around themes such as loyalty, truthfulness, respect, and friendship. Activities for the class or for the whole school may be built around these themes on a weekly basis. Any time ideas surrounding values or character are made a part of the curriculum, you would be wise to let parents and other interested parties know. Seemingly benign topics such as those listed above may be misinterpreted as an effort to indoctrinate students with values that conflict with those taught at home. One way to stop such misunderstanding is to provide thorough information to parents ahead of time.

The purpose of values-clarification activities is for students to see what they believe and what their classmates believe.

Teachers should let parents know when they are going to include activities on values or character in the curriculum.

Diagnostic Meetings

Another type of class meeting is the diagnostic meeting, which does not relate as directly to group problems or issues as social problem-solving and open-ended meetings. You can use diagnostic meetings to evaluate your students' understanding of some aspect of the curriculum. For example, you might use diagnostic meetings to discuss current events in relation to concepts you are studying in United States history. Group discussions of a Supreme Court decision, a congressional hearing, or a foreign policy decision can help you determine students' understanding of the way the three branches of the U.S. government operate. Even if you are teaching secondary-level courses in science or math, diagnostic meetings are a legitimate way to regularly evaluate your students' understanding of what they are studying. When diagnostic meetings are part of your regular routine, you can call open-ended and even problem-solving meetings when they are needed.

Regardless of which types of class meetings you hold, their central purpose is to provide opportunities for your students *to develop communication skills,* including vocabulary, verbal and nonverbal expression, listening, and taking

Diagnostic meetings help you see what your students have learned or how well they understand certain concepts.

The main reason for class meetings is for students to learn to communicate better.

Students need communication skills for all their subjects.

turns. "The more we teach children to speak clearly and thoughtfully, the better we prepare them for life. When a child can speak satisfactorily for himself, he gains confidence that is hard to shake" (Glasser, 1969, p. 144). In addition to improved confidence, the verbal skills your students learn and practice in class meetings can help them gain a better understanding of how others think and feel. Developing communication skills is an integral part of the language arts and social studies curriculum and important to all curricular areas.

AFFECTIVE EDUCATION TECHNIQUES

While class meetings provide a forum for sharing ideas and feelings and solving problems, there are other techniques to help students develop better understanding and appreciation of their own and others' feelings. Feelings influence behavior. When students feel discouraged, frustrated, or angry, their behavior tends to reflect those negative feelings. When students feel confident, successful, and happy, their behavior reflects those more positive feelings. If you want your students to develop a greater awareness of their feelings and of the effect their feelings have on their behavior, you can design your own affective education activities and materials or use existing commercial resources.

One of the main purposes of affective education is to build self-esteem in students.

Building student self-esteem is integral to affective education approaches. Students who feel better about themselves usually do better academically and behave more helpfully. Of course, many of the approaches we have considered earlier—such as designing inviting, comfortable classroom environments; infusing culturally inclusive material into your curriculum; enthusiasm; and effective instructional approaches (high expectations, high success rates), to name just a few—contribute to students' self-esteem. Sometimes, however, you may also need to directly help students feel better about themselves and others.

You can use a tremendous variety of activities to encourage self-esteem in students.

The possibilities for affective education are limited only by your familiarity with existing materials and your creativity. They can include a wide variety of activities, such as students choosing positive descriptive labels for themselves and others, interviewing and collecting biographical information about one another, brainstorming positive attributes of classmates (a *fuzzy shower* or star of the week), discussing what makes them feel good, and drawing composite group portraits using one another's features. Some teachers encourage students to keep journals or diaries to record their thoughts and feelings; sometimes they provide written comments on students' journal entries (Shatzer, 1991).

Commercially Available Affective Education Programs

There are many commercially available affective education programs, especially at the elementary level. These programs include activities to help students recognize, understand, and appreciate how their own and others' feelings are related to behavior. Stimulus activities include stories, tape recordings, pup-

There are many affective education programs on the market.

petry, role playing, and games that can be used in group formats to stimulate thinking and discussion. Three widely used programs are *Developing Understanding of Self and Others—Revised* (DUSO–R) (Dinkmeyer, 1982); *Thinking, Feeling, Behaving: An Emotional Education Curriculum for Children* (Vernon, 1989); and *Toward Affective Development* (TAD) (Dupont, Gardner & Brody, 1974). DUSO–R I and II are designed for students in kindergarten through fourth grade; *Thinking, Feeling, Behaving* is for grades 1–6 and for grades 7–12, and TAD is for grades 3–6.

These programs are to help students control themselves and feel better about themselves and others.

Several affective education programs are designed to help students recognize negative thinking habits and learn more positive thinking skills to help them control their feelings and feel better about themselves and others. Examples are *Bright Beginnings* (Anderson, 1990) for ages 5–6; *PUMSY in Pursuit of Excellence* (Anderson, 1987) for ages 6–9; and *Thinking, Changing, Rearranging* (Anderson, 1982) for ages 9–17. These programs use puppetry, posters, stories, songs, and activities in group formats to study topics like developing internal controls and making responsible choices.

Recently the Issaquah School District in Washington has developed the ASSIST (Affective Skills Sequentially Introduced and Systematically Taught) curriculum for elementary classrooms (Huggins, 1986, 1991a, 1991b, 1991c, 1991d). ASSIST includes cognitive/affective activities that are designed to improve student self-concept and social skills. The curriculum is organized in six manuals, each with a different focus:

- Building Self-Concept in the Classroom
- Creating a Caring Classroom
- Teaching Friendship Skills
- Teaching Cooperation Skills
- Helping Kids Handle Anger
- Teaching About Sexual Abuse

In these manuals you will find activities to promote self-esteem, understanding of others, and interpersonal adjustment that could be incorporated into health, social studies, and/or the language arts curriculum.

Creating a Caring Classroom (Huggins, 1991a) organizes activities into the following nine sections:

- Warm-up activities
- Climate-building activities
- Classroom management procedures
- Praise and rewards
- Individual behavior-improvement plan
- Holiday activities

- Relaxation techniques
- Guided imagery
- Magic tricks

For each activity, the program developers have identified an objective and included a description of the strategy, a list of any needed materials, and a description of the procedure. Forms, questionnaires, certificates, and other materials used with any activity are included and you may copy them for students or use them as overhead transparencies.

Some programs teach about cultural differences.

Some commercially available programs have been specially developed to promote understanding and appreciation of cultural differences. For example, *Helping Kids Learn Multi-Cultural Concepts* (Pasternak, 1979) suggests approaches and topics that teachers can use in elementary classrooms. *Comparing Cultures* (Pickering, 1990) includes project topics, materials, resources, and procedures that teachers of young adolescents can use in their language arts and social studies classes. A new magazine, *Teaching Tolerance,* published by the Southern Poverty Law Center (at no cost to educators), offers ideas and information about programs and materials that promote appreciation of individual, cultural, and ethnic diversity that can be used with different age levels and in different curricular areas.

Affective education activities help students learn to communicate.

Affective education activities like these provide opportunities for students to practice and develop verbal and nonverbal communication skills. You can justify including them (like class meetings) in your academic curriculum on that basis. Also, since most students like to learn more about themselves and their classmates, they will probably find these activities interesting and engaging—features that are in short supply in too many classrooms (Goodlad, 1984, 1994).

THE ARTS

You can use the arts to encourage your students' emotional and social development.

What were your most positive, satisfying, memorable school experiences? Our own memories include helping create class murals, playing in the school band and orchestra, participating in sports and clubs, and performing in class and school plays. We suspect your most memorable school experiences also include special activities like plays, art projects, field trips, athletic events, and concerts. Many students' educational high points involve group projects or activities and a large dose of fun. The arts—visual arts, music, and sometimes drama—are usually part of the elementary, middle, and secondary school curriculum, and you can use them to promote the emotional and social development of your students. Frequently, the emphasis in art instruction is on skill development rather than on using the arts to help students understand and express feelings. Of course you can use the arts to simultaneously promote skill development and personal insights.

Visual Arts

You can use drawing, painting, sculpting, ceramics, and an infinite variety of other visual arts activities in group formats. Groups of students can paint group portraits, combining features of individual students into a single portrait. Groups of students can collaborate to plan and prepare murals that illustrate aspects of the curriculum they are studying while they practice communication and social skills. Keep in mind that these projects can use more skills than drawing. (Many students will wail, "But I can't DRAW. . . .") Using torn paper, collage techniques, painting, outline drawing, and other graphic forms including computer graphic presentations can include those students who don't like to draw. In addition, student art can be a major feature of your classroom decor. Most students like to have their artwork seen and appreciated by others, and they feel involved in the class when their work is displayed.

You don't need a degree in art history to help your students understand and appreciate the feelings and emotions in visual arts. Works as varied as Eduard Munch's *The Scream* or Norman Rockwell's *Vacation* can lead to questions such as "What is happening here?" "What is this person feeling?" "Have you ever felt this way?" These strategies have the added benefit of encouraging students to see works of visual art as expressions of thought and emotion as well as examples of artistic skill and technique. Many resources are available to help you integrate the visual arts into your curriculum (Campbell, Campbell & Dickinson, 1992; Herman & Hollingsworth, 1992).

Music

You can also use music to teach cooperation, to encourage self-expression, and to stimulate group discussions about the effect of music on moods and emotions. As in the visual arts, students can identify and illustrate how the music makes them feel. Such musical experiences help students not only develop vocabularies of feelings and practice communication skills, but also understand connections between feelings and behavior. You can stimulate interesting discussions and activities about musical styles, connections between young people and musical changes and innovations, music and rebellion, or child prodigies such as Mozart and Michael Jackson.

When you use music to enhance your curriculum (songs of the Civil War, folk music of countries you are studying), as a learning strategy (math songs, jingles that serve as mnemonics), or as a relaxing time together (listening or singing—yes, you *can* sing in the classroom when it isn't music class), you add a motivating and group-building feeling while you encourage musical appreciation and skills. One kindergarten teacher decided that reciting the Pledge of Allegiance did not mean much to her five-year-olds, so she began teaching them patriotic songs as an alternative. Now her students leave kindergarten knowing not only the Pledge of Allegiance, but also "It's a Grand Old Flag,"

"God Bless America," and a whole list of others—a repertoire that makes them popular at school assemblies and Fourth of July celebrations!

Drama

You can use drama to add to your curriculum or simply to help students learn to cooperate and communicate.

You can also infuse drama activities into many areas of the curriculum, especially language arts and social studies. There are many educational ways to use drama. Students can write scripts, plan sets, design costumes, rehearse, and perform in group skits and even class-wide plays on any topic in your academic curriculum. Theatrical activities also provide opportunities for students to develop and practice cooperation and communication skills.

Drama can channel the energies of attention-seeking students in a constructive way.

Most students enjoy performing for an audience. Unfortunately, some students perform in ways that disturb and distract other students, though sometimes their classmates serve as an appreciative audience. Teachers may call attention to the misbehavior when they try to interfere with it, but that attention inadvertently reinforces it. Dramatic performance is an acceptable way for students to get attention and feedback.

Acting can help students understand how other people feel.

One of the most valuable aspects of drama is its potential for helping students learn to take on the role of the other—to imagine others' experiences, feelings, and perspectives. This is a fundamental social skill that involves sensitivity and empathy for others.

Acting can help students understand and express their feelings.

Drama Therapy and Psychodrama. Drama therapy and psychodrama are techniques used by trained and registered therapists to help individuals express deeply felt and often suppressed emotions. These strategies are typically used in therapeutic settings such as treatment centers and hospitals, rather than classrooms. However, the success of drama therapy indicates the power of dramatic expression to help people understand themselves. You can use drama to help students explore and express their feelings and thoughts, to see what their behavior looks like to others, or just to have fun performing. You might, for example, have students act out emotions like anger, joy, fear, or surprise without using words and ask the other students to identify them. After the initial astonishment that everyone did not get it *immediately,* students see that just because they *think* they are looking or acting fearful or joyful or surprised, others may not see it that way. If you are interested in using drama in your classroom, there are resources for teachers that describe theater games, warm-up activities, and dramatic play (Salman, 1992).

Puppetry. Puppetry is another application of dramatics. Your students can design and make puppets using relatively inexpensive materials (paper bags, construction paper, paste, and crayons). They can then write stories or scripts about their puppets to perform in individual or group productions in class or for other classes.

Using puppets can help students express their feelings and practice cooperating.

Puppetry has several potential benefits. Students are often able to express feelings and thoughts that they might not otherwise feel comfortable doing. Puppetry also offers opportunities to practice communication and social skills, such as cooperation. For example, you can expand the story-telling activity to include writing books about the puppets and their adventures. Your students can create covers and illustrations for their scripts, they can publish their books by having them bound, take them home to share with their families, and/or place them in a classroom library. In our experience, there are few activities students find more rewarding than writing books.

Culinary Arts

You can use cooking to practice reading and math as well as social skills.

You might also find opportunities to involve your group through the culinary arts. Many facets of food preparation can promote inter- and intra-personal skills as well as integrate aspects of the academic curriculum. For example, students practice reading and math skills when they read recipes and use measures (sizes, weights, temperatures). Most people enjoy cooking, and especially eating.

You can use cooking in your science curriculum.

While it may seem easier to include food-related activities in the elementary curriculum, even secondary teachers can find ways of using food preparation in their classes. For example, in social studies, English, and foreign language you can relate foods to historical periods and events, to literature, and to countries and ethnic groups. Even in curricular areas like math you can help abstract concepts and calculations come alive for your students by studying shapes and measures in preparing food. The sciences offer unlimited possibilities for integrating food preparation into the curriculum. Students can study nutritional and chemical ingredients in foods, the changing properties of ingredients that result from mixing and changing temperature, etc. Of course, in addition to the rewarding potential of preparing and eating food, fixing it and sharing it with others (other classes, teachers, parents, a soup kitchen or shelter) can help students develop a concern for others.

EXERCISE AND RELAXATION

Students need time to move around.

You may be able to sit quietly and work independently for a much longer period of time than most children and adolescents. For some students with attention deficit disorders, sitting quietly is a near impossibility. Students tend to be more engaged in learning when they participate in a variety of instructional approaches and activities (Kounin, 1970). They need opportunities to engage in large muscle activities and vigorous physical exercise as well as to relax.

You can plan for students to get exercise during physical education classes and recesses (at the elementary level) when your students choose their own activities. These opportunities to "blow off steam" as well as to learn and practice physical skills are extremely important and can affect student behavior in the classroom. While you need to provide sufficient structure in the form of rules to prevent injuries on the playground, the freedom should provide relief from classroom pressures.

Teachers should rarely keep students from going out to recess.

Some teachers threaten students with losing recess if they misbehave. While the threats may work in the short run, we think you should be slow to keep students in during recess. Recess helps students cool off, unleash energies and frustrations, or wake up. When you take it away, you may actually encourage the troublesome behavior and make the student resent you.

Plan transitions between recess or gym and academic work.

You can smooth your students' transitions from highly physical activities of the playground and gym to the less physical activities of class by planning transitions that allow students to calm down. To help your students relax, you can establish routines for transition times. For example, you might read a story while your students put their heads on their desks for two or three minutes, or you might use guided imagery ("Everyone close your eyes and imagine you are lying on a beach on the coast of Florida. You can hear the waves gently slapping against the shore and seagulls calling one another. It's warm and there is a gentle breeze. . . ."). These relaxation techniques seem to work best when they are used over many months with the same teachers involved (Richter, 1984).

BIBLIOTHERAPY

Teachers can use stories to help students deal with problems in their lives.

As we stressed earlier, your students' lives outside of school have an impact on their behavior in your classroom. As you become aware of your students' emotional and social difficulties, you may look for ways to help them deal with their experiences. **Bibliotherapy** involves using books therapeutically to help readers increase their self-knowledge and self-esteem, gain relief from conflicts, understand themselves and others, and find ways to resolve their problems if possible.

Bibliographic resources can help you find the right book for a particular need.

You may already be familiar with literature that is relevant to certain topics and is appropriate for the reading level of your student. You can also consult your school librarian or language arts specialists. *The Bookfinder: A Guide to Children's Literature About the Needs and Problems of Youth Aged 2–15* (Dreyer, 1989, 1992) is a bibliographic resource to help you find literature that is relevant to students' problems. *The Bookfinder* provides bibliographical information on over a thousand entries, a description of the topic, a summary of the content, a commentary on the book's main message, and the general reading level. Teachers, parents, and other adults can match books to individual student needs. Topics include abandonment, birth order, foster homes, homosexuality, loneliness, moving, obesity, peer pressures, pregnancy, stepparents, speech problems, and truancy. You can use bibliotherapy with individual students by quietly encouraging the student to read a book you have found and providing an opportunity for the student to talk with you or a school counselor.

In cases where you have several students or an entire class who are dealing with a similar concern (e.g., peer pressure, friendship, transitions, disabilities), you can locate a book to read and discuss with the whole group.

As We See It: *The Authors Talk*

Mary Kay: There certainly seem to be a lot of books out now on the topics we discussed above. It's hard to keep track of all the different "concern" books that are on the shelves.

Bob: As we said, *The Bookfinder* is a good resource for tracking them.

Mary Kay: True. I do worry, though, that sometimes we put too heavy a burden on literature. We need to be sure that students are encouraged to read *anything* and *everything* from comic books and magazines to *War and Peace* so they become true readers.

Bob: It is easy to get caught up in the disaster of the month mentality when discussing books in school—or the political correctness debate, or the cultural literacy harangues.

Mary Kay: I think sometimes we don't give kids enough credit for being able to separate fact from fantasy or to choose their own role models without our intervention. Caryn James (1994), writing in the *New York Times Review of Books*, said "As a girl, I read *Little Women* the way I read fairy tales. I wanted to be the princess in *Cinderella* too, but I didn't think I'd grow up to be royal. . . . It never occurred to me that Amy was a pathetic weakling or that *Cinderella* should have come with a warning label: 'This story contains a woman who depends on a man. It may be dangerous to your economic self-sufficiency later on.'"

Bob: True. When kids are learning to manage their own behavior, it's probably best for them to see a variety of ways of doing things—some right and some wrong—and literature can provide many of those perspectives.

Mary Kay: You're so good at bringing me back to the task at hand . . .

Bob: And I'm not dangerous to your economic self-sufficiency.

PEER MEDIATION

Peer mediation is a way of resolving arguments.

Peer Mediation is an approach for helping students deal with disputes (Schrumpf, Crawford & Usadel, 1991a, 1991b; Glasser, 1965, 1986, 1990).

In this program, peer mediators either intervene in conflicts directly as they encounter them (in class, on the bus, in lunchrooms, in hallways, on the playground, etc.), or disputants and others ask them to mediate conflicts.

Conflict often develops when students are each trying to meet their own psychological needs.

Because participation in mediation is voluntary, the mediator's first step is to ask the disputants if they wish to have their conflict mediated. If they do, the process begins. If not, the mediator does not try to intervene. Several forms are used to guide and document the process, including a mediation request form, a brainstorming worksheet, an agreement form, and a record-keeping form. Peer mediation assumes that interpersonal conflicts develop from individuals' efforts to meet four basic psychological needs identified earlier: *belonging* (to love, share, and cooperate with others); *power* (to achieve, accomplish, be recognized and respected); *freedom* (to make choices); and *fun* (to laugh and play). Because individual students have different psychological needs, resources, and values, some conflict is inevitable. Conflicts can result in students avoiding or confronting one another; they can show in arguments, threats, fights, or covert hostilities.

No one needs to lose for a conflict to be resolved.

Students often expect that conflicts can only be resolved when one person wins and the other loses (so-called *win-lose* solutions). Proponents of peer mediation, however, believe that conflicts between students need not be destructive. Instead, they suggest strategies for negotiating disputes and finding solutions that combine, rather than compromise, the needs of disputants. The goal is to produce *win-win* solutions where *both* disputants have their needs met and the participants learn ways to handle future disagreements better.

Peer mediation involves working with experts and being trained.

Peer mediation is usually implemented on a school-wide basis, so it requires collaboration among faculty, staff, and students. It has several phases. First, you and your colleagues form an advisory committee to plan and guide the program's implementation. At the secondary level, student leaders may also serve on the advisory group. This advisory committee builds support for the program within the school and larger community.

Peer mediators can be elected or chosen.

Next, the school needs to choose the peer mediators, a critical feature of the program. There are two ways for students to become mediators, either through *selection* by the advisory group from applications or through *election* by classmates. In elementary schools, mediators are usually two or three students selected or elected from each of the upper grades. In middle or high schools, mediators may be selected from interested applicants or from representative groups such as student councils, or they may be chosen by their homerooms. In our experience, students are careful to select peers whom they consider responsible and effective communicators. In fact, they tend to choose mediators that teachers themselves would have picked.

Then an expert in peer mediation will need to teach mediators and trainers (faculty and staff with mediation experience). There is usually one teacher or other adult for every three to four mediators and they receive training in full- or half-day workshops. They learn the peer mediation philosophy, practice effective communication skills in role playing exercises, and learn the peer mediation procedure. Then they orient other faculty, staff, and students to the program.

The peer mediation procedure has six steps.

The program includes the following steps (Schrumpf, Crawford & Usadel, 1991a, pp. 12–13):

1. Open the session.

2. Gather information.

3. Focus on common interests.

4. Create options.

5. Evaluate options and choose a solution.

6. Write the agreement and close.

During all the steps of an actual peer mediation session, the mediator attempts to be an unabiased, active listener who shows respect for disputants and ensures confidentiality of those involved. A valuable feature of peer mediation is that *all* students receive training in their classrooms, where they discuss the process and talk about ways to de-escalate confrontation. The training allows them to see how their behavior, whether as participants or bystanders, influences conflicts. This reinforces the concept of the classroom as an ecosystem.

Peer mediation can help students learn to take responsibility for solving conflicts.

Although it is difficult to assess the long-term benefits of peer mediation, we think that when it is properly planned and implemented it can help students develop self-management skills. Equipped with training, support, and procedures, students assume more responsibility for finding their own solutions to conflicts. Since the central assumption is that students themselves produce the solutions, participating students must examine their feelings and behavior, generate solutions themselves, and make real commitments to follow through on these solutions.

Peer mediation gives students chances to use and develop verbal and nonverbal communication skills.

As with other cognitive-affective approaches, peer mediation offers opportunities for students to practice verbal and nonverbal communication. Peer mediation removes some responsibility from teachers and other adults for controlling student behavior and resolving conflicts and gives it to the most interested parties—the students themselves.

BEHAVIORALLY ORIENTED APPROACHES TO GROUP INTERVENTIONS

SOCIAL SKILLS TRAINING PROGRAMS

Social skills training programs have been developed to deliberately and systematically teach social behavior that will be accepted and rewarded by others. These programs are designed primarily for students with emotional and behavioral disorders, including social skills problems. Many students with emotional/behavioral disorders are not choosing to misbehave, but have not yet learned skills that enable them to be successful in social interactions. You might also sometimes have several students who, though not formally diagnosed as having emotional/behavior disorders, nevertheless have social skill deficits.

Social skills training programs draw heavily on social learning explanations of behavior (Bandura, 1977), which emphasize the importance of *vicarious learning*—learning from observing others' (models') behavior. They also include a cognitive component called *cognitive behavior modification* (Meichenbaum, 1977) to teach students to think about their behavior. The usual sequence of steps in these programs is:

1. An adult *modeling* the behavior while talking aloud (describing the behavior)

2. Students *imitating* the behavior while talking aloud

3. Student(s) *practicing* the behavior *while whispering the instructions* to themselves (faded guidance by the adult)

4. Students *performing* the behavior *while silently instructing themselves*

Social skills training programs have been developed for both elementary and secondary level students. At both levels, however, trained support service personnel, such as special education teachers, school social workers, counselors, or psychologists, are likely to provide social skills training outside your classroom to students who can benefit from the instruction.

Turtle Technique and Think Aloud

Techniques of talking to themselves can help young students control themselves.

Two approaches for elementary students that require relatively little preparation or special instruction for the social skills instructor are *The Turtle Technique* (Robin, Schneider & Dolnick, 1976) and *Think Aloud* (Camp & Bash, 1981). The turtle technique uses self-instruction (self-talk) to help young students control their impulsive and aggressive behavior. You can teach your students to use the turtle response when they are angry or frustrated. Pulling their arms and legs close to their body, they put their heads down on their desks and imagine they are turtles who are withdrawing into their shells instead of verbally and/or physically striking out at others. The teacher first models the technique to the individual student or small group, then guides them as they practice responding to typical problem situations. You can also teach the students to use relaxation techniques such as those we discussed in Chapter 7 and have students practice them in volatile situations. Additional aspects of the turtle technique are generating alternative, more socially acceptable behaviors; learning to anticipate likely consequences of one's behavior; and changing impulsive, aggressive behavior through step-by-step action plans.

Impulsive young students can restrain and change their behavior by aking themselves a series of questions.

Think Aloud is intended to help impulsive children in the primary grades deal with difficult situations by teaching them to practice self-talk to solve problems in either small-group or class-wide programs. In *Think Aloud,* teachers model and then have their students practice asking and answering the following series of questions:

1. *What is my problem?* or *What am I supposed to do?*

2. *How do I do it?* or *What is my plan?*

3. *Am I using my plan?* and

4. *How did I do?*

Working with small groups of students, you or other support personnel provide specific scripts with illustrations and activities to model thinking aloud. There are twenty-three lessons in the program, each with a goal, specific teaching strategies, expected outcomes, and materials. *Think Aloud* reportedly improves impulsive students' performance on cognitive measures, promotes more socially acceptable behavior, and reduces aggressiveness (Camp & Bash, 1981).

Other Social Skills Programs

Other commercially available social skills programs for elementary level students are *Getting Along with Others: Teaching Social Effectiveness to Children* (Jackson, Jackson & Monroe, 1983); *Skillstreaming the Elementary School Child* (McGinnis & Goldstein, 1984); The *ACCEPTS Program* (Walker, et al., 1983); and *Taking Part* (Cartledge & Kleefeld, 1991).

There are training programs to teach specific social skills to students who need them.

Each of these social skills training programs includes strategies to explicitly teach important social skills to small groups of students who markedly lack them. In *Skillstreaming the Elementary School Child,* for instance, there are thirty-six social skills in two general categories:

- *Introductory skills,* such as listening, asking for help, following instructions, beginning a conversation, and giving compliments

- *Skills for dealing with feelings,* such as apologizing, knowing one's feelings, recognizing/understanding others' feelings, dealing with anger and fear, sharing, staying out of fights, and dealing with group pressure

Skillstreaming groups meet regularly, usually for about twenty to thirty minutes three times each week, with two trainers (usually special educators, social workers, counselors, trained paraprofessionals, or psychologists). Additional time is allotted for students to record the skills they are practicing. The Skillstreaming lesson format consists of several steps:

There are several steps to the skillstreaming program.

1. *Demonstration* of the skill by the trainers, who use *self-talk* to model the elements of the skill

2. Trainer-led *discussion* of when and where the skill could be used

3. Student practice *imitating* the modeled behavior using self-talk

4. Trainers and other group members provide *feedback* about performance

5. Training is *transferred* to other settings.

Group members are assigned homework, practicing the skills in real-life situations in school and outside. They evaluate their performance and report back to the group. As an incentive for students to work on these skills, students may receive token reinforcements that are added to a group reward pot.

Students can get rewards for working on these skills.

There are social skills programs for secondary school students too.

There are several programs for the secondary level also, including *The Walker Social Skills Curriculum: The ACCESS Program* (Walker, Todis, Holmes & Horton, 1988); *Asset: A Social Skills Program for Adolescents* (Hazel, Schumaker, Sherman & Sheldon-Wildgen, 1982); and *Skillstreaming the Adolescent* (Goldstein, Sprafkin, Gershaw & Klein, 1980), which uses a format similar to the elementary level version of *Skillstreaming* described above.

The *Social Skills Intervention Guide* (Elliott & Gresham, 1991) includes social skills that can be taught to both elementary and secondary level students. The guide includes forty-three social skills organized into the following five groups (whose first letters spell the acronym *CARES*):

Social skills can be divided into five categories.

1. *Cooperation Skills:* ignoring distractions, making transitions without wasting time or disrupting others, paying attention, and following teacher's instructions

2. *Assertion Skills:* giving compliments, making positive self-statements, initiating conversations with peers, inviting others to join activities

3. *Responsibility Skills:* asking an adult for help, questioning rules that may be unfair, responding to a compliment

4. *Empathy Skills:* saying nice things to others when they have done something nice, asking before using other people's things, listening to adults when they are talking or giving instructions

5. *Self-Control Skills:* cooperating with peers without prompting, responding to peer pressure appropriately, responding to teasing from peers appropriately, receiving criticism well

There is a series of steps to follow to learn a social skill.

The basic training format involves several steps: tell, show, do, follow through, and generalization. First the group leader defines, discusses with the group, and explains why the skill is important (*tell*). Next, the leader models positive and negative examples of the skill, demonstrating the steps for enacting the skill (*show*). Then students use the behavior in role plays while the leader provides feedback about their performance (*do*). Finally, the leader gives students homework assignments to practice skills in other settings with other students (*follow through* and *generalization*).

Social skills training programs like these are often used in special education programs for students with identified behavioral and learning disabilities and programs for students at-risk for social behavior problems. If you have students who are participating in social skills training outside your class, you will want to be aware of the training procedures, provide opportunities for them to practice the skills, and consistently support their improved social skills. Although you may need to make some adaptations to your normal routine, social skills training can contribute to improved behavior and to the atmosphere of your class as a whole.

GROUP BEHAVIOR MODIFICATION

Sometimes teachers need to teach a whole class to behave better.

Sometimes you may decide that the social behavior of your class as a whole needs improvement. For example, you may be concerned about uncooperativeness or rudeness in your classs, about students making disparaging remarks, taking property without asking, or not sharing or helping one another. There may be frequent arguments, scuffling, and fights at recess, in hallways, or the lunch room. You may decide to promote a more positive classroom atmosphere and to encourage your students to behave in a more helpful way. Two approaches for dealing with problems that involve your class as a whole are **group contingency management** and **token economies.**

GROUP CONTINGENCY MANAGEMENT

Earlier we discussed instructional and behavior management approaches that contain features of group contingency management. In Chapter 4, for example, we looked at cooperative learning procedures that include group recognition and rewards for academic performance. In the last chapter we discussed how you can use contingency management to modify problem behavior of *individual* students. In group contingency management, your focus expands to your entire class or to a subgroup of the class that poses most of the problems. The goal of group contingency management is to increase student behavior that contributes to the class as a whole.

When an entire group needs to change its behavior, it should first decide on a target behavior.

If you decide to use a group contingency management plan, your entire class can follow the steps we outlined in Chapter 7 for individual contingency management interventions. Your first step is to conduct a problem-solving class meeting where the entire group can identify problems and desirable alternative, or target, behaviors. Students can then discuss a rationale for

Students need a reason to change and a reward for changing.

As students get used to the program they can take over more and more of the decisions as well as keep track of their progress.

changing the behaviors, determine group goals, select group rewards and payoff criteria, evaluate their progress, and participate in the rewards as a group when they achieve their goals.

The degree of student participation in design, negotiation, and implementation of the group contingency program depends on their ability or readiness to participate in each aspect of the intervention. Initially, you will probably need to assume a more directive role in designing and managing the plan. Eventually, as your students become familiar with the procedure, they can assume more responsibility. At first, for example, you may need to identify the target behaviors, specify the rewards and exchange rates, and monitor progress. Later, your class may select behaviors to work on, negotiate rewards and exchange rates, and monitor its own progress. Table 8.1 outlines the elements of one group contingency management program that could be used in an elementary classroom to promote two categories of behavior—following group directions and interpersonal interactions.

In Table 8.1, we grouped possible desirable target behaviors into two categories—following group directions and interpersonal interactions. *Following group directions* includes getting ready for a new activity, lining up to go somewhere as a group, moving through the school, and arriving and leaving on time. *Interpersonal interactions* include helping, sharing, encouraging, complimenting, and reminding. For each behavior, you will need to discuss operational definitions with your students so that everyone has the same idea of what constitutes helping, sharing, and each of the other behaviors.

Although students earn points for their own behavior, the points go into a group pot. Because they are the group's, the reward should be something

TABLE 8.1
Group Contingency Management Program

	FOLLOWING GROUP DIRECTIONS	INTERPERSONAL INTERACTIONS
Target behaviors	Getting ready Lining up Moving through school Arriving on time Leaving on time	Helping Sharing Encouraging Complimenting Reminding
Point value	1 point per student for each behavior	1 point per student for each behavior
Reinforced	At end of activity At bell When students go/return from lunch/recess/gym	Whenever observed At scheduled sum-up time
Bonuses	When all group members perform, double points are awarded to class	When teacher judges entire group has behaved positively

like a group activity. Time for a class game at the end of the day, a Friday popcorn party, or a field trip are possibilities. You might suggest several alternatives or ask your group to suggest reasonable rewards for the entire class. Again, you can negotiate the terms (number of points, length of time) with your class. You can use virtually any group activity that students consider rewarding (and you are capable of providing) as a contingent group reward. Valued rewards need not be costly. See the Classroom Closeup "Working Together to Shave the Teacher" for an example.

As we mentioned in our discussion of individual contingency management plans in Chapter 7, charting performances can provide both visual feedback and reinforcement. In group contingency programs, also, you can monitor and visually display your group's progress toward their goals to inform and motivate your students. When you graph the points they have earned or add tokens to a group jar or pot, you show the group its progress. You might, for example, have a Class Bank, with students making daily deposits

Classroom Closeup

Working Together to Shave the Teacher

In one group contingency program, students had chosen a regular reward when they earned 250 points for following group directions and interacting positively. They chose free time and a popcorn party for Friday afternoon. Although they looked forward to that time and worked hard to earn it, Mr. Peterson was looking for a novel, motivating, and available group activity for a contingent reward that would increase his class's cooperative behavior and would require more sustained effort. During a class meeting, one student jokingly said he'd like to see the teacher without a beard. Mr. Peterson responded to the class, "OK. I'll shave my beard if you can earn a total of a thousand points in the next three weeks. What do you think?" The class thought it was a great idea and accepted the challenge to increase

their usual points by about 30 percent. Together, they made a bulletin board with a drawing of Mr. Peterson's face and covered it with a thousand paper whiskers. At the end of each day points (whiskers) earned by the class were ceremoniously "shaved" from the drawing. After just two and a half weeks of enthusiastic effort, the class reached its goal. They went with their teacher to a nearby barbershop, where they cashed in their tokens and watched the real beard disappear.

Of course, Mr. Peterson had already decided to shave his beard, but he also recognized that it might be a motivating contingent reward for his class. Not only did his class improve their performance in following directions and treating one another better, but the class atmosphere was more joyful and upbeat as the students worked together to achieve their goal. Both their behavior and attitudes improved. ✳

into their joint account and writing checks to purchase the predetermined group activities.

A variation of group contingency management that adds a competitive feature is the "Good Behavior Game," which has been used to reduce disruptive behavior (Barrish, Saunders & Wolf, 1969; Harris & Sherman, 1973) and to increase group on-task behavior (Darch & Thorpe, 1977). The class is divided into two or more teams. Each team receives marks on the chalkboard when members of the team perform specified, desirable behaviors or is given marks when members perform unwanted behaviors. At the end of each day, the team with the most marks for desired behavior (or least marks for undesired behavior) earns a special privilege or activity. While this competition may be motivating for some students, we think you should be aware of possible pitfalls of introducing a negative feature to contingency management. Taking away points for misbehavior may allow one or two students to purposely sabotage the efforts of the group. If you see this happening, drop the take-away portion of the game and just provide points for positive behavior.

Teams can have fun seeing who can earn the most points for good behavior.

Also, if you use a competitive version of group contingency management, we recommend that you avoid a winner-take-all situation. One team's winning should not require that the other teams lose. When this happens, a nonwinning team may conclude that its efforts are unrewarded and unrecognized. When only one team can win, the other team or teams may be so far behind that students conclude that they have nothing to gain by behaving well. A better strategy is to negotiate a reasonable goal for each team to meet each day and to provide the rewards for every team that meets the goal. The team with the highest number of points could receive a bonus reward—a special activity or recognition—or have its name posted on a Team of the Day or Team of the Week poster. Public posting of team performance is an effective and relatively simple way to provide visual feedback on class or team performance (Jones & Van Houten, 1985).

Every team should be able to win some points.

If you use team competition in group contingency management, make sure to change the members of each team regularly. You can accomplish this by either randomly assigning students (those with birthdays in certain months, specific letters in their names, numbers of letters in their names) or devising a rotation system.

It is a good thing to change members of a team regularly.

Some group contingency programs and token economies (see page 288) use response cost—taking away already earned points for infractions (Kazden, 1982; Walker, 1983). Students can earn tokens for specific, desired behaviors and lose tokens for specific, undesired behaviors. As we mentioned in Chapter 7, response cost is a feature of some *individual* contingency management programs, but is generally not appropriate in *group* token programs. When individual students lose points that other members of their group have earned, students can get angry and undermine the positive nature of your program. In any group contingency management program, your message should be posi-

Losing points for misbehavior does not work well in group programs.

tive: behavior that contributes toward group goals is rewarded, but unwanted, individual behavior will not detract the group's progress.

Guidelines for Group Contingency Programs

If you believe a group contingency program would help your class and promote more positive, cooperative interactions, these guidelines will help you:

1. *The basis of your program should be "catching your students being good."* Too often we pay attention to undesired behavior and catch students doing something bad. Unfortunately, even negative teacher attention can reinforce the behavior (Walker & Buckley, 1972). A group reinforcement program such as that described above helps both you and your students notice and acknowledge positive behavior.

2. *A group reinforcement program encourages your students to help each other.* Too often we expect our students to operate as independent entities in our classrooms. Given our crowded classrooms, this is unrealistic. To encourage mutual caring, assistance, and cooperation, you need to offer opportunities for your students to learn and practice those skills.

3. In a group reinforcement program, *you serve as a model of the positive and appropriate behaviors* you hope to see in your students. As we have stressed throughout this book, your students learn more from what you do than from what you say. Also, when you deliberately model behavior you would like to see, such as helping, sharing, encouraging, and complimenting, *your* attitudes and behavior will likely become more positive.

4. *Your students should assume more responsibility for their own behavior.* Rather than relying on external control, you will place more responsibility directly on your students' shoulders. You can encourage them to ask for and offer help to each other. Students learn that they have responsibilities to the entire group.

5. Even though your students assume greater responsibility for managing their behavior, *you continue to be the classroom leader in a group reinforcement program.* Although you negotiate features of the program with your students, you determine their level of involvement and control the overall structure. As classroom leader you facilitate, arbitrate, moderate, and intervene as needed.

TOKEN ECONOMIES

Class-wide token economies are similar to group contingency management programs, except that individuals, rather than the entire group, earn rewards. Token economies are behavior modification systems in which you award token

With token economies each student earns a reward.

reinforcers such as points, poker chips, play money, or some other form of currency to reward specified behaviors. You might identify target behaviors for *each* individual student, behaviors that are important for *all* students, or a combination of *both* individual and group target behaviors. Once earned, your students can exchange their tokens, at a convenient, prearranged time, for valued, backup reinforcers.

This program takes a lot of time and energy.

Like group contingency management programs, class-wide token economies are extremely high-cost interventions requiring substantial investments of time and energy to plan, prepare, and implement. You will need to allow time to set up and operate the token system as well as teach the students how it works; how to get tokens and backup reinforcers; how to monitor, record, and keep records; and how to trade tokens for backup reinforcers. Consequently, you should use class-wide token economies only when you clearly need a contingency management program that involves all your students.

If you decide to use class-wide token economies, you will need help from people with experience.

However, if your class includes many students who have not responded to less intensive efforts discussed in earlier chapters, a token system is an option; little academic learning can happen until the classroom is safe and orderly. As a practical matter, when this type of intensive group intervention is necessary, you will need the help of a paraprofessional, a team-teacher, special educators, or other support services personnel who have expertise in this approach.

Class-wide token economies have been used for years in special education programs for students with behavior and learning problems (Broden, Hall, Dunlap & Clark, 1970; Kazden, 1982; Kazden & Bootzin, 1972; Wolery, Bailey & Sugai, 1988) as well as in some regular classrooms (Kerr & Nelson, 1989; McLaughlin & Malaby, 1972). Some entire schools have been involved in token economies.

The essential steps for a class-wide token economy are similar to those we outlined for individual contingency management in Chapter 7:

1. Selecting target behaviors and developing a rationale for intervening

2. Observing and recording baseline date

3. Selecting backup reinforcers

4. Selecting tokens

5. Determining procedure for monitoring performance

6. Arranging for exchange of tokens for backup reinforcers.

Target Behaviors

Choose target behaviors that matter and that can probably be changed.

Target behaviors are most often behaviors that contribute to the efficiency and smooth functioning of your class. You can select target behaviors that you consider important for individual students and/or you may ask students at a class meeting about behaviors that are important for group functioning. When there are several possibilities, you may wish to focus your initial efforts on just a few behaviors (perhaps two or three that are important for the group; and one or two individualized target behaviors for each student) that have a high probability for success. You can tackle other target behaviors later, when students are familiar with the program and have experienced success.

Students need to know exactly what each target behavior means.

You will need to describe target behaviors so your students recognize exactly what they need to do to earn tokens. Clearly explain the quantitative or qualitative standards of performance so you and your students have the same understanding of the target behavior. For example, you might measure student performance in quantitative terms such as *products* (completed homework assignment, grades on assignments) or *specific behaviors* (coming to class on time, having books and instructional materials). Or you might set up an *amount of time* (remaining on-task for twenty minutes, not talking without permission during a work period) or *frequency* (number of times on time to class).

You must be consistent in judging your students' performance.

You can also use qualitative measures of target behaviors. For example, if you choose "cooperating with classmates" as a target behavior, you might give ratings of 2 (excellent), 1 (OK), or 0 (uncooperative) for how cooperative you think the students are. Of course, your students must have a clear idea of the performance standards necessary to receive these ratings, and you must evaluate performance consistently.

Target behaviors can include behaviors you expect of all students, such as:

- Sitting at assigned place within one minute of entering the classroom
- Picking up work folder
- Turning in completed assignments

In some cases, you might also include additional, target behaviors for individual students, such as:

- Having pencils sharpened before class
- Bringing all necessary materials to class
- Keeping hands and feet to oneself
- Using appropriate language in class

Backup Reinforcers

Backup reinforcers must be valuable to students if they are to be effective. Unlike the group contingency program discussed earlier, backup reinforcers in token economies are not limited to group rewards. Instead, each student earns individual rewards. These backup reinforcers may represent any of the forms of reinforcement we discussed in the last chapter: *tangible objects* (e.g., stickers, candy and other edibles, school supplies, toys), *activities* (e.g., computer time, independent reading time, extra recess, videotapes, game periods),

Teachers can use a wide variety of rewards.

privileges (line leader, teacher helper, messenger, classroom helper) and/or *social events* (popcorn parties, field trips, games). Backup reinforcers need not be costly, but you must be able to give them out easily at the time you establish for exchanging tokens.

As in individual contingency management plans, you might use a *menu* of reinforcers, offering a variety of objects and/or activities so that students have choices. Some backup reinforcers have a relatively low value and require fewer tokens; others are more valuable and cost more. Some teachers have a class store, where students use tokens to purchase tangible reinforcers (food, trinkets, supplies) at the end of a class period or school day or at a designated time during the week. You can let students manage the store (an opportunity that must be earned, of course), ordering and stocking supplies, making sales, keeping records, etc. If you are using a token system for the entire class, you will need to carefully consider the cost of reinforcers. Even small items become expensive when multiplied by thirty students, some of whom may earn points very quickly. The more activities or use of special materials you can offer, the healthier your budget.

You can introduce an element of chance into token economies by periodically holding lotteries or raffles. Lotteries offer students incentives for extra performance beyond the usual rewards they can earn in the token economy. They can write their initials on slips of paper, coupons, or movie tickets used as tokens and place them into a container (Good Job Jar, Social Studies Lotto). You can have periodic drawings for the special prizes that you have identified and displayed. Students who contribute more tokens have a higher probability of winning the lottery prizes. Although your special rewards might be tangible (school supplies, a coupon for a sandwich at a fast food restaurant, grab bag), they could be activities and privileges, such as being class messenger the next day, serving as line leader, taking care of class plants and animals, choosing a class activity, being your assistant; or recognitions, such as Student of the Week.

To maintain student involvement following a drawing, you can keep nonwinning lottery tickets in the pot so your students still have a chance to win future drawings. Depending on your judgment of your students' needs, you can hold drawings daily, weekly, or when the container is filled. You may also decide to have more than one winner, with a third, second, and first place winner each receiving more valued rewards.

Selecting Tokens

A variety of objects, some we have already mentioned, can serve as tokens, including strips of construction paper color-coded to represent either different values or different target behaviors. You can use play money, or your own home-made currency, poker chips, movie tickets, or washers of different sizes. Or you can use stickers, stamps, or checkmarks that are easy to mark on point cards like the daily report cards we described in Chapter 7.

Some rewards are worth a lot less than others.

Be aware of the total cost when you are buying enough items for the whole class.

You can set up a lottery to give students a greater incentive.

Efficiency in dispensing, collecting, and exchanging tokens is an important consideration. The following factors can help you choose appropriate tokens: age and skill level of students; likelihood that students will destroy, eat, or cheat (by duplicating); expense, durability, and convenience; and the use of other types of tokens in your classroom and school (Kerr & Nelson, 1989).

Students need to have ample opportunities to earn tokens. If they are not earning tokens, it probably means that the backup reinforcers are not sufficiently desirable, the performance standards are too high, or the opportunities to exchange tokens for backup reinforcement are too infrequent. Especially when you are first implementing a token economy, there should be little delay between earning and cashing tokens. As students become comfortable with the procedure, you can lengthen the delay.

Make sure, especially at first, that students can cash their tokens quickly and easily.

Monitoring Performance

Class-wide token economies require careful monitoring of student behavior. You will need a way to accurately and efficiently record individual student performance. There are several possibilities. You may, for instance, give each student an individual token holder (small plastic cups for chips or coins, paper envelopes taped to desks for paper strips), or point cards.

Students need a way to keep track of how they're doing.

Older students can use checkbooks to record their token income and expenses. Tokens are assigned monetary values which can be deposited in students' checking accounts and recorded in their checkbooks. Students write checks for backup reinforcers and then deduct the amount from their checkbooks. An advantage of the checkbook procedure is that it is like a real checking account, with checks to write and accounts to balance. When you use checkbooks, you combine a motivation system with valuable life skills.

Regardless of your token system format, you can include students in the data management process. They can be responsible for recording their points, tabulating totals, and preparing the token cards. In this way, self-monitoring and self-recording are an integral part of your motivational system since students are usually rewarded by seeing their progress. You might even have students prepare graphs of their performance that are displayed in the room.

If you use point cards, you can send copies home to parents so they know how their child is doing.

You can also use your daily point cards to communicate with parents about their child's behavior. If you use carbon paper or carbonless copy forms, you can file originals as a record of student performance and send copies home to parents. Some teachers ask parents to initial the point cards and return them with their child the next day. Even this process can be part of your token economy if you award tokens for the returned, signed copies.

Exchanging Tokens

It is important, especially when you are first implementing a class-wide token economy, to let students exchange their tokens for backup reinforcers often.

This helps them associate the value of the tokens and the backup reinforcers. Usually they can save all or some of their tokens over time for more costly rewards. For example, they may need to earn a minimum of twenty-five tokens each day to earn an activity time, but be able to earn up to twenty-five additional points each day. Students can record the extra points in their accounts and spend them at a class store at the end of the week. They can spend their points for items they can already afford or save them until they have enough to buy more costly items or activities. For example, a small sticker might cost ten points, a colorful pencil, fifty points, a pad of paper, one hundred and fifty points, and a Walkman radio a thousand points. Students might have the option of spending some or all of their tokens at each exchange opportunity or saving for more valued reinforcers. Don't panic when you find students saving up (hoarding?) large numbers of points. One of the unique aspects of token economies is that the tokens or points themselves quickly take on meaning beyond the actual value. For some students, being able to say "I have three thousand points!" is worth much more than anything those points could buy. In fact, points taking on this sort of value can be an indication that your system is working—students are valuing their contribution to the class (as measured by their points or tokens) over any actual reward that is provided.

A helpful feature of a class-wide token economy is that it can give you on-going information about your students' behavior. You have a built-in record of student performance on the target behaviors.

LEVEL SYSTEMS

An additional feature of some contingency management plans is a **level system** in which students progress through levels (Bauer & Shea, 1988; Bauer, Shea & Keppler, 1986; Barbetta, 1990; Smith & Ferrell, 1993). Each level includes more challenging target behaviors and, usually, more valued reinforcers. At a lower level, for example, target behaviors might include "staying at seat" or "raising hand before talking." Reinforcers at this level may be more tangible—edibles (food, candy) or objects (small toys, stickers). At higher levels, target behaviors are more complex, such as "cooperating with others" or "offering help to classmates," and reinforcers are more social and activity-oriented, such as privileges, class games, or parties. As individual students demonstrate their ability to meet the expectations of one level, they are promoted to the next level. Each level entails higher expectations for academic and/or social behavior and greater expectations for student self-management and self-monitoring. It relies increasingly less on extrinsic reinforcment and more on social and intrinsic rewards. Based on their performance, students earn promotions to higher levels, and they can be demoted if they do not meet the expectations of their level.

Some students like to save a great number of tokens.

Students can move to higher levels with more valuable prizes.

Higher levels have more intrinsic rewards.

TIME-OUT

Time-out has often been misunderstood and misused.

A strategy that often accompanies token economies, but can also be used independently, is *time-out*. Time-out is frequently used, misused, misunderstood, and abused. This procedure, commonly discussed in behavioral texts, teacher education texts, and books on intervention strategies for emotionally and behaviorally disordered students, has a broad range of definitions and usefulness. Time-out has been defined in a variety of ways, most suggesting that the student is denied access to the reinforcing environment (Alberto & Troutman, 1995) or spends time in a less reinforcing environment (Brantner & Doherty, 1983) contingent on certain behaviors. "Actually, time-out involves a combination of extinction, punishment, positive reinforcement, and negative reinforcement inasmuch as it incorporates multiple contingencies for several possible behaviors" (Nelson & Rutherford, 1983, p. 56). Two basic conditions for time-out are (1) the student must find the environment from which he or she is being excluded reinforcing; and (2) the time-out environment itself must *not* be reinforcing. In other words, if you exclude Esther from an activity in your classroom that she doesn't want to participate in anyway, timeout will not be successful. And if you place Chester in the hall for time-out, where he can watch all sorts of activity and chat with students on their way to and from the library, it will not be successful.

Time-out doesn't work when the student didn't want to do what the class was doing.

Time-out doesn't work when the student goes to an interesting place.

Time-out can be used in three different ways: nonexclusionary, exclusionary, and isolation. *Nonexclusionary time-out* means excluding the student from reinforcement, but not from the environment. If Franklin is whispering and giggling with a friend while you are conducting a science lesson, you might continue to reward students around Franklin with praise and attention ("You're really getting this aren't you? You'll be ready for the lab soon"), or, in the case of a token economy, with points or other reinforcers. You don't comment directly to Franklin that his behavior is inappropriate, you simply don't pay attention to him at all. The intent here is not to call attention to Franklin's behavior, but to wait for him to realize that he is not receiving reinforcement while other students are, causing him to stop whispering and pay attention. Of course, as soon as you see him behaving appropriately, you reinforce that behavior ("I'm glad you're listening, Franklin, we really need your help on this.") The advantage of this type of time-out is that it is relatively nonintrusive, doesn't call attention to the negative behavior, and allows Franklin to return to the fold with a minimum of disruption. This is the type of time-out used most often in regular classrooms.

One form of time-out is to praise other students and ignore the misbehaving student.

Another form of time-out is to move the distracting student to another part of the room.

If the behavior is more disruptive, or if nonexclusionary time-out is unsuccessful, you may need to move to the next level, *exclusionary time-out*. In this form, the student is removed from the activity (remember, the activity or the environment must be reinforcing for this to work). You frequently see teachers of young children use this technique when they ask a child to sit in the "thinking chair" or the "time-out chair" (there are even commercially manufactured "time-out benches" available!). The teacher directs the student to sit in the chair until he or she can regain control over the behavior. In this instance, the student is asked to leave the specific activity in which the group is engaged, but stays in the room observing what is going on. This form of time-out is useful for young children and for behaviors that are not unusually disruptive to the rest of the group. Obviously, if a child is yelling and screaming in the back of the room, this is difficult for the whole class and exclusionary time-out would not be an appropriate intervention.

You need to be aware that students may find their own ways to make the time-out environment reinforcing even when the teacher has tried to eliminate such aspects. A colleague once told us about observing a child in a preschool classroom who was placed in exclusionary time-out (the time-out chair at the back of the room). He stayed in his chair very well and was quiet and nondisruptive. But he spent his time dismantling the timer used to keep track of the minutes he spent there. At the end of his time-out period, he had completely taken apart the timer and was engrossed in seeing if he could put it back together (he couldn't).

Isolation is the most drastic form of time-out.

The most intrusive form of time-out is *isolation*. This form is rarely used in regular education classes and must only be implemented when appropriate facilities are available. This strategy involves placing the student in a separate time-out room until the student controls or diminishes his or her behavior. If, for example, Jason has violent outbursts where he verbally or physically assaults other students, he may need to go to the time-out room until he can control his behavior. This involves having a special time-out room for Jason to go to, however. Such a room must be safe, supervised, and have appropriate light and ventilation. We've heard stories of educational personnel using bathrooms, hallways, even the kneehole in the teacher's desk or a refrigerator box as a time-out facility. Clearly, these are NOT appropriate settings. If you do not have access to a safe, supervised, well-lighted and ventilated facility, you should not use isolation time-out. This technique should *never* be used under the "best we could do" conditions. It must be used completely correctly or not at all.

Teachers should never send a student to a separate time-out room unless the room meets all the safety criteria.

Keep a record of every time you use time-out.

Some general guidelines on the use of time-out can be found in Table 8.2. They apply to students regardless of age, disability, or severity of behavior. In addition, if you plan to use exclusionary or isolation time-out, be sure that you discuss it with administrators, support staff, and parents. You will need to define what you plan to do, establish the guidelines and setting, and get agreement from these stakeholders in your classroom. You should also keep a log of your time-out use. A simple form that includes the student's name, date, reason for time-out, time in, and time out will show you if any patterns are developing and will help you discuss the situation with parents and others. Your time-out log can alert you to overuse with specific students, indicate whether specific students are having trouble at certain times of the day (one of our colleagues discovered a student in his behavior disorders class frequently

TABLE 8.2
Guidelines for the
Use of Time-out

1. The environment from which the student is removed must be reinforcing.
2. The time-out environment must limit access to reinforcement.
3. A student should not remain in time-out for a long period. A rule of thumb is one minute per year of age.
4. Time-out is not suspension or expulsion. A student should return to the group without lengthy discussion.
5. Time-out, like any intervention, does not work for everyone. Monitor your use of this technique, and if the same students appear to be in time-out over and over, consider a different approach.
6. Never use isolation time-out unless you have the proper facilities, supervision, and agreement of stakeholders.

seemed to go to time-out right after lunch—the teacher discovered that the student was having a brief nap in the time-out room . . .), and show what behaviors are resulting in time-out in your classroom.

Time-out should only be used for serious and threatening misbehavior.

Teachers most often use time-out for physical aggression, verbal aggression, and destruction of property (Zabel, 1986), and these are probably appropriate reasons. Such an intrusive procedure should not be used for small infractions or for failure to complete work. Appropriate and effective use of time-out procedures depends on the analytical abilities and the sensitivity of the teacher. When implemented correctly, this technique can help students understand the consequences of their behavior and begin to modify it.

SUMMARY AND REVIEW

We all live in groups—families, neighborhoods, communities, cities, states, nations . . . the list continues. For most children, school is one of the most significant groups in their lives. Helping students learn to live, function, and thrive in a group situation is critical to their success in life and work. Therefore, the time you spend enhancing your students' skills and abilities in this area is of major importance.

In this chapter, we have focused on classroom management interventions that involve groups of students. Some of these group interventions are intended to directly influence the affective and social behavior of the group. Others, such as cooperative learning, are intended to promote academic learning as well as to develop communication and social skills. Class meetings, affective interventions, peer systems, and group contingency management are all methods of fostering group interaction, decision making, and modification. One of the most important things you will model as a teacher is your attention to group dynamics. If students learn that the progress of the group is as important as their own achievement, that the well-being of the group directly influences their own attitudes and opportunities, and that decisions made by a group are decisions that often are helpful and necessary to them as individuals, they will be well equipped to participate in useful ways as they move through the many groups that will be a part of their lives.

REFLECTING ON CHAPTER 8

Group intervention strategies can be extremely successful, but they can also be unpredictable. Annie had a successful experience, as recorded in her journal, but perhaps we should consider some alternative outcomes.

- In discussion with your classmates, identify the potential pitfalls of several group strategies. What could be done to minimize them?
- Are there aspects of any of these interventions that might be of concern to parents or watchdog groups?

The issue of values is alarming people all over the country, but schools still see the need for character education or discussions of specific behaviors. How can we make these situations less politically volatile?

Discuss some of your own memories of school experiences, particularly those surrounding the arts. You may be surprised at how many of your classmates were involved in similar activities.

Key Terms

cognitive-affective approaches (p. 269)

behavioral approaches (p. 269)

bibliotherapy (p. 281)

peer mediation (p. 282)

group contingency management (p. 288)

token economies (p. 288)

level systems (p. 297)

Building Your Own Knowledge Base

Campbell, B., Campbell, L., & Dickinson, D. (1992). *Teaching and learning through multiple intelligences.* New Horizons for Learning, 4649 Sunnyside North, Seattle, WA 98103. This book contains information and activities for incorporating Gardner's theory of multiple intelligences into the classroom.

Elliott, S. N., & Gresham, F. M. (1991). *Social skills intervention guide: Practical strategies for social skills training.* Circle Pines, MN: American Guidance Service. Provides guidelines and exercises for systematically teaching cooperation, assertion, responsibility, empathy, and self-control (CARES) to small groups of students in special or regular education (grades 1–10) who have deficient skills in these areas.

Hayes, J. (1988). *A heart full of turquoise.* Mariposa Publishing, 922 Baca Street, Santa Fe, NM 87501. A collection of Pueblo tales that are excellent to tell in the classroom.

Raffini, J. P. (1993). *Winners without losers: Structures and strategies for increasing student motivation to learn.* Boston: Allyn and Bacon. Raffini discusses and suggests classroom structural arrangements and strategies for fostering students' intrinsic motivation, enhancing self-esteem, building cooperative relationships, and stimulating student involvement and enjoyment of school. Includes ideas for all grade levels.

References

Alberto, P. & Troutman, A. (1995). *Applied behavior analysis for teachers* (4th ed.). Columbus, OH: Merrill/Macmillan.

Anderson, J. (1982). *Thinking, changing, rearranging.* Eugene, OR: Timberline Press.

Anderson, J. (1987). *PUMSY in pursuit of excellence.* Eugene, OR: Timberline Press.

Anderson, J. (1990). *Bright beginnings.* Eugene, OR: Timberline Press.

Bandura, A. (1977). *Social learning theory.* Englewood Cliffs, NJ: Prentice-Hall.

Barbetta, P. (1990). Red-light–green-light: A classwide management system for students with behavior disorders in primary grades. *Preventing School Failure, 34,* 14–19.

Barrish, H. H., Saunders, M., & Wolf, M. M. (1969). Good behavior game: Effects of individual contingencies for group consequences on disruptive behavior in a classroom. *Journal of Applied Behavior Analysis, 2,* 119–124.

Bauer, A. M., Shea, T. M., & Keppler, R. (1986). Levels systems: A framework for the individualization of behavior management. *Behavioral Disorders, 12,* 28–35.

Bauer, A. M., & Shea, T. M. (1988). Structuring classrooms through level systems. *Focus on Exceptional Children, 21,* 1–12.

Brantner, J. P., & Doherty, M. A. (1983). A review of timeout: A conceptual and methodological analysis. In S. Axelrod & J. Apsche (Eds.), *The effects of punishment on human behavior* (pp. 87–132). New York: Academic.

Broden, M., Hall, R. B., & Dunlap, A., & Clark, R. (1970). Effects of teacher attention and a token reinforcement system in a junior high special education class. *Exceptional Children, 36,* 341–349.

Camp, B. W., & Bash, M. A. (1981). *Think aloud: Increasing social and cognitive skills, a problem-solving program for children.* Champaign, IL: Research Press.

Campbell, L., Campbell, B., & Dickinson, D. (1992). *Teaching and learning through multiple intelligences.* Seattle, WA: New Horizons for Learning.

Cartledge, G., & Kleefeld, J. (1991). *Taking part: Introducing social skills to children.* Circle Pines, MN: American Guidance Service.

Darch, C. B., & Thorpe, H. W. (1977). The principal game: A group consequence procedure to increase classroom on-task behavior. *Psychology in the Schools, 14,* 341–347.

Dinkmeyer, D. (1982). *Developing understanding of self and others—revised* (DUSO–R). Circle Pines, MN: American Guidance Service.

Dreikurs, R. (1968). *Psychology in the classroom* (2nd ed.). New York: Harper & Row.

Dreikurs, R., Grunwald, B., & Pepper, F. (1982). *Maintaining sanity in the classroom: Classroom management techniques* (2nd ed.). New York: Harper & Row.

Dreyer, S. S. (1989). *The Bookfinder: A guide to children's literature about the needs and problems of youth aged 2–15* (vol. 4). Circle Pines, MN: American Guidance Service.

Dreyer, S. S. (1992). *The best of The Bookfinder: Selected titles from volumes 1–3.* Circle Pines, MN: American Guidance Service.

Dupont, H., Gardner, O. W., & Brody, D. S. (1974). *Toward affective development* (TAD). Circle Pines, MN: American Guidance Service.

Elliott, S. N., & Gresham, F. M. (1991) *Social skills intervention guide.* Circle Pines, MN: American Guidance Service.

Glasser, W. (1965). *Reality therapy.* New York: Harper & Row.

Glasser, W. (1969). *Schools without failure.* New York: Harper & Row.

Glasser, W. (1986). *Control theory.* New York: Harper & Row.

Glasser, W. (1990). *The quality school.* New York: Harper & Row.

Goldstein, A. P., Sprafkin, R. P., Gershaw, N. J., & Klein, P. (1980). *Skillstreaming the adolescent.* Champaign, IL: Research Press.

Goodlad, J. (1984, 1994). *A place called school: Prospects for the future.* New York: McGraw-Hill.

Harmin, M., Kirschenbaum, H., & Simon, S. (1973). *Clarifying values through subject matter.* Minneapolis, MN: Winston Press.

Harris, V. W., & Sherman, J. A. (1973). Use and analysis of the "good behavior game" to reduce disruptive classroom behavior. *Journal of Applied Behavior Analysis, 6,* 405–417.

Hayes, J. (1988). *A heart full of turquoise.* Santa Fe, NM: Mariposa.

Hazel, J. S., Schumaker, J. B., Sherman, J. A., & Sheldon-Wildgen, J. (1982). *Asset: A social skills program for adolescents.* Champaign, IL: Research Press.

Herman, G. N., & Hollingsworth, P. (1992). *Kinetic kaleidoscope: Exploring movement and eneregy in the visual arts.* Tucson, AZ: Zephyr Press.

Huggins, P. (1986). *Building self-concept in the classroom.* Longmont, CO: Sopris West.

Huggins, P. (1991a). *Creating a caring classroom.* Longmont, CO: Sopris West, Inc.

Huggins, P. (1991b). *Helping kids handle anger: Teaching self control.* Longmont, CO: Sopris West, Inc.

Huggins, P. (1991c). *Teaching cooperation skills.* Longmont, CO: Sopris West, Inc.

Huggins, P. (1991d). *Teaching kids about sexual abuse.* Longmont, CO: Sopris West, Inc.

Huggins, P. (1993). *Teaching friendship skills: Intermediate version.* Longmont, CO: Sopris West.

Huggins, P. (1993b). *Teaching friendship skills: Primary version.* Longmont, CO: Sopris West.

Jackson, P. (1990). *Life in classrooms.* New York: Holt, Rinehart, & Winston.

Jackson, N. F., Jackson, D. A., & Monroe, C. (1983). *Getting along with others: Teaching social effectiveness to children.* Champaign, IL: Research Press.

James C. (1994). Amy had golden curls; Joe had a rat. Who would you rather be? *New York Times Book Review,* December 25, p. 3.

Jones, D. B., & Van Houten, R. (1985). The use of daily quizzes and public posting to decrease the disruptive behavior of secondary school students. *Education and Treatment of Children, 8,* 91–106.

Kazden, A. E. (1982). Response cost: The removal of conditioned reinforcers for therapeutic change. *Behavior Therapy, 3,* 533–546.

Kazden, A. E., & Bootzin, R. R. (1972). The token economy: An evaluative review. *Journal of Applied Behavior Analysis, 5,* 343–372.

Kerr, M. M., & Nelson, C. M. (1989). *Strategies for managing behavior problems in the classroom* (2nd ed.). Columbus, OH: Merrill.

Kohn, A. (1993). Punished by rewards: A rejoinder. *Beyond Behavior, 5,* 4–6.

Kohn, A. (1993). *Punished by rewards: The trouble with gold stars, incentive plans, A's, praise, and other bribes.* Boston: Houghton Mifflin.

Kounin, J. S. (1970). *Discipline and group management in classrooms.* New York: Holt, Rinehart & Winston.

McGinnis, E., & Goldstein, A. P. (1984). *Skillstreaming the elementary school child.* Champaign, IL: Research Press.

McLaughlin, T. F., & Malaby, J. E. (1972). Intrinsic reinforcers in a classroom token economy. *Journal of Applied Behavior Analysis, 5,* 263–270.

Meichenbaum, D. (1977). *Cognitive-behavior modification: An integrative approach.* New York: Plenum.

Morrow, L. W., & Morrow, S. A. (1985). Use of verbal medication procedure to reduce talking-out behavior. *Teaching: Behaviorally Disordered Youth,* 23–28.

Nelson, C. M., & Rutherford, R. B., Jr. (1983). Timeout revisited: Guidelines for its use in special education. *Exceptional Educational Quarterly, 3,* 56–57.

Pasternack, M. G. (1979). *Helping kids learn multi-cultural concepts: A handbook of strategies.* Champaign, IL: Research Press.

Pickering, J. W. (1990). *Comparing cultures.* Portland, ME: J. Weston Walch.

Raffini, J. P. (1993). *Winners without losers: Structures and strategies for increasing student motivation to learn.* Boston: Allyn and Bacon.

Richter, N. C. (1984). The efficacy of relaxation training with children. *Journal of Abnormal Child Psychology, 12,* 319–344.

Robin, A., Schneider, M., & Dolnick, M. (1976). The turtle technique: An extended case study of self-control in the classroom. *Psychology in the Schools, 13,* 449–453.

Salmon, L. S. (1992). *Applause! Activities for building confidence through dramatic arts.* Tucson, AZ: Zephyr Press.

Schrumpf, F., Crawford, D., & Usadel, H. C. (1991a). *Peer mediation: Conflict resolution in schools,* Program Guide. Champaign, IL: Research Press.

Schrumpf, F., Crawford, D., & Usadel, H. C. (1991b). *Peer mediation: Conflict resolution in schools.* Student Manual. Champaign, IL: Research Press.

Shatzer, J.R. (1991). Writing with emotionally disturbed children. *Beyond Behavior, 2,* 12–15.

Smith, S. W., & Ferrell, D. T. (1993). Levels system use in special education: Classroom intervention with prima facie appeal. *Behavioral Disorders, 18,* 251–264.

Teaching Tolerance. Southern Poverty Law Center, 400 Washington Ave., Montgomery, Alabama.

Vernon, A. (1989). *Thinking, feeling, behaving: an emotional education curriculum for children,* Grades 1–6. Champaign, IL: Research Press.

Vernon, A. (1989b). *Thinking, feelings, behavior: An emotional education curriculum for children, Grades 7–12.* Champaign, IL: Research Press.

Walker, H. M. (1982). Applications of response cost in school settings: Outcomes, issues, and recommendations. *Exceptional Education Quarterly, 3,* 47–55.

Walker, H. M., & Buckley, N. K. (1972). Teacher attention to appropriate and inappropriate classroom behavior: An individual case study. *Focus on Exceptional Children, 5,* 5–11.

Walker, H. M., McConnell, S., Holmes, D., Todis, B., Walker, J., & Golden, N.(1983). *The Walker social skills curriculum: The ACCEPTS program.* Austin, TX: Pro-Ed.

Walker, H. M., Todis, B., Holmes, D., & Horton, G. (1988). *The Walker social skills curriculum: The ACCESS program.* Austin, TX: Pro-Ed.

Wolery, M., Bailey, D. B., Jr., & Sugai, G. M. (1988). *Effective teaching principles and procedures of applied behavior analysis with exceptional students.* Boston: Allyn and Bacon.

Zabel, M. K. (1986). Time-out use with behaviorally disordered students. *Behavioral Disorders.*

Building Support Systems

To be an effective classroom manager you will sometimes need to work

with others within your school as well as with students' families. You will need to make use of resources within the community and be sensitive to your own needs as well. The two chapters in **Part Four, Building Support Systems,** *will help you find and develop support from others as well as take care of yourself.*

Chapter 9, **Partnerships with Colleagues, Parents, and Others,** *describes the roles of colleagues both inside and outside schools who can provide support, services, and resources that contribute to your classroom management success.*

Chapter 10, **Taking Care of Yourself,** *examines factors that can contribute to teacher stress and burnout as well as ways to cope with the challenges of teaching and managing a classroom, to minimize the defeating effects of stress, and to prevent professional burnout.*

Roles and Responsibilities of Colleagues

- Other teachers
- Building administrators
- Special educators

Agencies and Services Outside of Schools

- Therapists
- Evaluation of eligibility for special education
- Neglect and abuse
- Foster homes, group homes, and residential treatment centers
- Physicians and other medical professionals
- Development and implementation of IEP's
- Referral procedures

Inclusion of Exceptional Students in Regular Classrooms

- Working with paraprofessionals
- Working with your colleagues
- Working with teacher assistance teams

Partnerships with Colleagues, Parents, and Others

Partnerships Outside of Schools

- Diversity among families
- Types of family involvement with schools
- Positive communication with parents
- Disagreements with parents
- Parents with limited English proficiency

Consultation, Collaboration, and Teamwork with Your Colleagues

- Ingredients of successful consultation
- Collaboration and teamwork in the school ecosystem

Chapter 9

Partnerships with Colleagues, Parents, and Others

Annie's Journal

Minutes of the IEP meeting held for Danny LaMar Fontaine
April 4, 1995

Present:
Dr. Alice Wright, principal, Madison School
Ms. Annie Harris, teacher, Madison School
Mr. Franklin Wood, E/BD teacher, District 801
Dr. Miranda Fox, school psychologist, District 801
Ms. Rachel Cohen, school social worker, District 801
Mr. and Mrs. Calvin Nelson, parents

Dr. Wright convened the meeting with introductions and a brief description of each of the professions represented at the meeting. She reminded all present that this was the second time a meeting had been convened, the first being in response to Danny's aggressive behavior at school. That meeting resulted in referral to the Madison School Teacher Assistance Team in February. Results of the TAT's suggestions and interventions showed that while Danny enjoys the group discussions that he has had with Dr. Fox and the small group she coordinates, he has not been able to restrain his aggressive behavior toward other children. This behavior has resulted in a referral for special education services. Mr. and Mrs. Nelson (Danny's mother and stepfather) agreed to the evaluation, which has been completed. The group has now convened to discuss what further programming options should be considered. Dr. Wright pointed out that while it has only been a short time since the TAT's recommendations were implemented, the situation has become more urgent; Danny had a fight with another student in the hall three weeks ago, the second fight in which Danny has been in-

volved this term. The other student was seriously hurt in this fight. Dr. Wright asked Dr. Fox to discuss the findings from the various assessments and observations that have been conducted.

Dr. Fox reported that, according to Danny's achievement tests, his teacher's reports on his academic performance, and his work portfolio, he is performing below grade level in reading and math. His reading is halting and slow, although he knows all the letters and sounds and is able to figure out what the words say, given enough time. Ms. Harris reports that he is beginning to enjoy reading more, is willing to listen to the stories she reads to the class, and particularly enjoys the stories she tells to the group. When asked to read on his own, however, he often slams the book closed and says the work is dumb. In math, the pattern is similar: he seems to have the computation skills but lacks patience with performing the task. In addition, Danny seems unable to reason logically or to figure out what procedure to use solving narrative problems. Performance in other academic areas is hindered by his reading problems.

The major concern for Danny, however, is in the social-skills area. Dr. Fox reported that, based on her observations, Danny seems to be a social isolate who responds with aggression to any perceived challenge to his desires. While he has one or two friends in his class, these friendships are uneasy, at best. The relationships seem to be based on a leader-follower model, with Danny calling the shots and the other boys doing what he tells them to. The behavior rating scales Dr. Fox, Ms. Harris, and Ms. Cohen completed showed agreement on the aggressive, acting-out nature of Danny's behavior across several settings. The bus driver and lunchroom supervisor have also had to send discipline referrals on Danny to the office this term.

Mr. and Mrs. Nelson were asked about Danny's behavior at home, and they reported that, while they do not see as much trouble there, Danny does get into physical fights with his two younger brothers several times a week. Mrs. Nelson feels that this is "just boy behavior" and that he will grow out of it. She also reports that since she works an evening shift (3 to 11 P.M.) at the hospital (she is on the maintenance crew), she is not home in the evening and doesn't see the boys then. Mr. Nelson is also frequently absent after school and during the evening since he works as a handyman and lawn-care assistant with a changing schedule.

Ms. Cohen suggested that since the boys seem to spend a significant amount of time home alone, the committee might suggest some options for the family. Danny's two younger brothers (one brother, one stepbrother) are six and four, and Danny, who is nine, is really too young to care for them. Mrs. Nelson replied that her sister, who lives in the neighborhood, looks in on the boys during the evening if no one is home. Ms.

Cohen asked if they had considered Madison School's after-school program. Danny and his six-year-old brother, DeWayne, would be eligible at no cost to the family. The boys would be given a snack and supervised activities until 5:30. Mrs. Nelson said that that would be good for them but that it would leave the youngest boy, Martin, alone. The situation was discussed, and it was decided that Mrs. Nelson would talk with her daycare provider to see what it would cost for Martin to stay until 6:00. She will also talk with her sister about having the boys regularly at her apartment for dinner two nights a week. Mr. and Mrs. Nelson felt they could schedule their work times so that one of them could be home the other evenings.

Discussion then returned to Danny's difficulties in school, and Dr. Wright asked the group for recommendations. Mr. Wood described his special education class, which is designed for students with emotional and behavioral problems who also have academic difficulty. He said he felt that this would be an appropriate setting for Danny since the class is small and he is able to monitor individual children closely, both in terms of behavior and of academics. Ms. Harris said she felt her class was also willing to work with Danny, and she would not like to see him lose all connections with students he had come to know this year.

After much discussion and an invitation from Mr. Wood to Mr. and Mrs. Nelson to observe his class, it was agreed that Danny will spend his mornings in Mr. Wood's class, where the emphasis will be on improving his fluency in reading and his logical thinking and reasoning in math, as well as on specific social-skills instruction. In the afternoons he will return to Ms. Harris's class, where he will participate in story reading and storytelling, social studies, and other activities. Danny will continue to meet with Dr. Fox's group to discuss feelings and concerns. Dr. Fox, Mr. Wood, and Ms. Harris will meet on a weekly basis to discuss Danny's progress. Annual goals for Danny are as follows:

1. Danny will improve his fluency in reading, raising the rate at which he reads silently and orally. (Wood)

2. Danny will improve his math problem-solving skills, applying the appropriate computational strategy to problems presented. (Wood)

3. Danny will improve his social interaction with peers by completing a social skills training program (Wood), describing and applying what he has learned. (Harris)

4. Danny will improve his ability to verbalize his anger and concerns. (Fox, Harris)

Short-term objectives were discussed and established for each of the goals. All parties signed the IEP document, and the meeting was adjourned. Meeting time: 2 hours.

FOCUS QUESTIONS

✳ What are your feelings as you finish reading this document? Do you feel optimistic about Danny's future?

✳ The team was surprised to find out that the boys spent so much time alone. How did team members handle the information? Will their suggestions be successful? How will the team follow up on the recommendations? What is the school's responsibility?

✳ What problems do you see with implementing this plan? What kinds of resources and support will the team need to see that it works?

SOURCES OF SUPPORT AND EXPERTISE IN CLASSROOM MANAGEMENT

As we have emphasized throughout this book, your classroom exists within school and community ecosystems. Consequently, your students' learning and behavior affect and are affected by those larger ecosystems. Consider, for example, the many adults in schools who serve in a variety of roles as they interact with you and your students. They include other classroom teachers, teachers with expertise in specific areas (music, art, physical education, instructional media, special education, bilingual education), paraprofessionals, administrators and supervisors, psychologists, counselors, social workers, custodians, secretaries, nurses, food-service workers, bus drivers, and playground and lunchroom supervisors. Others, such as substitute teachers, student teachers, tutors, volunteers, parents, and visitors, may at times be in your school and classroom. Any of these people may be involved in your program. Many of them have skills and expertise that can help you manage your classroom.

Outside of school, as well, there are many people that may influence you and your students. Parents, guardians, foster parents, and other family members are, of course, critical influences on your students' classroom behavior. Often they can be your best allies. Other human resources for classroom management include physicians, therapists, clergy, social workers, and recreation specialists, who provide services through private or public agencies.

In this chapter we are concerned with sources of support and expertise in classroom management you can find both inside and outside your school. We will identify the roles and responsibilities you and your colleagues have and suggest ways to access the expertise and resources these persons can offer. We will also examine your role in preintervention assessment, referral, and development of **individual education programs** (IEPs) for students who may benefit from services beyond those that can typically be offered in regular classrooms. And we will continue to discuss your critical role in providing services for exceptional children.

ROLES AND RESPONSIBILITIES OF COLLEAGUES

Teachers today need to be able to work with a lot of specialists.

Increasingly, appropriate education for diverse learners requires you to be able to collaborate with other service providers within and outside of school. Especially for students who have learning or behavior difficulties, classroom teachers need to draw on the expertise and services that are available from their colleagues. Although you will usually retain primary responsibility for your students' education, you cannot, and should not expect to, have all of the specialized skills and materials or time to meet every student's special educational needs. Colleagues working within your school can be some of your best resources in classroom management.

Teachers need to know who is available to help with different student needs.

In Chapters 1 and 4 we discussed how important it is for you to be familiar with the personnel and resources available in your building and school district. Even before your students arrive, you should meet your colleagues and learn as much as you can about their roles, their services, and the procedures for accessing those services. Available school personnel vary from school to school and district to district, depending on state and local policies, budgets, and school or district needs for personnel. Of course, the skills of the persons who serve in those support roles also vary. In this section, we identify personnel who are usually (or often) available and their potential roles in assisting you with classroom management issues.

OTHER TEACHERS

In the past, teachers were on their own with their students.

Traditionally, teachers have operated fairly independently within their own classrooms. The traditional classroom consists of a teacher and a group of students somewhat isolated from the rest of the school. This independence contributes to the autonomy of individual teachers, who have substantial influence over features of their classroom ecosystem, but it also contributes to their isolation from other adults (Goodlad, 1984). Although many teachers work as members of instructional teams or with teacher aides, some are cut off from ongoing contact with other adults and have almost total responsibility for their classrooms. Many teachers have little opportunity to speak with another adult during an entire school day (Eisner, 1988).

This condition has both advantages and disadvantages. On the one hand, teachers typically have considerable freedom in their approaches to instruction and classroom management. Administrators may offer little interference as long as there are no complaints and everything seems under control. On the other hand, behind the closed classroom door there is also a risk of mistakes going undetected and uncorrected. The downside of teacher autonomy is the absence of the expertise and support that other professional educators can provide. The traditional classroom teacher carries the burden of total responsibility for effectively meeting the multiple, diverse needs of all students and

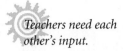

Teachers need each other's input.

for managing the classroom. It is increasingly apparent that an individual teacher cannot meet all of his or her students' needs alone. Your fellow classroom teachers may be your most valuable resources for information, ideas, and support concerning classroom management. You can also be an important resource for your colleagues.

BUILDING ADMINISTRATORS

Principals can help get support services for your students.

A principal's attitude toward the educational process affects the whole school.

The typical administrative structure in public schools includes a principal, who serves as the instructional leader for the building, perhaps together with assistant principals, curriculum coordinators, and department heads in larger schools. Principals are also instrumental in obtaining resources and services that support instruction and classroom management. The effective-schools literature discussed in Chapter 4 consistently points to the essential role of building principals in providing the instructional leadership necessary for creating effective schools. Principals' educational philosophies influence the entire school atmosphere. Their attitudes about acceptable and desirable student behavior, appropriate methods for handling behavioral problems, teachers' responsibilities, and their own roles are significant influences on the attitudes and approaches of faculty, staff, and students, as well as on parent and community support and involvement.

A few days before the beginning of one of the authors' first year of teaching, the principal briefed the new teacher about disciplinary procedures. Pulling a wooden paddle from behind his desk, he told the new teacher that any serious behavior problems would be dealt with in his office. (That encounter occurred more than twenty years ago, and, fortunately, most school districts have discontinued corporal punishment.) A principal can serve a very supportive role, though. Indeed, building administrators are in the *key* position to exert a schoolwide influence on the attitudes and behavior of the faculty, students, support staff, and community toward classroom management.

Another major responsibility of building principals is to evaluate teacher performance, and assessing your skills in classroom management is often central to their judgments. Administrators, whether principals or department heads, can also encourage and direct a teacher. When teachers suffer stress and burnout, lack of administrative support is often a major cause (Cherniss, 1988; Zabel & Zabel, 1982). When an administrator does give a teacher the support he or she needs, it can make all the difference. See the Classroom Closeup "The Ice Cream Fight" for a description of an experience in which a department head helped a new teacher.

Helping teachers is an important part of a principal's job.

One principal we know sees supporting teachers who are inexperienced or are having problems with classroom management as a major part of her job. Like most principals, she wants her teachers not only to survive but also to grow and thrive in their jobs. She also recognizes that classroom management

Classroom Closeup

The Ice-Cream Fight

My teaching career began in a Queens high school in the middle of a term. To say that my classes were undisciplined is to put it mildly. LeRoy serenaded the class with a trumpet mouthpiece every day. I could never quite catch him with it, and when accused of making disturbing noises, he put on his dramatic "Who, me?" act to further entertain the class. Two of my students were blind. They didn't like each other and did their best to punch each other out. I tried to keep them apart, but if one sensed the other was near, there would be a pitiful flailing of arms and cursing. I dragged myself home every night in utter defeat and tears.

On a memorable occasion, three-quarters of the class got into an ice-cream fight. Kids who couldn't remember to bring a pencil organized themselves to come to class with piles of ice-cream sandwiches, which they promptly spread over one another and the room. Although I knew a teacher was supposed to handle her own dirty linen, I made a desperate call to the department chairman. He gave me some valuable advice. He didn't tell me to punish the kids or to barter with them or to offer them contingency contracts. He told me to become a better teacher. He gave me specific suggestions on how to improve my curriculum. I have never forgotten that discipline "technique." . . . That department chairman invested a lot of time in me. He came to my class every Monday and watched how I applied a suggestion for getting across curriculum from the previous Monday's conference. Then he added another item to the list. Slowly, layer upon layer, he helped me to build mastery of the material I was teaching. He borrowed veteran teachers' notes for me, he taught demonstration lessons, he arranged for me to observe other teachers. (Ohanian, 1994, p. 183) ✳

is complex and challenging. Consequently, she spends many hours sharing ideas, offering reassurance, counseling, and helping solve individual and group problems in a supportive way.

SPECIAL EDUCATORS

Most regular classrooms have a few students who are receiving special-education services.

Federal legislation has required special education services for students with disabilities for more than twenty years, yet there is great latitude in how those services are provided at the district and school level. Nationwide, about 13 percent of public-school students are identified as having an educational disability of some type, and more than 90 percent of these receive at least some of their education in regular classrooms (U.S. Department of Education, 1993). Thus, you can expect that several of your students (an average of three or four students in a class of thirty) will be involved in special education; you will probably be working with special educators. In order to make use of the special educators' expertise, you need to understand their service-delivery roles and their areas of competence.

Special Education Service Delivery Models

Traditionally, special educator roles have been defined according to the services they offer along a continuum of special education services (Deno, 1970; Reynolds & Birch, 1982). These services are provided to meet the special needs of individual students as established by multidisciplinary teams of educators, administrators, relevant support personnel, and parents. A student may receive those services only following a formal evaluation of eligibility.

Educational-service delivery models are usually defined by the extent to which they offer services that are separate from the regular education programs. See Figure 9.1 for a continuum that shows less to more restrictive programs of the delivery models.

Students with more severe disabilities receive services in a more restricted or separate environment than those with mild disabilities.

According to this continuum of services model, students whose disabilities are more severe are expected to receive services in more restrictive settings. Those with more mild and moderate disabilities are served in less restrictive settings. Because the vast majority of educational disabilities are considered mild or moderate, most students with disabilities are served predominently in regular classrooms with support, assistance, and consultation from special educators and support services personnel. In many districts, even students with pronounced disabilities are placed in regular classrooms.

FIGURE 9.1   Continuum of Programs of the Delivery Models

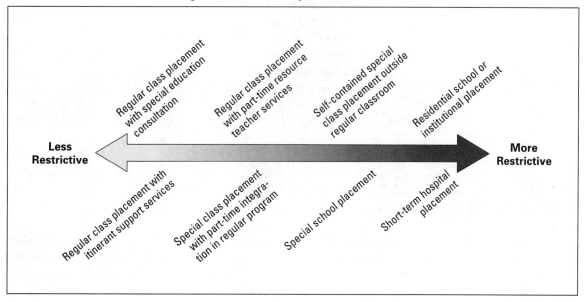

Special Education Disability Classifications

Specialists are certified in particular types of disabilities.

Special educators are usually trained and certified to work with students who have particular types of disabilities. Thus, there are specialists in learning disabilities (LD); speech and language disorders (S-L); mental retardation (MR); serious emotional disturbances (SED); multiple disabilities; hearing, visual, and physical impairments; as well as traumatic brain injuries, autism, deaf and blind, and other health impairments. Over 90 percent of identified students with disabilities fall into the first four classifications (LD, S-L, MR, and SED). Currently, Congress is considering adding an AD(H)D (attention deficit hyperactivity disorder) classification, although some students with ADD or ADHD who have educationally significant disabilities are already identified in LD or SED classifications. Federal mandates do not require special services for students who are gifted or talented, but some states and many school districts also provide special programs for gifted students, and teachers with training and expertise in this area are a part of regular and special education faculties.

Some specialists are trained in several areas of disability.

In many cases, special educators have expertise across several types of exceptionality. In some teacher-preparation programs, teachers receive multi-categorical or cross-categorical training, most often in the high-incidence areas of learning disabilities, serious emotional disturbances, and mental retardation. Cross-categorical teachers may work in any of the service-delivery models, but most often serve in consulting or resource-teacher roles.

Your school will probably have special educators assigned to your building who help and consult with regular classroom teachers and who may work collaboratively in team-teaching arrangements. Their role is to work with you and others to provide appropriate special education for students who have met eligibility requirements. Technically, special educators may not provide direct services to students who have not yet been formally identified. However, they may participate on teacher assistance teams and offer information and general consultation to classroom teachers. In addition, other special educators in self-contained programs may also be in your school, but your involvement may be limited to situations where students from their programs are integrated part-time into your classroom or to informal interactions you have with them.

INCLUSION OF EXCEPTIONAL STUDENTS IN REGULAR CLASSROOMS

Since public schools started providing special education services, there has been ongoing discussion and debate about the desirability and feasibility of providing special services within regular classrooms. Most advocates, parents, policy makers, and teachers agree that, to the greatest extent possible, students

People disagree about whether or not special education ought to be offered in the regular classroom.

with disabilities, or exceptional students, should be educated in regular programs with typical classmates. Some of the central arguments for mainstreaming or inclusion of students with disabilities are that

- Both disabled and nondisabled students benefit from integration,
- There is no justification for segregating most disabled students from regular classrooms,
- There are harmful social and intellectual effects from segregation, and
- Most special-education services can be provided in regular classrooms.

According to the Individuals with Disabilities Education Act (IDEA), the federal legislation that requires public schools to provide special education, students with disabilities must receive "an appropriate education" in the "least restrictive environment." However, it is not always easy to balance these two principles. They do not mean that all students, regardless of the type and extent of their disability, must be educated totally in the mainstream or regular classroom. What they do mean is that the multidisciplinary teams of educators, parents, and related-services personnel who design IEPs must develop an appropriate program that can be provided in the least restrictive environment possible. Usually, the least restrictive environment is a regular classroom with accommodations, adaptations, and support services. It is likely that you will participate in the IEP programming and placement planning and implementation. It is also likely that you will collaborate with special educators to provide appropriate education for students with disabilities in your classroom.

It is sometimes hard to balance the best education for a child with disabilities with the environment.

Decisions about appropriate placement must consider characteristics of *both* the individual child and the available personnel, resources, and settings (although lack of an appropriate program is not an excuse for not providing appropriate services). Among the questions to be answered are

- What are the student's special needs?
- What understanding and skills does the classroom teacher have?
- What assistance and support must be provided?
- What effect will the student have on the classroom?
- What accommodations must be made in the regular program to meet the student's needs?

None of these questions can be answered apart from a careful examination of the individual student and the school and classroom ecosystems. Today, some schools provide educational programming in regular classrooms for students with severe and multiple disabilities, while other schools have difficulty including even mildly disabled students.

Students with emotional disturbances are the hardest to include in the regular classroom.

As a group, no students offer greater challenges to integration than those with serious emotional disturbances (Rizzo & Zabel, 1988). Their behavior can be disruptive and nonresponsive to the group and to individual interventions discussed in the last few chapters. To successfully manage the behavior of students with serious emotional disturbances, you can call on colleagues in several support roles. Knowing when to ask for help is one of the critical skills of effective classroom management in today's schools.

WORKING WITH PARAPROFESSIONALS

Paraprofessionals, or teacher aides, have worked in special education programs for a long time, and are a rapidly increasing group of special-education personnel (U.S. Department of Education, 1993). As more students with disabilities are served in regular classrooms and as personnel budgets do not keep pace with growing enrollments, schools are increasingly looking to paraprofessionals to assist teachers and other professional staff.

Teacher aides have a wide variety of training and skills.

Educational training and experience of paraprofessionals vary widely. They are required to have little formal training as educators, although some have training in related fields like psychology and child development, and a few are certified teachers. Consequently, you will need to determine their understanding of child development and their instructional and classroom-management skills before making assignments in your classroom. Paraprofessionals can help you in many ways, or they can add to your responsibilities if they have minimal skills or if you are unable to supervise them. If they are to contribute to your classroom management, you will need to work together as a team. You must discuss your philosophy of classroom management with them, explain your management approaches, explicitly define responsibilities, and provide feedback to them about ways of dealing with specific incidents.

WORKING WITH YOUR COLLEAGUES

Three school personnel roles that can provide support and assistance to the classroom teacher are the school psychologist, counselor, and social worker. The specific responsibilities of your colleagues in these roles are often hard to define, and frequently they overlap since your school may not have all three types of personnel available. In one way or another, psychologists, counselors, and social workers provide services and offer expertise that should enable students to function more successfully in your classroom.

School Psychologists

Traditionally, school psychologists have been the ones primarily responsible for individual psychological and educational testing and for preparing psychological evaluations to determine student eligibility for special education. While psychologists still serve this assessment role, they are now apt to rely more on observing students in actual classroom situations than on paper-and-pencil tests in their offices to assess the students' functioning.

School psychologists often observe more than they test to see if students need special education.

Psychologists trained in ecological and authentic assessment can provide objective views of how classroom events influence and are influenced by individual students. Consequently, school psychologists are likely to take an active role in intervention efforts and to provide consultation and feedback to classroom teachers and other members of intervention teams about student behavior and learning problems. By studying a student's behavior, a psychologist can help you design, implement, and evaluate behavior-change interventions. In addition, some school psychologists provide individual and group therapy for students.

Psychologists can help teachers understand a student's problems and plan an intervention.

School Counselors

School counselors are more apt to be in secondary schools than elementary schools because in the higher grades they are needed to help with academic scheduling as well as career or vocational and college counseling. They are also typically trained in psychological counseling and may work with individuals or groups of students who are experiencing emotional trauma, such as parental divorce, depression, or drug or alcohol problems. For example, a school counselor may lead support groups for students who are at-risk due to stressful family situations, such as divorce. Counselors also sometimes provide drug- or sex-education programs to students in regular classrooms.

There are more counselors in high schools than in elementary schools.

School Social Workers

School social workers serve primarily as liaisons between the school, home, and community for students who are in special education programs, who are considered at-risk, or who have particular problems that require coordinating school, family, and community efforts. Social workers attempt to find resources and services outside of school to help children function effectively in school, and they too may provide individual or group counseling. For example, social workers sometimes lead social-skills training and affective education groups such as those discussed in Chapter 7.

Social workers connect home and school for students who have special needs.

School social workers provide a variety of services depending on identified student needs. For example, a social worker usually collects information and reports to IEP and placement teams about a student's previous educational, home, and medical history. Social workers sometimes coordinate the efforts of a child's family, social-welfare agency, and physicians to obtain needed medical services. They may help arrange for after-school childcare or recreation activities, teach parenting classes, or solicit and coordinate efforts from child-protection services for students who are suspected victims of abuse or neglect.

Like school psychologists and counselors, school social workers have many possible roles that are relevant to classroom management. Each school may make different use of these colleagues depending on the perceived needs in the school and the availability of persons with specific skills. In one way or another, these three types of professionals offer consultation and support to classroom teachers. In your school, you will need to find out what kinds of services and resources these professionals offer and then work jointly with them to provide services to benefit your students.

WORKING WITH TEACHER ASSISTANCE TEAMS

Teacher assistance teams can help you understand a student's problem and find ways to deal with it, sometimes without a comprehensive evaluation.

Through preassessment, **teacher assistance teams** can help you study persistent problems and develop solutions to avert the need for referral. We know that once a student is referred for a comprehensive evaluation, it is highly likely that he or she will be formally identified as disabled (Algozzine, Christenson & Ysseldyke, 1982). Although formal identification and the accompanying label of disability is necessary to obtain special services, this identification also carries risks. Official disability labels carry a stigma or a feeling of a spoiled identity, which can serve as a self-fulfilling prophecy of lower expectations and performance. In most cases, it is much easier to give someone a label of disability than to put it aside.

Teacher assistance teams include specialists, administrators, and the classroom teacher.

Every school should have a teacher assistance team, although it may operate under another name like *child study, prereferral* or *preassessment team.* Before they refer a student for a comprehensive evaluation to determine eligibility for special education services, schools must make substantial efforts to resolve behavioral and learning problems within the regular classroom. They must also document their preassessment interventions. Although the composition of teacher assistance teams varies from school to school, they should include experts on student behavior and learning. Typically, your colleagues in any of the roles discussed above and classroom teachers and administrators are involved.

Teacher assistance teams help students stay in the regular classroom.

When a student's behavior has not responded to approaches we discussed in the first eight chapters of this book or when you have significant concerns about the student's learning or behavior, you should ask for help from your teacher assistance team. In some cases it may provide direct assistance and services that will help you resolve the problem. For example, other teachers may suggest strategies that have worked for them in similar problems. A school psychologist may conduct observations that offer insights about how seating or grouping arrangements, feedback from other students, or distractions affect your student's behavior. A social worker may contact the student's parents to find out whether the child is getting enough sleep or food or if there are problems at home that may be carried over to school. A central function of teacher assistance teams is to keep the student in the mainstream classroom. Preassessment requirements force teachers to examine and implement interventions that go beyond normal classroom routine; they keep teachers from giving special educators the responsibility for solving problems.

You should not see asking a teacher assistance team for help as failure on your part. Recognizing when a student's needs go beyond what you are able to provide is a critical part of professional behavior. A common mistake teachers make is to wait too long to enlist the help of others, mistakingly believing that it is up to them to solve all classroom problems by *themselves.* As with most of life's difficulties, from an oil leak in your car to the flu, the sooner you recognize the problem and seek appropriate solutions, the more likely you will be to find solutions.

Teachers often wait too long to get help with a problem.

REFERRAL PROCEDURES

When a student's behavior does not respond to the documented preassessment interventions, you may decide to refer the student for a comprehensive evaluation. Referral is not an easy step for most teachers, who may see it as admitting they failed to change a student. However, some problem behavior is neither the result of classroom conditions nor amenable to change in that setting. When you, the other members of the teacher assistance team, the student's parents, and others who know about and have been involved in the situation all conclude that the student may have needs that cannot be met by the regular program, the next step is referral.

When students need more help, you may need to refer them for a more thorough evaluation.

Referral actually includes several substeps. Typically, your school will have referral information forms for you, the teacher assistance team, and the building administrator to document your preassessment interventions. The building administrator forwards this information to the special-services department of your district, which informs the student's parents or guardians of the referral, requests their permission to conduct a formal evaluation, and informs them of their rights and responsibilities to participate in the evaluation process, to provide information they believe is relevant, and to due process should they disagree with the evaluation. In most cases, this notification should come as no surprise if parents have been appropriately involved in the preassessment process.

EVALUATION OF ELIGIBILITY FOR SPECIAL EDUCATION

After obtaining parental permission, a comprehensive and multidisciplinary evaluation is undertaken to determine if the student meets the criteria for a diagnosis of disability. The types of assessment vary according to the problems described in the referral but must include information from a variety of sources and perspectives on the child's educational functioning. The evaluation normally includes individually testing the student's intelligence and academic achievement; collecting health, family, and school histories; measuring personality; and observing the child directly.

The purpose of an evaluation is to find out if the student has a disability.

There are a number of steps in an evaluation.

As the student's classroom teacher, you should be asked for information and evidence of the student's academic performance and behavior. In most cases, special educators or school psychologists will also conduct formal observations of your student's in-class behavior. In cases where behavior problems are a central concern, you and others (parents, other teachers, administrators) will complete *behavior rating scales.* There are dozens of commercially available, norm-referenced behavior rating scales that allow you to evaluate the student's behavior across a number of dimensions (e.g., aggressiveness, withdrawal, immaturity) in comparison with other students of the same age. On the basis of these ratings, the assessment team can determine how several persons involved with the child in different contexts view the child's behavior. They can also help identify the type of behavioral excess or deficit and reveal the extent of agreement among raters. Table 9.1 contains two sample items from each of the five factors on a rating scale, the Walker Problem Behavior Identification Checklist (Walker, 1983).

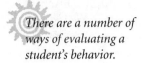

There are a number of ways of evaluating a student's behavior.

Follow-up on the Comprehensive Evaluation

Following the evaluation, special education services personnel schedule a meeting involving the student's parents, persons involved in the evaluation,

TABLE 9.1
Sample Items from Walker Problem Behavior Identification Checklist

FACTOR 1: ACTING OUT
Argues and must have the last word in verbal exchanges. Has temper tantrums.
FACTOR 2: WITHDRAWAL
Does not engage in group activities. Has no friends.
FACTOR 3: DISTRACTIBILITY
Has difficulty concentrating for any length of time. Continually seeks attention.
FACTOR 4: DISTURBED PEER RELATIONS
Comments that nobody likes him/her. Is hypercritical of himself/herself.
FACTOR 5: IMMATURITY
Is listless and continually tired. Weeps or cries without provocation.

Source: Items from *Walker Problem Behavior Identification Checklist, Revised.* Copyright © 1970, 1976, 1983 by Western Psychological Services. Reprinted by permission of the publisher, Western Psychological Services, 12031 Wilshire Boulevard, Los Angeles, California 90025.

and others who are familiar with the child or who may become involved in future educational planning. Again, the members of this identification team vary depending on who has information about the child's educational performance. At minimum, eligibility committees include

- The student's parents or guardians,

- A representative of the school district's special education services (administrator, school psychologist, coordinator) who can report and interpret the results of the comprehensive evaluation,

- The student's teacher(s), and

- Additional persons who have some involvement or knowledge and expertise to help determine eligibility (psychologists, social workers, counselors, physicians, nurses, building administrators, parent advocates, and sometimes the student him or herself).

After an evaluation, a team needs to decide what to do for the student.

As the student's classroom teacher, you should participate in any decisions regarding identification and placement of your students since your experiences and insights about the child are useful for educational planning (Zabel, Peterson & Smith, 1986). At the meeting, members of the multidisciplinary team discuss their findings and offer recommendations about formal identification of disability and eligibility to receive special education services. This decision is intended to reflect the consensus of the group. Possible outcomes are

1. Agreement that the child does meet eligibility criteria—has documented educational disabilities,

2. Agreement that the child does not meet eligibility criteria,

3. Disagreement about whether the child does or does not meet legal criteria, and

4. Agreement that additional information is necessary to make an eligibility decision.

When the team agrees that the student meets eligibility criteria, it begins to develop an IEP. When there are disagreements, as between school personnel and parents or guardians, the team may decide to continue the current program and periodically reevaluate the student's progress. In some situations, school personnel may recommend proceeding with identification and development of an IEP despite parent objections. If so, parents are reminded of their due-process rights and may contest the district decision. If these disputes are not resolved, a due-process hearing is scheduled before an independent hearing officer, who will collect and study the evidence and make a decision on the case. Although the eligibility decisions and IEP program development may appear straightforward, they rarely are. You and the other members of the committee must determine whether the student's problems interfere with educational performance, and, if they do, you must determine what is best for the student.

In evaluating emotional and behavioral disorders, we are always engaged in the study of relativity. There are no objective measures of behavioral deviance, no tests that will conclusively diagnose emotional and behavioral disorders. And, as we have stressed throughout this book, behavior cannot be considered independent of the context—the ecosystems—where it occurs. Ultimately these decisions rest on the team's best judgment about the severity of the problem behavior and the extent to which it can be appropriately handled in the regular classroom.

There are no objective standards or tests to tell whether a problem behavior is a disorder.

Conscientious teachers and members of multidisciplinary committees who are charged with making these important decisions must ask questions such as these:

- Is the student's behavior disturbed or just disturbing?
- Are we really concerned about the student's behavior or simply unwilling to tolerate it?
- How could we have dealt more effectively with the problem?
- What are the potential benefits of a special education program?

There are rarely definitive answers to any of these questions, but obtaining information, perspectives, and insights from the people who know the student seems to be the most sensible approach. In the Classroom Closeup "Placing a Troubled Student in a Special Program," a fifth-grade teacher, Chris Zajac, examines her mixed feelings about the decision to place one of her students, Clarence, into the Alpha class, a special program for behaviorally disordered students.

DEVELOPMENT AND IMPLEMENTATION OF IEPs

If the multidisciplinary team agrees on a student's eligibility for special education, the next step is developing an individual educational program. The IEP is both a process and a product. It is a *process* for involving relevant persons in the design, implementation, and evaluation of special interventions for a student with educational disabilities. It is a *product* in the sense of being a document that specifies the commitment among those persons to provide an appropriate educational program for the student.

An IEP has several elements that are required by law. They include

An IEP defines goals for a student and the means of arriving at these goals.

- A summary of the student's present performance level,
- Long-term educational goals,
- Short-term objectives for meeting each goal, and

Classroom Closeup

Placing a Troubled Student in a Special Program

It is remarkable how much of the time of how many adults in a school one child can command simply by being difficult. The meeting happened Thursday. Past the long desk in the office and into the windowless, overheated conference room at a little before noon went a parade of five experts on troubled children. Chris went in, too. The only person missing was Clarence's mother, though she had been officially notified again.

When, about an hour and a half later, the parade came out of the conference room, Clarence was no longer a member of Chris's class. . . .

Chris worried about Clarence. She had reason. To send him away was to tell him the same old news: he was a problem; he had failed. And to help Clarence by placing him in a special class among a number of other noto-

riously unruly children—might as well say his behavior would improve if he was made to join a street gang. . . .

And yet at the same time, removing Clarence from the class seemed like a just solution. He had not committed any acts of extreme violence; he hadn't thrown chairs at other children or come to school with weapons. But he did beat up and intimidate other kids. More and more since Christmas, he had begun to seem like a wrecker in the room. Was it fair to let one child's problems interfere with the education of nineteen other children, many of them just as needy as Clarence? When she looked back and imagined herself saying, "No! I don't want him taken away," she imagined herself feeling just as guilty as she would have if she'd said, "Yes, by all means, Alpha." In retrospect, sending Clarence to Alpha seemed like a decision to accomplish something that was probably right by doing something that was probably wrong. (Kidder, 1989, pp. 166–167) ✳

- A list of special-education and support services, materials, and interventions to be provided, including timetable and personnel.

Classroom teachers should play a central role in each aspect of IEP development. You have the most direct knowledge of your student's present performance level as well as of goals and objectives for that student. *Long-term goals* are the IEP committee's general estimates of desirable changes to be accomplished over a long period of time. *Short-term objectives* are statements of measurable steps for meeting long-term goals.

Classroom teachers must share in the IEP decisions.

In most cases, special education and support services will supplement the regular program in your classroom, so it is essential that you participate in determining what services will be provided, when, how often, and who will be responsible. A variety of special educators and support-services personnel may be responsible for providing services and obtaining resources that will be delivered outside or inside your room. Be sure you are clear about specific responsibilities you have in the IEP implementation. Before you sign the IEP, you should feel comfortable about the support and assistance you will have in delivering those responsibilities.

Today most special education programs happen in the regular classroom.

As we mentioned earlier, students with disabilities usually receive special education and support services in their regular classrooms. Although IEP teams sometimes conclude that the appropriate services require placing students in more restrictive settings, such as special classes and schools, increasingly special education services are provided in the regular classroom. Thus, in one way or another, you will work with the people who provide these services. These cooperative and collaborative relationships have far-reaching implications for your classroom ecosystem. Today, you are much less likely to operate apart from other professionals than teachers in the past.

Sometimes you will work with specialists right in your classroom.

Your collaboration may be relatively minimal, such as adapting your students' schedules and seeing that they get to and from resource rooms or counseling sessions. You may collaborate with other service providers to monitor student behavior and performance and to provide feedback to other members of the intervention team. You may use materials and resources to implement interventions that you and other service providers have jointly designed. In some cases, you will work next to specialists and paraprofessionals in your classroom to design and deliver IEP-designated programs.

Other School-Based Professionals

Besides administrators, psychologists, counselors, social workers, and special educators, there are a number of other specialists—sometimes called related-services personnel—whom you are likely to encounter.

There are many kinds of specialists who work with students separately and in your classroom.

Speech and Language Specialists.   When speech and language specialists work with your students, they usually do so right in your classroom. While they may need to work separately with a student some of the time, they often help integrate language practice into the everyday routines of your classroom. They may also conduct language activities with a variety of students as part of the regular classroom day.

Physical and Occupational Therapists.   Physical and occupational therapists may also come into your classroom on a regular basis to work with students who need specific fine- or gross-motor programs to enhance their development. Like the speech and language clinicians, these professionals may work sometimes with several members of your class and other times with the individual student to whom they are assigned.

ESL and Bilingual Teachers.   ESL (English as a Second Language) and bilingual teachers may teach their own separate classes or work with students who spend part or all of the day in your class. With the increasing numbers of students whose first language is not English, you are very likely to work with ESL or bilingual teachers. These programs vary from self-contained to pull-out to full-inclusion models, but in every case, the assistance and support of a trained ESL or bilingual teacher is critical to the student's success. Having students in your class whose first language is not English may at first seem an enormous challenge, and so it is. But it is also an extraordinary opportunity for you and your students to learn something of the language, culture, and experience of children in other parts of the world.

Students from other countries can greatly enrich your classroom.

CONSULTATION, COLLABORATION, AND TEAMWORK WITH YOUR COLLEAGUES

In the context of the classroom ecosystem, consultation, collaboration, and teamwork are important interactions as professionals work toward common goals (Dettmer, Thurston & Dyck, 1993; Heron & Harris, 1993). Although these approaches have similarities, with each you and your colleagues have a different level of interaction.

A consultant helps the classroom teacher know how to help a student.

- *Consultation* In consultation, someone with specialized knowledge, skills, or expertise—a consultant—provides information or resources to help solve instructional or management problems to a consultee, such as a classroom teacher. The consultee then provides the direct services to the clients (usually students). For example, a school psychologist might provide an observation form you can use to monitor the behavior of one of your students. Or a special education teacher might show you how to develop a contract with one of your students.

    Although the specialist is often placed in the role of consultant who provides expertise *to* others, as a classroom teacher, you will often consult *with* others. For example, you may have information and insights about your students that can help the specialists understand them better and design programs that are more likely to be effective. According to special education teachers of students with emotional and behavior disorders, for example, information from regular classroom teachers about their previous efforts is one of the most valuable types of assessment information for program planning (Zabel, Peterson & Smith, 1986).

Sometimes a specialist will work with you on a problem in your classroom.

- *Collaboration* While consultation is an *in*direct means of providing educational services, collaboration is a direct, joint effort of professionals addressing a problem. For example, a psychologist might conduct observations right in your classroom that could provide data for analyzing the student's behavior and then help you design, implement, and evaluate the interventions. Or a special educator might regularly conduct social-skills training with several members of your class.

- Teamwork   Teamwork involves two or more persons working regularly together, each performing a different role. For example, you might team up with a special educator and a paraprofessional to instruct and manage your classroom, with each team member having specific responsibilities. Together, you plan curricular goals for the class and for individual students, determine instructional approaches, develop materials, discuss approaches for dealing with problems, and clarify your roles. The special educator may work primarily with individual students or small groups, the paraprofessional may handle clerical duties (such as maintaining records and preparing instructional materials), and you may be primarily responsible for more large-group instruction.

Obviously, consultation, collaboration, and teamwork can take many forms, depending on the contexts in which they occur, the *processes* that are employed, and the *content* of the consultation (Dettmer, Thurston & Dyck, 1993). *Context* includes all the student, setting, and activity variables that we discussed earlier. Student characteristics include intelligences, needs, learning styles, achievement levels, social skills, sociocultural identifications, interests and experiences. For example, consultation settings may involve classroom, school, home, or community—each of which has its own characteristics.

Processes include the types of communication, coordination, and cooperative skills that enable participants to "listen to each other and interact, seek to identify the problem, share information and ideas, resolve conflicts, conduct observations, develop courses of action, coordinate activities, follow through on results, and assess the outcomes for further planning and implementation" (Dettmer, Thurston & Dyck, 1993, p. 27). Collaborative consultation processes can be informal or formal. No doubt much of your consultation and collaboration with others will be informal, consisting of conversations and spontaneous exchanges of ideas and information with other teachers, administrators, and support-services personnel within and outside of school. Formal consultation is more structured and consists of scheduled meetings, training activities, and delineated responsibilities. Formal consultation may be structured to meet the identified needs of your students, as specified, for example, in a student's IEP.

Content of consultation usually falls into one or more of the following categories: materials, methods and strategies, or alternatives. Materials include books, equipment, materials, and media that you use in instruction or classroom management. Methods and strategies are different instructional approaches, like the physical arrangement of your classroom, cooperative learning strategies, peer tutoring, small- and large-group recitation, and self-directed learning, as well as preventative approaches and the individual and group interventions we discussed in previous chapters. Alternatives include accommodations and adjustments, such as modifying materials and revising requirements and expectations.

THE INGREDIENTS OF SUCCESSFUL CONSULTATION

If collaborative consultation is to work, participants need more than technical expertise; they also need effective communication and coordination skills (Heron & Harris, 1993). Consultants must have the expertise—the knowledge, skills, and materials—that can add to the instruction and management of students. In addition, you and they must be *willing* to participate in consultative relationships—an unfamiliar role in which many teachers, accustomed to functioning more autonomously, are initially wary.

Good communication is one of the most important skills a school specialist can have.

Another key to successful consultation is effective communication. In Chapter 2 we discussed some of the complex, yet critical, issues of classroom communication primarily in terms of teacher-student interactions. As we saw there, communication is complex, and the more subtle nonverbal forms of interaction are as important as the verbal. Clearly, effective collaborators must establish rapport, recognize and respect one another's competence, develop a sense of common purpose and goals, delineate individual roles, and be able to amicably manage any conflicts that might arise.

A consulting team needs a lot of scheduled time to accomplish its purpose.

A third key ingredient is coordination. It is critical for collaborators to set aside time for collaborative planning and for scheduling activities. The consultation team, with administrative support, must schedule regular and sufficient amounts of time for planning and preparation if collaboration is to be successful. This is not easy since time is often the most precious commodity in schools.

The resources we have already described can help you and your colleagues develop collaborative relationships. One promising approach for serving students with disabilities in regular classrooms is called "Class Within a Class" (Reynaud, Pfannenstiel & Hudson, 1987). In this delivery model, special educators team with regular classroom teachers to provide services in the regular classroom for students identified as having disabilities, but the special educators work with typical students as well.

COLLABORATION AND TEAMWORK IN THE SCHOOL ECOSYSTEM

Everyone who works in a school affects the school.

Remember that at the beginning of this chapter, we said that everyone in a school who interacts with you and your students may play a role in classroom management? To some degree, everyone—including bus drivers, secretaries, lunchroom workers, custodians, security personnel, and volunteer tutors—contributes to the atmosphere and operation of your school ecosystem. Many

The nonprofessional staff needs to be respected and valued.

factors influence the support personnel; an important influence is the respect of the professional staff and the sense of community that you share.

Everyone involved in your school should be a valued member of the school team. There are times when you might actively involve support personnel in your classroom management efforts. For example, when you "antiseptically bounce" a student to the school office where the secretary allows him or her to cool off before being sent back, when the custodian works with one of your students as a reward in a contingency management program, or when a bus driver monitors the bus behavior of one of your students, you are including support persons directly in classroom management. We believe that communicating mutual respect, optimism, and enthusiasm among all school personnel helps build a sense of community and caring that has positive influences on your students' attitudes and behavior.

As We See It: *The Authors Talk*

Bob: Do you think we're painting too rosy a picture of the consultation-collaboration aspect of teaching?

Mary Kay: You mean are we making it sound too easy? I don't think so. We've pointed out how important good communication skills and open attitudes are to the process. You're right, though: creating a truly workable team isn't easy. And when you have team members at different levels of training and involvement, it can get difficult.

Bob: I'm wondering if we've made it sound as though everyone is doing this and just loving it. Actually, there are many teachers who *like* going into that classroom and closing the door—seeing their students as their own, feeling personally and solely responsible for their learning. I'm not sure that's all bad, either. We talk about what at-risk students who have been successful say, how so often it is one person (often a teacher) who made such a difference in their lives. Are those students going to say, "Yes, it was my third-grade assistance team that made all the difference?" I don't think so. As we add layers of professional expertise, are we in danger of losing the personal attachment that often makes the whole thing work?

Mary Kay: I guess it's going to be even more important for teachers to build those relationships with students. I think it is important for students to have one person they know is totally concerned about their welfare. And it's equally important for teachers to be able to feel that their own personal intervention matters to the student's success. Maybe that's the team's first responsibility—to see that those relationships don't get disrupted. Do you think we need to say that?

Bob: We just did.

PARTNERSHIPS OUTSIDE OF SCHOOL

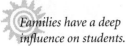

Families have a deep influence on students.

Outside of school, students' families are the major influence on their behavior. Our discussion in Chapter 3 provided an overview of several perspectives that stress the role of families, especially parents, on child behavior and development. Biological parents supply a child's genetic makeup. In utero experiences affect physical and cognitive development; early nurturing and stimulation lay the foundation for behavioral and psychological adjustment; parental models and reinforcement help form learned patterns of behavior; and family cultural and socioeconomic factors influence values, beliefs, and behavior. The influence of families on the learning and behavior of students in school cannot be overstated.

DIVERSITY AMONG FAMILIES

How is your family like and different from other families? There are as many different kinds of families as there are people who make them. We have considered how every classroom is an ecosystem of unique individuals, activities, and setting characteristics. So, too, every family is made up of a combination of persons with unique personal characteristics, histories, experiences, and interaction patterns. Also, like classrooms, families are dynamic—continuously changing in response to internal and external factors. Consider, for instance, how all families must adjust to the changing developmental characteristics of their members. Sometimes the basic structure of the family changes, with death or divorce or other disruptions. The variety of family structures includes the following types:

There are many kinds of family structures:

- Intact, with two biological parents,
- Single parent,
- Separated parents,
- Divorced parents,
- Foster family,
- Adoptive family,
- Recombined families of divorce.

This list is by no means complete; each of these configurations has many variations and some children may experience *all* of them. Many children and youth find themselves with a large number of parents, stepparents, grandparents, stepgrandparents, siblings, cousins, and other assorted relations.

More and more children are living in nontraditional families.

A growing proportion of American children live in nontraditional families. Recent predictions suggest that about one-half of all children will live in a nontraditional family situation before they are eighteen years old. Some of the demographic changes in the American family are dramatic. There are currently, for example, many more children who are born to single mothers (Children's Defense Fund, 1994) and who experience their parents' divorce (Wallerstein, 1985) than twenty to thirty years ago. In 1970, less than 10 percent of American births were to single mothers; by 1991, the percentage increased almost threefold to nearly 30 percent (Whitehead, 1993).

Implications for the Classroom

Children in nontraditional families often have more problems than those in traditional families.

Changing family demographics have many implications for the classroom: the nontraditional family often carries risks for a child. Every traditional family certainly does not provide an ideal environment for child development. Traditional, intact families can be abusive and neglectful, can experience chronic or acute financial problems, can experience overt and covert hostilities and conflicts, and can have accidents and illnesses. And it is true that nontraditional families often provide healthy, caring, nurturing environments for children. As a group, however, children in some types of nontraditional families are at greater risk for economic, emotional, and social problems that can affect their learning and behavior in school. For example, children in young, single-parent families are likely to be poor and thus have less access to medical care and adequate nutrition (Children's Defense Fund, 1994; Edelman, 1991). When parents divorce, there is apt to be less money, less care and attention from parents, and more academic and behavioral problems in school (Wallerstein, 1985). Consequently, classroom teachers must be sensitive to the effects of family situations on the behavior of their students, especially when the child is experiencing family crises.

Single-parent families are often poor and less nurturing than intact families.

TYPES OF FAMILY INVOLVEMENT WITH SCHOOLS

There are four types of possible family involvement with school, regardless of the type of family structure. Families tend to be *involved, unresponsive, overwhelmed,* or *hostile* in their relationships with school and teachers (Rizzo & Zabel, 1988).

Most families either think the school is doing a good job with their children or try to make changes in the system.

Most families are actively concerned about their child's education and involved at some level in supporting their child's learning and behavior in school. Involved parents have a generally positive attitude about education and about school and believe that it is beneficial for their children. Some are satisfied with the programs and atmosphere of the school and classrooms, while others are actively interested in improving their child's educational experience. Involved parents attempt to meet their child's basic needs. As best they can, they see that their child is adequately fed and clothed, is healthy, is supervised and cared for outside of school, has necessary school supplies and materials, gets to school on time, and completes schoolwork. In addition, some of these parents play an active role in their schools. They participate and

Some parents do a lot to help the school.

provide leadership in parent-school organizations; volunteer in school; provide extra support and materials for the classroom; chaperone field trips and class parties; attend teacher conferences, student activities, and performances; and respond to your communications. Involved parents value education and want their children to do well academically and behaviorally in your classroom. These are parents you can usually count on to support your instructional and classroom management efforts.

Some parents don't want to be involved with their child's school.

Other parents are unresponsive, some because they do not seem to care about their child's learning or behavior and others because they are intimidated by school personnel and try to maintain their distance. Some have had little formal education themselves, have limited English proficiency, or come from minority cultural backgrounds and may be reluctant to become involved with the schools. Some parents feel blamed by school personnel for their children's problems in school and withdraw from involvement.

Some parents don't take the time to be a part of their child's education.

Disorganized and unresponsive parents may appear on the surface to meet their child's needs, but may be so involved in social activities or careers away from the home that they have little time to be informed and involved in their child's schooling. Some of these families have the intelligence, education, and financial security to meet their child's needs, but are distracted by other concerns and are inconsistent in caring for their children. They may not adequately supervise their children, see that they are prepared for school, or make sure their children follow up on school responsibilities.

Some parents have too many problems to share in their child's learning.

Some parents are so overwhelmed with responsibilities and problems that they do not have the energy, resources, or competence to be involved in their child's education. For some, unemployment or underemployment creates chronic financial stress. Some families with low incomes or on welfare have insufficient resources to meet their children's basic needs. Families who live in neighborhoods where crime, gangs, drugs, and other adverse social conditions demand their attention and energy have little left to devote to their child's schooling.

Some overwhelmed families have personal problems with drugs and alcohol, illness, or emotional instability that undermine their ability to be involved with their children and schools. They may also be adversely affected by the chronic academic and behavioral problems of their children in and outside of school. Although they may have tried to address these problems in the past, they may have been repeatedly unsuccessful and then given up.

Some parents are opposed to school and undermine a teacher's efforts.

Occasionally you might encounter parents who are actually hostile toward school and teachers. Often the hostility is covertly expressed in the ways these parents communicate distrust and contempt for schools to their children, such as telling their children that they do not have to do anything you tell them. There are even some parents who openly express their disagreement with the ways things are done in your school and classroom and who complain to you and your supervisors about how you teach and treat their child. Although parent hostility is sometimes the result of perceived past or present mistreatment of their child by school personnel, these parents have often experienced academic and social problems themselves.

Fortunately, most parents want to be positively involved in their child's education. Parenting is hard work, and most parents do the best they can for their children. They can be your best allies in promoting student attitudes and behavior that are conducive to learning. Your behavior and communication with parents help maintain and strengthen existing parental involvement and support. With these parents, your job is to reinforce their efforts and channel their energies in ways that will benefit their children and your classes.

You can encourage unresponsive and overwhelmed parents to become more involved with their children's education by communicating how they can contribute to their child's growth. To help overwhelmed parents find support within the community for their basic needs, you can call upon other school personnel, such as social workers and psychologists. In some cases, you can even overcome parent hostility and generate a degree of trust by demonstrating your concern for their child.

POSITIVE COMMUNICATION WITH PARENTS

There are many ways to maintain and foster parent involvement and support. Parents tend to be most involved and supportive when your communication is regular and mostly positive. Then, when you must discuss problems, it will be in the context of the student's positive accomplishments and attributes. Always, remember to *listen* to parents, who generally know more about their child than anyone else does. It is also important to be aware of cultural attitudes toward school and teachers. Some Asian families, for instance, view the teacher as the expert and do not expect or want to be asked for their opinion on solutions. In this situation, you may need to provide some background as to why you are asking for their input and some time for them to adjust to this new way of collaborating.

You can encourage positive communication with parents in opportunities as varied as parent-teacher conferences, telephone calls, class newsletters, report cards, and notes home that communicate your concern for their child and your respect for them. We suggest three guidelines:

1. Keep communication as positive as possible.

2. Solicit parent perspectives and information.

3. Find ways to involve parents to the degree *they wish* to be involved.

When a student has significant learning or behavioral problems in your classroom, it is important that you inform the parents and ask for their help. Parents are sometimes unaware of their child's problems in school. It is a rare

You can encourage parents to stay involved by communicating with them.

Teachers can help parents who are having a hard time find help in the community.

It will be easier for parents to talk with you about problems that come up if you have shared good things about the student.

There are many ways to show parents that you care about their child.

Let parents know when their child is having trouble at school.

student who gets into trouble at school and then reports the details at home. One approach we have found helpful is to have an offending student call his or her parents at home or work to report misbehavior. You can dial the number, introduce yourself, say something like, "Mrs. Jones, I'm going to put Billy on the phone to tell you what he has been doing in our class this morning," and then hand the telephone to Billy. Although you would probably use this approach only when a student has been extremely unresponsive to your reasonable efforts, it can be an effective way to stop misbehavior. While most parents do not want to get such a call, you are communicating to them that their child's behavior is a concern both you and they need to address.

When parents hear only about wrong things their child does, they get discouraged and blame the school.

Parents tend to experience their children's successes and failures as a reflection of their own competence. We like to hear more positive than negative things about our children because we want them to do well and to feel good about themselves. Parents who hear only of failures and shortcomings, whether academic or social, may become discouraged about their child and feel resentment toward the person who delivers the negative information. They are likely to feel responsible for their child's shortcomings. They may respond both by punishing the child and by blaming others (teachers, principal) for the problems.

Letters

Welcome letters are a good way to start communicating with parents.

You should take every opportunity to communicate with parents. A good way to initiate communication is to mail a welcome letter to your prospective students before school starts or to send it home with them on the first day. See Table 9.2 for suggestions about what to include in a welcome letter.

A newsletter is a good way to share information and ideas with parents.

Your welcome letter can be followed by regular newsletters that include updates of activities, schedules, and announcements. Some schools have newsletters that include similar information of schoolwide interest. You may regularly, or occasionally, attach a sheet about *your* classroom to the school newsletter. Computer programs are available with class-newsletter formats, and students can be responsible for writing, editing, printing, and distributing them. In newsletters you can recognize students for special accomplishments, report on individual and class activities, write brief profiles of students and their families, and include creative writing and illustrations.

Notes

You can send a note home every week, telling what the student has accomplished.

In addition, you can communicate with parents about student performance and behavior in brief notes or certificates in photocopied Happy Grams. We suggest some form of weekly, positive communication to parents about each of your students, highlighting their participation in classroom jobs (as lunch counters, tutors, message carriers, line leaders, and classroom custodians) and special accomplishments or helpful behavior (good citizen, neat desk, hard

TABLE 9.2
Suggestions for
Welcome Letters

> Your letter may include all or any of the following information:
> - Description of yourself, including your background
> - Themes or activities your class will be pursuing
> - Daily schedule
> - List of needed materials and supplies
> - Significant dates (holidays, in-service days, parent-teacher conferences, open-house evenings)
> - Request for volunteers for activities like seasonal parties and field trips
> - Encouragement of parent ideas and concerns
> - Names, professional roles, and telephone numbers of some school personnel
> - Your phone number and preferred times for parents to call

worker). Occasionally, you may also call a student's home to share news of a success.

Sample Work

Most parents want to see some of their child's academic work, and you may have students collect representative samples to take home each week. In some cases, you may attach a form for parents to sign indicating they have seen their child's packet and inviting their comments. Portfolios of student work may also be shared at parent-teacher conferences, where you can explain and discuss the student's progress.

Students can bring home samples of their work to show their parents.

Conferences

You can use parent-teacher conferences to give and receive information about student performance and behavior, to discuss future plans, and to enlist parent support. Conferences can be valuable opportunities for communication, but they are often uncomfortable for both parents and teachers. It helps reduce any stress if both teacher and parents can see that the conference is more than you providing information and evaluating their child but is an *interchange* of information and ideas. Meeting and talking with parents often provide insights into the child's behavior and clues for effective communication and management.

If conferences are in the evening, more parents may be able to come.

To encourage parents to come, try to schedule conferences when parents might be able to attend, with both day and evening times available. Most elementary schools offer both day and evening conference times and allow parents to choose a specific time. Many middle and high schools schedule regular report-card distribution events, when parents can meet teachers and discuss their student's performance. At the elementary level, you can help parents begin to focus on important issues by sending home a brief preconference questionnaire. For example, you might ask about their child's favorite and least favorite subjects, what their child likes (and dislikes) about school, and what concerns they or their child have.

Establishing rapport and trust is a major goal of any conference.
Michael Newman/ Photo Edit)

It's important to help parents trust you.

The most important goal of a parent-teacher conference is to establish rapport and trust. If it is held in your classroom, the atmosphere should be inviting. You can display examples of student projects and artwork. (We do *not* suggest, however, using an approach one of us used in our first year of teaching—asking the students to draw pictures of their families and posting them on the student's desk for the parents to find. Some families were definitely *not* amused at the depiction of their home life—particularly the group in which the father was portrayed as sitting behind a newspaper saying, "What's for dinner?" and the mother was represented by a balloon coming from the side of the picture saying, "Let's go out.") After welcoming parents, you can briefly tour the room, showing where their child works and what goes on in different areas of the classroom. You should sit around a table or in a way that encourages communication for your discussion. Always begin and end the conference with some positive evaluations or stories about the student.

When you must discuss academic or behavior problems, avoid attaching blame. Instead, try to communicate your concern and enlist parent ideas and support for devising reasonable plans for dealing with the problems. Solicit and respect parents' views of their child, encourage them to express their concerns, and attempt to deal with concerns jointly.

Parents sometimes turn to teachers for understanding and support. Although you may be able to offer ideas and communicate that you care, you must avoid trying to be a counselor or therapist. Some problems are beyond your expertise and may exhaust your emotional resources and time. Consequently, you should be sensitive about how you can help and recognize the limits of your expertise and skills. When parents need more support than you feel comfortable providing, you can refer them to other school personnel, like social workers, counselors, and psychologists, who can direct them to support services outside of school.

Ask for a parent's ideas in coping with a problem.

Teachers should recognize their limits and not try to be family counselors.

PARENTS WITH LIMITED ENGLISH PROFICIENCY

It is difficult to communicate with parents when they speak little English and you do not speak their primary language. In these situations, you must find ways to translate written and verbal communication. Your school district's ESL (English as a Second Language) or bilingual-program personnel should be able to translate written communications, and your building administrator can arrange for school district translators for verbal communications. If none are available in the schools, you may have to enlist volunteer translators among your bilingual parents or members of the community. In some cases, your students may serve as translators, but avoid this if possible. After all, this conference is between you and the parents and the importance of the information being conveyed may be diminished if it is filtered through the student him or herself.

You may need help communicating with parents who don't speak English.

DISAGREEMENTS WITH PARENTS

Parents sometimes have legitimate concerns about what is in the best interests of their child. Some parents may disagree, for example, with the ways you manage your classroom. Some may believe that you are too open and lenient, others that you are too structured and strict. You may have parents who believe rigid rules and aversive consequences are appropriate for disciplining children. You may have parents who believe that more nurturing, flexible environments are best for their children.

Sometimes these differences reflect different cultural perspectives and values. For example, a recent study of Puerto Rican parents' views of mild mental retardation and learning disabilities indicates conflicts between par-

Parents will sometimes disagree with how you manage your classroom.

ents' and schools' views of disabilities (Harry, 1992, 1994). These parents dismissed the school's designation of their child as mentally retarded because the Spanish they spoke identified mental disability with the vernacular term *loco,* meaning crazy, which parents considered both inaccurate and stigmatizing. Parents found *learning disabled* more acceptable because it implied that the disability was not intrinsic to the child, but indicated the language of instruction (not their native Spanish) and instructional approaches were inappropriate.

Parents and guardians have established legal rights to participate in identification, program planning, and placement decisions when their child is involved in special education. Parent participation means that adoptive parents, step-parents, and foster parents have the same rights as biological parents when they are the students' principal custodians or caregivers (Turnbull, Turnbull, Shank & Leal, 1995). Those rights are based on the recognition that parents have interests and knowledge that contribute to their child's education.

AGENCIES AND SERVICES OUTSIDE OF SCHOOL

In addition to your students' families, there are people and resources outside of school that may contribute to your students' learning and behavior. They include foster families, group homes, mental health and social service agencies, such as social and rehabilitation services and child-protection agencies.

NEGLECT AND ABUSE

Sometimes teachers find out that students are being neglected at home.

Teachers frequently learn of home situations that are detrimental to the health and development of students and are indicative of neglect. You may have students you believe are inadequately supervised, whose basic needs for food, shelter, hygiene, clothing, and medical care are not being met, or students who encounter potentially dangerous situations. Some of your students may have access to alcohol or other illegal drugs that you suspect they are using.

When such situations occur, you should share your concerns with appropriate members of your school staff, such as your principal and school social worker, who can then help determine a course of action. An initial step should be contacting parents or guardians to find out whether they are aware of these conditions and are able to do anything about them. If they cannot, you and your colleagues must contact potential sources of assistance for the child and family from public or private agencies in the community.

If you think a child is being abused, you must report it to the principal.

You may suspect physical or sexual abuse based on injuries, the child's behavior, or what a student tells you. When you see or hear evidence of abuse, you are legally obligated to report it to your building administrator, who must contact the office of child protection or other appropriate social agency to investigate the possibility. Reporting suspected abuse is obviously not a pleasant task, and there may be times when you are uncertain. However, we think it is usually better to report possible abuse and be mistaken than to risk allowing abuse to continue. Teachers are sometimes the only responsible adult a child can turn to who can initiate steps to report suspected child abuse.

People have different ideas about how to raise children.

In many cases, there is a fine line between abuse and socially sanctioned discipline by parents. An especially difficult situation involves cultural variations in discipline techniques (MacIntyre & Silva, 1992). Some parents may approve of discipline practices you consider abusive. You will need to become aware of culturally different approaches to child rearing and discipline practices, and you may need to ask other members of the cultural community about the acceptability of the behavior. However, if you feel a student is being harmed or in danger of being abused—no matter what the cultural or religious reason—you need to talk with your principal and school social worker about taking appropriate action.

FOSTER HOMES, GROUP HOMES, AND RESIDENTIAL TREATMENT CENTERS

Some children live apart from their families.

Some of your students may live in foster homes, group homes, residential treatment centers, or institutions. Children are placed in foster homes when their parents are unable to provide adequate care and supervision, or when there is established abuse or neglect. It is estimated that about 500,000 children in the United States live in foster homes—see the Classroom Closeup "Foster Care in the United States." Group homes, residential treatment centers, and institutions are places for children to live when they have been removed from their parents' custody by the courts or state social-service agencies. This is often due to the family's neglect or abuse or to the child's emotional and behavioral problems. These homes may be operated by public agencies or by private agencies with state financial support. Children in group homes usually go to public schools. Residential treatment centers and institutional or hospital programs sometimes operate their own schools, although residents of these programs also often attend public schools.

Children who live away from home have gone through hard times.

Children and youth in these living arrangements have frequently experienced considerable disruption and trauma in their family lives. In most cases, these out-of-home placements offer greater stability and support for healthy development than their previous home environments. However, these placements are still inherently stressful for children. Because they are usually temporary, children are faced with adapting to changing living situations and to uncertainty about their futures. Some have lived in several out-of-home placements that for one reason or another have not worked out. Consequently, you can expect to see some emotional and behavioral fallout from these experiences. Your classroom can be an island of relative stability and predictability in these students' lives. In addition to your awareness and sensitivity

Classroom Closeup

Foster Care in the United States

In 1991, there were four hundred and thirty thousand children in foster care in the United States, at a cost of some six billion dollars, and, with more children being born each year into tenuous families or into circumstances where a child lacks even a single parent, the number seems certain to grow. In the last decade of the twentieth century, black, Native American, and Hispanic children are vastly overrepresented in foster care, and their stays tend to be longer than those of white children.

Approximately eighty percent of the children coming into care are estimated to have lived with a single parent, and an increasing number of babies entering care are suffering from severe physical disabilities, notably AIDS and drug addiction. An increasing number of adolescents in care are displaying the emotional consequences of long-term placement and multiple placements—of being moved from foster family to foster family or from foster family to institution and back, without ever really having had a place to call home. (Sheehan, 1993, p. 23) ✳

about the child's unstable background, you will need to establish communication with the child's primary caregivers—foster parents, houseparents, or child-care workers—as you would with any parents.

PHYSICIANS AND OTHER MEDICAL PERSONNEL

Physicians and other medical personnel provide services that can influence your students' learning and behavior. It is likely, for example, that you will have students with attention deficit hyperactive disorders who are treated with psychoactive medications. These medications are meant to help the child (less activity, greater attention) but may also produce undesirable behavioral and physical side effects (lethargy, headaches, and irritability) (see Chapter 3). If the treatments are to be beneficial, you will need to work with the physician to monitor and report their apparent effectiveness. You should talk with the student's parents about the intended effects and possible side-effects of drug and other treatments so you can be alert to behavior changes and provide feedback to parents and physicians.

If any of your students are on medication, you may need to be in touch with their doctors.

THERAPISTS

Some of your students may be involved in therapy for emotional or behavioral problems that influence their behavior in your classroom. Some may be identified as having emotional and behavioral disorders and also receive special education and other support services in school. Oftentimes, however, students

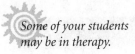

Some of your students may be in therapy.

may be in therapy for emotional or behavioral problems that are not considered to have significant educational implications.

It is hard to characterize what is meant by *therapy*. There are many types of therapists, with different kinds of professional training, theoretical orientations, and treatment approaches. Although anyone may call himself or herself a therapist, the officially sanctioned professionals are psychiatrists, clinical psychologists, psychiatric social workers, and counselors with the requisite training and licenses. A *psychiatrist* is a physician who specializes in treating mental disorders and may prescribe medications as well as offer psychological therapies. A *clinical psychologist* has a Ph.D. in psychology, a *psychiatric social worker* usually has a master's degree in social work (M.S.W.), and a *counseling psychologist* has advanced training (M.S. or Ph.D.) in either counselor education or counseling psychology. In addition to a specified course of academic training, these specialists are licensed by their professional organizations and the state to offer therapy. Therapists may have private practices or work in public mental health agencies or hospitals.

Therapists represent a variety of specializations. For example, some work primarily with children, families, or preadolescents; some specialize in substance-abuse or marital problems. Treatment approaches also vary and are hard to categorize. Play therapy, affective-cognitive therapies, behavioral therapy, and family therapy are often used with children. Table 9.3 provides an overview of therapeutic approaches to suggest the general orientations and treatment approaches some of your students may experience. Although you will not always know when a student is involved in therapy, when you do, you

TABLE 9.3
Common Forms
of Therapy

Play therapy	Play therapy is sometimes employed with young, less verbal children. Using dolls to represent persons in the child's life, the therapist allows the child to act out interactions that provide clues to underlying feelings and conflicts (Axline, 1947).
Talk therapy	There is a variety of *cognitive/affective* or talk therapies in which the therapist and client talk about problems to help the client understand how feelings and thoughts influence his or her behavior. The focus of cognitive/affective approaches is to help the client change feelings and thinking in order to change behavior patterns.
Behavioral therapy	*Behavioral therapy* focuses directly on problem behavior that interferes with a client's functioning or acceptance by others (Meichenbaum & Goodman, 1979). Behaviorists help their clients learn new, more effective behaviors, using behavior-modification approaches like those described in Chapters 7 and 8. Sometimes behavioral therapists train parents (Kazdin, 1985; Patterson, Chamberlain & Reid, 1982). *Cognitive behavior modification* involves teaching strategies for self-monitoring and self-managing behavior, social perspective taking, and social problem solving (Lochman, White & Wayland, 1990).

TABLE 9.3
Continued

Family therapy	Family therapy is practiced in many forms but generally involves all the members of a family ecosystem who are engaged in dysfunctional behavior (Minuchin, 1970). Family therapy focuses on the family system rather than on the individual child. The therapist helps family members identify destructive, dysfunctional attitudes and interactions and develop alternative patterns of behavior.
Arts therapy	There are also a variety of arts therapies, specifically visual art, music, drama, and movement. These therapists sometimes work within a school system, although they are more likely to work in private practice or in a public mental health organization. They help children and adults make use of their creative natures to unlock feelings and abilities that may not find expression in more conventional approaches.

You may need to communicate with a student's therapist.

should be aware that what happens in therapy is likely to affect the student's behavior in your classroom. Sometimes, you may be asked to participate in the treatment effort by providing feedback, for example, about changes in the child's behavior. Also, you and other members of your school's preassessment team may believe that a student could benefit from counseling outside of school and refer parents to community mental health or private counseling.

SUMMARY AND REVIEW

It may seem overwhelming to consider all the individuals with whom you will be involved as a teacher. After all, you probably chose teaching as a career because you like children and not because you like meetings. But as our students' lives become more complex, so does providing an appropriate education for them. It seems that providing someone with an education is no longer a one-person job.

The days of of the lone, kindly teacher operating behind closed doors and not emerging until spring are over forever. Teaching has become a collaborative, complex task, one that calls on numerous disciplines, professionals, and service providers. Some may mourn the lost autonomy of the individual classroom teacher, but when we view the increased services, highly developed specialized programs for individual children, and collaborative, integrated programs that take students from preschool through high school, we see the change as positive.

REFLECTING ON CHAPTER 9

Annie found herself overwhelmed at the IEP meeting for Danny, with so many different people and roles in attendance. But when new information came up, such as the many afternoons and evenings Danny and his brothers spent alone, she was glad that professional expertise was available. You can begin to gather information about the various professionals with whom you will be working.

- Talk to students in your institution who are preparing for careers in psychology, counseling, speech and language, social work, or educational administration. What similarities and differences do you see when you compare their training programs with yours? Is information on collaboration and consultation a part of their training?

- Begin thinking about ways you might interact with parents. With a group of your fellow students, assume that notes have gone home about an upcoming open house at your school. Write notes responding to the open-house invitation as though you were parents who are involved, overwhelmed, or unresponsive. How would you respond to each of these notes?

- Find out what types of out-of-home placements are common in your area. Are there institutions, group homes, residential centers or other living arrangements nearby? If so, where do these students go to school?

Key Terms

individual education program (IEP) (p. 315)

teacher assistance team (p. 324)

Building Your Own Knowledge Base

Cartwright, M., & D'Orso, M. (1993). *For the children: Lessons from a visionary principal.* New York: Doubleday. An account of Cartwright's eleven years as principal of an inner-city elementary school and her efforts to get teachers, students, and parents to work together to improve educational opportunities.

Morgan, S. (1994). *At-risk youth in crises: A team approach in the schools* (2nd ed.). Austin, TX: Pro-Ed. Discusses ways schools can develop prevention and intervention programs to help students cope with life crises such as parent divorce, substance abuse, depression, abuse, and suicide.

Wood, J. W. (1993). *Mainstreaming: A practical approach for teachers* (2nd ed.). New York: MacMillan. Includes information and practical ideas to help teachers work together with their colleagues to provide appropriate educational programs for students with disabilities in inclusive classrooms.

References

Algozzine, B., Christenson, S., & Ysseldyke, J. E. (1982). Probabilities associated with the referral to placement process. *Teacher Education and Special Education, 5,* 19–23.

Axline, V. (1947). *Play therapy.* Cambridge, MA: Riverside Press.

Cartwright, M., & D'Orso, M. (1993). *For the children: Lessons from a visionary principal.* New York: Doubleday.

Cherniss, C. (1988). Observed supervisory behavior and teacher burnout in special education. *Exceptional Children, 54,* 449–454.

Children's Defense Fund. (1994). *The state of America's children: Yearbook 1994.* Washington, DC: Children's Defense Fund.

Deno, E. (1970). Special education as developmental capital. *Exceptional Children, 37,* 229–237.

Dettmer, P., Thurston, L., & Dyck, N. J. (1993). *Collaborative consultation.* Boston: Allyn and Bacon.

Edelman, M. W. (1991). *Families in peril.* Washington, DC: Children's Defense Fund.

Eisner, E. W. (1988). The ecology of school improvement. *Educational Leadership, 45,* 24–29.

Goodlad, J. (1984). *A place called school: Prospects for the future.* New York: McGraw-Hill.

Harry, B. (1992). Making sense of disability: Low-income, Puerto Rican parents' theories of the problem. *Exceptional Children, 59,* 27–40.

Harry, B. (1994). Behavioral disorders in the context of families. In R. L. Peterson & S. Ishii-Jordan (Eds.), *Multicultural issues in the education of students with behavioral disorders.* Cambridge, MA: Brookline Books.

Heron, T. E., & Harris, K. C. (1993). *The educational consultant: Helping professionals, parents, and mainstreamed students* (3rd ed.). Austin, TX: Pro-Ed.

Kazdin, A. E. (1985). *Treatment of antisocial behavior in children and adolescents.* Homewood, IL: Dorsey Press.

Kidder, T. (1989). *Among schoolchildren.* Boston: Houghton Mifflin.

Lochman, J. E., White, K. J., & Wayland, K. K. (1990). Cognitive-behavioral assessment and treatment with aggressive children. In P. C. Kendall (Ed.), *Cognitive behavioral therapy with children and adolescents.* New York: Guilford.

MacIntyre, T., & Silva, P. (1992). Culturally diverse child-rearing practices: Abusive or just different? *Beyond Behavior, 4,* 8–12.

Meichenbaum, D., & Goodman, J. (1979). Training impulsive children to talk to themselves: A means of developing self-control. *Journal of Abnormal Psychology, 77*, 115–126.

Minuchin, S. (1970). The use of an ecological framework in the treatment of a child. In J. E. Anthony & C. Koupernik (Eds.), *The child in his family.* New York: Wiley.

Morgan, S. (1994). *At-risk youth in crises: A team approach in the schools* (2nd ed.). Austin, TX: Pro-Ed.

Ohanian, S. (1994). *Who's in charge? A teacher speaks her mind.* Portsmouth, NH: Boynton/Cook Publishers, Heinemann.

Patterson, G. R., Chamberlain, P., & Reid, J. B. (1982). A comparative evaluation of a parent-training program. *Behavior Therapy, 13*, 638–650.

Reynaud, G., Pfannenstiel, I., & Hudson, F. (1987). *Park Hill secondary learning disability project: An alternative service delivery model implementation manual.* Kansas City, MO: Park Hill School District.

Reynolds, M. C., & Birch, J. (1982). *Teaching exceptional children in all America's schools* (rev. ed.). Reston, VA: Council for Exceptional Children.

Rizzo, J. R., & Zabel, R. H. (1988). *Educating children and adolescents with behavioral disorders: An integrative approach.* Boston: Allyn and Bacon.

Sheehan, S. (1993). *Life for me ain't been no crystal stair.* New York: Pantheon Books.

Turnbull, A. P., Turnbull, H. R., III, Shank, M., & Leal, D. (1995). *Exceptional lives: Special education in today's schools.* Englewood Cliffs, NJ: Merrill/Prentice-Hall.

U.S. Department of Education (1993). *Implementation of Public Law 94-142: The Individuals with Disabilities Education Act.* Washington, DC: ED/OSERS, Division of Educational Resources.

Walker, H. M. (1983). *Walker Problem Behavior Identification Checklist.* Los Angeles: Western Psychological Services.

Wallerstein, J. S. (1984). Children of divorce: Preliminary report of a 10-year follow-up of young children. *American Journal of Orthopsychiatry, 54*, 444–458.

Wallerstein, J. S. (1985). Children of divorce: Recent research. *Journal of the American Academy of Child Psychiatry, 24*, 515–517.

Whitehead, B. D. (1993). Dan Quayle was right. *The Atlantic Monthly* (April), 47–84.

Wood, J. W. (1993). *Mainstreaming: A practical approach for teachers* (2nd ed.). New York: MacMillan.

Zabel, R. H., Peterson, R. L., & Smith, C. R. (1986). Availability and usefulness of assessment information for behaviorally disordered students: A replication. *Diagnostic, 12*, 26–36.

Factors that Contribute to Teacher Stress and Burnout

• The realities of in-school contributors to stress
• Dimensions of burnout and stress
• Contributors to stress and burnout from outside of school
• Factors associated with burnout

Taking Care of Yourself

Stress Reduction and Burnout Prevention

• Finding opportunities for professional growth
• Preventing burnout
• Learning to cope successfully with stress
• Building supportive relationships
• Cultivating empathy

Chapter **10**

Taking Care of Yourself

Annie's Journal

MAY: May. May baskets . . . May poles . . . May Day (as in HELP!). I can't believe I've gotten this far. There are lots of cliches about time flying (but isn't that supposed to be when you're having fun?) and one day at a time, but let me tell you, there were days in September when I thought this month would *never* come. There were even days in *April* when I thought this month would never come!

But I seem to have made it—still standing—probably not the same person I was when I started—more tired than I ever thought possible. . . . I remember finals week in college, when we'd spent a lot of time talking about how stressed and exhausted we were and how we really needed some time to get away. . . . I remember all that and I have just one thing to say to myself back then: *ha!* You thought you were worn out then? Listen, . . . you haven't been *tired* until you've spent nine months with twenty-three or so active young persons—taking them on field trips, counting noses every ten seconds because you're terrified that someone will wander off, attaching noses for the Halloween play, wiping noses during the endless months of December, January, and February—each of which is at least sixty days long—and trying to make sure that those twenty-three or so noses are not out of joint, poked into someone else's business, or bleeding. This is, of course, in addition to stimulating the area *above* the nose and teaching them everything they need to know to be successful nine- and ten-year-olds, everything their fifth-grade teacher will expect them to know, everything their parents think they should know, everything I think they should know, and everything every reform-minded politician thinks they should know. Whew. I feel better just having said all that.

Having had my time to vent, I have to admit I am amazed that this year is ending. Maybe I should spend time thinking about all that has happened and how I feel about it. To really do that, though, would take a lot longer than I have to write this entry. I think I've experienced every emotion a person can have this year. Some of the highs were amazing, like Justin and Samantha walking across the stage to accept the All-District— yes, that's right the *All-District*—fourth-grade math prize; Lee's mother telling me she thought my talks with Lee were all that held her together during her parents' divorce; listening to the class meeting where they all talked about helping Danny; and having Dr. Wright tell me that I was a valued member of the faculty and she looked forward to working with me in the future. I've had some awful lows too, though, like walking down the hall with Danny after the fight when he slugged Mrs. Garcelon; coming to school to find that Tamica had moved—no advance warning, no goodbye; watching Danny come to school and go to Mr. Wood's room instead of mine; and finding Keisha crying in the bathroom the day after winter break because she had just found out that her mom has cancer.

Funny how Danny ends up on both sides of my emotional chart. He is still in my room in the afternoons, but our relationship has changed. He's more like a visitor than part of the class. Those first days after his IEP were hard on all of us. I'm sure the kids were wondering who was going to get sent away next. Tremaine, especially, was really angry at me—which he showed by not looking at me or talking to me unless he absolutely had to. I guess I still feel as though I failed Danny—if I had been able to meet his needs better the change wouldn't have happened. I'm afraid that's on the negative side of this year's blotter.

But I've won a few, too. Matt has really blossomed as a writer and has had a story accepted for the state literary journal. Justin, who wasn't interested in anything at the beginning of the year, won the math prize with Samantha. Carla still talks all the time, but at least she knows it and has the grace to look sheepish when I glare at her. I don't think of my class as a solid mass like coral anymore, the way I did at the beginning, but as a group of individual beings that cause all those highs and lows for me.

I've had some situations that were neither victories nor defeats, like the situation with Nketi's parents. Ever since the infamous cooperative-learning conference, we've had an uneasy truce. I kept him in the group, but I also made sure he was part of the science enrichment team that met every week. He actually conducted an interesting study with the gifted teacher that he presented to the class, involving genetics and breeding fruit flies. The kids weren't impressed but I was. I tried to help his social skills, but I don't think that was too successful. I haven't heard from Dr. Mom and Dr. Dad since the last report card conference, though, so I guess that's a plus.

You read a lot about burnout—and I guess I don't feel like that (not yet, anyway). I feel tired, and I feel a bit drained, but I also know I want to do this again next year. It's helped during this year to write in this journal, to talk with Charlotte and Frank about what's going on, and to sometimes just go home and forget about it. My family knows my kids almost as well as I do, I talk about them so much (it kind of scares me to realize that the kids are talking about *me* at home, just the way I do). I wish there had been another first-year teacher (other than Tracy who left) at our school this year. I really felt like the new kid a lot of the time.

There are lots of things I'd like to do differently next year—more time on journals, more poetry, better spelling activities, more time for storytelling, maybe some drama activities, more math tutors from the high school, better report card procedures and portfolios, more parents at conferences—more, more, more. I wonder where I think I'm going to find *more* time to organize all this? I think I might take a class this summer, that is if I don't decide to just sleep through the whole months of July and August. . . . And I want to get a better camera so when I go to Canada this summer I can bring back slides for social studies, and I need to read about working with high-achieving kids . . . and about kids with real behavior problems . . . and about multiple intelligences . . . and about authentic assessment. Oh, my.

I guess I'm a teacher now—although I wouldn't say that to anyone else yet. I have a feeling I'm going to be almost as nervous next August as I was at the beginning of this year. I suppose that's good. At least next year I won't have to worry about what to wear to the in-service meeting.

FOCUS QUESTIONS

✳ After a year of teaching Annie doesn't feel like the same person she was last August. What changes have you seen in her?

✳ What do you think are Annie's most important qualities for succeeding as a teacher?

✳ What do you think were the most demanding and exhausting events in Annie's year? What were the most rewarding?

A STRONG START

Throughout this book we have emphasized the ecological nature of classroom management. We have explored student diversity, examined the influence of physical and psychological environments, studied a variety of approaches for creatively and humanely managing individual and group behavior, and suggested how other persons within and outside of school can be included in classroom management. The other key element of the classroom ecosystem is you, the teacher. Teaching is hard work that can exact a physical, emotional, and intellectual toll. Reflecting the responsibilities that our society places on schools, classroom teachers are expected to operate in multiple roles with increasingly diverse students.

As we discussed in our first chapter, beginning teachers often experience *reality shock* as they come face to face with the demands of their jobs. They often cite discipline as their most pressing concern and worry about how they will organize and maintain safe and orderly learning environments to help students learn and behave. Your early teaching experiences will lay the foundation for the attitudes and approaches you will use during the rest of your career. They are also critical to your survival. Most teachers who leave the profession do so during the first few years. After that initial period there is relatively little turnover among experienced teachers (Murnane et al., 1991).

There are many reasons people leave teaching early in their careers. Some are related to their ability to manage their classrooms and some to the teacher's age, gender, amount of previous experience, level taught, salary, and academic achievement (Haberman & Rickards, 1990; Heyns, 1988; Murnane et al., 1991).

Teachers who are not yet thirty, inexperienced, and female are at especially high risk of leaving the profession. This group, the largest group of new teachers, is much more likely to leave than either males or more experienced older females. Sometimes they leave to raise their own children or to follow their spouse's job opportunities. Of course, some of them return to teaching later.

New teachers who are young women are the group most apt to leave teaching in the first few years.

Still, early teaching experiences also often serve as the impetus for teachers to leave, some never returning. Referring to career patterns of both regular classroom and special education teachers, one researcher concludes, "While some find their first years of teaching exciting and satisfying, others find it frustrating and overwhelming. Those who cannot cope, leave. As both types of teachers learn how to manage a classroom, the burdens can diminish, allowing the rewards to grow" (Singer, 1992).

In recent years there has been considerable attention to how classroom conditions affect stress and burnout and to how these, in turn, affect teachers' functioning. Studies have also considered contributing features inside and outside schools as well as approaches for dealing with stress. Concern about stress and burnout has struck a responsive chord among teachers, who refer to themselves or colleagues as stressed or burned out. In this chapter, we will examine some of the factors that contribute to teacher stress and burnout and suggest strategies to help you avoid these states.

FACTORS THAT CONTRIBUTE TO TEACHER STRESS AND BURNOUT

Burnout is a term borrowed from studies of other human services or helping professions, such as nursing, social work, child-care, nursing-home work,

A person is burned out when job stresses are to hard to handle.

medicine, and police work. All of these occupations serve clients with problems, frequently under difficult conditions. Burnout refers to a person's chronic inability to cope with stress and shows in the psychological and physiological distress that result from occupational conditions (Cherniss, 1980; Freudenberger, 1974). See Table 10.1 for a list of symptoms of this distress. These symptoms result in diminished job performance, frequent absenteeism, and, in some cases, attrition. The phenomenon has been observed among human-service providers whose jobs involve them on a regular basis with clients who have problems. Human-service professionals are at risk for burnout because they are "required to work intensely and intimately with people on a continuous basis. They learn about people's psychological, social, and physical problems and are expected to provide aid or treatment of some kind. Some aspects of this job involve 'dirty work' . . . tasks particularly upsetting or embarrassing to perform" (Maslach & Pines, 1977, p. 100).

Because the terms *stress* and *burnout* are often used loosely, we think a few cautionary comments are in order. Living is always stressful, but under certain conditions people sometimes experience more stress than they can handle. This *dis*tress can adversely affect their physiological functioning, emotions, and behavior. Also, while you may hear someone refer to persons as *burned out*, burnout is not an all-or-nothing condition: someone is not necessarily either burned out or functioning well. It is more accurate to consider burnout as a relative condition; some persons are more, or less, burned out (or distressed) than others and burnout researchers, in fact, measure burnout by degrees.

Burnout is relative; feelings and circumstances change from day to day.

In addition, a person's feelings of stress are not static. Teachers and other human-service providers have good and bad days. Situations inside and outside the classroom will influence your feelings. Even the most upbeat, optimistic, effective teachers occasionally encounter discouraging, frustrating situations and may, at least temporarily, experience periods of general malaise.

The Classroom Closeup "Am I Burnt Out?" shows that even a generally confident, effective teacher may occasionally feel burned out. Mrs. Zajac, the teacher Tracy Kidder wrote about, was feeling frustrated and discouraged after months without progress with her student, Clarence, who had serious behavior disorders (see Chapter 9, page 329, about the decision to place Clarence outside her classroom). Together with a placement team, she had reluctantly and guiltily agreed that he should be placed in a special-education program in another school.

TABLE 10.1
Symptoms of Psychological and Physiological Distress

- Unhappiness or depression
- Lack of enthusiasm or interest in work
- Lack of energy
- Distancing from clients and colleagues
- Psychosomatic conditions, such as headaches, backaches, and lack of energy
- Excessive use of alcohol or drugs

Classroom Closeup

Am I Burnt Out?

Over the years Chris had gotten in the habit of wondering when she would burn out. It was like waiting to catch the flu and, at the first intimations, like waiting to see if flu would turn into pneumonia this time. Now in the room . . . she kept having a feeling of doubleness. She didn't want to be here. The real Chris wasn't here. Now and then she lost her temper at one or another of the children for offenses that would not have upset her before, and her voice sounded harsh and shrill to her, like the voice of someone else, someone she didn't like. The little leaps of the clock's minute hand, which had seemed to happen much too quickly once, now seemed to come after endless delay. On the surface, her lessons seemed adequate but plain. In her mind, as she taught some of them, she thought, "I'm really boring myself. I'll just get through this one. I'm not really here. I don't know what's wrong." She told herself, "It's March. I do this every year. I say, 'Uh-oh, it's March. I'm supposed to feel terrible.'" But in the middle of a social studies lesson on Tuesday, she felt as if she were listening to someone else drone on before the class, and she asked herself, "Oh, God, am I losing it? Am I burnt out?"   (Kidder, 1989, p. 175) ✸

Circumstances alone don't make someone burned out; reactions do.

Stress and burnout are not simply a result of job conditions, such as certain kinds of clients and problems, the number of hours on the job, and the amount of paperwork. We think the experience of stress is as much a reflection of an individual's reactions to those conditions as it is to the conditions themselves. Different persons react differently to the same conditions. For example, one teacher may react negatively to students' apparent lack of respect, while another may see this behavior as a challenge.

THE REALITIES OF IN-SCHOOL CONTRIBUTORS TO STRESS

Teaching is a human-services profession. You will work intensely and intimately with your students. Recall that two of the central characteristics of classroom ecosystems we discussed in Chapter 1 are crowded conditions and lack of privacy (Doyle, 1986; Jackson, 1990). As a teacher you learn a great deal about your students—about their abilities and disabilities, their temperaments and personalities, their strengths and weaknesses, and their lives inside and outside of school. In addition, you are expected to *do* something to change and help them, often in the face of tremendous odds presented by countervailing influences in their lives. Despite large classes, insufficient resources, and inadequate support, you are responsible for teaching your students.

Teachers sometimes need to deal with difficult students.

Not all of your teaching responsibilities will be pleasant and rewarding. Students are sometimes sick, belligerent, unmotivated, annoying, or aggressive, yet you must deal with them in the very public arena of the classroom. Often their problems are not readily resolved. Teachers also have responsibilities to the parents, administrators, and colleagues. Dealing with problems, demands, and expectations—both yours and others'—can be draining and discouraging.

DIMENSIONS OF BURNOUT AND STRESS

Sometimes when people get burned out they get very tired and can't get rested.

Burnout can be defined along three dimensions: **emotional exhaustion, deper-sonalization,** and **personal accomplishment** (Maslach & Jackson, 1986). *Emotional exhaustion* refers to feelings of being emotionally and physically drained, of having little left to give. A person who is emotionally exhausted lacks energy, seems unable to get enough sleep, and appears to have insufficient reserves of strength to cope with stress. *Depersonalization* refers to psychological distancing from clients, creating barriers to guard against emotional involvement in the clients' problems, and seeing oneself as essentially different from them. Depersonalization may be expressed in criticism, cynicism, putdowns, or mockery of clients. To a certain extent, depersonalization is an adaptive method of coping with the demands of helping people with problems. It helps the professional defend against becoming overwhelmed by responsibilities. However, in more extreme cases, it becomes a kind of noncaring. *Personal accomplishment* refers to how effective a human-service professional feels he or she is with clients. People who feel little personal accomplishment may believe their efforts are worthless and have little benefit on their clients' lives.

Sometimes when people get burned out they get critical and cynical.

People who feel effective in their work are less likely to become burned out.

Over the past decade researchers have studied stress and burnout among regular-classroom and special-education teachers and have identified factors involved in burnout (Cherniss, 1980; Frank & McKenzie, 1993; Greer & Wethered, 1984; Kyriacou, 1987; Zabel & Zabel, 1982; 1984). Researchers studied special educators because their clients—students with disabilities—are assumed to present greater challenges than typical students and because of especially high attrition rates among special educators. The high attrition has been partly explained by the very rapid growth of the field since the Education for All Handicapped Children Act of 1975 was passed. Some people were drawn to special education because so many jobs were available, but many of them were not suited to teaching and soon left. More recent evidence indicates that the patterns of attrition among regular and special educators are actually quite similar (Singer, 1992), with younger, less-experienced teachers more likely to leave.

Some people leave teaching for another job or to have children.

As we mentioned earlier, attrition and burnout are related but are not the same. Teachers sometimes leave their jobs because of stress and burnout, but they also leave for other reasons, such as other job opportunities or raising a family. Although it is unfortunate when teachers quit their jobs because of burnout, it is even worse when burned-out teachers stay. Discouraged, pessimistic, exhausted teachers are not good for their students or for themselves.

FACTORS ASSOCIATED WITH BURNOUT

There are certain aspects of a job that are connected to burnout.

There are patterns to burnout, although cause-effect relationships per se have not been established: some factors are associated with higher scores on measures of burnout (Zabel & Zabel, 1982, 1984). Conditions of the job that are related to burnout include student caseload, perceptions of support from other sources, types of students, and service delivery models.

Number of Students and Perceptions of Support

Although the number of students itself is not decisive, teachers who believe they have too many students feel more burned out than those who say the number of students is about right or too small. In addition, *perceptions of support* from colleagues, parents, and especially from administrators are important. Teachers who say they are receiving more support from those sources feel less burned out than teachers who feel they have less support.

Types of Students

Students with emotional and behavioral problems can be very trying for a teacher.

Teachers of students with emotional and behavioral disorders have a higher level of burnout than other special educators. This is not surprising and has implications for regular-classroom teachers as well. By definition, students with behavior problems arouse strong emotions, even from teachers who are trained to work with them, and by definition, their behavior is extreme. Compared to other students they tend to be either excessively aggressive or withdrawn and depressed. They may be described as disruptive, lacking self-control, distant, odd, and bizarre. Some of these students are verbally and physically assaultive toward other students and even toward teachers. Clearly, these kinds of behavior patterns present management problems for teachers, whether the students are in regular or special classrooms.

Service Delivery Model

Another significant factor in special education teacher burnout is the service delivery model (institutional, self-contained, resource, itinerant, or self-contained). Generally, teachers who work at either end of the continuum of services (serving as consultants or teaching in institutions) score higher on burnout measures than those in the middle. While it seems logical that teachers in institutional settings might be more stressed by working with more seriously disabled students, the high burnout scores for itinerant and consulting teach-

Consulting teachers who go from class to class or school to school often suffer stress.

Classroom teachers can miss feeling personally satisfied when they work on a team.

Most teachers care more about intrinsic rewards, such as helping a child grow, than about salary or benefits or status.

ers, who generally work with mildly disabled students in regular classrooms, are more surprising. There are a number of possible explanations for this finding: itinerant or consulting teachers often have high caseloads; they work in collaborative relationships with colleagues; and they may have difficulty identifying with a group of students, a classroom, or even a school. Also, until recently, few special-education teachers were trained to operate in collaborative arrangements. As such, they were less likely to experience the sense of personal accomplishment that can balance emotional exhaustion and depersonalization. Because regular-classroom teachers also receive little preparation to work as members of a team, we suspect that they are experiencing similar distress.

You may remember the three potential sources of rewards for teachers we discussed: extrinsic, ancillary, and intrinsic (Lortie, 1975). *Extrinsic rewards* include salary and benefits and the perceived status of being a teacher. *Ancillary rewards* include convenience of work location, schedule, and working conditions. *Intrinsic rewards* are primarily a teacher's satisfaction from achieving positive results with students. If you were to examine your motivations for becoming a teacher, what would they be? Would you think first of extrinsic, ancillary, or intrinsic rewards? We think it is likely that you would first mention potential intrinsic motivators, such as wanting to make a difference in children's lives, desiring to help children learn and achieve, enjoying working with people, and contributing to your students' growth and development. You might also mention ancillary rewards, such as longer vacations and the availability of teaching jobs in a variety of locations. However, these potential ancillary rewards probably have less influence on your career choice than the intrinsic rewards. We suspect you are also less likely to be primarily motivated by extrinsic rewards (or you are unfortunately misinformed!), since teacher salaries tend to be lower than those for occupations with similar levels of training, although teaching is considered an honorable profession and teachers are esteemed in our society.

Expectations About Teaching

Many teachers believe their jobs represent a kind of service to their society—a way to contribute to the future. Like persons attracted to other human-service professions, teachers "may have particular types of personality traits and respond to similar types of motivation. It could be argued that they seek employment opportunities that focus more on people than on things, and that they put high importance on empathy, understanding, and service to others. Such work can hold the promise of a 'noble calling' and is often invested with great meaning and high expectations" (Greer & Greer, 1992, p. 169).

We believe that most teachers are intrinsically motivated to do well with their students. Our society needs teachers who care about their students and

Some teachers are idealists who get disappointed in the classroom.

are motivated by a desire to help them develop and achieve. However, this idealism also predisposes teachers to disappointment, feelings of ineffectiveness, and even professional burnout. In fact, professionals who tend to be sensitive, dedicated, idealistic, and empathic seem especially vulnerable to burnout. This is a particular concern for young, inexperienced teachers.

This disparity between expectations and reality can be seen in Figure 10.1, Model of Teacher Stress and Burnout. According to the model, teacher stress occurs in a series of dynamic components: expectations, school experiences, feelings, behavior, and others' reactions. Within each component, a teacher's experiences are depicted along a positive to negative continuum, because, once again, burnout is a relative rather than an absolute condition.

When a teacher's expectations are very different from reality, it can cause stress.

Your expectations about teaching affect and are affected by the other components of burnout. Expectations reflect your experiences as a student yourself, your individual personality traits, your professional training, and what has been called your "beliefs-attitudes-values system" (Kyriacou & Sut-

FIGURE 10.1 Model of Teacher Stress and Burnout

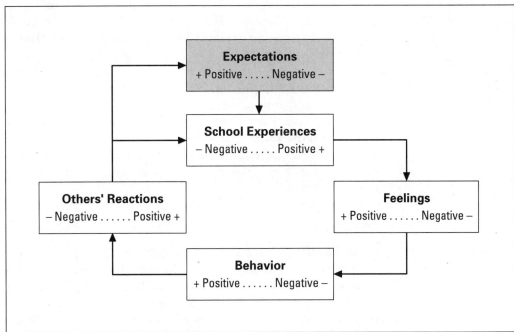

Source: Zabel, Boomer & King (1984), adapted from Long & Duffner (1980). Used by permission.

cliffe, 1978). You approach teaching with expectations about your students, school and classroom facilities, resources, materials, and relationships with parents, colleagues, and supervisors. Most important, you have expectations about your competence—your ability to teach effectively.

Experiences

Experiences in your classroom are at least partly defined by your expectations, although once on the job you may notice the difference between your expectations and your experiences. Students, facilities, resources, materials, parents, colleagues, and supervisors may or may not conform to your expectations. For example, some of your students may not readily respond to you, some may not seem as motivated as you expected, others may have academic difficulties that are less responsive to your instruction than you expected, and some may not behave in what you consider reasonable ways.

Feelings

When students do poorly you may feel ineffective.

Classroom life may seem more complex than you anticipated, and you may find you are not as prepared for the multiple roles of teaching as you had believed. Because intrinsic rewards of teaching are based largely on your students' accomplishments, you will tend to judge your effectiveness by student performance and behavior. Feeling ineffective, also called *helplessness* (Greer & Wethered, 1984; Greer & Greer, 1992), *inconsequentiality* (Farber, 1983), or *incompetence* (Lortie, 1975), is one of the main reasons teachers feel burned out. For many teachers, being able to maintain discipline or classroom control is critical to how competent they feel.

The correspondence or conflict between your expectations and actual experiences generates feelings that will be relatively positive or negative. You may feel positive about your ability to manage your classroom when students behave pretty much according to your expectations. If, on the other hand, they do not, you may feel frustrated, confused, or angry. The result may be emotional exhaustion.

Behavior

People's behavior usually reflects how they are feeling.

According to the stress and burnout model, your feelings generate corresponding behavior. That is, more positive feelings generate more positive behavior; negative feelings generate more negative behavior. If you feel positive about your performance, you will be energized to work enthusiastically to continue your perceived successes and you will communicate your enthusiasm to your students and colleagues. On the other hand, if you are discouraged, frustrated, and embittered, you are likely to have less energy, enthusiasm, and caring. You may become cynical and blame your students and others for your problems.